Timothy L. Warner

DATE DUE

Sams **Teach Yourself**

Scratch™ 2.0

in 24 Hours

SAMS 800 East 96th Street, Indianapolis, Indiana, 46240 USA

Sams Teach Yourself Scratch™ 2.0 in 24 Hours

Copyright © 2015 by Pearson Education, Inc.

ISBN-13: 978-0-672-33709-3
ISBN-10: 0-672-33709-6
Library of Congress Control Number: 2014933847
Printed in the United States of America
First Printing: July 2014

Trademarks

All terms mentioned in this book that are known to be trademarks or service marks have been appropriately capitalized. Sams Publishing cannot attest to the accuracy of this information. Use of a term in this book should not be regarded as affecting the validity of any trademark or service mark.

Scratch is a registered trademark of MIT.

Warning and Disclaimer

Every effort has been made to make this book as complete and as accurate as possible, but no warranty or fitness is implied. The information provided is on an "as is" basis. The author(s) and the publisher shall have neither liability nor responsibility to any person or entity with respect to any loss or damages arising from the information contained in this book.

Special Sales

For information about buying this title in bulk quantities, or for special sales opportunities (which may include electronic versions; custom cover designs; and content particular to your business, training goals, marketing focus, or branding interests), please contact our corporate sales department at corpsales@pearsoned.com or (800) 382-3419.

For government sales inquiries, please contact governmentsales@pearsoned.com.

For questions about sales outside the U.S., please contact international@pearsoned.com.

Editor-in-Chief
Greg Wiegand

Executive Editor
Rick Kughen

Development Editor
Mark Renfrow

Managing Editor
Kristy Hart

Senior Project Editor
Betsy Gratner

Copy Editor
Karen Annett

Senior Indexer
Cheryl Lenser

Proofreader
Katie Matejka

Technical Editor
Patrick Mangan

Publishing Coordinator
Kristen Watterson

Cover Designer
Mark Shirar

Compositor
Nonie Ratcliff

Contents at a Glance

Table of Contents

About the Author

Timothy Warner is an IT professional and technical trainer based in Nashville, Tennessee. Tim began his programming career in 1982 when his dad bought the family a Timex Sinclair 1000 home computer and he began teaching himself BASIC programming. Today Tim works as a technical trainer for Skillsoft, a premier provider of live instructor-led training. You can reach Tim directly via his LinkedIn profile at https://www.linkedin.com/in/timothywarner.

Dedication

*To my beautiful, amazing daughter, Zoey Elizabeth, who loves technology
and Scratch programming as much as her daddy does.*

Acknowledgments

For a variety of reasons, this book was challenging to write. I extend my biggest debt of gratitude to my valiant and open-minded editors, Rick Kughen and Mark Renfrow. Thanks also to my publishers, Greg Wiegand and Paul Boger—you guys are great. Thank you to the always helpful and efficient Pearson production and administrative staff, including Kristen Watterson, Betsy Gratner, and Kristy Hart.

Technical books like this put a special burden on its content editors. Thanks so much to Patrick Mangan, my technical editor, and to Karen Annett, my copyeditor, for your thoroughness in making the manuscript as best as it can be.

Thanks to my family—Susan, Zoey, and our menagerie of pets—for putting up with my occasional grumpiness as I burned through the rough spots of this project.

Finally, thanks to you, my readers: Without you, I have no teacher-student circuit to complete, and I would write into the void. That's no fun, so I want you to know how grateful I am that you're reading this book and participating in this learning journey with me.

We Want to Hear from You!

As the reader of this book, *you* are our most important critic and commentator. We value your opinion and want to know what we're doing right, what we could do better, what areas you'd like to see us publish in, and any other words of wisdom you're willing to pass our way.

We welcome your comments. You can email or write to let us know what you did or didn't like about this book—as well as what we can do to make our books better.

Please note that we cannot help you with technical problems related to the topic of this book.

When you write, please be sure to include this book's title and author as well as your name and email address. We will carefully review your comments and share them with the author and editors who worked on the book.

Email: consumer@samspublishing.com

Mail: Sams Publishing
         ATTN: Reader Feedback
         800 East 96th Street
         Indianapolis, IN 46240 USA

Reader Services

Visit our website and register this book at informit.com/register for convenient access to any updates, downloads, or errata that might be available for this book.

Introduction

"My task, which I am trying to achieve is, by the power of the written word, to make you hear, to make you feel—it is, before all, to make you see."

—Joseph Conrad, *Lord Jim*

So you want to learn programming? If you were here, physically right in front of me, I would ask you the following questions:

▶ What was it that got you interested in learning to do computer programming? An iOS or Android app? One of your teachers at school? A family member or friend?

▶ Where do you envision taking your programming skills? Are you considering programming as a career, a money-making venture, or simply a fun, satisfying hobby?

Regardless of your motivations, I'm happy to welcome you to the always challenging, sometimes fun, sometimes tedious world of learning to write computer programs. In choosing Scratch 2.0, you've made an excellent choice for your first programming language, if you are a beginner.

Why? Because Scratch is a visual, drag-and-drop programming environment that allows you to be creative without having to get bogged down in learning strange syntax rules like you do in more formal languages such as JavaScript or Python.

By the time you've finished this book and completed all of the Try It Yourself exercises, you'll not only be an expert with Scratch programming, but you'll also have a number of real-world programming best practices under your belt.

Please note that I don't dismiss Scratch as a "toy" programming language. In this book, you'll make various projects that other people can actually play and enjoy. We're talking about programs like games, educational interactions, or multimedia storybooks—the proverbial sky is the limit.

Who Should Read This Book

Any author worth his or her salt always writes with the audience in mind. As far as I'm personally concerned, I envision my readers as coming from one (or more) of the following experience contexts:

▶ **Brand new to programming**: Welcome! You don't need any prior experience with programming to gain value from this book. The only related experience I hope you have is a lot of time spent playing video games and using other multimedia apps so you have some ideas to pursue in Scratch.

▶ **Considering a career change**: Perhaps you are a K-12, junior college, or university student who has perhaps a bit of past programming experience, and you are pondering a full-time career as a software developer. Learning Scratch serves as an excellent diagnostic to gauge your aptitude and interest in the subject matter.

▶ **Just tinkering**: Maybe you are a technology buff who always wondered what work went into developing a software project. You have no real career aspirations in programming— you just enjoy tinkering and having fun. Well, welcome! You are bound to have a blast learning Scratch!

If you find that you don't belong in any of the previous three classifications, then don't worry about it. Set your sights on learning as much as you can and, above all else, having fun, and you'll be fine!

How This Book Is Organized

Can you learn how to program with Scratch 2.0 in 24 one-hour sessions? Absolutely! The following chapter-by-chapter breakdown details how the material is structured:

▶ Hour 1, "What Is Scratch?" formally defines what Scratch is, how it came to be, and how you can use the platform to learn real, honest-to-goodness computer programming skills.

▶ In Hour 2, "Creating Your First Project," you create your first Scratch project. If you are to become an expert Scratch programmer, then you need to get right into the mix.

▶ In Hour 3, "Working with Costumes and the Stage," you turn your attention to sprites and their potentially many costumes. You also formally meet the Stage and its accompanying backdrops.

▶ In Hour 4, "Using Motion Blocks," you begin a detailed consideration of every script block in Scratch 2.0. Here, you use Motion blocks to make stuff happen on the Stage.

▶ In Hour 5, "Using Looks Blocks," you learn how Looks blocks enable you to make sprites interact with your players.

▶ In Hour 6, "Using Sound Blocks," you add audio to your Scratch projects.

▶ In Hour 7, "Working with Pen Blocks," you learn to draw on the Stage by using the fun Pen blocks.

▶ In Hour 8, "Using Events Blocks," you get comfortable with event-driven programming and using Events blocks to orchestrate action in your Scratch projects.

▶ In Hour 9, "Using Control Blocks," you use the powerful Control blocks to program potentially complicated branching and looping logic.

▶ In Hour 10, "Using Operators Blocks," you apply (ugh!) mathematics and logical thinking by means of Scratch's Operators blocks.

▶ In Hour 11, "Using Sensing Blocks," you start to operate with both analog and digital processes and interact with the player more intimately through the Sensing blocks.

▶ In Hour 12, "Using Data Blocks," you learn how to implement dynamic data (that is to say, variables and lists) into your Scratch 2.0 projects.

▶ In Hour 13, "Using Cloud Data," you take what you learned about local variables in Hour 12 and scale them out to the cloud by using cloud data—exciting, cutting-edge stuff here, people!

▶ In Hour 14, "Adding Multimedia to Your Project," you add multimedia (recorded audio, video) to your Scratch projects.

▶ In Hour 15, "Creating Your Own Blocks," you learn how to build your own custom blocks using the built-in tools in the Scratch 2.0 editor.

▶ In Hour 16, "Documenting Your Project," you pick up some real-world programming best practices as they relate to source code documentation and unit testing.

▶ In Hour 17, "Publishing Your Project," you take your work and publish your project on the Scratch website to enable other people from all over the world to play your game.

▶ In Hour 18, "Using the Scratch Offline Editor," you discover how you can work on your Scratch projects even if your computer is not connected to the Internet.

▶ In Hour 19, "Troubleshooting Your Project," you learn valuable tips and tricks for debugging your Scratch 2.0 projects, ensuring that they are free from errors and give players the best possible experience.

▶ In Hour 20, "Remixing a Project," you "stand on the shoulders of giants" by building new Scratch 2.0 projects based on the work of other Scratchers.

▶ In Hour 21, "Creating Your Own Sprites and Backdrops," you put on your artist's beret and learn how to draw your own sprite costumes and Stage backdrops by using both the built-in Paint Editor as well as a third-party image-editing program.

▶ In Hour 22, "Implementing Buttons and Multiple Screens," you put your Scratch project on another level of quality by including multiple game screens and button controls.

▶ In Hour 23, "Connecting Scratch to the Physical World," you use third-party add-on products to link your Scratch programs with stuff happening in the real world. (Think temperature, touch, volume...this is some fun stuff, trust me!)

▶ In Hour 24, "Capstone Project: Arcade Game," you consolidate what you learned through the previous 23 hours by writing and publishing a fully functional game.

Downloading the Sample Files

As you'll learn soon enough, the Scratch programming community is all about resource sharing. To that end, the solution files for every Try It Yourself exercise in the book are provided for you in the solution archive. To access the archive, go to www.informit.com/title/9780672337093 and click the Downloads tab.

Conventions Used in This Book

In my experience as an author and a teacher, I've found that many readers and students skip over this part of the book. Congratulations for reading it! Doing so will pay off in big dividends because you'll understand how and why we formatted this book the way that we did.

Try It Yourself

Throughout the book, you'll find Try It Yourself exercises, which are opportunities for you to apply what you're learning right then and there in the book. I do believe in knowledge stacking, so you can expect that later Try It Yourself exercises assume that you know how to do stuff that you did in previous Try It Yourself exercises.

Therefore, your best bet is to read each chapter in sequence and work through every Try It Yourself exercise.

About the is.gd Hyperlinks

Whenever I want to point you to an Internet resource to broaden and deepen the content you're learning, I provide a uniform resource locator (URL, also called an Internet address) in the form: http://is.gd/uaKpYD

You might wonder what the heck this is. The way I look at the situation, if I were reading this title as a print book and needed to type out a URL given to me by the author, I would rather type in a "shortle" URL than some long, crazy URL with all sorts of special characters, you know what I mean?

The most important thing I have to tell you concerning the is.gd short URLs is that the ending part is case sensitive. Therefore, typing the previous URL as http://is.gd/UaKpyD isn't going to get you to the same page as what I intended.

NOTE
_____

URL Shortening Services

Is.gd is just one of many URL shortening services; others include bit.ly, goo.gl, and TinyURL.com. I like is.gd because the service is free and the owner operates with high integrity. For more information on is.gd, visit their FAQ page: http://is.gd/faq.php#owner.
_____

TIP
_____

Notes, Tips, and Cautions

This book uses the Note formatting (see the previous URL Shortening Services note) to frame supplemental content that adds to the current topic of discussion. Or, perhaps the Note represents a clarification or an expansion of the information. This extra information could also be formatted as a Tip, which identifies tips, tricks, or other pieces of expert advice, or a Caution, which warns you of potential hazards. Call it potpourri!
_____

About the Code Images

For most Try It Yourself exercises, you'll see one or more source code images that are annotated with alphabetical letters. The Try It Yourself steps are then cross-referenced with parts of each code image. Hopefully, you find this format convenient to your learning. Remember not to fall into the trap of blindly copying the provided code; instead, remember that learning to program requires (yes, *requires*) lots and lots of trial and error.

System Requirements

You don't need a heck of a lot, computer-wise, to perform all of the Try It Yourself exercises in this book. However, if you do not meet the necessary system requirements, then you are stuck. To that end, make sure that you have the following met prior to beginning your work:

▶ **A standard computer**: It doesn't matter whether your computer runs Windows, OS X, or Linux. Likewise, you can use either a desktop or laptop computer. However, Scratch 2.0

won't run on any device that does not fully support Adobe Flash. That rules out, at the least, iOS devices such as iPhones, iPads, and iPod touches.

▶ **An Internet connection**: Scratch 2.0 is a web application, so you need to be connected to the Internet to complete the exercises. Yes, in Hour 18, you'll learn about the Scratch 2.0 Offline Editor. However, the Offline Editor does not support all Scratch 2.0 features, and in this book you learn to use *all* of the features in the product.

▶ **An Adobe Flash-enabled web browser**: Again, it doesn't matter whether your web browser of choice is made by Microsoft, Apple, Google, or another vendor—what does count is whether the browser has the Adobe Flash plug-in installed. Point your browser to the Adobe website (http://is.gd/pCNCvd) to perform a check; if you don't have the plug-in, you can install it at Adobe.com for free.

Okay—that's enough of the preliminaries. It's time to learn to program with Scratch 2.0!

HOUR 1
What Is Scratch?

What You'll Learn in This Hour:

▶ What is an educational programming language?

▶ Understanding Scratch history

▶ Creating your Scratch profile

▶ Browsing the Scratch websites

▶ Previewing popular Scratch projects

Have you ever wanted to build a computer game from scratch? Do you sometimes wonder how the programs that you use every day work beneath the hood? Do you love to be creative, undergo experiments, and share your findings with others?

If so, then perhaps learning how to program using Scratch 2.0 is for you. Creating a software project involves three discrete actions.

First, you need to *imagine* what your software program will do. This process is almost entirely creative. Have you seen a game somewhere and thought to yourself, "I can do better than that"? Following are several project types that may serve to spark your imagination:

▶ **Animations:** Imagine a cartoon that you make yourself that features various creatures behaving in absurd and hilarious ways.

▶ **Games:** Imagine an arcade game like the old retro console video games of the early 1980s.

▶ **Simulations:** Imagine a program that enables the player to simulate performing a moon landing, albeit on a simplified scale (or not!).

▶ **Music:** Imagine an interactive xylophone. Or pedal steel guitar. Or steel drum.

▶ **Art:** Imagine a slideshow featuring some of the greatest works of art of the twentieth century, annotated with historical and cultural information.

- ▶ **Stories**: Imagine bringing the stories told to you by your parents during your childhood alive in a multimedia format that you can share with your kids.

- ▶ **Tutorials**: Imagine a program that teaches you common phrases in Spanish. Or Italian. Or Esperanto.

The key word here is *imagine*. It's a cliché, but the sky is literally the limit when it comes to what you can do with your own computer programs. You are the architect, so you get to decide exactly how the program works and for what audience the project is intended.

Next, you need to *program* the software project. Here is where you take your dream and shape it into an attainable reality. To do this, you need development tools and processes.

The operative principle during the build phase is *experimentation*. To create software, you have to be comfortable trying things out, testing them, identifying flaws, and iterating and reiterating that process until the software is excellent in your own eyes.

You're reading this book, so that must mean that you plan to use Scratch to create your program. That's a very intelligent choice on your part (congratulations!) because for many people Scratch is the ideal learning programming language.

You'll learn more about what a *learning programming language* is momentarily.

Finally, you'll want to *share* your completed software project with other people. For many software developers, myself included, this is where the ultimate payoff resides. To witness people playing your game and enjoying themselves is a deeply satisfying experience.

The associated term at play here is *social*. Offering your computer program to the world and accepting feedback, whether positive, neutral, or negative, is an inherently social transaction.

I suppose you could simply build computer programs for your own enjoyment and nobody else's, but that's probably not much fun. You can exert a positive effect on the rest of the world by sharing your creative endeavor; it's "just" a software program, but it's *much* more than that.

For instance, I've made a very nice living for myself by using Microsoft Word, the industry-leading word processor, to chronicle my thoughts in documentary form. You must not take for granted that programs like Microsoft Office, Microsoft Windows, Apple OS X, and so forth are nothing more than programs themselves that were programmed by other human beings.

What Is an Educational Programming Language?

According to Wikipedia (reference: http://is.gd/n9rltF), an *educational programming language* is designed primarily as a learning instrument and not so much as a tool for writing programs for real-world work. Extending this definition by using the same source (http://is.gd/BxNVGw), a *programming language* is a formal language that is designed to communicate instructions to a machine such as a computer.

You are here today to learn all about Scratch, but you should know that Scratch is not the only learning programming language on the block. Consider the following list:

▶ **BASIC**: This language, which stands for **B**eginner's **A**ll-purpose **S**ymbolic **I**nstruction **C**ode, was invented in 1964 to help non–computer science students learn a bit about computer science. The program is still going strong today in many different forms.

▶ **Alice**: This is free software developed at the University of Virginia that features an easy-to-understand environment for building 3D models. Figure 1.1 shows the Alice interface.

▶ **Logo**: This is a graphical educational programming language that has been around almost as long as BASIC. Logo influenced Smalltalk, which is the language behind the first version of Scratch.

▶ **Python**: This is a "tricky" choice because people and organizations use Python every day to do real work. Python is not in any way a "toy" programming language. However, its extreme ease of use makes it function exceptionally well as a learning programming language.

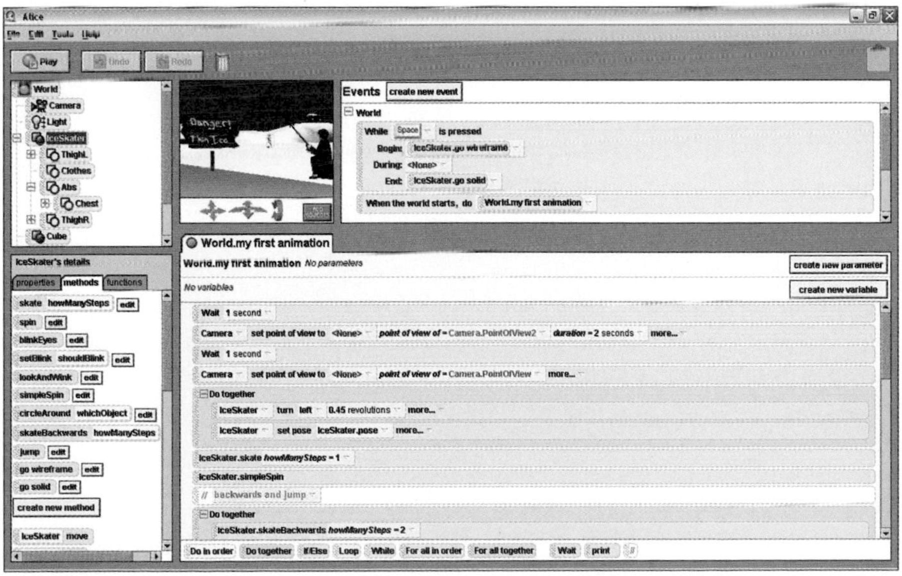

FIGURE 1.1
Alice is an excellent way to learn the fundamentals of 3D programming.

You might be wondering, "Why should I bother learning Scratch if, as an educational programming language, it isn't taken seriously by the world?" That is a good question, and I have an answer for you.

Using Scratch as your entry point into computer programming is wise because doing so will teach you the fundamentals of building computer programs without bogging you down in mathematics, lateral thinking, and other "scary" processes that dissuade many people from investigating programming in the first place.

As you'll learn, Scratch hides complexity behind an interface that might appear to some almost childish. That having been said, you'll be surprised at how powerful the Scratch tools truly are. You can build some impressive projects. And what's more is that you can carry your Scratch knowledge forward and apply it directly to learning any of the aforementioned languages, or even "real" programming languages, such as JavaScript, Ruby, or C.

Understanding Scratch History

Let's turn our attention to Scratch specifically, shall we? To begin with, Scratch is the name of several things:

- ▶ The programming language and Integrated Development Environment (IDE)
- ▶ The team at the Lifelong Kindergarten Group that owns the Scratch project
- ▶ The cat who serves as the project mascot, as well as the default sprite in a Scratch project

The Scratch programming language was developed in 2003 by the Lifelong Kindergarten Group (http://is.gd/LYZJWm) at the Massachusetts Institute of Technology (MIT) in Cambridge, Massachusetts, under the directorship of the brilliant Dr. Mitchel Resnick.

Scratch is used in K-12 schools all over the globe as a way to introduce basic computer programming concepts to children. However, and I can't stress this enough, do not be put off by the fact that the primary target audience of Scratch is preadolescents and adolescents. As a matter of fact, Harvard University uses Scratch in some of its introductory programming courses, and even training sites aimed at experienced programmers like Pluralsight.com offer Scratch training for programming "newbies."

NOTE

About That "Imagine, Program, and Share" Thing...

Recall that this hour began by describing the computer software creation process with the three descriptive verbs imagine, program, and share. That was intentional. As it happens, *Imagine, Program, Share* is the official motto for Scratch!

Although Scratch uses a cartoon cat as its mascot, the name Scratch actually derives from the disk jockey (DJ) technique of scratching, whereby the DJ moves vinyl records back and forth on a turntable to create new and different hip-hop music.

The metaphor works like this: The DJ uses creativity and experimentation to create his or her music, and then shares that music with patrons at a club. Likewise, the Scratcher uses these same elements to share his or her Scratch program with patrons located all over the globe.

Later in the book, you'll discover another DJ-related term that relates to Scratch—the remix.

Before visiting the Scratch website and creating your user profile, let's spend a moment reviewing the version history of the Scratch development environment.

The first stable version of Scratch was version 1.4, released in 2009; Figure 1.2 shows the interface.

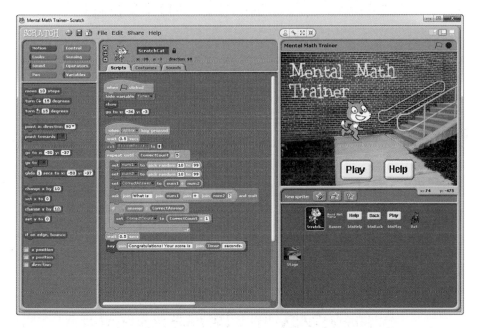

FIGURE 1.2
The Scratch 1.4 user interface. You'll find that the Scratch 2.0 interface is quite similar to this.

Scratch 1.4 is a desktop application that runs on Microsoft Windows, Apple OS X, and Debian/Ubuntu Linux. Although Scratch 1.4 has been replaced by Scratch 2.0, you can still download, install, and use Scratch 1.4 for free by visiting the Scratch website at http://is.gd/iIuIQK.

I myself was a big fan of Scratch 1.4 because the software was stable and fun to use. Like many Scratchers (incidentally, Scratch users are affectionately known within the community as *Scratchers*), I was concerned when the Scratch Team announced the impending availability of Scratch 2.0. Why was I scared? In a nutshell, Scratch 2.0 is a major upgrade to the Scratch platform.

Scratch 2.0 was released on May 9, 2013, to a good degree of fanfare. The biggest difference between Scratch 1.4 and Scratch 2.0 is that the latter is a cloud-based application. Figure 1.3 shows the Scratch 2.0 interface.

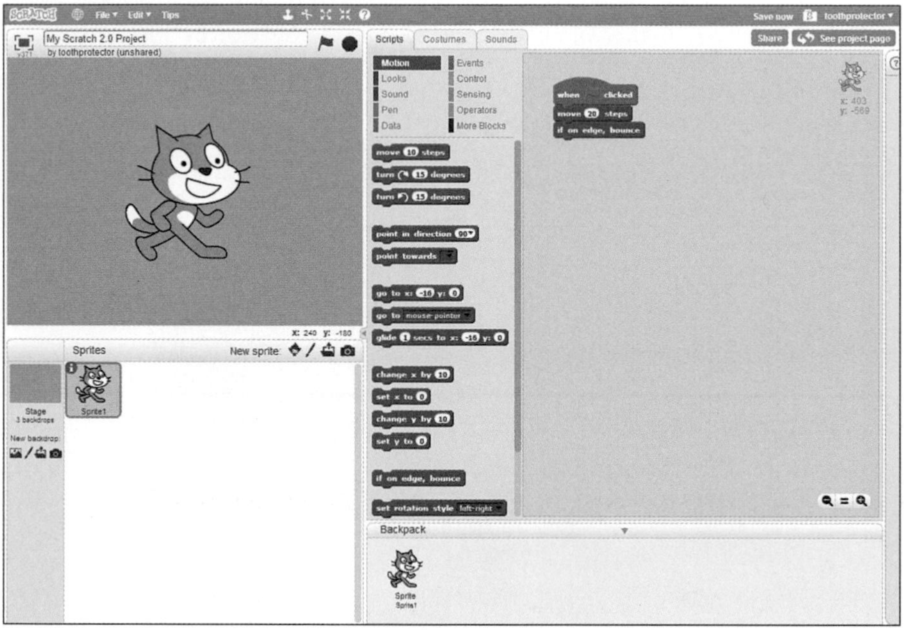

FIGURE 1.3
The Scratch 2.0 user interface. Under the hood, this is an Adobe Flash application that runs in any modern full-fidelity web browser.

This means that Scratch 2.0 runs not locally on the Scratcher's computer, but online on one of MIT's web servers. Moreover, the underlying technology used in Scratch 2.0 is Adobe Flash, which does not run on many mobile platforms, most notably Apple's iDevices (iPhone, iPad, iPod touch).

"But what if I don't have an 'always on' Internet connection?" many Scratchers asked incredulously. The Scratch Team's answer to the offline access question is the Scratch 2.0 Offline Editor, shown in Figure 1.4.

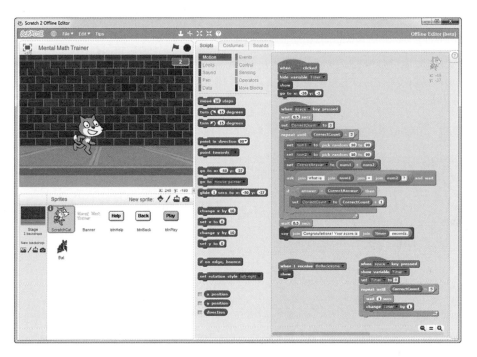

FIGURE 1.4
The Scratch 2.0 Offline Editor, which enables you to work on Scratch projects when you don't have an Internet connection.

The Scratch 2.0 Offline Editor includes all the features of the standard cloud-based project editor, but has the advantage of being locally installed on the user's computer and is, therefore, available even without an Internet connection. You'll spend time working with the Offline Editor in Hour 18, "Using the Scratch Offline Editor." If you can't wait until then, you can download the Offline Editor from (where else?) the Scratch website: http://is.gd/sB2h1k.

As of this writing, the Scratch Offline Editor is officially listed as "beta" (which is to say, prerelease) status. Don't let that fact worry you, however. I've tested every exercise we undertake in this book by using the beta editor, and I've seen no issues at all.

Before moving on, a few quick words need to be said about compatibility between Scratch 1.4 and Scratch 2.0 projects. Here's the deal, friends: Although you can run Scratch 1.4 and the Scratch 2.0 Offline Editor on the same computer at the same time, you cannot load Scratch 2.0 projects into Scratch 1.4.

Conversely, you can open Scratch 1.4 projects in Scratch 2.0, but they will be converted to the Scratch 2.0 format once you've uploaded them to the cloud.

Alrighty then! With no further ado, it's time to visit the Scratch website and become a member of the community. After all, that's how you can become a real, live Scratcher!

Creating Your Scratch Profile

One of the most important websites in this entire book is the Scratch project home page at scratch.mit.edu. If you haven't bookmarked that site in your web browser yet, then please do so.

Using Figure 1.5 as a guide, take a quick tour of the Scratch home page by reviewing my descriptions of the figure annotations:

▶ **A:** The Scratch button takes you back to the home page.

▶ **B:** The Create button instantly creates a new project, provided you are logged in to the site with your Scratch account.

▶ **C:** The Explore button enables you to browse other Scratchers' projects and try them out.

▶ **D:** The Discuss button takes you to the discussion forums, where you can get your questions answered and help other Scratchers solve their problems with the platform.

▶ **E:** The Help button takes you to the documentation page.

▶ **F:** The Search button allows you to perform keyword searches across the entire Scratch website.

▶ **G:** The Join Scratch button is what you use to create your free Scratch user account.

▶ **H:** The Sign In button is used to log in to the site with your Scratch username and password.

▶ **I:** The Try It Out button allows you to play with the Scratch Project Editor without having a user account.

▶ **J:** The See Examples button transports you to the same place that the Explore button does.

▶ **K:** The Join Scratch button does the same thing as clicking the Join Scratch button described above in G.

▶ **L:** The Featured Projects area is a good place to view popular Scratch projects.

▶ **M:** The Featured Studios area allows you to browse popular project collections known as studios.

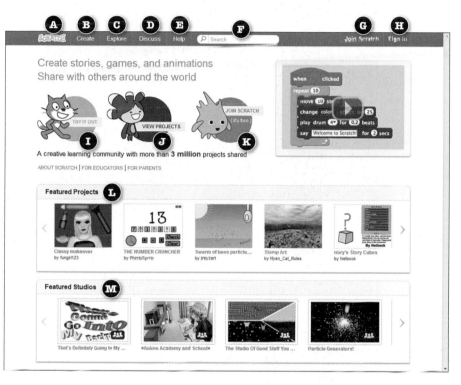

FIGURE 1.5
The Scratch home page (scratch.mit.edu).

TRY IT YOURSELF ▼

Create Your Scratch Account

Creating a free Scratch user account is required for you to save your work on the Scratch website, participate in discussions, and otherwise be a part of the Scratch community. To get started, you will need to think of a unique username, a strong password, and have a valid email address. Follow these steps:

1. From the Scratch home page at scratch.mit.edu, click Join Scratch in the top navigation bar.

2. In step 1 in the Join Scratch dialog box, type a Scratch username and enter and confirm a strong password. A *strong password* is defined as a password that is nearly impossible for someone to guess. The password should not be any word found in a dictionary and should consist of a mixture of uppercase letters, lowercase letters, numbers, and nonalphanumeric characters. For your username, it is advisable for security reasons not to include any personally identifiable details, such as your name or birth year. Click Next to continue.

▼

3. In step 2 in the Join Scratch dialog box, type your birth month, birth year, gender, country, and email address. If you prefer to remain anonymous, you can put in fake information. However, your email address must be valid so you can use it to recover a lost password, track support requests, and so on. Click Next to continue.

4. The Thanks for Joining Scratch! dialog box appears (shown in Figure 1.6), which lets you know that you have successfully created your account. Click OK Let's Go! to dismiss the Join Scratch dialog box.

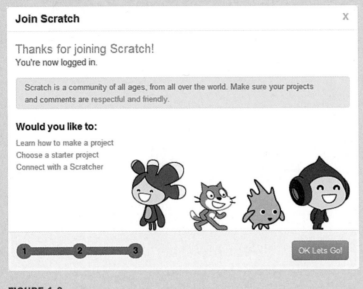

FIGURE 1.6
It's fast, free, and easy to create your own Scratch user account.

Once you have your Scratch account, you can always (and should always) sign in immediately after reaching the Scratch website. To do this, simply click Sign In in the top navigation bar, type your username and password, and then click Sign In.

What can you do with your new account? For one thing, and most important, you can click Create to build new Scratch projects. You also can manage all aspects of your public profile.

Populate Your Scratch Profile

Let's spend some time getting to know the Scratch user account controls. To get started, make sure you are logged in to the Scratch website with your new account credentials, and then follow these steps:

1. As shown in Figure 1.7, open your user account menu and note the options. Profile takes you to your public profile page. My Stuff takes you to your personal project gallery. Account Settings allows you to change your password and/or your contact email address. Sign Out, well, signs you out of the website!

2. Again, using Figure 1.7 as a guide, check out the various and sundry components of your profile page. If you haven't done so already, open your user menu and click Profile.

   To the left of your username, notice the placeholder for a profile image. Hover your mouse over the placeholder and click Change. You can then upload a profile pic. Be creative here! You don't have to use your actual likeness. For my *toothprotector* Scratch account, I use a picture of the associated Atari 2600 game cartridge from which I derived my username.

3. Optionally, fill out the About Me and What I'm Working On fields in the Profile page by clicking within each box and typing your information.

4. At this point, your Shared Projects bucket should be empty; you'll eventually have one or more projects ready to share with the world—be patient!

5. As you browse the public project gallery, you'll likely find projects that are simply fun to play or, more to the point, inspire you to emulate their great attributes. You can add these preferred projects to your Favorites list for easy future reference. You can also choose to follow other Scratchers, which keeps you notified as to any new projects they share with the community.

   Do you see the little envelope icon to the left of the user menu in the top navigation bar? If you don't see it on your computer screen, take a look at Figure 1.7 again until you notice it. Click that button and you'll find yourself at the Messages screen.

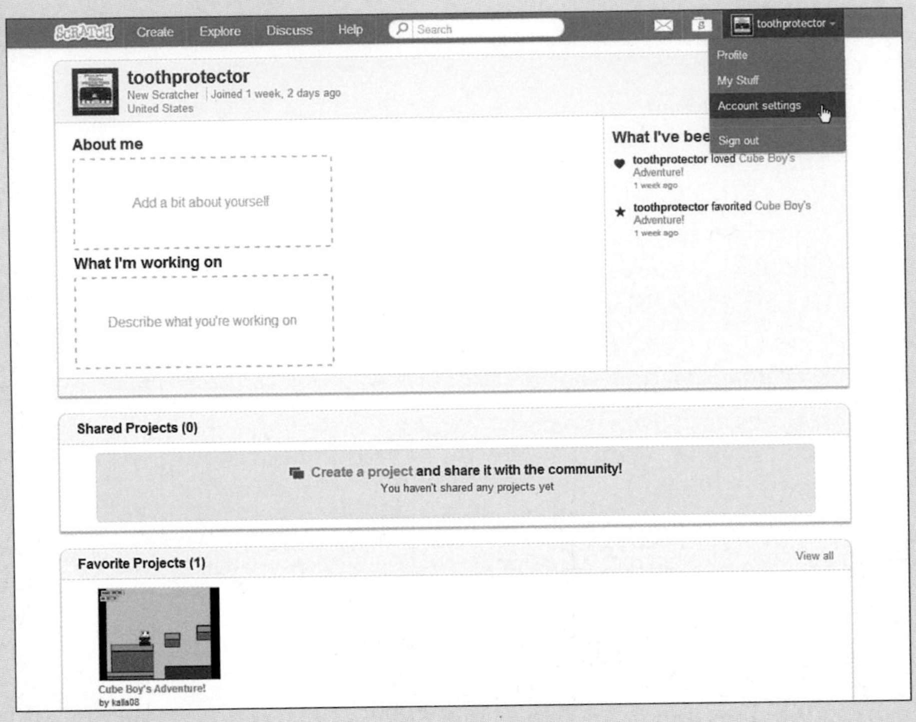

FIGURE 1.7
The Scratch user account menu is visible in the top right, and the user profile page is shown in the background.

The Scratch Messages area is not an Internet email application like Yahoo! mail. Instead, it provides you a way to view messages and alerts from the Scratch Team and/or other Scratchers. The interface also logs any comments associated with your Scratch account. Unfortunately, as of this writing, the Messages page does not allow you to send messages directly to other Scratchers.

If you do want to communicate with a Scratcher, your best bet is to visit his or her profile page and leave a comment.

Browsing the Scratch Websites

The Scratch Team maintains a number of Scratch-related websites besides the primary one you've been dealing with thus far.

To start with, click Discuss from the Scratch website top navigation menu. Have you used discussion forums (also called message boards) before? Here, you can find categorized conversations on a variety of subjects, including the following:

- ▶ New Scratchers

- ▶ Help with scripts

- ▶ Project ideas

- ▶ Questions about Scratch

- ▶ Advanced topics

Figure 1.8 shows the discussion board interface. What's so cool about the discussion forums is that simply having a Scratch account entitles you to participate in any of these discussions. If you have a question, go ahead and ask it! First, though, use the Search box to see if your question has already been answered.

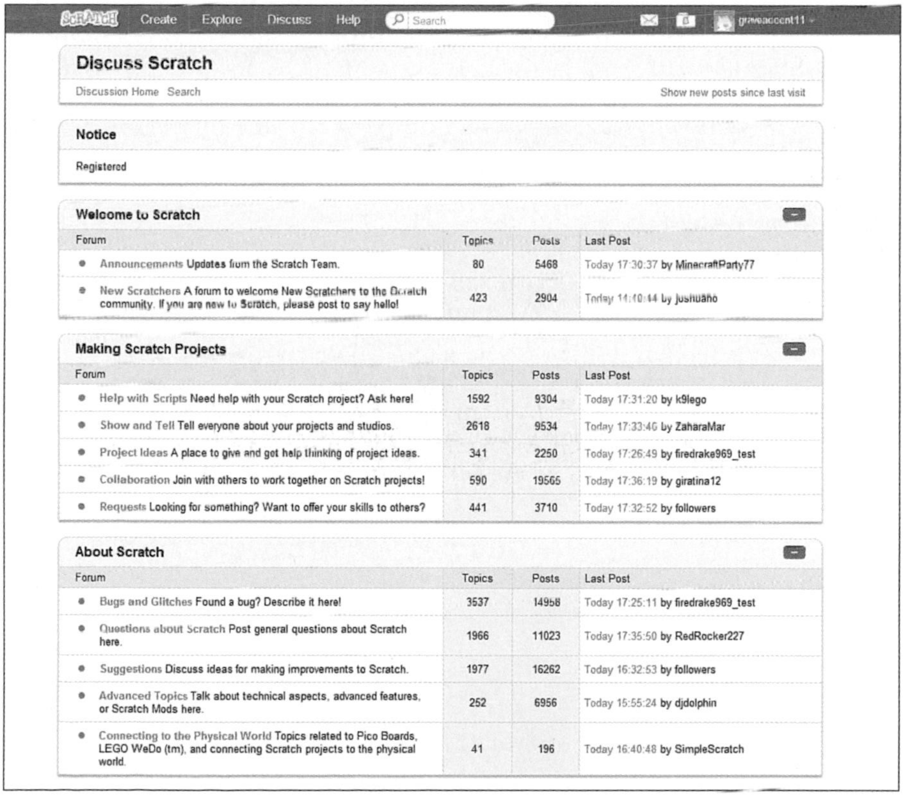

FIGURE 1.8
Participating in the Scratch discussion forums can help you feel like a part of the community.

The Scratch Team members moderate these online conversations, so you can both benefit from their expertise as well as enjoy their pruning of spam or off-topic conversation stubs.

Now let's click Help from the top navigation bar to visit the Scratch Help page (http://is.gd/zOLryH). Wow—this page is literally covered with links to provide you with assistance no matter what your professional role and/or experience with the product.

If you are a teacher, then you'll want to click the link to the Scratch Ed website (http://is.gd/Ciw37B), where instructors can collaborate and share knowledge regarding how to integrate Scratch into their classrooms or online training.

Personally, I spend a lot of time at the Scratch Wiki (http://is.gd/zi2pLU), shown in Figure 1.9. You might have used Wikipedia.org before—a *wiki* is a user-edited online encyclopedia. To that point, the Scratch Wiki is an online knowledge base focused entirely on Scratch technology.

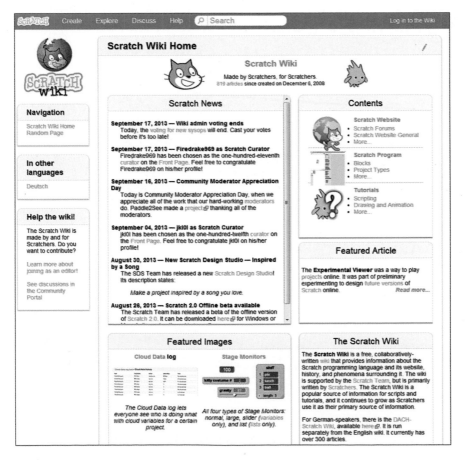

FIGURE 1.9
The Scratch Wiki is your go-to information source whenever you have a question about the product.

Once you finish this book and put in the necessary work hours with Scratch, you might want to consider becoming a contributor at the Scratch Wiki. Note that you cannot use your ordinary Scratch user account to log in to the Scratch Wiki and make edits to pages. Instead, you have to submit a request to the Scratch Team in Massachusetts.

Previewing Popular Scratch Projects

Okay, now for the really fun stuff. From the Scratch home page, click Explore to visit the Scratch project gallery, shown in Figure 1.10.

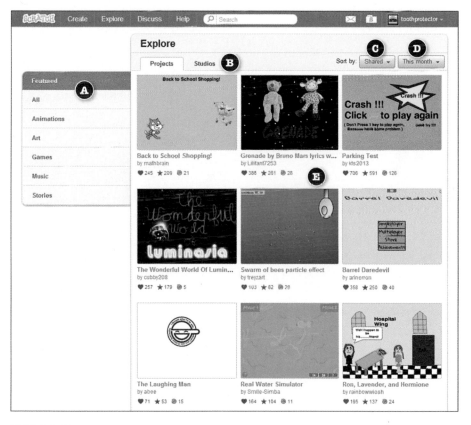

FIGURE 1.10
The Scratch Explore gallery is a fantastic place to find inspiration and simply to have fun.

The Explore area is crucial for a number of reasons, two being (1) this is where your users will discover and use your own projects and (2) this is where you can derive inspiration by studying the work of others.

As you'll see in just a moment, you can do more than play other Scratcher's projects—you can actually enter inside them to view their underlying source code.

Please cross-reference the annotations in Figure 1.10 with the following list, which serves to introduce you to the major interface elements of the project gallery:

▶ **A:** Use this control to filter the type of projects you want to browse in the gallery. Choices include All, Animations, Art, Games, Music, and Stories. You can also perform a keyword search on tags to locate specific types of projects; you'll learn all about tags later in the book.

▶ **B:** Use these tabs to see either individual projects or project studios.

▶ **C:** You can sort the gallery view by opening the Shared drop-down and selecting from the following criteria: Most Viewed, Most Loved, or Most Remixed.

▶ **D:** The view choices here are This Month or This Week. If you want to see older projects, your best bet is to perform a keyword search from the top navigation bar.

▶ **E:** Click any project in the project window to visit the project's home page.

▼ TRY IT YOURSELF

Check Out a Published Scratch Project

To prepare for this Try It Yourself exercise, use the Scratch Explore page to locate a project that is of interest to you. Click the project to navigate to its project page, and then complete the following steps to get a feel for how Scratch projects work:

1. Click the Green Flag icon on the project Stage to being the program. Be sure to read the Instructions and Notes and Credits areas to learn how the program works. For instance, many authors will list the control scheme for the program in the Instructions window.

2. Take some time to read through some comments. Feel free to leave one of your own if you want.

3. If the project is popular enough, you will see a list of one or more remixes. In Scratch nomenclature, a remix is another Scratcher's project that was built from your project's source code. Remixing (along with giving proper credit) is fundamental to the Scratch community ethos.

4. Click See Inside and prepare to be amazed! As shown in Figure 1.11, you'll be teleported "magically" to the Scratch Project Editor, where you can view all of the original source code behind that Scratcher's project!

   Of course, all the block stacks and sprite lists will just look like gobbledygook to you at this point; that is entirely to be expected. Simply appreciate the fact that you can not only appreciate other community members' work, but you can actually learn from their best and worst coding practices.

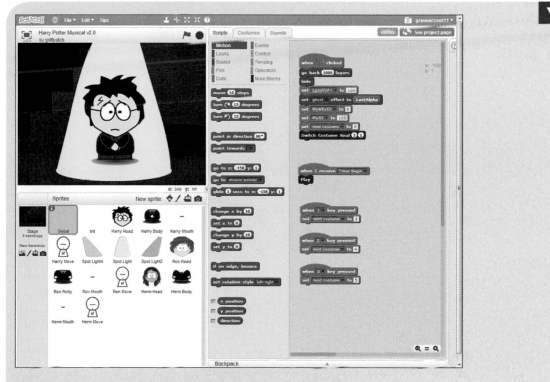

FIGURE 1.11
Scratch's open source nature enables you to learn from the coding of other Scratchers in the community.

Summary

In this hour, you learned what educational programming languages are and found out why Scratch is one of the ideal languages to use when you want to discover computer programming and computer science.

You then went from being a Scratch community bystander to being a full-fledged member. You did this simply by creating a free Scratch user account. Having an account unlocks the power and full functionality of Scratch. While logged in to the site, you can view other Scratchers' source code, participate in discussion forum threads, leave comments—the list goes on and on.

This hour concluded with a consideration of the major Scratch websites. You've just seen the core websites—you should definitely spend some time on the Web researching Scratch, and you're guaranteed to find plenty more.

Coming up in the next hour, you'll learn how to create and manage sprites and costumes.

Workshop

Quiz

1. Which Scratch website page allows you to manage your shared projects?

    A. Explore

    B. My Stuff

    C. Account Settings

2. Which of the following actions on the Scratch website does *not* require that you have a Scratch user account?

    A. View other Scratchers' project source code.

    B. Respond to a discussion forum post.

    C. View the Scratch Help pages.

3. Where should a teacher go in the Scratch website hierarchy to find shared lesson plans for teaching Scratch to K-12 students?

    A. Scratch Ed

    B. Scratch Wiki

    C. Scratch Explore

Answers

1. The correct answer is choice B. The My Stuff page is your "home base" for managing Scratch projects that you create, both those that are shared with the Scratch community as well as those that are private and under development by you. The Explore page is where you go to browse other Scratchers' projects. The Account Settings page allows you to manage your account password and email address.

2. The correct answer is choice C. You can view just about all of the content on the Scratch website without having to define a user account. However, if you actually want to participate in the action, you need to have an account and be logged in to said account. Specifically, although you can view the source code of any Scratch project without a login, you need an account if you want to remix or otherwise borrow from that project.

3. The correct answer is choice A. The Scratch Ed website is squarely targeted to educators at all levels. Here, instructors can swap stories, share lesson plans, and discuss how Scratch works in a teacher/student educational setting. The Scratch Wiki is more of a general-purpose information repository regarding all things Scratch. The Explore page, as previously mentioned, is the gallery of published Scratch projects that are available for playing, analyzing, and remixing.

Challenge

To get a clear idea of how Scratch community collaboration works, create a second Scratch user account simply for testing purposes. If you don't have another email address, it is fast and free to get another one via, say, Google Gmail (http://is.gd/sjPlfG).

Once you have a second Scratch account defined, search for and locate your first account. Practice sending and receiving messages between the two accounts. Try the same thing with comments. Create a blank project, share it (publishing is covered in Hour 17, "Publishing Your Project"), and then view the project by using your other account.

Once you're finished with your testing, you might want to delete your second Scratch account both to (1) reduce confusion on your part in having to juggle multiple identities and (2) reduce the Scratch Team's burden of maintaining unused user accounts on its site.

To delete a Scratch user account, you need to reach out to the Scratch Team directly and ask the team to remove your Scratch account from the system. You can contact the team through the Contact Us page at http://is.gd/JUNXdk.

HOUR 2
Creating Your First Project

What You'll Learn in This Hour:

▶ Navigating the Scratch Project Editor
▶ Formally introducing Scratch blocks
▶ Previewing your project
▶ Using My Stuff

By now, you have an idea as to what Scratch is all about, and you've also become a member of the Scratch community by creating a user account. What's next?

In this hour, you start by becoming familiar with the Scratch Project Editor, which is the primary interface for creating Scratch projects. Because Scratch 2.0 is a cloud-based application, you must have an active Internet connection to develop projects using the online Project Editor. Keep in mind, though, that you'll learn how to use the Scratch Offline Editor in Hour 18, "Using the Scratch Offline Editor."

Once you create your first project, you learn how to preview your work by viewing its corresponding project page. You also discover how to leverage the My Stuff page to manage your Scratch projects.

Let's get to work!

Navigating the Scratch Project Editor

To begin your first project, go to the scratch.mit.edu website, log in to your Scratch account, and then click Create on the top navigation bar. This action switches your view to the Scratch Project Editor, all loaded up with a fresh, unsaved project.

Figure 2.1 shows the primary user interface elements of the Scratch Project Editor. Use Figure 2.1 as a guide as you learn about each part of the main screen:

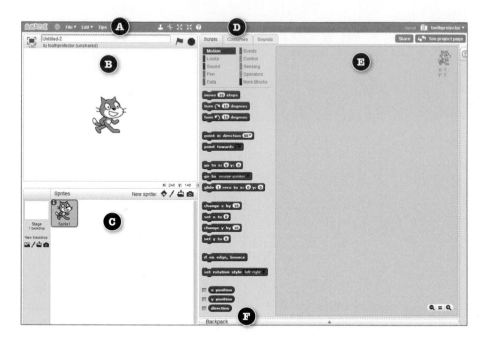

FIGURE 2.1
You will spend the vast majority of your project creation time working in the Scratch Project Editor.

▶ **A:** You can use the menu bar to perform various project- and sprite-related management tasks.

▶ **B:** The Stage is where all of the action of your project occurs.

▶ **C:** The Sprites list shows the sprites, which are the characters and elements that appear on the Stage.

▶ **D:** The Blocks palette is where you add the programming logic behind your Scratch project.

▶ **E:** The Scripts area is where you stack blocks to perform actions on the Stage.

▶ **F:** The Backpack enables you to move content both within a project and between projects. This is a favorite feature of Scratch 2.0, which you'll come to love as well.

Once you have the "lay of the land" with the Project Editor overall, it's time to get initially acquainted with each workspace component in a bit more detail. Using Figure 2.2 as a guide, examine the menu bar in more detail:

FIGURE 2.2
The Scratch Project Editor menu bar contains lots of useful command shortcuts.

▶ **A**: The Scratch logo button takes you to the Scratch home page.

▶ **B**: The Globe button enables you to change the interface language.

▶ **C**: The File menu enables you to save your work, download the project to a local file, or upload a project file from your computer to the cloud.

▶ **D**: The Edit menu enables you to adjust the Stage size or access the Undo function.

▶ **E**: The Tips button toggles a pop-out window that provides general Scratch help.

▶ **F**: Click the Duplicate button and then click a block or a sprite to clone it. This function can save you a lot of development time.

▶ **G**: Click the Delete button and then click a sprite or a button to immediately remove it from the project. *Warning*: There is no confirmation for this action, although you can click Edit, Undelete to get your deleted object back.

▶ **H**: Click the Grow button and then click a sprite to make it grow in predefined increments.

▶ **I**: Click the Shrink button to do the exact opposite of the Grow button.

▶ **J**: Clicking the Block Help button and then clicking any Scratch block opens a contextual Help window that provides assistance focused on that block's usage.

▶ **K**: The Save status toggles between Save Now and Saved depending upon the current save state of your project.

▶ **L**: The My Stuff button takes you to your My Stuff page, where you can manage all of your Scratch projects.

▶ **M**: The User menu enables you to manage all aspects of your Scratch user account.

Now let's turn your attention to the Sprites list because there is quite a bit of activity in that part of the Project Editor. Refer to Figure 2.3 for the annotated image, and then check out the following additional information:

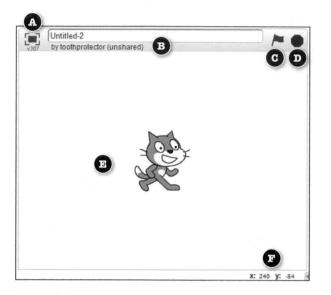

FIGURE 2.3
The Stage and Sprites lists are where you define and modify the characters and action of your Scratch project.

▶ **A:** The Stage button toggles between the default Stage size of 480 pixels wide by 360 pixels tall and Full-Screen mode.

▶ **B:** Using the Title field, you can change the name of your Scratch project at any time.

▶ **C:** Use the Green Flag to start (in the sense of executing) a Scratch project.

▶ **D:** The Stop button stops the execution of the Scratch project immediately.

▶ **E:** On the main Stage, the origin point of the Stage is at its dead center; sprite location is determined by using the Cartesian coordinate system.

▶ **F:** Sprite coordinates give you the Cartesian (x and y) coordinates of your mouse pointer.

Finally, take a look at the Scripts area more closely. Use Figure 2.4 as your guide with these descriptions for your studying pleasure:

▶ **A:** The Share button makes your project viewable by all members of the Scratch community, regardless of whether they have a Scratch user account.

▶ **B:** Using the See Project Page button, you can toggle the view between the editor and the project's public information page.

▶ **C:** This area shows a small representation of the currently selected sprite along with its x,y location coordinates. You can find a current sprite's location by double-clicking the sprite in the Stage or in the Sprites area.

▶ **D**: You can also use the Magnification tools. The left (minus) button zooms the Scripts pane out, the right (plus) button zooms in, and the middle button resets the zoom level to 100 percent, the default value.

▶ **E**: This button exposes the Backpack, which allows you to move or copy resources—both within a single project or between multiple projects.

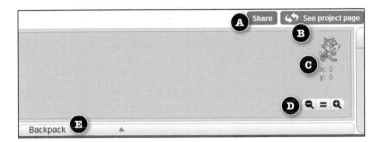

FIGURE 2.4
The Scripts area is where you actually program the action in your Scratch projects.

Okay, then—let's get to work. Before doing any real work in your new project, you need to give it a name and make sure that it is saved to the Scratch servers at MIT.

TRY IT YOURSELF ▼

Save a New Scratch Project

Although the good folks at the MIT Lifetime Learning Lab automatically (or "automagically," depending upon your perspective on information technology) save your work periodically, you should give the project a meaningful name to make it easy for you and your audience to remember. Follow these steps:

1. Above the Stage, remove the placeholder project title (*Untitled-1* is the default title), and provide a descriptive project name. Don't worry, you can always change the title later.

2. From the menu bar, click File, Save Now.

3. You can verify that your file has been successfully saved to the cloud by looking at the right side of the menu bar. When the file is current, the menu will read Saved, as shown in Figure 2.5. When you have made a change that hasn't yet been saved, the menu will read Save Now. To manually save your work, click File, Save Now or click the Save Now text directly in the menu bar.

   However, don't get too stressed out if you forget to manually save your work—the project will be autosaved to the cloud within 10 seconds or so.

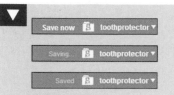

FIGURE 2.5
The Project Editor interface lets you know at a glance whether your project is current or should be saved. By the way, toothprotector is my Scratch username.

NOTE

Up in the Cloud

By default, all your Scratch projects are saved in what's commonly called the cloud. What exactly does this mean? In information technology jargon, the cloud refers to an Internet-connected server that does not belong to you. Specifically, your project exists on one of the content servers owned by the MIT Media lab in Massachusetts. Because we as Scratch users don't need to know or care specifically where these servers are or how they work, we use the generic term *cloud* to refer to remote file storage. You'll revisit the cloud in much more detail in Hour 13, "Using Cloud Data."

The Scratch Team's autosave interval is undocumented as of this writing. My best guess is that each action you take in a project, whether it's modifying a costume, adding a block, and so forth, is assigned a numeric weight. When the project counts to a certain threshold value, then an automatic save is performed. The take-home message here concerning saving is the same as for any computer application:

Get into the habit of saving your work early and often.

If you have any previous experience with programming, you are probably surprised that we haven't asked the question, "What kind of a program do you want to build?" To be sure, one of the main tasks of the software developer (also known as a programmer) is to clearly define the goals of the project prior to beginning work on it.

That said, once you have your "sea legs" with regard to Scratch and understand how to use and apply its tools, you can sit down and map out your projects. In fact, the project management side of building computer software is discussed later in the book in Hour 16, "Documenting Your Project."

For now, though, don't think about things too much and just have fun! After all, that's why the Lifetime Learning folks at MIT developed Scratch—as an enjoyable way for people to apply their creativity and learn programming without having to be mired in "the boring stuff."

Animate the Scratch Cat

In this Try It Yourself exercise, you dive right in and make the Scratch Cat, the first, default sprite in your Scratch project, move around the stage. Perform all this work from the Scratch Project Editor on your newly saved project by following these steps:

1. Make sure the Scratch Cat sprite is selected by double-clicking the Sprite1 icon in the Sprites list.

2. In the Blocks palette, ensure that the Scripts tab is visible, and click Events to expose the Events blocks.

3. Click the [when clicked] Hat block and drag it to the empty Scripts area. You can check your work against the completed script shown in Figure 2.6.

4. Now navigate back to the Motion tab and drag a [move 10 steps] block out to the Scripts pane.

5. Here's the magic: Move the [move 10 steps] block just beneath the [when clicked] block until it snaps in place. That was easy, wasn't it?

6. Double-click the [move 10 steps] block and change the value 10 to something more substantial, like 100.

7. You're all done! To test the script, click the Green Flag icon on the Stage. To run the project again, click the Green Flag again. Feel free to click and drag the Scratch Cat to reposition him (her?) on the Stage. Alternatively, if you find your project's current state to have become hopelessly confusing, you can click File, Revert to reset the project to its initial defaults.

FIGURE 2.6
One of the great beauties of Scratch is that the environment hides the complexity of building and applying programming logic.

In case you wondered, you can detach connected blocks in the Scripts pane by clicking and dragging away the lower block in a stack. For practice, try detaching and then reattaching the [move 10 steps] block that you added during the previous Try It Yourself exercise.

Congratulations, friend! You just completed your first simple Scratch project! If questions like, "Why doesn't the position of the Scratch Cat reset to the center of the Stage each time I click the

Green Flag?" come to your mind, then you get a gold star—that is the kind of question asked by inquisitive programmers.

You'll learn how to reset the project environment so that the program runs consistently each time it is started later.

Formally Introducing Scratch Blocks

Gentle reader, I would like you to meet some good friends of mine. These buddies have helped form the "engine" of several successful and fun Scratch projects. With no further ado, I give you...Scratch blocks.

All kidding aside, it is imperative that you develop an intimate familiarity with all of the available block types that are included in Scratch. Let's begin by differentiating the six basic block types (check Figure 2.7 for reference):

▶ **A**: The Hat blocks are used to start a script. This is clear when you see the notch on the bottom of the shape, but not at the top.

▶ **B**: The Stack blocks are the workhorse of the Scratch block library. The top and bottom notches indicate that you can stack these blocks to any degree that you require.

▶ **C**: The Boolean blocks represent conditional logic. For instance, you can ask the question "Did the user click Sprite A?" and the Boolean answers are either "Yes" or "No," or "True" or "False."

▶ **D**: The Reporter blocks hold character or numeric data.

▶ **E**: The C blocks are also called *wrap blocks* and enable you to perform branching and/or looping logic in your Scratch projects.

▶ **F**: The Cap blocks are used to stop scripts; notice the smooth bottom that literally prevents you from snapping additional blocks after it.

You've probably noticed that the blocks contained within the 10 categories in the Blocks palette are color-coded. This is by design; the Scratch Team felt that keeping related blocks color-matched would lend to faster learning.

As you work through this book, you'll come to know how to use every single block category and individual block in the product. The 10 categories are described in the following list:

▶ **Motion**: These medium-blue blocks are used to control a sprite's movement on the Stage.

▶ **Looks**: These light-purple blocks are used to manage a sprite's appearance.

▶ **Sound**: These pink blocks are used to introduce audio media into your Scratch project.

▶ **Pen**: These dark-green blocks are used to control the Scratch 2.0 drawing pen.

▶ **Data**: These orange and dark-red blocks are used to store and display variable data, both locally in your Scratch program and globally in the MIT cloud.

▶ **Events**: These brown blocks are used to sense events and to trigger scripts to run.

▶ **Control**: These gold blocks are used to control the execution of your Scratch scripts.

▶ **Sensing**: These light-blue blocks are used to detect various digital and analog inputs.

▶ **Operators**: These light-green blocks are used to perform mathematical operations in your Scratch programs.

▶ **More Blocks**: These dark-purple blocks allow you to create your own custom blocks in Scratch 2.0.

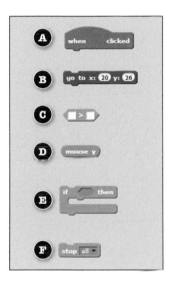

FIGURE 2.7
In time, you'll intuitively understand the purpose of each Scratch block by examining its shape and color. Note that in this figure I grabbed a representative example of each block type; at this point, don't pay attention to the specific function provided by each block shown.

Previewing Your Project

The fastest way to preview your project is simply to click the Green Flag icon in the upper-right corner of the Stage. However, Scratch 2.0 has another trick up its sleeve; namely, you can preview what your published project looks like even before you make the program available to the public!

NOTE

What's with All This "Project" Stuff?

You'll notice that throughout this book I'm careful not to call your Scratch program a *game*, an *interactive book*, or anything else very specific. This decision on my part is intentional: We need to honor the fact that Scratchers develop programs in Scratch for a variety of reasons and to accomplish a number of different goals. Thus, it is the path of least resistance when we speak generally of Scratch to use the equally generic descriptors *project* and *computer program*.

After you save your work (or let the Scratch environment save it for you automatically as discussed previously), click See Project Page above the Scripts area. You'll be magically transported to your program's very own project page, as shown in Figure 2.8.

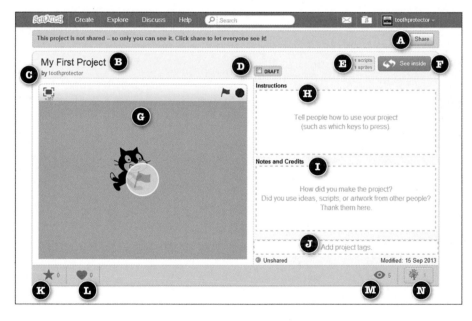

FIGURE 2.8
You can customize the appearance of your project page long before you make your program publicly visible (and playable).

Figure 2.8 shows the interface elements of the project page. Use the figure as a guide with the following list:

▶ **A:** Click the Share button to make your Scratch project publicly viewable.

▶ **B:** You can change the project title either here or in the Project Editor.

▶ **C:** Clicking the Author link takes you to your author page at the Scratch website.

▶ **D:** Enabling the Draft option lets other Scratchers know that the project is currently being updated.

▶ **E:** The Script assets indicator tells you how many scripts and how many sprites are contained in your project.

▶ **F:** Click the See Inside button to open the project in the Scratch Project Editor.

▶ **G:** On the Stage, you can start and stop the project just like you can in the Project Editor.

▶ **H:** The Instructions area is where you can tell your audience what your project is and how to use it.

▶ **I:** The Notes and Credits area is a catchall area where you can ask players for feedback, give attributions, and so forth.

▶ **J:** By applying descriptive keywords (project tags) to your project, you make it easier for people to find your project on the Scratch website.

▶ **K:** Click this button to add a reference to the project to your user account's Favorites list.

▶ **L:** Click this button to add a Love reference to the target project. A project's Love count affects the project's visibility on the Scratch website.

▶ **M:** The Total Views button lets you know the relative popularity of the project. Unfortunately, the total views number includes your own views.

▶ **N:** View the remix tree to see what other Scratchers, if any, have built projects that are based upon your work.

Please note that my interface descriptions are current as of this writing in spring 2014. However, the Scratch project is under constant development, so you might notice changes. Don't be disheartened! Once you gain your "sea legs" with Scratch, you'll come to appreciate most, if not all, of the evolving enhancements to the interface.

You will learn how to prepare your Scratch projects for publication in Hour 16 and Hour 17, "Publishing Your Project."

TRY IT YOURSELF ▼

Explore the Scratch Project Page

In this Try It Yourself exercise, you check out the project page of a particularly popular Scratch project. If this project isn't available on the Scratch website by the time you read this, then simply search for another project and use that instead. Follow these steps:

▼

1. Visit the project page of Scratcher kalla08's game Cube Boy's Adventure by pointing your web browser to http://is.gd/UFTmLt.

2. The game directions are pretty straightforward; read them by reading the text in the Instructions and Notes and Credits boxes. Don't forget to click the Green Flag and play a few rounds for yourself!

3. Go ahead and Favorite and Love the project by clicking the appropriate buttons beneath the game Stage. Observe how the counters increment by one.

4. Read through some of the comments and consider leaving your own remark, perhaps a compliment to the author.

5. Speaking of the author, click the Scratcher's username listed beneath the project title to view his or her profile page. Figure 2.9 shows kalla08's profile.

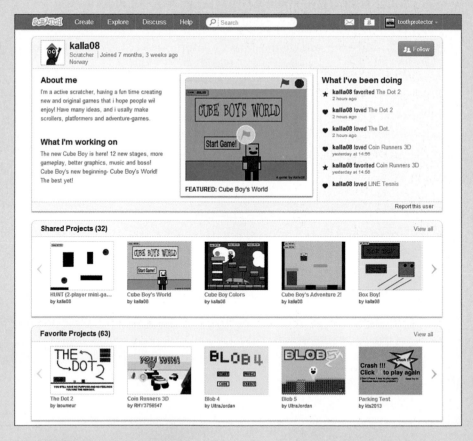

FIGURE 2.9
This Scratcher has a robust and completely populated Scratch profile. It really makes a difference!

6. Return to the game's profile page and see how many Scratchers remixed (modified a copy of) the project. Hour 20, "Remixing a Project," discusses remixing in detail. You can view the project's remix tree by clicking the appropriate button; Figure 2.10 shows this project's remix tree.

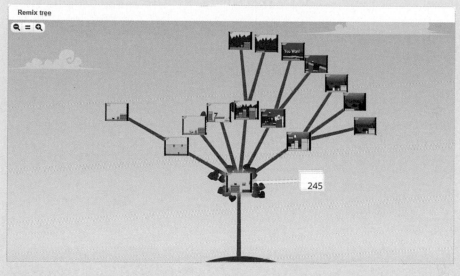

FIGURE 2.10
One measure of a Scratch program's success is how many people want to create their own remix, or modified version, of it. Look at the left side of the "tree"; the picture shows both direct remixes of your project as well as when a Scratcher remixes a remix!

Using My Stuff

Each Scratcher has his or her own My Stuff page where all saved Scratch projects are aggregated. Therefore, you can refer to your My Stuff page as your project manager page.

To get to My Stuff, click the My Stuff icon in the top right of the Scratch website navigation bar. It sort of goes without saying, but you need to be logged in to the site with your Scratch user account to get to My Stuff. Figure 2.11 shows you the My Stuff interface.

As has become the habit, take a look at each major component of the My Stuff page using Figure 2.11 as your guide:

 ▶ **A:** Use Sort By to adjust the order of your projects by modification date, number of views, number of loves, number of remixes, or alphabetically.

 ▶ **B:** Use the New Project button to create a new blank project with a single click.

▶ **C:** The New Studio button creates a new studio. A studio is a named collection of multiple Scratch projects, yours and/or any other Scratcher's.

▶ **D:** Use the View filter to customize the view to show all projects, shared projects, unshared projects, your studios, or the trash can.

▶ **E:** Clicking the project title link in My Stuff takes you to the program's project page, not the Project Editor.

▶ **F:** Clicking the Share button makes your project publicly available on the Scratch website.

▶ **G:** The See Inside button opens the project in the Scratch Project Editor.

▶ **H:** The Delete button sends your project to the trash.

▶ **I:** The Load More button shows you the next screenful of projects in your My Stuff folder.

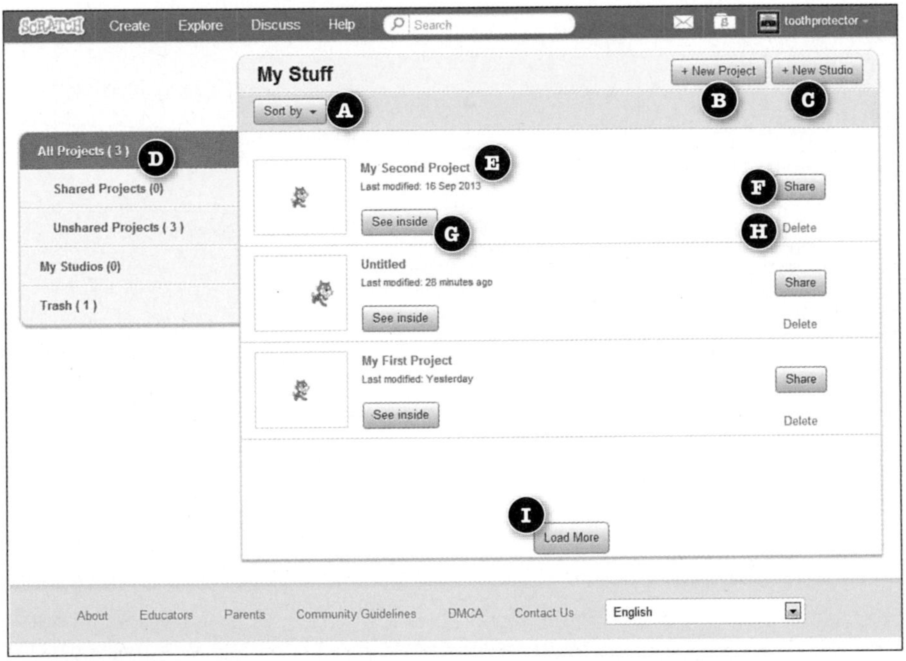

FIGURE 2.11
My Stuff is your one-stop shop for managing all of your Scratch projects, whether they are published or unpublished.

You might discover, much to your consternation, several "Untitled" projects show up in your My Stuff view. This is bound to happen as you experiment with the Scratch Project Editor. Because Scratch autosaves your work, you might find entries in your My Stuff page that you never intended to save. No problem—to delete a project from my stuff, simply click Delete. Be sure you're clicking the Delete button that corresponds to the project you want to remove because there is no Undo once the project page is refreshed

Don't be afraid to delete projects because they are not deleted permanently yet. Instead, deleted Scratch projects go into the Trash folder, where you can permanently delete the project or restore it to your active projects. In fact, let's practice using the My Stuff interface and the trash in particular.

TRY IT YOURSELF ▼

Get Comfortable with My Stuff

In this Try It Yourself exercise, you create a new Scratch project and then manage it by using My Stuff. Follow these steps:

1. Create a new Scratch project named Test Project.

2. Click My Stuff from the Scratch Project Editor to display the My Stuff page.

3. Note that the My Stuff defaults to the All Projects view. Click Unshared Projects and verify that Test Project exists in this list.

4. For Test Project, click Delete to send the project to the trash.

5. Navigate to the Trash view. Note that you can click Empty Trash to purge all contents of the trash can. Figure 2.12 shows you this screen.

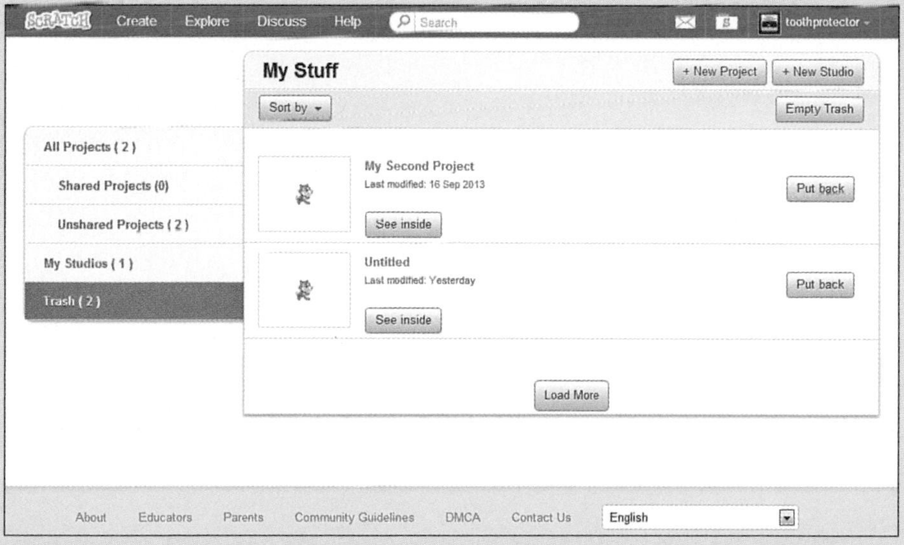

FIGURE 2.12
You can retrieve deleted projects from your My Stuff trash can.

▼

6. Take the Test Project out of the trash by clicking Put Back.

7. Navigate back to the All Projects or Unshared Projects views and verify that the project has been successfully restored.

One trash-related point to consider: The My Stuff page does ask for confirmation when you click Empty Trash. However, as of this writing, there is no confirmation prompt when you either send a project to the trash or retrieve a project from the trash.

Summary

By this point, hopefully your appetite for learning computer programming is fully whetted. You are now a (hopefully active) member of the Scratch community. You have some initial familiarity with the Scratch Project Editor, which of course you'll broaden and deepen as you move through the remaining hours of this book.

Although some readers tend to skip over them, it is important to work through the Quiz sections that close each hour of learning. Why? The Quiz helps you to mentally underline some of the kernel concepts you learned this hour.

By contrast, the Challenge empowers you to apply the theory in a practical context. You know what they say (whoever *they* are): Practice makes progress!

Workshop

Quiz

1. Which of the following is *not* a valid way to start a new Scratch project?

    A. Click New Project from the Scratch Explore page.

    B. Click Create from the Scratch home page.

    C. Click New Project from the My Stuff page.

2. What kind of Scratch block is used to start project scripts?

    A. Cap block

    B. Hat block

    C. Stack block

3. How are projects saved to the cloud in Scratch 2.0?

   A. Projects are saved automatically; no manual intervention is required.

   B. Projects are saved automatically, and can also be manually saved by the Scratcher.

   C. Projects are saved manually; be sure to periodically click File, Save Now in the Scratch Project Editor.

Answers

1. The correct answer is choice A. You cannot create a new project from the Explore page; these pages are intended to help you locate, preview, and potentially remix other Scratchers' projects. Instead, you can create a new Scratch project either by clicking Create from the Scratch home page or by clicking New Project from your My Stuff page.

2. The correct answer is choice B. We use Hat blocks to start scripts in Scratch projects. By contrast, Cap blocks are used to stop scripts. Stack blocks are used to implement most commands within a Scratch project.

3. The correct answer is choice B. Scratch 2.0 projects are automatically saved to the cloud every so often. However, this autosave feature is no substitute for you regularly performing manual saves by clicking File, Save Now in the Scratch Project Editor.

Challenge

See if you can figure out a way to move the Scratch Cat horizontally (back and forth in a left-to-right and right-to-left direction) across the Stage. As an added bonus, research how you might reset the Scratch Cat's position on Stage each time that the Green Flag is clicked. Don't worry if you find yourself hopelessly stuck—you'll learn how to do all this and more in a little while.

HOUR 3
Working with Costumes and the Stage

What You'll Learn in This Hour:

▶ Understanding sprites

▶ Adding and managing costumes

▶ Understanding the Stage

▶ Adding and managing backdrops

▶ Let's assemble the pieces, shall we?

Suppose you want to build a Scratch project that tells the story of *Goldilocks and the Three Bears*. How would you go about building the scene?

For starters, you would need to create sprites to represent each of the major players in the story; namely, Goldilocks and the three bears.

What might not be so obvious is that you also need sprites to represent all of the other assets of the scene, for instance:

▶ The cabin

▶ The dining table

▶ Chairs

▶ Bowls of porridge

There's more to the story, but the point is clear: Sprites form the foundation of any Scratch project. In this hour, your primary objective is to define sprites and learn how to use them in Scratch 2.0.

You also learn how to control the backdrop environment on the Stage. Once you get the hang of using sprites and Stage backdrops, you will truly start to have some major fun with Scratch. It's time to get started!

Understanding Sprites

In Scratch, a *sprite* is a graphical object that performs actions in a project. Every new Scratch project includes a single default sprite, the Scratch Cat. As you'll see in a moment, the Scratch Cat includes two costumes by default that serve to change the sprite's appearance. Specifically, the two default Scratch Cat costumes are also useful for simulating sprite movement on the Stage (more on that point momentarily).

Open up a new, blank project and take a close look at the Sprites list. Using Figure 3.1 as a guide, check out the major moving parts of this interface component:

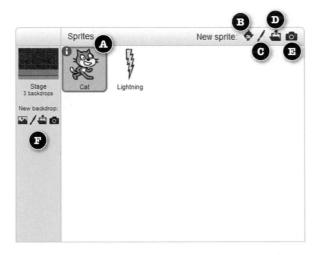

FIGURE 3.1
The Sprites list is the "bucket" that contains all of the sprites you use in your project.

> ▶ **A:** This is the sprite itself. Take note of the *i* icon in the upper-left corner of the sprite; you learn how to edit sprite properties a bit later on in this hour. If you right-click the sprite, you can duplicate the sprite, delete it, save the sprite to a local file, or hide the object from the project.

> ▶ **B:** The Choose Sprite from Library button shows the Sprite Library, from which you can create a new sprite based upon preconfigured objects maintained by the Scratch Team.

> ▶ **C:** The Paint New Sprite button displays the Paint Editor, where you can draw a new sprite from scratch (pun certainly intended).

> ▶ **D:** The Upload Sprite from File button enables you to transfer an image file from your computer to the cloud, where it is available to your project.

▶ E: The New Sprite from Camera button gives you the chance to use your webcam to snap a pic that will form the basis of a new sprite.

▶ F: This panel does not have anything to do with sprites. Instead, you use these controls to manage Stage backdrops. You learn more about this later in this hour.

Adding a New Sprite to the Project

This section shows you how to use the Sprite Library to add a new sprite to your project. It then covers how to delete a sprite, should you need to do so.

Use the Sprite Library

Save the project as Hour 3. Then, follow these steps:

1. In the Sprites list, click the Choose Sprite from Library button in the New Sprite area.

2. The Sprite Library appears, as shown in Figure 3.2. Use the Category, Theme, and Type filters to display only certain types of sprites.

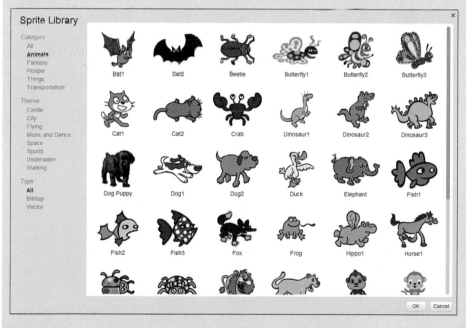

FIGURE 3.2
The Scratch Team gives us quite a few sprites to get us started in the Sprite Library.

▼   **3.** For this hour's project, you need a particular sprite. Navigate to the Flying theme type and click Butterfly1. Next, click OK to add the sprite to your Sprites list.

NOTE

Finding New Sprites

As your imagination becomes increasingly fired up by your experimentation in Scratch 2.0, you'll probably run into the question, "The Sprite Library is fine, but where can I find more resources online?" Well, I'm glad you asked! You should visit the Scratch Resources website (http://is.gd/hRfOyN), log in with your Scratch credentials, and perform a site search for the type of asset you are interested in.

The Scratch Resources site is a place for Scratchers to share their sprites, Stage backdrops, and media files with other Scratchers, all for fun and for free. One note: As of this writing, the Scratch Resources site appears to be suffering from some programming bugs. Such is the nature of open-source projects, I'm afraid.

Deleting a sprite is supereasy. Simply right-click the sprite in question and click Delete from the shortcut menu. One word of warning: Scratch does not prompt you to confirm your choice—the instant you select the Delete command, the sprite disappears.

That said, as long as you act quickly, you can recover the sprite by clicking Edit, Undelete. You'll also be pleased to observe that when you undelete a sprite, any associated costumes and/or scripts that you associated with that sprite are brought back. However, once you exit the Sprite Editor, none of your deleted objects can be resurrected.

Renaming and Viewing Information About a Sprite

By default, most sprites don't have very descriptive names. When you consider how often you'll reference your sprites in your project scripts, it makes sense that you learn how to rename and otherwise manage their properties.

In the Sprites list, click your desired sprite to select it, and then click the Information icon, which shows up as a small *i* icon in the upper-left corner of the sprite.

You'll then see all of the sprite's metadata appear in the same pane. Use Figure 3.3 along with the following list to inspect each user interface element:

▶ **A:** This button closes the Information panel and returns you to the Sprites list.

▶ **B:** This shows a thumbnail representation of the sprite based upon the current costume.

▶ **C:** This field allows you to rename the sprite. It's a good idea for you to do this to make it easier to identify the sprite in your code.

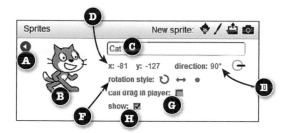

FIGURE 3.3
Each sprite has an Information panel where you can rename and otherwise control the default behavior of the object.

▶ **D**: This shows the current position of the sprite on the Stage. You'll learn more about Stage location coordinates later on.

▶ **E**: You can (and should) click and drag the Direction control to test functionality. A value of 90 degrees is the default orientation of the sprite; this control changes that orientation along a 360-degree plane.

▶ **F**: The Rotation Style control specifies what happens when the sprite bounces off the edge of the Stage. The first icon specifies full rotation, which means the sprite can face any of 360 degrees. The second icon indicates left/right orientation. The third icon represents no rotation.

▶ **G**: The Can Drag in Player control disallows or permits your users to override sprite movement in the project. Leave this option disabled unless you want your users to be able to manually drag sprites around the Stage.

▶ **H**: The Show property easily shows or hides the sprite.

Incidentally, Scratch has blocks that enable you to set sprite properties dynamically.

TRY IT YOURSELF ▼

Manage Your Sprites

You can turn your current project into a pretty cool animation in which you (1) Animate Scratch Cat as he or she walks across the Stage, (2) have Scratch Cat turn into a butterfly when it makes contact with a Lightning Bolt sprite, and (3) animate the butterfly as it continues its "strut."

▼ You can compare your work this hour to the solution file that is included with this book; the filename is Hour03a.sb2.

Follow these steps:

1. In the Sprites list, add the Lightning Bolt sprite. You can do this by creating a new sprite from the Sprite Library; search in the Things category for the sprite named Lightning.

2. Access the sprite properties to change the name of the Scratch Cat to Cat.

3. We want the Cat to rotate only in the left/right directions, so set the Rotation Style property accordingly. Also, make sure that the Can Drag in Player property for both the Cat and the Lightning is set to Off.

Adding and Managing Costumes

When I was a boy, I used to make "flipbook" animations by drawing stick figures in the margin of my textbooks. Have you seen those before? What you do is alter the stick figure's shape just a little bit on each page. When you flip the pages rapidly, the flickering pages simulate animation. You might know that this elementary technique is how the first cartoons were made.

In Scratch, you can use costumes to simulate animation (among many other things). Essentially, each sprite in Scratch has at least one costume, which you are free to edit and/or add to. In fact, the default Scratch Cat sprite has two costumes that, when played repeatedly à la a flipbook, make it appear as if the Scratch Cat is walking. It's a cool effect, and you'll see it in action momentarily.

By the way, the official name for this type of animation is *stop motion* animation.

Speaking of the Scratch Cat, select the object in the Sprites list and then click the Costumes tab in the top middle of the Scratch Editor. Using Figure 3.4 as your guide, check out the proverbial "dials and switches" in the Paint Editor:

▶ **A:** These are the same four controls you saw earlier for creating sprites. When you think of it, adding a costume to a sprite is akin to adding another sprite to the project.

▶ **B:** This is the costume list. Notice that you see not only the costume's name, but also its dimensions in pixels.

▶ **C:** You can (and should) name costumes so you can instantly identify them by their names. Trust me, once you get heavily into scripting, you'll thank me for giving you this tip.

▶ **D:** Here, you can undo or redo your last several actions just like you can in most applications.

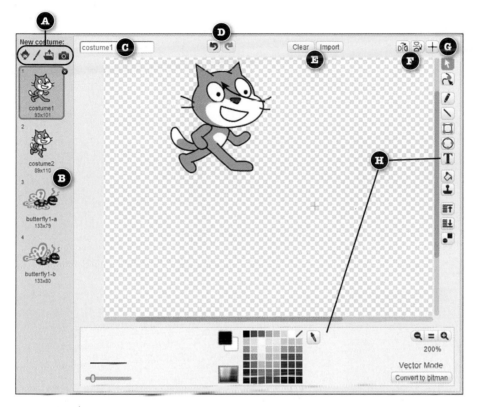

FIGURE 3.4
You use the Scratch Paint Editor to manage the "costumes wardrobe" of your sprites.

▶ **E:** The Clear button removes the costume, leaving you with a blank costume. To understand this, click the button and then immediately click Undo. The Import button allows you to import a graphic image from your computer to add it as the current costume.

▶ **F:** The Flip Left/Right and Flip Up/Down buttons enable you to do just that—quickly swap the orientation of the costume.

▶ **G:** Click the Set Costume Center button and then click on the costume where you want its center of rotation to be. The default (dead center) setting is fine for most costumes.

▶ **H:** You will get to know these drawing tools in intimate detail when you get to Hour 21, "Creating Your Own Sprites and Backdrops."

If you would, repeatedly click back and forth between the two Scratch Cat costumes. Do you see how the sprite appears to "walk"? In a little bit, you'll use Scratch script blocks to "wire up" the sprite to animate across the Stage.

▼ TRY IT YOURSELF

Work with Costumes

You need to add two more costumes to your Cat sprite to enable the object to transform from a cat into a butterfly. Make sure you have the Cat selected in your Sprites list and then perform these steps from the Costumes tab:

1. Click the Choose Costume from Library button and import the sprite named butterfly1-a. You can find this sprite from the Flying theme area.

2. Perform step 1 again, this time importing the butterfly1-b sprite. Your finished costume list should match what is shown in Figure 3.5.

3. As mentioned earlier, click back and forth between the two cat costumes and the two butterfly costumes to get a feel for how they are used to simulate movement. Which Scratch blocks do you think you need to use to make the animation happen?

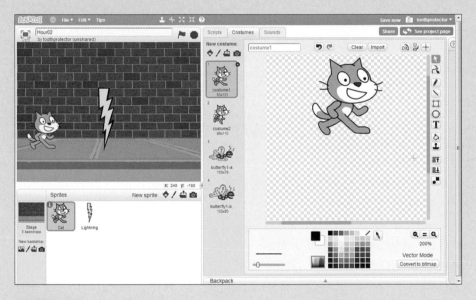

FIGURE 3.5
The state of your project thus far.

Understanding the Stage

In Scratch, the Stage is the surface on which your sprites "come to life." Specifically, the Stage represents the background of your project, and is sized at 480 pixels wide by 360 pixels tall (the dimensions are often given as 480×360).

Moreover, sprite position on the Stage is indicated by using the Cartesian coordinate system. Take a look at Figure 3.6—do you remember using x,y coordinates in school?

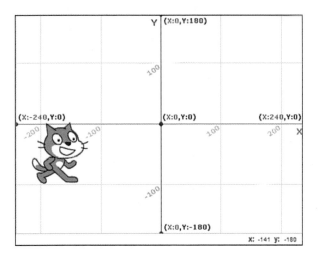

FIGURE 3.6
The Scratch Stage uses the Cartesian coordinate system to describe sprite position. What you're looking at is actually a built-in backdrop called xy-grid that can be found in the Backdrop Library.

If not, it's like this: A sprite's position is described by a pair of numerical coordinates. The x-axis denotes the left/right (horizontal) plane, and the y-axis denotes the up/down (vertical) plane. As you can see in Figure 3.6, the coordinates (0,0) specify the dead center of the Stage.

If you are one of the many math-shy people of the world, don't be afraid. We'll gradually immerse ourselves into x,y positioning as we work. Before long, you'll be an old hand at it.

NOTE

Pixels? Cartesian What?

On a computer monitor or television, the pixel (short for *picture element*) is the smallest addressable element on screen. For the purposes of this text, all you need to remember is that on the Scratch Stage you have 480 of them horizontally and 360 of them vertically.

Because the Stage's point of origin is (0,0), this means that your sprites can move 240 pixels either to the right (positively) or to the left (negatively). Furthermore, a sprite can move 180 pixels up (positively) or down (negatively). More on the positive and negative stuff later....

The Cartesian coordinate system comes to us by way of the brilliant French mathematician/philosopher René Descartes (1596–1650).

What can take some time getting used to is having your Stage "cluttered" up with sprites as you figure out how you want the project to proceed. Remember that you can always hide sprites temporarily by opening their Information panel and deselecting the Show property.

Another potential point of confusion: How can you place sprites on the Stage properly? Well, that's actually pretty easy—all you have to do is use your mouse and click, drag, and drop. Try doing this with the Lightning Bolt sprite that you added earlier.

Specifically, open the Lightning Bolt's Information panel and notice what changes as you relocate the sprite on the Stage. Hint: You should observe the sprite's x,y coordinate change. Remember that position (0,0) represents the dead center of the Stage.

As you move the sprite from left to right, you should notice the x coordinate value grow in the positive direction. The opposite will occur when you move the sprite from right to left.

Along those lines, observe the y value changing when you move a sprite up and down on the Stage.

Adding and Managing Backdrops

Your Scratch project can have a blank, white Stage, or you can have several different looks that dynamically change through the running of your project.

Here's an analogy for you to consider: Costumes are to sprites as backdrops are to the Stage. You can have only one Stage per project, so it is crucial that you understand how to add backdrops if you want your Scratch project to have more than one scene.

▼ TRY IT YOURSELF

Add Backdrops to the Stage

Double-click the Stage to expose the Backdrops panel of the Scratch Editor interface, shown in Figure 3.7, and then follow these steps:

1. Take a moment to get your bearings. You should notice all of the familiar controls that you used earlier when you imported sprites into your project. As it happens, Stage backdrops use the same Paint Editor as do sprite costumes. Notice the default backdrop, which has the default name *backdrop1*.

2. Click Choose Backdrop from Library to access the Backdrop Library. For this hour's project, select the brick wall1 backdrop from the Outdoors category and click OK to continue.

3. Now go back to the Backdrop Library and import the xy-grid backdrop from the All category. It should be the very last backdrop in the grid. This backdrop is excellent for learning and testing purposes, especially as you get comfortable working with the Cartesian coordinate system.

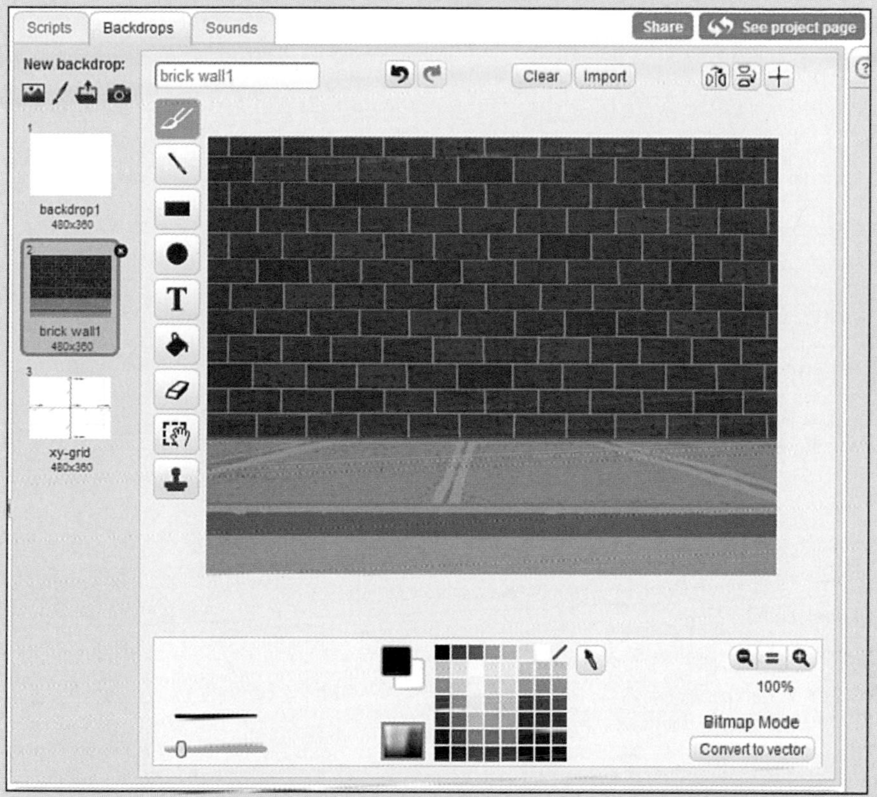

FIGURE 3.7
You use the same Paint Editor to manage Stage backdrops that you used earlier to manage sprite costumes.

4. Right-click the brick wall1 backdrop and notice the options that appear in the shortcut menu. You can duplicate the backdrop, delete it from the project, or save a copy of the object to your computer.

5. Note that you can change the names of your backdrops so you'll recognize them more easily when you access them programmatically via the Script Editor. For now, though, you can leave the names alone.

Let's Assemble the Pieces, Shall We?

Now that you have been introduced to the basics of Scratch sprites and the Stage, it's time to build a simple project that uses script blocks to wire everything together!

Here's the goal of the game: The Scratch Cat will walk from stage left. Once the Cat makes contact with the Lightning Bolt, the Cat will "magically" transform into a Butterfly, which will continue flying until the sprite is almost offscreen.

Before you start playing with blocks, first use something programmers call *pseudocode* to figure out what you want to happen in the project. The following four points outline in plain language how our project will run.

1. Make sure that every time the project is started, the Scratch Cat's position resets to the left side of the Stage.

2. Make the Scratch Cat "walk" from left to right by switching its costume.

3. Once the Cat makes contact with the Lightning sprite, switch to the butterfly costume.

4. Animate the Cat the same way as before, this time swapping the two butterfly costumes.

Let's get to work!

NOTE

What Is Pseudocode?

You'll use pseudocode a lot in this book. Why? Because programmers know that it makes the most sense to think about what you want your program to do before you start horsing around with programming language keywords (or, in our case, Scratch script blocks).

The word *pseudo* means *false* or *fake*, and what it means is that you can simply focus for a moment on goals, procedures, and logic by using natural language.

Once you have the project's framework outlined in pseudocode, it is much easier to translate that human-readable outline into an actual, honest-to-goodness computer program.

▼ TRY IT YOURSELF

Build the Hour 3 Project

You can find the completed Hour 3 Project file in this book's companion files. To open the project and upload it to your online Scratch account, you need to install the Scratch 2.0 Offline Editor (http://is.gd/sB2h1k). Hour 18, "Using the Scratch Offline Editor," covers all things Offline Editor-related.

Fire up a new Scratch project and work through the following steps to complete the exercise:

1. Make sure your Cat sprite is "wearing" costume1, and position the sprite on the Stage at approximately (–161, –127).

2. Position the Lightning Bolt sprite at approximately (–5, –20).

3. Double-click the Stage and set the current backdrop to brick wall1.

4. Double-click the Cat and bring the Scripts pane forward. You'll do all your script programming on the Cat for this project.

5. Your first task is to kick off the project with the `when ⚑ clicked` Hat block. You then need to reset the position and orientation of the Cat so that the project starts consistently each time. Connect the blocks like you see in Figure 3.8; the `when ⚑ clicked` block comes from the Events category, the `go to x: 0 y: 0` and `point in direction 90▾` blocks come from the Motion category, and the `switch costume to costume2 ▾` block comes from the Looks category.

FIGURE 3.8
It's important to script your project so that the environment is reset each time the user clicks the Green Flag.

6. You can perform stop-motion animation in Scratch by (1) having the sprite move a few steps, (2) waiting a small amount of time, usually a fraction of a second, (3) switching to the next costume, and (4) repeating these steps. For this project, a step interval of 10 steps with a 0.3 second delay in between works well.

   In programming, you want to avoid coding repetitive actions over and over again. To that point, you can use the `repeat until` C block to have the Cat walk until a certain condition is met; namely, the sprite making contact with the Lightning Bolt. Check out Figure 3.9 to learn how to put the blocks together.

FIGURE 3.9
This is an important block stack for you to master because it forms the basis of all stop-motion animation in Scratch 2.0.

The `touching ▾ ?` Boolean block is found in the Sensing category, and you'll observe how nicely it fits into the hold in the `repeat until` C block. Also note how you can drag your

▼

move/wait/switch blocks into and out of the C blocks. Scratch is pretty fun to play around with, isn't it?

7. Now what will happen once the Cat touches the Lightning Bolt? Well, we want the Cat to change costumes and continue to move across the Stage. Create one more block stack using Figure 3.10 as your guide.

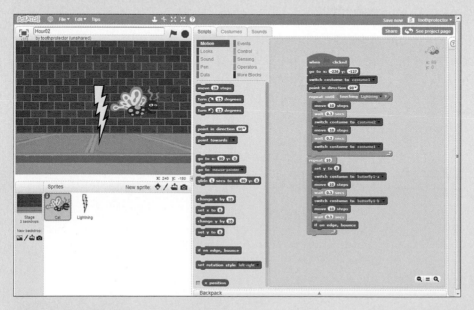

FIGURE 3.10
This block stack describes the behavior of the "transformed" sprite in your project.

I chose a 10-cycle repeat here because I wanted the Butterfly to "bounce" off the right side of the Stage and begin to move left. That is the great beauty of the 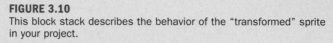 block from the Motion category.

8. Snap together the three code stacks that you just created to match the completed code listing shown in Figure 3.11.

FIGURE 3.11
The completed Hour 3 project.

Before wrapping up, let's go over how to open the completed Hour 3 project file on your own computer. Yes, you'll learn how to use the Offline Editor in detail later in the book, but I want to save you some unnecessary page flipping.

The Scratch 2.0 Offline Editor is an Adobe AIR application that you can install directly from the Scratch website. Simply visit http://is.gd/sB2h1k and click Install Now to transparently download and install the application to your Windows, Mac, or Linux computer.

Once the Offline Editor installation process completes, go ahead and open it up. You shouldn't be surprised to note that the Offline Editor looks and behaves exactly like its cloud-based counterpart.

Click File, Open and browse to where you stored the solution file on your computer. The completed project appears as shown in Figure 3.12. Done and done!

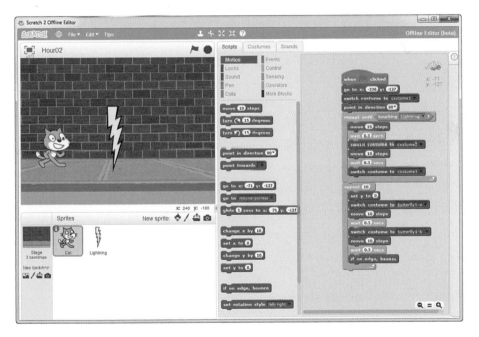

FIGURE 3.12
The Scratch 2 Offline Editor is an excellent way to study the solution files from this book.

It might take you a while to get the hang of connecting, disconnecting, and reconnecting script blocks. Suppose you want to remove a Move/Switch/Wait block set from the repeat until C block. How do you do that?

You'll find that when you click and drag a block in Scratch, that block as well as any blocks connected underneath it come along for the ride.

As a programming best practice, you'll want to remove any "loose" or unneeded blocks from the Scripts pane. To get rid of them, simply drag the unwanted blocks into the middle pane—you'll see the block(s) disappear immediately.

Summary

Wow—you covered quite a bit of ground in this hour, didn't you? At this point, you should have a nice level of familiarity with sprites, costumes, the Stage, and backdrops. You also seamlessly integrated some fairly complex programming logic into your scripts.

You might have noticed that this hour didn't spend a lot of time explaining the purpose of each block; this is intentional because you'll spend a lot of time doing so in subsequent hours.

In this hour, the goal was to give you some more experience in moving and connecting blocks according to your pseudocode-based program design plan. More will be revealed in time—it's a promise!

Workshop

Quiz

1. Which of the following statements best describes how stop-motion animation works in Scratch 2.0?

    A. Using multiple sprites with a single costume

    B. Using a single sprite with multiple costumes

    C. Using one or more sprites with multiple backdrops

2. The use of the repeat until C block is an example of conditional logic. Why do you think this is the case?

    A. Because in conditional logic you test a case against a True/False result

    B. Because in conditional logic you loop through a procedure a fixed number of times

    C. Because in conditional logic you always perform a mathematical computation

3. Which of the following Scratch blocks could be integrated into your project to trigger a scene change on the Stage?

    A. Next costume

    B. Switch costume to

    C. Switch backdrop to

Answers

1. The correct answer is choice D. In this hour, you learned how to animate sprites by alternating between multiple costumes. Although you could use more than one sprite for this, that procedure is unnecessarily complex because each sprite can have as many costumes as needed.

2. The correct answer is choice A. In conditional logic, you test a case against a True/False result. For instance, this hour the test was "Is the Cat sprite touching the Lightning Bolt?" If the answer to that question is False (not touching), then you take the actions defined in the C block. When the case evaluates to True (touching), you exit the C block and continue with the rest of the script.

3. The correct answer is choice C. The switch backdrop to block from the Looks category enables you to swap the current Stage backdrop for another one.

Challenge

The `if on edge, bounce` block you used in this hour's project makes the Butterfly "hit" the right side of the Stage and then begin moving to the left. How can you ensure that the Butterfly does not rotate into an upside-down position?

Here is another challenge for you to work on: Edit the program such that the Butterfly changes back into the Cat once the Butterfly reaches the Lightning Bolt on the return journey.

Finally, try adding in another Stage backdrop and programming the backdrop to change whenever a cat-to-butterfly or butterfly-to-cat transition takes place.

HOUR 4
Using Motion Blocks

What You'll Learn in This Hour:

▶ Getting to know the Stage more intimately

▶ Bouncing around the Stage

▶ Tracking a sprite to the mouse

▶ The Hour 4 project: Drawing in Scratch 2.0

In this hour, you become fully acquainted with the methods that Scratch 2.0 gives us to move sprites around the Stage. You used a few of the Motion blocks in previous hours, but now is the time to take your understanding to the proverbial next level.

Log in to the Scratch website and fire up a new, blank project. Rename the Scratch Cat to Cat (you remember how to do that, right?), and spend a moment getting to know the blocks in the Motion palette of the Scripts pane.

Use Figure 4.1 as a reference as you discover "what's what" in Table 4.1.

TABLE 4.1 Scratch Motion Blocks

Figure 4.1 Callout	Block Type	Function
A	Stack	Moves the sprite x steps in the current direction
B	Stack	Rotates the sprite's direction by x degrees clockwise
C	Stack	Rotates the sprite's direction by x degrees counterclockwise
D	Stack	"Physically" faces the sprite in one of four directions: 90 (right), –90 (left), 0 (up), 180 (down)
E	Stack	Points the sprite toward the mouse pointer or another sprite
F	Stack	Positions a sprite to x,y coordinate
G	Stack	Instructs the sprite to "follow" the mouse pointer or another sprite

Figure 4.1 Callout	Block Type	Function
H	Stack	Smoothly moves the sprite to given x,y coordinate
I	Stack	Adjusts the sprite's x position by x pixels
J	Stack	Changes the sprite's x position to x pixels
K	Stack	Adjusts the sprite's y position by y pixels
L	Stack	Changes the sprite's y position to y pixels
M	Stack	Instructs the sprite to reverse direction when it hits the edge of the Stage
N	Stack	Sets the sprite's rotation style to (1) left-right, (2) don't rotate, or (3) all around
O	Reporter	Denotes the sprite's current x position on the Stage
P	Reporter	Denotes the sprite's current y position on the Stage
Q	Reporter	Denotes the sprite's current direction

Hey—do me a favor and load up the xy-grid Stage backdrop from the Backdrop Library. Recall that you learned how to load Stage backdrops in Hour 3, "Working with Costumes and the Stage."

You use this particular backdrop throughout this chapter because it serves to make our sprite movements easier to visualize on the x,y grid.

Also, notice what happens when you select the check boxes immediately to the left of the [x position], [y position], and [direction] reporter blocks. These are called Stage monitors, and they are useful both for troubleshooting purposes as well as for displaying useful information to the user who is playing your game.

Stage monitors are used a lot in projects to display important game-related metadata, such as a score. Later in the book, you'll learn how to use cloud-based variables that are actually usable by multiple players at once. It is pretty cool technology!

Stage monitors are illustrated in Figure 4.2. There'll be much more to say (and do) about Stage monitors throughout the rest of the book. To turn off a Stage monitor, simply revisit the Motion block palette and remove the check boxes from the appropriate reporter blocks.

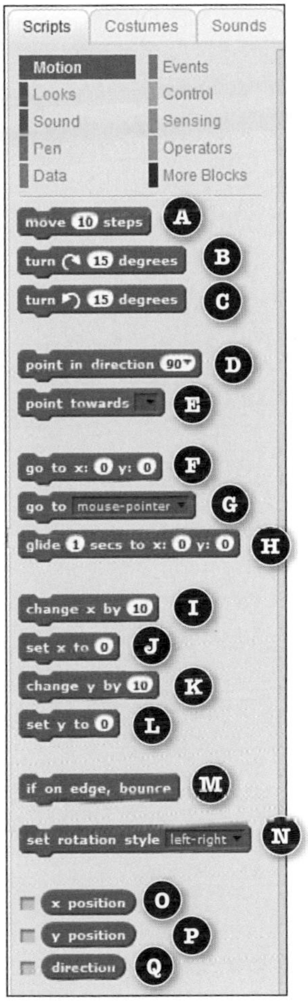

FIGURE 4.1
Scratch Motion blocks.

Getting to Know the Stage More Intimately

We're going to dive right into several examples here because I don't want to waste precious whitespace in this book flapping my proverbial gums about theory. Programming is about practice just as much as (and in some cases more than) it is about the theory.

To set the stage (pun intended) for these exercises, make sure you have the xy-grid backdrop loaded, rename the Scratch Cat sprite to Cat, and import the Baseball sprite from the Sprite Library.

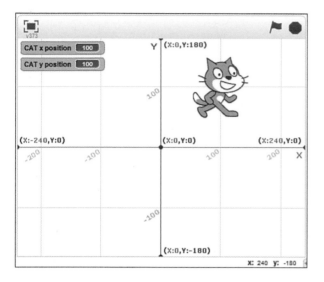

FIGURE 4.2
Stage monitors are great for monitoring key sprite values while your project runs.

Because you won't need the Baseball sprite until later, open the sprite's Information panel (remember that you do this by selecting the sprite in the Sprites list and clicking the little *i* icon in the upper-left of the sprite) and deselect the Show option.

Let's do this!

▼ TRY IT YOURSELF

Glide the Cat with Your Keyboard

A guiding principle for me as a game designer is that I insist on handing control to the user as early and often as possible. To that end, let's program Scratch such that your keyboard arrow keys move (or more to the point, glide) the Scratch Cat across the Stage.

You can find this completed work file in the companion files on www.informit.com/title/ 9780672337093; the filename is Hour04a.sb2. To complete this exercise, perform the following steps in order.

1. Begin by setting up the environment such that the project begins consistently each time that the Green Flag is clicked. To do this, have the Cat go to (0,0), point to the right, and have a left-right rotation style. Use Figure 4.3 as a script reference for this entire Try It Yourself exercise.

2. Use your mouse to reposition the sprite, and then click the Green Flag to ensure that the sprite relocates correctly.

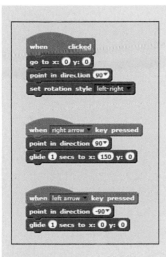

FIGURE 4.3
The "gliding the Cat with your keyboard" script code.

3. Now you "wire up" the left arrow and right arrow keyboard controls. As shown in Figure 4.3, you need two when key pressed Hat blocks. For each block, open up the drop-down list and select the appropriate control key. Note that you can map a script block to just about any key on the keyboard.

   When the right arrow key is pressed, you want the Cat to glide (move smoothly) to the right to position (150,0).

   Likewise, when the left arrow key is pressed, you want the Cat to glide back to the (0,0) "home" position. Don't forget about customizing the sprite's pointing direction. It's these little things that make the difference between an amateur game and a professional one.

4. Once again, click the Green Flag and test functionality. This is a simple example, but it gets you thinking in terms of sprite movement possibilities as well as how important it is to give your players something to do in your projects.

So what did you think? Pretty cool stuff, right? With no further ado, let's up the complexity ante by trying another experiment. Open up another blank project with all the same sprite/backdrop assets as you used in the previous Try It Yourself exercise.

In this next Try It Yourself exercise, you enable the user to move the Scratch Cat wherever he or she wants on the Stage.

Take Control of Scratch Cat

In this Try It Yourself exercise, you allow the player to move the Scratch Cat anywhere on the Stage by using the up, down, left, and right arrow keys. In case you wondered, you can indeed integrate mouse control in your Scratch projects as well—hold your horses, you'll get to that technique soon enough.

As always, you can find the completed solution file in the companion files; the filename is Hour04b.sb2. In addition, Figure 4.4 shows the script code to help you if you get stuck completing the following steps.

1. If you have the Baseball (or another sprite) in your list and you want to hide the sprite programmatically, select that sprite, add a when flag clicked block and add a hide stack block from the Looks palette.

2. Take a look at Figure 4.4. The code here is similar to what you did in the previous Try It Yourself exercise, with the addition that you are changing the sprite's rotation style. Feel free to change the point in direction and move steps blocks to make the Cat move longer or smaller distances each time an arrow key is pressed.

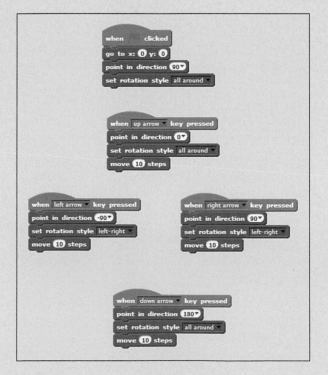

FIGURE 4.4
The "taking control of Scratch Cat" script code.

▼

3. Do you see what is happening with the positive and negative values for the change stack blocks? For instance, if you set the `change x by 10` to 100, then the sprite jumps 100 pixels in the positive (either rightward or upward) direction. Likewise, if you set the `change y by 10` block to 100, the sprite jumps 100 pixels in the upward (positive) or downward (negative) direction.

Experiment with the set rotation style blocks until you are positive that you understand how they work.

As you just saw, the glide stack block is of fairly limited capability when compared with the move, go to, change, or set blocks.

Instead, you want to concern yourself with moving sprites by using a specific x,y coordinate, as well as ensuring that the sprite's directionality and rotation style are appropriate.

How would you approach the situation where you want the player to have more fine-grained control over the Scratch Cat's movement? For instance, suppose that each time the player presses an arrow key, you want the Cat to move only 10 steps.

To accomplish this goal, simply swap out the `change x by 10` and `change y by 10` stack blocks and instead use the `move 10 steps` block, specifying a move of 10 steps. Click the Green Flag to see how it works, and adjust parameters accordingly. *Tip*: Try holding down an arrow key and observe how it affects sprite movement.

Bouncing Around the Stage

Did you know that Scratch allows you to easily clone a project? For instance, you should set up a new project that is based upon the previous examples. Try this: In the Scratch Editor, click File, Save as a Copy. After a moment's pause, you have a new project that is identical to your previous one. You can simply rename the copy, and you're good to go.

Many Scratchers work diligently to make sprites bounce realistically. To be sure, the Scratch 2.0 tools are powerful enough to provide for some cool effects that simulate velocity, gravity, and so forth. However, this hour focuses on basic sprite bouncing mechanics.

If you are interested in ideas for creating realistic bouncing in Scratch, check out this cool discussion thread from the Scratch Forums: http://is.gd/IZDoX3.

At this point, your project should include two sprites, the default Scratch Cat and the Baseball. You don't need the Cat now, so you might be tempted to delete the sprite entirely. Not so fast! You've invested some time and effort in customizing the sprite's code.

A faster way to tuck unwanted sprites out of the way, temporarily or permanently, is to attach a

hide block from the Looks palette to the sprite's when green flag clicked Event block, as shown in Figure 4.5. It's as easy as that!

FIGURE 4.5
You can control a sprite's visibility either through its Information panel, or programmatically with the Hide and Show stack blocks.

The Scratch C blocks from the Control palette are useful when you want to repeat an action forever or a certain amount of times. For instance, select the Baseball sprite and create the block stack labeled A in Figure 4.6. While you're at it, don't forget to use the Show block to make the Baseball sprite visible on the Stage.

Do you see any problems with that code? I can spot a couple right off the bat:

▶ The sprite bounces off the edge of the Stage, but gets trapped in a particular left-right or top-bottom pattern because there is no simulated rotation.

▶ The sprite's starting position is neither fixed nor random; Scratch simply uses the last location of the sprite.

Okay. Now try modifying your block stack to match what is shown in block stack B in Figure 4.6. What do you see? Any room for improvement?

The B example is pretty good, actually. Here's what's going on:

▶ The sprite is reset to (0,0) every time the project is run.

▶ I dropped a pick random 1 to 10 reporter block from the Operators palette and dropped it into the point in direction stack block. Each time the Green Flag is clicked, the ball points in one of 360 degrees, making for a new trajectory during each program run.

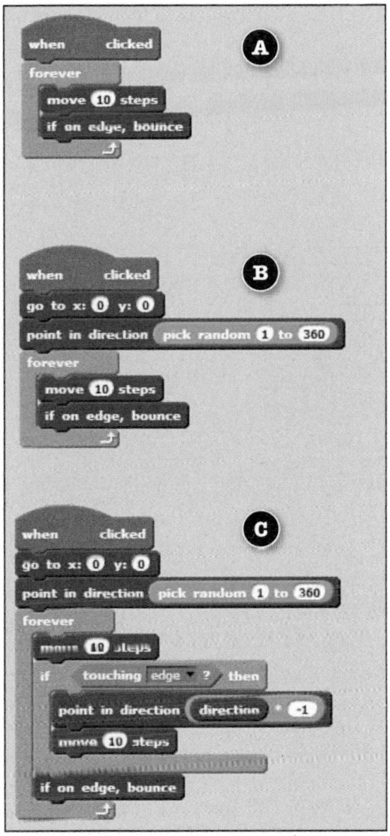

FIGURE 4.6
Experiments in bouncing a sprite in Scratch 2.0.

NOTE

Scratch Shapes Are Important

Take a look at Motion blocks such as point in direction or turn degrees. Do you see the whitespace? Sure, you can type in values yourself, but you can also insert reporter blocks.

Similarly, go check out some of the Control blocks. Do you see the hexagonal cutouts? Sure enough, those are open spaces into which you can insert Boolean blocks.

Please don't ignore this wonderful functionality in Scratch. Not only are related blocks color-coded, but the cutout holes (as I affectionately call them) enable you to add automation and dynamism to your Scratch projects.

Finally, take a look at example C in Figure 4.6. There are quite a few moving parts in this one:

▶ An if C block is nested inside the forever C block to test for the condition "what if the Baseball sprite hits the edge of the Stage?"

▶ You can find the `touching  ▼ ?` Boolean block in the Sensing palette; it fits nicely in the hexagonal cutout in the if C block.

▶ The point in direction block simply takes the sprite's current direction and reverses it. Recall that any positive number multiplied by –1 is simply the same number made negative. For instance, $240 × –1 = –240$.

▶ The `if on edge, bounce` stack block ensures that the sprite does not get "hung up" on the Stage edge.

The take-home message from this part of the book is to convince you that there is rarely (I would say "never," but I want to hedge my bets) a single correct way to accomplish any programming task.

As you just saw, you can use any of the three aforementioned methods to bounce a sprite. Let me be the first to guarantee you that with a little effort you can find three more ways in Scratch—that's just how computer programming works, and it is one of the many reasons why I find the work so fulfilling. In many ways, creating computer programs is all about solving puzzles.

Tracking a Sprite to the Mouse

Remember the earlier discussion about how important it is to give the player as much control in your Scratch project as possible? Think of it this way: How do you feel when you play a game and wind up passively watching more than you do actually playing? I get bored with that, and quickly.

Let's now take a look at how you can move a sprite by using the mouse. Practically every computer user nowadays understands intuitively how to control a mouse.

Suppose you want to control the Scratch Cat in your current project by using the mouse. To begin with, create another copy of your current project and go ahead and hide the Baseball so you don't have to worry about that thing bouncing around the Stage whenever you click the Green Flag.

Next, let's resize the Cat so the sprite is more manageable onscreen. To do this, make sure that the Cat's Show property on its Information panel is selected (a bit obvious, but I don't want to leave any useful information out).

As shown in Figure 4.7, click the Shrink button on the top toolbar and then click the Cat repeatedly until it reaches the desired size. If you make the Cat too small, repeat the same procedure, this time clicking the Grow button. When you're finished resizing, simply click an unused part of the Stage.

FIGURE 4.7
The Shrink and Grow buttons make it easy to resize sprites.

You'll be amazed at how simple it is to bind a sprite to the movement of the mouse pointer. Check out the code stack labeled A in Figure 4.8.

By the way, you won't need any of the arrow key events that you used earlier this hour. Remember that you can delete code blocks by dragging them into the center palette area and letting go.

Click the Green Flag to test. As nice as this function is, many Scratchers are disappointed that there appears to be no way (yet) to hide the computer's mouse pointer. In other words, you have to live with the sprite appearing underneath the mouse pointer. Oh, well.

Notice also in the code stack labeled A in Figure 4.8 that the Cat sprite is explicitly shown using the `show` stack block. Trust me—you'll get a *lot* of mileage out of the `show` and `hide` stack blocks in your Scratch projects. In fact, according to the Scratch Team, these are perhaps the most popular blocks universally across the entire user base.

At this point, with all our talk and work of sprite movement and keyboard/mouse control, you probably wonder about collision detection. For example, think of how many video games rely upon something happening when two sprites bump into each other.

If you are thinking these questions, then good for you, faithful student! This means that you are beginning to think like a true programmer.

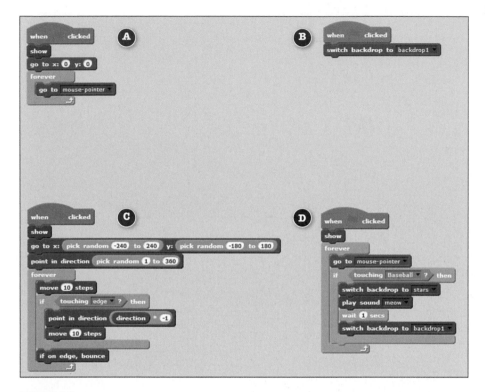

FIGURE 4.8
Scratch code to control sprites with the mouse (and for the Implement Collision Detection Try It Yourself exercise).

▼ TRY IT YOURSELF

Implement Collision Detection

In this Try It Yourself exercise, you program Scratch such that if the Cat collides with the bouncing ball, the backdrop flashes to black momentarily. To prepare for this exercise, make sure you have the Cat "wired up" to the mouse pointer as per the previous Try It Yourself exercise. You also need all the bounce code you used for the Baseball sprite.

The name of the solution file is `Hour04d.sb2`. To complete the exercise, follow these steps:

1. Select the Stage and import the backdrop named stars from the Backdrop Library. You can delete the xy-grid backdrop; ensure that you have only the default, white backdrop1 and the stars backdrop.

2. On the Scripts pane for the Stage, add code such that the white backdrop (backdrop1 is the default name if you haven't deleted it) is always loaded first. You can see this code stack labeled B in Figure 4.8.

3. Modify the Baseball sprite's code as shown in the code stack labeled C in Figure 4.8. Notice that the ball's starting position is adjusted because, otherwise, the Cat and the ball would overlap at (0,0) every time that the Green Flag was clicked.

   This bears a little further discussion, actually. Remember that the Stage is 480 pixels wide, which is to say –240 pixels from the left edge of the Stage to the origin (center), and then 240 more pixels to the right edge of the Stage.

   Likewise, the Stage is 360 pixels tall, which equates to 180 pixels in either direction above and below the point of origin. Hopefully, you can now see the logic behind creating the x and y random values for the ball's initial position.

4. Now modify the Cat's code, as shown in the code stack labeled D in Figure 4.8. Here, you'll see a couple of goodies that you'll be happy to have in your Scratch tool bag.

   First, you can use the `switch backdrop to backdrop1` block to swap in the stars background. Second, you can have Scratch play a built-in or prerecorded sound using the `play sound meow` stack block. Third, you can build in a 1-second pause in which the sprite is "paralyzed," and then reinstate the original, white background.

   This is some excellent game theory in action. The goal of this mini-dodgeball game is to avoid the baseball. If you are unfortunate enough to connect with the ball, then you get a jarring multimedia surprise and are knocked out of action temporarily.

The Hour 4 Project: Drawing in Scratch 2.0

For this hour's capstone project, you have the Scratch Cat draw a geometric shape on the screen. This involves using some of the Pen tools in Scratch. I know, I know...we haven't formally defined the Pen tools. That's fine—you'll learn about them later in Hour 7, "Working with Pen Blocks."

My instructional approach here is to "sneak" in concepts you haven't yet learned while you're mastering the current tools under consideration. This gives you an extra dose of confidence so that when we formally define the "snuck-in" topics, you'll think to yourself, "Cool! I already have experience doing this."

TRY IT YOURSELF ▼

Draw with a Sprite!

This Try It Yourself exercise isn't very interactive, but it gives you practice with using sprite movement and the Cartesian coordinate system. Create a new, blank project file, and load up the xy-grid backdrop.

▼ The solution file, which can be found in this book's companion files, is titled `Hour04e.sb2`. Complete the following steps, using Figure 4.9 as a guide, which shows you the code in context:

1. Start by creating the initial environment. You can reset any residual pen "stuff" from previous runs of the project by including the ~~pen up~~ and ~~clear~~ blocks from the Pen palette (see the code section labeled A in Figure 4.9). Then, explicitly show the Cat and position it at (–200,0).

2. To draw with a sprite, "drop" the pen by invoking the ~~pen down~~ block (see the code section labeled B in the figure). You can customize the pen's behavior with the ~~set pen size to 1~~ and ~~set pen color to~~ blocks.

3. You are going to have the sprite draw two concentric diamond shapes. Here's an excellent tip for quickly duplicating sprites: Create a couple of the ~~glide 1 secs to x: 0 y: 0~~ blocks, stack them up, click the Stamp button on the top toolbar, and then click the first of the ~~glide 1 secs to x: 0 y: 0~~ blocks. The stamper clones that selected block as well as any that are connected below it. Pretty neat, eh? The glide stacks are shown in the code labeled C in the figure.

4. For the second, inner diamond, change the pen color (see the code section labeled D in the figure), and then go "around the horn" using a slightly different set of coordinates (see the code section labeled E in the figure). If you don't know the Cartesian coordinate system cold by the end of this exercise, I would be genuinely surprised!

5. Finish up by hiding the Cat once it's finished doing its work (see the code section labeled F in the figure).

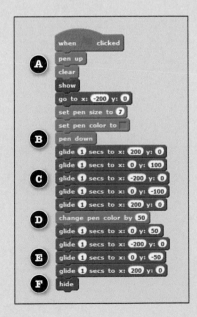

FIGURE 4.9
The source code for the Draw with a Sprite! Try It Yourself exercise.

NOTE

Cleaning Up the Scripts Pane

Thus far, the project scripts haven't been anything too intense. However, before too long, you'll find that a sprite's Scripts pane can get cluttered with several long block stacks.

You can use the zoom controls in the lower right of the Scripts pane to zoom your scripts view in and out. Because the script blocks themselves are vector images, they will remain ultracrisp no matter how far in (or out) you zoom. The middle button resets the view to the default 100 percent magnification.

Alternatively, try right-clicking inside the Scripts pane and selecting Clean Up from the shortcut menu. This simple action can work wonders in terms of making what otherwise would be a tangled mess of script stacks relatively readable and attractive.

Remember, as always, that other Scratchers will want to study your source code, and the actions you take to make your code easier to understand will go a long way in making yourself a valuable member of the Scratch community.

Summary

At this point, you know enough about Scratch 2.0 programming that you can create some pretty functional (or just *fun* for short) projects. Hopefully, your imagination is in full swing. Remember that the Scratch motto is *Imagine, Program, Share*.

You'll get to the *share* part of that statement later on. For now, continue cultivating your imaginative skills, conceiving of what games, interactions, stories, or tutorials you might want to create in Scratch.

Don't forget what a wonderful resource the Scratch project gallery (http://is.gd/tsr9gM) is for aspiring Scratch programmers. It is incredibly helpful not only to play other peoples' games, but also to peek inside their source code and make use of their experiences.

In the next hour, you'll move on to the Looks blocks, which give you complete control over the appearance of your sprites and Stage backdrops.

Workshop

Quiz

1. If a sprite is programmed to glide from (10,100) to (10, −100), what direction did the sprite move on the Stage?

    A. Right

    B. Up

    C. Down

2. Which of the following stack blocks is used to have a sprite track with the player's mouse pointer?

    A. Point in direction

    B. Go to

    C. Point towards

3. In Scratch 2.0, which of the following blocks can be used to code an action or series of actions that triggers when the user presses a particular key on the keyboard?

    A.  block

    B. `when I receive message1` block

    C. `when this sprite clicked` block

Answers

1. The correct answer is choice C. A movement from x=10, y=100 to x=10, y = –100 is a downward move.

2. The correct answer is choice B. We use the `go to mouse-pointer` block to "tie" the player's mouse pointer to a sprite on the Stage. Believe me, this is a useful trick to have in your Scratch programming tool belt. There are many games that require the gamer to control icon movement with his or her mouse. This question is tough because you can use the point towards stack block to have a sprite always face the mouse pointer; that is a useful trick for many Scratch 2.0 games.

3. The correct answer is choice A. We use the `when space key pressed` block to bind most keyboard keys to Scratch scripts.

Challenge

Create a Scratch game whose objective is to see how long you can keep the Scratch Cat in motion without making contact with another sprite that is programmed to follow the Cat. Here are the game design goals:

▶ Control the Scratch Cat with the mouse.

▶ Use an appropriately "spacey" background. You can use something from the Backdrop Library or import an image of your own.

▶ Bring in another sprite and code that sprite to follow the Cat around the Stage.

▶ Program the game such that all scripts stop execution if and when the Cat and the other sprite touch each other.

The solution to this challenge is included in the book's companion files as `Hour04f.sb2`. Figure 4.10 shows a screenshot.

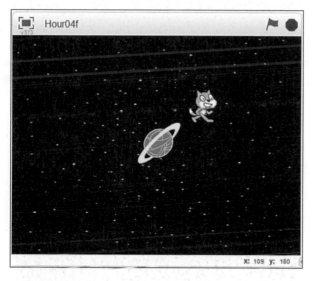

FIGURE 4.10
The Hour 4 Challenge game screen.

Hint: Google is your friend. Learn to turn to online research when you need to understand how to accomplish something in your computer programming projects.

For instance, you might wonder, "Tim wants me to program the game to stop all script execution when two sprites collide. We didn't discuss that in the book so far!"

Don't fret. Instead, pop open a browser and run a search for something like the following:

scratch how to stop script

Alternatively, if you get stuck in figuring out how to get the sprite to follow the mouse, you can try a search query like:

scratch sprite follow mouse

The vast majority of professional programmers turn to search engines every single working day to quickly find answers to questions. There is no shame in research; instead, it is a practical necessity when you work in as dynamic and quickly changing a field as information technology is.

HOUR 5
Using Looks Blocks

The main theme for this hour is that of involving your user in your Scratch project. I've always enjoyed video games of the first-person shooter (FPS) variety; however, I have remarkably low patience for long, drawn-out cut scenes that have no player interaction. I just want to get to the good stuff and to start playing the darned game!

Likewise, you should always keep your player in mind as you develop your Scratch projects. Believe me, they don't want to sit there twiddling their thumbs while you present all of your nifty animations. Instead, they want to control the behavior and perhaps the outcome of the project—and you can make that happen.

The Looks block palette in Scratch 2.0 includes lots of goodies that put the power and control into your players' hands. In this hour, you learn how to communicate with your player both by using speech and thought bubbles. You also learn how to ask the player questions, get his or her feedback, and act accordingly on that feedback.

By the end of this hour, you'll have the ability to grow, shrink, fade, or otherwise modify your sprites in novel and effective ways. Let's get to work.

Getting to Know the Looks Blocks

You know the drill by now: Fire up a new, blank project, select the Cat sprite, and click the Looks tab from the Scripts palette. Next, study Table 5.1 to familiarize yourself with the purple Looks blocks.

TABLE 5.1   Scratch Looks Blocks

Block Image	Block Type	Function
say Hello! for 2 secs	Stack	Makes a time-limited speech balloon appear above the selected sprite
say Hello!	Stack	Makes a persistent speech balloon appear above the selected sprite
think Hmm... for 2 secs	Stack	Makes a time-limited thought balloon appear above the selected sprite
think Hmm...	Stack	Makes a persistent thought balloon appear above the selected sprite
show	Stack	Displays the sprite immediately
hide	Stack	Hides the sprite immediately
switch costume to costume2	Stack	Changes the sprite's costume to another one
next costume	Stack	Transitions the sprite from the current costume to the next one in the sprite's costume list
switch backdrop to backdrop1	Stack	Changes the Stage backdrop to a particular one
change color effect by 25	Stack	Changes the current value of a particular sprite's graphical effect by a percentage; the effects are color, fisheye, whirl, pixelate, mosaic, brightness, and ghost
set color effect to 0	Stack	Sets the sprite's effect to a percentage
clear graphic effects	Stack	Restores all of the sprite's graphical effects to their default zero value
change size by 10	Stack	Changes the sprite's default size (100) to a larger or smaller value
set size to 100 %	Stack	Sets a sprite's size to a given magnification level
go to front	Stack	Brings the sprite to the top layer of the Stage "stack"
go back 1 layers	Stack	Moves the sprite back one layer on the Stage

Block Image	Block Type	Function
☐ costume #	Reporter	References the sprite's current costume ID number
☐ backdrop name	Reporter	References the current backdrop's Name property
☐ size	Reporter	References the sprite's current size

Make sure that you have the Scratch Cat sprite selected on Stage and spend some time double-clicking each of the Looks blocks. You'll observe that you can try out that block's functionality without having to compose an actual script.

For instance, double-click the ☐ say Hello! block. Now change the "Hello!" text to something else and test it out again.

This "click and try it" procedure is especially fun with the graphical effects stack blocks. Have fun, friend—that is largely what computer programming is all about!

By way of review, recall that stack blocks have a notch on top and a bump on bottom, just like a jigsaw puzzle piece. This is meant to indicate that you can easily stack these blocks together, one after the other, to chain actions and trigger events.

Reporter blocks are shaped like flattened-out ovals and hold values. You use reporter blocks by dropping them into a space within another block.

Boolean blocks (shaped like flattened-out hexagons) are a special type of reporter block. Whereas reporter blocks can hold alphanumeric data, Boolean blocks can contain only True or False values. You can insert Boolean blocks into the appropriately shaped holes in other Boolean blocks.

Hopefully, you are beginning to see the beauty and logic in how Scratch uses color-coded blocks to help you think like a programmer without getting bungled up in arcane syntax.

NOTE

Imitation Is the Sincerest Form of Flattery

You should know that Scratch is no longer the only game in town (pun most certainly intended) with regard to block-based, learning programming environments. Google released Blockly (http://cbt.gg/1969Kus) as a web-based, graphical programming editor whose color-coded blocks look and behave suspiciously like those in Scratch.

As you can imagine, some members of the Scratch community have mixed feelings about Google's "appropriation" of Scratch's main design and usage paradigms. On the other hand, competition between software vendors can often lead the way to increased innovation. For a nice comparison among most of today's graphical and/or block-based programming learning environments, check out Alfred Thompson's Computer Science Teacher blog at http://cbt.gg/1969T10.

For the first project example in this hour, let's play around with a sprite's appearance. To set the foundation for this exercise, do the following in the Scratch Editor:

- ▶ Rename the Scratch Cat to Cat.

- ▶ Import the Stage backdrop named route66 and make it the active backdrop.

- ▶ Turn on the ⬜ costume # and ⬜ size reporter blocks to make them appear as Stage monitors. To do this, simply enable the check box to the immediate left of each reporter block in the Looks block palette. You can see what this looks like in Figure 5.1.

FIGURE 5.1
Stage monitors make Scratch reporter data visible on the Stage. This is extraordinarily useful when you debug your project code or when you want to display information (such as a game score) to the user.

▼ TRY IT YOURSELF

Lookin' Good!

In this Try It Yourself exercise, you become familiar with how you can dynamically alter the appearance of a sprite by using Looks blocks. You start by having the Cat "say" something to the player, and then you make the sprite do a bunch of contortions, including growing, recoloring, warping, spinning, and then fading out.

The completed solution file is named Hour05a.sb2.

Complete the following steps using Figure 5.2 as a guide, which shows you the code in context:

1. Bring out a Green Flag block and ignore the code section labeled A in Figure 5.2 for now. Note the say and think blocks; the difference between these is the appearance of the bubble that appears by your sprite. For the purposes of this exercise, you want the Cat to say "Watch this!" for 2 seconds (see the code section labeled B in the figure).

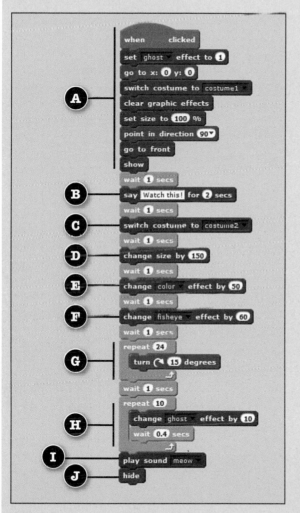

FIGURE 5.2
Source code for the Lookin' Good! Try It Yourself exercise.

2. After a 1-second pause, switch the Cat's costume (see the code section labeled C in the figure). Remember that the wait blocks are found in the Control palette.

3. Sprites start out at a size value of 100. Thus, if you bring out a `change size by 10` block and use a value of 150 (see the code section labeled D in the figure), the sprite will grow by 150 percent. In other words, the sprite's size will go from 100 to 250.

▼

4. Change the sprite's color effect by a factor of 50 (see the code section labeled E in the figure). A sprite's default color effect is 0, so any value you add or subtract alters the sprite's shade. A single sprite costume can take on 200 different color schemes by using the `set color ▾ effect to 0` block. Thus, if you set the change color effect block to 200, you'll see no difference in the sprite's color.

5. Take a moment to just play around with other effects (see the code section labeled F in the figure). The fisheye effect is pretty cool; the higher you set the value about the default value of 0, the more warping you see in the sprite.

6. Spin the sprite in a 360-degree (full) rotation (see the code section labeled G in the figure). There are probably several ways in which you could accomplish this goal. For my money, repeating a 15-degree turn 24 times (perform the arithmetic; you'll find that 15 multiplied by 24 equals 360) gets the job done efficiently enough.

7. Instead of having the Cat simply disappear with a `hide` block, add some pizzazz to the project (see the code section labeled H in the figure). The ghost effect is excellent if you want to fade in or fade out a sprite. Here, increase the sprite's ghost (transparency) effect by 10, 10 times. In Scratch 2.0, a costume can have 100 different transparency levels. If you run a +10 ghost level 10 times, then by the end of the loop the sprite is fully transparent.

8. You'll get into adding and managing audio in your Scratch projects in the next hour. For now, simply play the default meow sound to signify the conclusion of the project (see the code section labeled I in the figure).

9. Add a hide block just for grins (see the code section labeled J in the figure). In programming, being explicit with your code is generally superior to being implicit.

10. Now return to the code section labeled A in Figure 5.2. This is discussed last so the blocks used make sense to you. If you try to rerun the project without this "cleanup" code, the project will look a mess and be pretty much unusabvle.

It can't be stressed enough how important it is that you put code at the very front of your Scratch project that resets the environment. Here, you are resetting the sprite's ghost effect, Stage position, costume, size, directionality, and visibility. Strictly speaking, the set ghost effect block isn't needed in addition to the clear graphic effects block, but it's added here for completeness.

What do you think of the Stage monitors? Pretty cool, aren't they? Here's something else for you to try: Double-click each Stage monitor and notice what happens.

Sometimes the value you are reporting in a Stage monitor doesn't need a label, or perhaps you added the label to the Stage itself. For instance, I like the larger, no-label view in some of my games.

You won't need monitors for the rest of this hour, so feel free to return to the Looks palette and uncheck the `costume #` and `size` reporter blocks.

Interacting with the Player

I don't know about you, but when I'm playing a game or interactive presentation, I want to do something. The last thing you want to do as a Scratch developer is to bore your players.

Thus, the more options you give to your players, the more you ask (or require) them to take action on their part, the more involved they'll be in your project.

One great way to interact with the player is to have a sprite "ask" the player for input.

By prompting the user for input and then adding programming logic to react to that input, you accomplish many goals, including the following:

▶ The project becomes more dynamic instead of the same exact thing every time that it is run.

▶ The user feels that the project is personalized for him or her.

▶ The project has a longer "shelf life" because it has more than one outcome, and the outcome is at least partially dependent upon user input.

Here's how it works: First, navigate to the Sensing palette and bring out an `ask What's your name? and wait` block. You can add any text you want to the admittedly small text area.

During your program execution, a prompt box will appear at the bottom of the Stage, allowing the user to type some data and press Enter.

That answer from the user is captured and stored in the `answer` reporter block.

NOTE

Player, User, or Something Else?

This text has stressed to you many times the importance of coding your Scratch project with the user in mind. Just to be clear: When the text refers to "the user" or "the player," it's referring generically to the individuals who will access your project on the Scratch website.

▼ TRY IT YOURSELF

Ask the User

In this Try It Yourself exercise, you have the Scratch Cat ask the player if he or she wants the Cat to grow or shrink in size. Depending upon the player's answer, the Cat then obeys the player's command.

You should create a new project that is set up the same way as what you had in the previous exercise. One important change: Add a second backdrop to the Stage, and name it end. You can use the Fill tool, which you'll learn about in Hour 21, "Creating Your Own Sprites and Backdrops," to create a black screen. You can then use the Text tool to add a simple "The End" banner, which you can see in the solution file.

The completed solution file is called Hour05b.sb2.

Complete the following steps, using Figure 5.3 as a guide, which shows you the code in context:

1. Make sure that the Cat sprite is selected, and head over to the Scripts area. In the code section labeled A in Figure 5.3, you have the "cleanup" code that ensures that the sprite shows up in the same spot and is the same size every time that the Green Flag is clicked.

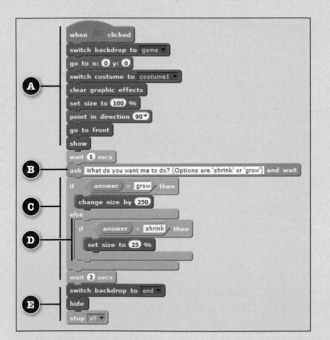

FIGURE 5.3
Source code for the Ask the User Try It Yourself exercise.

2. You want to be as descriptive as possible when you bring out the ask block (see the code section labeled B in the figure). For instance, adding What do you want me to do? (Options are 'shrink' or 'grow') tells the player exactly what is expected of him or her.

3. The main "engine" of this project occurs in the code section labeled C in the figure. You want to test for two conditions. The first condition will say "If the player types 'grow,' then the sprite should grow 250 percent. If the player types 'shrink,' then the sprite should shrink to 25 percent of its original, default size."

You can turn that pseudocode into real code by using the if else Control block.

4. You can embed if or if else C blocks to test for more than one condition. In the code section labeled D in the figure, if the test for *grow* fails, then you proceed to the second, embedded if statement. Here, you catch the event of the player typing *shrink*.

5. Because the code in the code section labeled E in the figure needs to run regardless of whether the player grew or shrunk the sprite, you place these blocks outside of the C block structure. In this case, you switch to your second backdrop, hide the Cat sprite, and stop program execution.

As you worked through the Ask the User Try It Yourself exercise, you probably had the thought, "What if the user were to type something other than *grow* or *shrink*?"

If you did have that question, then good for you! That's what it takes to think like a computer programmer. This case of the user typing something you don't anticipate is called an *exception*. Unhandled exceptions are one of the biggest reasons why programs crash.

Asking a user for input, as you can see in Figure 5.5, can be risky because that user can possibly submit invalid or unhandled input to your project.

Exception handling is covered in greater detail in Hour 19, "Troubleshooting Your Project"; for now, take a look at Figure 5.4 to see one way to handle this particular exception.

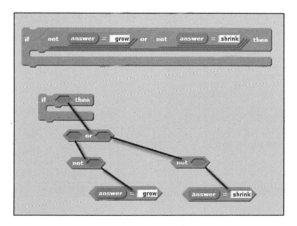

FIGURE 5.4
Trapping exceptions with Scratch blocks might not always be pretty, but it is possible. This code picks up the case where the player enters anything other than the required keywords.

FIGURE 5.5
Asking the user for input is a great way to build buy-in and interest for your Scratch project.

You need to become comfortable with the notion of nesting reporter blocks into Boolean blocks, and Boolean blocks into other Booleans. Remember that reporter blocks store variable data; you can pop them into any block that has a white, rectangular cutout.

By contrast, Boolean blocks look like flattened hexagons and have hexagonal cutouts as well as reporter cutouts.

Getting Sprites to "Talk" to Each Other

A common question among Scratchers who have made some progress in their work is, "How can I get sprites to affect each other?" For instance, what if you want Sprite B to move when Sprite A touches it?

In Scratch, you use *broadcasts* to pass messages among sprites. You can even communicate between sprites and the Stage by sending and receiving broadcasts.

You will find the `broadcast message1 ▾` and `broadcast message1 ▾ and wait` blocks in the Events palette.

You'll also see a `when I receive message1 ▾` Hat block that you use to catch outgoing broadcasts.

Trust me—before too long, you'll appreciate how powerful broadcasts are; they will be an indispensable addition to your Scratch programming toolkit.

Here are a few key points to keep in mind regarding Scratch broadcast messages:

▶ A sprite can both send and receive the same broadcast message.

▶ Broadcast messages can be received by all sprites (and the Stage).

▶ Broadcasts are most commonly used to (1) connect different events, (2) run two scripts in the same frame, and/or (3) prepare a scene with multiple sprites.

NOTE

Can You Broadcast to Specific Sprites?

Unfortunately, Scratch 2.0 has no built-in method for using broadcasts to target specific sprites. As you've seen, the default behavior is to make broadcast messages available to all assets in a project.

However, the adventurous can hop on over to the Scratch Wiki (http://is.gd/wwryoS) to learn a workaround (less charitably called a *hack*) to this behavior.

Essentially, you can tag each sprite with a unique ID by using private variables and then define a global variable that determines who should receive a particular broadcast.

If this procedure sounds frighteningly complex, don't worry about it for now. After all, you have yet to work with variables—you will, though, trust me!

To get set up for the Move from Room to Room Try It Yourself exercise, fire up a new, blank project that contains the following assets:

▶ **Sprite**: Default Scratch Cat; rename sprite to Cat.

▶ **Sprite**: Magic Carpet (look in the Transportation section of the Sprite Library); rename to Carpet.

▶ **Stage backdrops**: Add the room1 and room2 backdrops from the Indoors category of the Backdrop Library. You can delete the default backdrop for this exercise.

TRY IT YOURSELF ▼

Move from Room to Room

For this Try It Yourself exercise, you try your hand at a very brief and very simple interactive story. You first have the Scratch Cat move from one room to another (a very cool trick that you'll enjoy). Next, you have the Cat ask the user to press a key on the keyboard to move a second sprite (the Carpet) out of the way.

The Cat and Carpet scripts are illustrated in Figures 5.6 and 5.7, respectively.

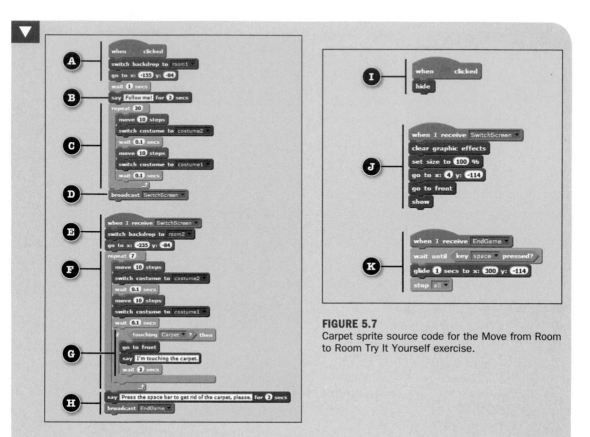

FIGURE 5.6
Cat sprite source code for the Move from Room to
Room Try It Yourself exercise.

FIGURE 5.7
Carpet sprite source code for the Move from Room
to Room Try It Yourself exercise.

The completed solution file is named Hour05c.sb2. Work through the following steps in order to complete this exercise. Let's get to work!

1. Begin by coding the Cat's scripts. Reset the story environment by ensuring that the room1 backdrop is active and the Cat is placed appropriately on the Stage, as shown in the code section labeled A in Figure 5.6.

2. Have the Cat say something to the player to help him or her feel more engaged with the story (see the code section labeled B in Figure 5.6).

3. The repeat block shown in the code section labeled C in Figure 5.6 defines the Cat's animation across the first backdrop. How to do this was covered earlier in the book; simply move the sprite 10 steps, switch its costume, and insert a short pause.

4. Now you get to the heart of the matter. Bring out a `broadcast message1` block, open up the drop-down, and select New Message from the menu. You can name a broadcast anything; for this purpose, make it SwitchScreen. (See the code section labeled D in Figure 5.6.)

5. In the code section labeled E in Figure 5.6, you see something that might strike you as surprising; namely, that sprites can actually "listen for" and receive their own messages! In just a moment, you have the Carpet sprite listen for this broadcast as well.

   For now, switch the Stage backdrop to the second room and place the sprite appropriately on the Stage. This action, combined with the previously defined sprite movement, gives the player the impression that the sprite traveled from one room to another.

6. Add in some animation blocks to get the Cat moved to the Carpet (see the code section labeled F in Figure 5.6). (We haven't addressed the Carpet yet, I realize that.)

7. Insert an `if then` C block to test for the Sensing condition where the Cat sprite touches the Carpet sprite. If that statement evaluates to True, then bring the Cat sprite to the very top layer on the Stage and have it say *"I'm touching the carpet."* (See the code section labeled G in Figure 5.6.)

8. After a 2-second pause, have the Cat sprite say *"Press the space bar to get rid of the carpet, please."* You then need to create a second broadcast named EndGame that will be picked up by the Carpet. (See the code section labeled H in Figure 5.6.)

9. Now switch your focus to the Carpet sprite and cross-reference these steps with Figure 5.7. Place the Carpet sprite at (4, -114) on the Stage. Reminder: Coordinates are given as (x,y). Simply hide the Carpet until the Cat reaches the second room (see the code section labeled I in Figure 5.7).

10. Next, listen for the SwitchScreen broadcast. At that time, reset the style and position of the Carpet sprite, and explicitly show it on the Stage. (See the code section labeled J in Figure 5.7.)

11. Finally, listen for the EndGame broadcast, which is, you'll remember, the broadcast that is triggered if the Cat sprite touches the Carpet sprite. (See the code section labeled K in Figure 5.7.)

   Use the wait until block to test for the key space pressed Boolean condition (that block is found in the Sensing palette). If True, then code the carpet to glide horizontally across the screen to an X value that lies beyond the 480 pixels of the Stage. You then invoke the `stop all` Control block to end the interaction.

Summary

By now, hopefully you are comfortable with the relationships between sprites, their costumes, the Stage, its backdrops, and how you can use broadcasts to connect scripts among sprites and the Stage.

Don't feel discouraged if you feel that you've learned nothing more than "toy code" thus far. You have all the time in the world to build full projects from beginning to end in the final two hours of this book.

Also, there is no way around the sheer time, repetition, and practice that is required for you to know your way around the Blocks palette.

You know that you are well on your way to becoming an honest-to-goodness computer programmer when your mind starts thinking in terms of "Ohh, I just thought of how to have the program do such-and-such" as opposed to, "Now where is the wait for block again?"

The next hour continues the fun. There, you'll learn how to integrate sound effects into your Scratch projects.

Workshop

Quiz

1. When you define a broadcast in Scratch, which assets can receive the broadcast message and therefore take action upon it?

   A. Only the sending sprite

   B. Only the receiving sprite

   C. Only the Stage and its backdrops

   D. The Stage and all sprites

2. Which of the following is a valid way to test for two or more conditions in a Scratch script?

   A. A Boolean block

   B. A nested if C block

   C. A repeat C block

   D. A broadcast block

3. Which of the following Scratch graphical effects can be used to fade in or fade out a sprite on the Stage?

    A. Color

    B. Pixelate

    C. Mosaic

    D. Ghost

Answers

1. The correct answer is choice D. In Scratch 2.0, any broadcasts that are sent out from a sprite or the Stage are receivable by both the Stage as well as all sprites in the project. Recall that the sending sprite can also receive its own message. However, a sprite or the Stage is not obligated to receive a message.

   The Scratch Wiki (http://cbt.gg/1bop3og) includes a hack or workaround that does enable you to effectively target specific sprites with broadcast messages.

2. The correct answer is choice B. By default, an if C block tests for the truth or falsity of a single condition (although you can certainly embed multiple operator blocks —you'll see how to do that in Hour 10, "Using Operators Blocks." An easy approach to solving this problem that you discovered in this chapter is nesting one or more if C blocks inside of the outer, original C block.

3. The correct answer is choice D. The ghost graphic effect works well for fading in or fading out a sprite on the Stage. Changing the color effect can make a sprite look like it's flashing. The pixelate effect makes a sprite look retro or old-fashioned. The mosaic graphic effect is useful for transitioning a sprite between costumes.

Challenge

Okay, here is a fun project for you to try out. This challenge gives you some more experience using graphical effects, implementing broadcasts, and responding to the player's keyboard input.

Here are the design goals for this project:

▶ Have the Scratch Cat instruct the player to press the spacebar (or another key of your choosing) to transform the sprite into a butterfly.

▶ Use graphical effects to pixelate the Cat and have it "become" a butterfly.

▶ Have the butterfly "tell" the gamer that he or she can use the arrow keys to move the butterfly around the Stage.

▶ Code the butterfly for player control.

Figure 5.8 shows a screenshot of my version of this game, and you can also examine the solution file Hour05d.sb2.

FIGURE 5.8
A screen capture from the Hour 5 Challenge project (Hour05d.sb2).

Remember that you need to download and install the free Scratch Offline Editor (http://is.gd/ sB2h1k) to view the solution files. You'll learn everything there is to know about the Offline Editor in Hour 18, "Using the Scratch Offline Editor."

Before finishing this hour, though, it's only fair to discuss the pixelate graphic effect just a little because you didn't use it at all earlier in this hour.

As you can see in Figure 5.9, all you have to do is to wrap a change pixelate effect by block inside of a repeat C block. Test out this sample code block on one of your sprites and experiment with different pixelate intensities.

Also, please understand that there is no shame at all in turning to the Scratch project gallery (http://is.gd/tsr9gM) for help when you get stuck. For example, you can search for projects that include the word pixelate in their title or description, or you can do a tag search for the same term.

Most Scratchers are actually complimented when other Scratchers remix their projects. That's what the community effort of Scratch is all about, after all.

FIGURE 5.9
Pixelating a sprite has a cool retro effect that is useful for transitions.

HOUR 6
Using Sound Blocks

What You'll Learn in This Hour:

▶ Understanding notes and MIDI instruments

▶ Understanding the Backpack

▶ Playing the drums

▶ Using the Sound Library

▶ Recording and editing your own audio

This hour, take a leaf from the Beach Boys and "add some music to your day." More specifically, you learn how you can enhance your Scratch projects by implementing sounds.

Think of it: How many times have you played a completely silent video game? The inclusion of some kind of audio, whether it is a musical background track or event-driven sound effects, is almost a no-brainer for any recreation-oriented programming project.

By the end of this hour, you'll understand Scratch's somewhat convoluted methods for composing MIDI audio. You'll also know how to record your own audio and add prerecorded audio clips into your project and wire them up to sprites appropriately.

In the Scratch Editor, fire up a new, blank project, select the Scratch Cat, navigate to the Scripts tab, and click the Sound palette. Spend a few minutes studying Table 6.1 and double-clicking the blocks to get a feel for their general operation.

Don't worry if you're confused by all the musical nomenclature; pretty soon you'll understand all you need to know about beats, tempo, and so forth.

TABLE 6.1 Scratch Sound Blocks

Block Image	Block Type	Function
play sound meow ▾	Stack	Plays a sound
play sound meow ▾ until done	Stack	Plays a sound all the way to the end of the file
stop all sounds	Stack	Stops any playing sounds in the project
play drum 1▾ for 0.25 beats	Stack	Plays a drum sound for a specified number of beats
rest for 0.25 beats	Stack	Pauses the audio for the specified number of beats
play note 60▾ for 0.5 beats	Stack	Plays a note from a MIDI instrument for the specified number of beats
set instrument to 1▾	Stack	Sets the active MIDI instrument
change volume by -10	Stack	Adjusts the volume; negative numbers reduce the volume, and positive values increase it
set volume to 100 %	Stack	Sets the volume to a specific level (0 is silent, 100 is maximum volume)
volume	Reporter	Gives current volume level of active audio
change tempo by 20	Stack	Adjusts the tempo by a specified beats-per-minute (BPM) value
set tempo to 60 bpm	Stack	Sets the tempo to a specific BPM value
tempo	Reporter	Gives the current tempo BPM value

Without any further ado, let's get busy and make some music!

Understanding Notes and MIDI Instruments

Scratch 2.0 includes a built-in library of Musical Instrument Digital Interface (MIDI) virtual instruments. MIDI is a technical standard that defines a standard method for electronic musical instruments to communicate with each other.

For instance, open the Set Instrument block `set instrument to 1▾` drop-down menu. At the time of this writing, there are 21 virtual instruments, with each virtual instrument given its own ID number:

- ▶ (1) Piano
- ▶ (2) Electric Piano
- ▶ (3) Organ
- ▶ (4) Guitar
- ▶ (5) Electric Guitar
- ▶ (6) Bass
- ▶ (7) Pizzicato
- ▶ (8) Cello
- ▶ (9) Trombone
- ▶ (10) Clarinet
- ▶ (11) Saxophone

- ▶ (12) Flute
- ▶ (13) Wooden Flute
- ▶ (14) Bassoon
- ▶ (15) Choir
- ▶ (16) Vibraphone
- ▶ (17) Music Box
- ▶ (18) Steel Drum
- ▶ (19) Marimba
- ▶ (20) Synth Lead
- ▶ (21) Synth Pad

Now pull a `play note 60▾ for 0.5 beats` stack block into the Scripts area and attach it to the bottom of the Set Instrument block. In music theory, a *note* is a notation that represents the pitch and duration of a musical sound.

If you open up the first drop-down menu in the `play note 60▾ for 0.5 beats` block, you'll see a list of note values along with their IDs. Now, as much as I'd like to delve into music theory with you (I've been a musician for over 30 years), we just don't have the whitespace for it.

Therefore, I draw your attention to Figure 6.1, which shows you how these Scratch note ID values map to notes on a piano keyboard.

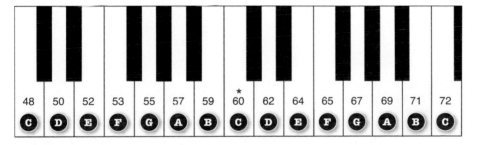

FIGURE 6.1
Scratch MIDI notes as mapped to a traditional piano keyboard (key of C major). The key with the asterisk represents middle C.

Thus, if you know a bit about how to play the piano, you can compose your own songs in Scratch by stacking play note blocks mapped to the appropriate pitches!

The *beat* value represents the atomic unit of time, or the pulse of your musical composition. It might be helpful for you to study Table 6.2, which shows you the relationship between common time (also called 4/4 time, with four beats per musical measure and a quarter note representing one beat) and the Scratch note's beat value.

TABLE 6.2   Relationship Between Beat Number Values and the 4/4 Time Signature

	Whole Note	Half Note	Quarter Note	Eighth Note	Sixteenth Note
Scratch beat value	4	2	1	0.5	0.25

The following Try It Yourself exercise will help you get more of a feel for this admittedly tedious theory.

To get set up for the upcoming exercise, create a new project and include the following assets:

▶ Scratch Cat, renamed to Cat

▶ Crab sprite from the Sprite Library, renamed to Crab

▶ Stage backdrop `stage2` from the Indoors category in the Backdrop Library

▼ TRY IT YOURSELF

Sing in the Choir

In this Try It Yourself exercise, you put on a brief "vocal" recital featuring the Cat and Crab sprites. The source code is shown in Figure 6.2. The completed solution file for this exercise is `Hour06a.sb2`. Let's get to work! Follow these steps and check your work with the annotations in Figure 6.2:

1. Position the two sprites appropriately on the Stage. I placed them right next to each other, but feel free to be creative!

2. Select the Cat and head over to the Scripts area. As usual, begin by resetting the environment (shown in the code section labeled A in Figure 6.2). Note the use of the new `stop all sounds` and `set volume to 100 %` stack blocks. You want to set the initial volume to 50 percent so you can play with increasing the volume later in the running of the project.

3. The quasimusical piece you're doing will make use of three `repeat 10` C blocks (see the code section labeled B in the figure). Choose MIDI instrument 15 (Choir), and play four notes with a value of one beat apiece.

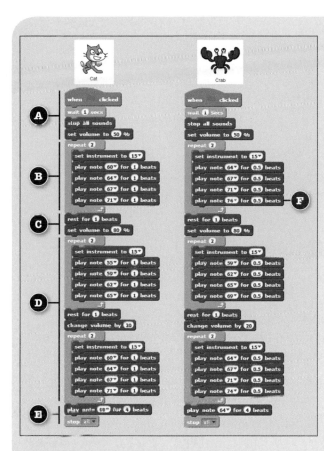

FIGURE 6.2
Source code for the Sing in the Choir Try It Yourself exercise.

You can save yourself quite a bit of dragging and dropping by clicking the Stamp tool and then clicking the `repeat 10` C block. This creates a duplicate of the selected block as well as any blocks connected underneath it. Convenient, eh?

4. Add a one-beat rest and then bump up the volume 20 percent (see the code section labeled C in the figure).

5. In the code section labeled D in the figure, notice that you can also adjust the volume by using the `change volume by -10` stack block. Here, you bump up the volume 20 percent more, effectively "maxing out" the project volume. (Do the addition—you'll notice that you are now at a volume of 100 percent.)

6. Finish the composition by droning the middle C for four beats and then stopping script execution, as shown in the code section labeled E in the figure.

▼

7. Now select the Crab sprite and build a matching script for it. Notice that you are using complementary notes. To save yourself work, you should make use of Scratch's Backpack feature to copy the Cat's entire script stack to the Crab's script area. The Backpack feature is described a bit later in this hour in the "Understanding the Backpack" section. Check your work by examining the code section labeled F.

8. Click the Green Flag to hear the concert. Unfortunately, the MIDI implementation in Scratch 2.0 isn't the best, and even though you set both scripts to start at the same time, you'll probably find some latency (delay) that staggers their playback. There isn't much you can do about the latency; it's a limitation of the Scratch environment and the MIDI weaknesses inherent in Adobe Flash technology.

Understanding the Backpack

I've worked with Scratch for a few years now, and one of the most annoying things about Scratch 1.4 was that you could not copy and paste scripts or sprites within a single project or between multiple projects.

Great news for those Scratchers who shared my frustration: Scratch 2.0 now includes an awesome new feature called the Backpack that does just that.

To use the Backpack, simply drag an element into the Backpack pane that appears at the bottom right of the Scratch 2.0 Editor interface. Figure 6.3 shows what this looks like.

You can drag and drop just about any Scratch asset into the Backpack, including:

▶ Sprites

▶ Individual costumes

▶ Stage backdrops

▶ Script block code

▶ Sound files

Once you have an asset in the Backpack, you can switch to your target (doesn't matter if the target object is in the current project or another one because the Backpack maintains its contents), and drag the Backpack element into the appropriate location.

To get rid of a saved Backpack item, right-click the element in the Backpack and select Delete from the shortcut menu.

One caveat: As of this writing, the Backpack feature has not made its way to the Scratch Offline Editor. Thus, you have to use the browser-based Editor to take advantage of Backpack.

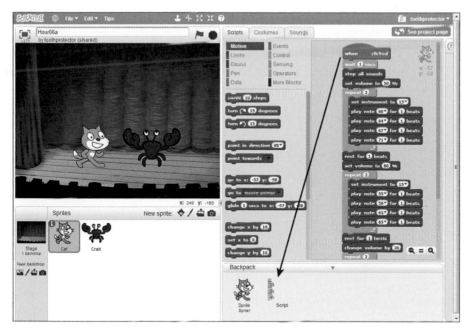

FIGURE 6.3
The Backpack is one of the best productivity enhancements in Scratch 2.0.

Playing the Drums!

When I was a boy, I banged on my mom's pots and pans to the accompaniment of the first two KISS *Alive!* record albums (anyone remember those?). Yeah, I suppose I fancied myself a drummer at the time.

There is something primal about a drum beat though, don't you agree? The good news for you as a Scratcher is that Scratch 2.0 includes a clunky but otherwise serviceable method for adding drum sounds to your projects.

Why do I describe the system as *clunky*? Well, for one thing, you have to contend with the beat and rest block system introduced earlier in this hour.

The Scratch 2.0 MIDI instrument library includes 18 drum models; you can see them by opening up the drop-down menu in **play drum 1▼ for 0.25 beats**. Here is a complete rundown of the 18 drum types along with their ID values:

- ▶ (1) Snare Drum
- ▶ (2) Bass Drum
- ▶ (3) Side Stick
- ▶ (4) Crash Cymbal
- ▶ (5) Open Hi-Hat
- ▶ (6) Closed Hi-Hat

▶ (7) Tambourine   ▶ (13) Bongo

▶ (8) Hand Clap   ▶ (14) Conga

▶ (9) Claves   ▶ (15) Cabasa

▶ (10) Wood Block   ▶ (16) Guiro

▶ (11) Cowbell (can't have enough of this!)   ▶ (17) Vibraslap

▶ (12) Triangle   ▶ (18) Open Cuica

While in this discussion, you should understand tempo, which is manifested in Scratch with change tempo by and set tempo to stack blocks. *Tempo* refers to the speed (counted in beats per minute, or BPM) at which a passage of music plays.

The following Try It Yourself exercise will give you some practice time with Scratch drums as well as help you become familiar with how tempo works. Here's the preliminary setup:

▶ Select the Scratch Cat sprite and rename to Cat.

▶ Select the Drum1 sprite from the Things category in the Sprite Library and rename to Drum.

▶ Set the Stage backdrop spotlight-stage from the Indoors category of the Backdrop Library (you can delete the default backdrop; you don't need it here).

▶ Make the drum smaller by selecting it in Scratch Editor, clicking the Shrink button in the toolbar, and then repeatedly clicking the Drum sprite on the Stage.

▶ Position the Cat and the Drum beneath the spotlight.

▶ Enable the tempo (Sound palette) and answer (Sensing palette) Stage monitors.

▼ TRY IT YOURSELF

Drums on Demand

In this Try It Yourself exercise, you have the Scratch Cat ask the player to select a drum model. You then take the user-submitted value and feed it into a play drum block at a given tempo. You can see the interface and source code in Figure 6.4, and the completed solution file is named `Hour06b.sb2`. Work through the following steps to finish this exercise:

1. Select the Cat, switch to the Scripts area, and add a [when clicked] block. You'll insert a 1-second delay before you get to the main logic of the project.

2. In the code section labeled A in Figure 6.4, you can see that the game will continue to ask the player for drum models and play 10 sixteenth-note beats over and over again until the player clicks the Stop button.

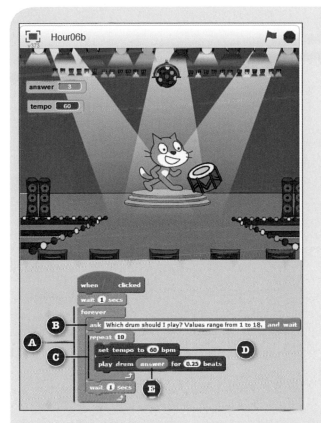

FIGURE 6.4
The Drums on Demand Try It Yourself exercise with the source code listed.

3. Use the ask block to ask the player "Which drum should I play? Values range from 1 to 18." It's crucial that you give the player the upper and lower bounds of the drum's legal values. (See the code section labeled B in the figure.)

   You get bonus points if you can figure out a way to handle the exception where a user tries to submit 0 or 19 as a drum value. If you just can't stand the suspense, check out Figure 6.5 for a possible solution to this problem.

4. Now play the drum loop. (See the code section labeled C in the figure.)

5. Next, you, as the programmer, manually set the tempo. (See the code section labeled D in the figure.) You should experiment with altering this value and then rerunning the project. In Hour 12, "Using Data Blocks," you'll work with variables, which allow you to capture multiple answers from the player and pop them in the project dynamically. For instance, it would be cool to ask the player what tempo he or she wanted to play the beats at.

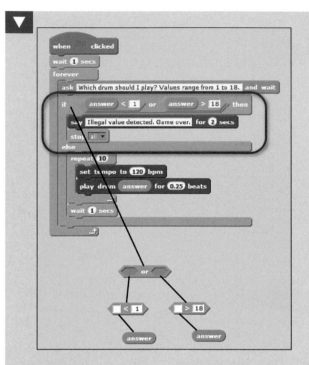

FIGURE 6.5
One way to handle the problem of the player entering an illegal value in the Drums on Demand Try It Yourself exercise. To help your understanding, the Boolean block is broken apart below so you can see its components.

6. Pop in the answer reporter block as an argument variable to the play drum stack block. (See the code section labeled E in the figure.) This is the heart of what makes this project cool. Again, as a developer, you can play around with the beat value to test out different drum effects.

Using the Sound Library

Thus far, you have learned how to make your own music by leveraging Scratch's built-in library of MIDI virtual instruments. What if you already have an idea of a sound you need (perhaps a sound effect for a game you're developing)? How can you find an appropriate clip?

NOTE

There Are Always More Sounds Available Online

You need to be careful about downloading other people's music without their permission because intellectual property theft is illegal in the United States and many other countries. A good, safe resource is the Scratch Resources site (http://is.gd/0zQFvW). Here, you can search for audio clips, download them for free, and in most cases the authors want nothing more than simple attribution in your project that acknowledges their work. You can easily add that attribution on your project's public page at the Scratch website.

One option is the built-in Sound Library. You can attach an audio file to a sprite or to a Stage backdrop. Simply select a sprite or backdrop, navigate to the Sounds tab, and click the Choose Sound from Library button.

The Sound Library includes several dozen sound clips, organized into categories as has been the case with sprites and Stage backdrops. Once you bring a sound clip into the Sounds pane, an array of options becomes available to you. Use Figure 6.6 and the following list to review the controls:

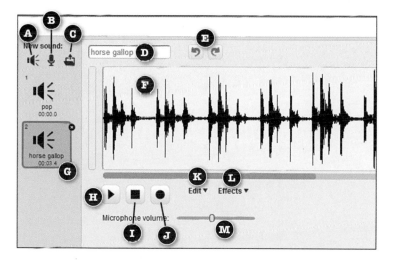

FIGURE 6.6
Managing sound properties in a Scratch 2.0 project.

- ▶ A: Choose Sound from Library
- ▶ B: Record New Sound
- ▶ C: Upload Sound from File
- ▶ D: Rename the Sound Clip
- ▶ E: Undo, Redo last action
- ▶ F: Waveform
- ▶ G: Right-click to delete or save clip to your computer

▶ H: Play

▶ I: Stop

▶ J: Record

▶ K: Edit menu

▶ L: Effects menu

▶ M: Microphone volume

If you right-click a sound clip in the Sounds pane and select Save to Local File, you have the option to download the sound clip to your computer in WAV format. The WAV format was invented by Microsoft and IBM and tends to be a larger file than an MP3 due to its uncompressed nature.

As you can see in Figure 6.7, once you have more than one sound clip attached to a sprite or Stage backdrop, those sounds become available on the appropriate Sounds script blocks.

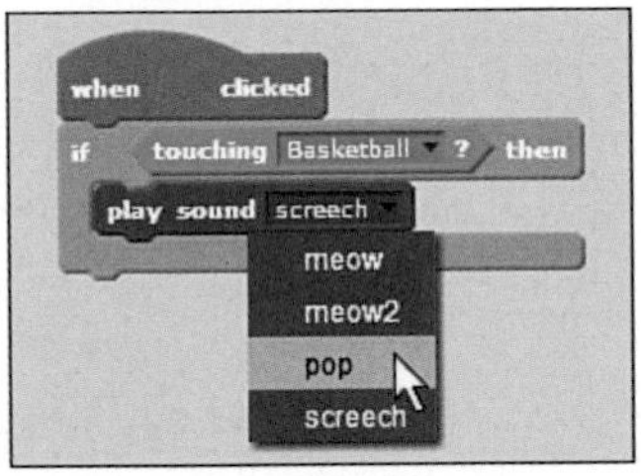

FIGURE 6.7
Having more than one sound attached to a sprite gives you more audio options.

Recording and Editing Your Own Audio

The included Sound Library in Scratch 2.0 is functional, but if you have a concrete image of the audio clip you need for your current project, there is nothing standing in your way of recording it yourself.

The only requirement to creating your own audio, of course, is that you need some sort of microphone. Nowadays, many computer monitors, especially laptop computer monitors, have built-in microphones. Another option is an inexpensive USB headset.

In any event, make sure that your microphone is functional, and get ready to do some recording!

You'll use the same Scratch 2.0 environment for the remainder of this hour. Use the following specifications to set up your work file:

▶ Delete the default Scratch Cat sprite (right-click the sprite and select Delete from the shortcut menu).

- Bring in the Button2 sprite from the Things category in the Sprite Library; rename the sprite to Cursor.

- Bring in the Planet2 sprite from the Space theme in the Sprite Library; rename the sprite to Planet.

- For the Stage, bring in the Stars sprite from the Space theme in the Backdrop Library.

- Rename the blank white backdrop to white.

Because this is the most complex project thus far, let me tell you in advance what it's going to do. This is a simple "twitch" video game in which you move your space paddle around the star field with your mouse and attempt to hit a rogue planet.

If you do hit the planet, the planet disappears and randomly respawns elsewhere on the Stage.

At this point, we'll begin to be concerned about keeping score or ending the game based upon a predefined condition. In this lesson, you'll learn a bit about how to use a variable to accomplish the first goal (display a score). You'll do much more with variables in Hour 12.

You'll learn how to code the end conditions of a Scratch project in Hour 8, "Using Events Blocks."

TRY IT YOURSELF

Record and Edit Your Own Audio Clip

In this Try It Yourself exercise, you create a simple audio clip that will play every time your Contact! game is started by clicking the Green Flag. Although you can add the audio to any sprite or the Stage, you add this clip to the Cursor sprite. Okay! Work through the following steps to complete the exercise:

1. Ensure that your microphone is plugged in and functional. Next, click the Cursor sprite, navigate to the Sounds tab, and click the Record New Sound button.

2. Click the Record button, pause for a second or two, and then say "Three...two...one...contact!" Just for grins, you can find my own file, `321.wav`, in the solution file set.

   You might find that the input volume, also called gain, results in a too-soft audio clip. If so, please adjust the Microphone Volume slider to the right to boost the incoming signal.

3. Rename the clip to 321. Right-click the clip to prove to yourself that you can save the clip to your computer as a WAV file if you want to.

4. Now you can edit the clip. Use the horizontal slider that appears beneath the waveform until you see a gap of silence. Next, click and drag your mouse inside the waveform to select a span of time. Selected audio shows up with a light blue highlight.

Finally, click Edit, Cut to remove the clip. If you make a mistake, simply click Edit, Undo to restore your cut. Figure 6.8 shows the interface.

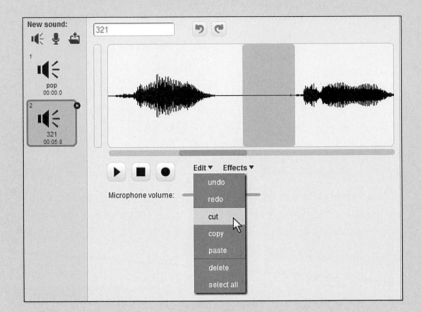

FIGURE 6.8
The Scratch 2.0 Editor gives you basic audio editing tools.

5. Now open the Effects menu. From here, you can perform the following actions on your audio selection: Fade In, Fade Out, Louder, Softer, Silence, and Reverse. The Reverse effect is particularly cool—try it out, and then click Undo to get your original forward audio back!

Awesome! Now you can build the game. Before you do, you can create a variable to hold the game score. Specifically, you want to keep track of how many times your Cursor sprite makes contact with the Planet sprite.

Navigate to the Data tab and click Make a Variable. In the New Variable dialog box, name the variable Score, and ensure that For All Sprites is selected. In other words, you are creating a data placeholder named Score that is available to all sprites in the project.

As you can see in Figure 6.9, a new variable spawns a number of new blocks, which are described here:

▶ The <variable> reporter block enables you to use the variable value as a Stage monitor or as an input to another block.

► The set <variable> block allows you to set the value to a variable manually.

► The change <variable> block allows you to increase or decrease a variable's value according to some condition (you'll use this method for the current game).

► The show variable <variable> block turns on a Stage monitor for the variable.

► The hide <variable> block turns off a Stage monitor for the variable.

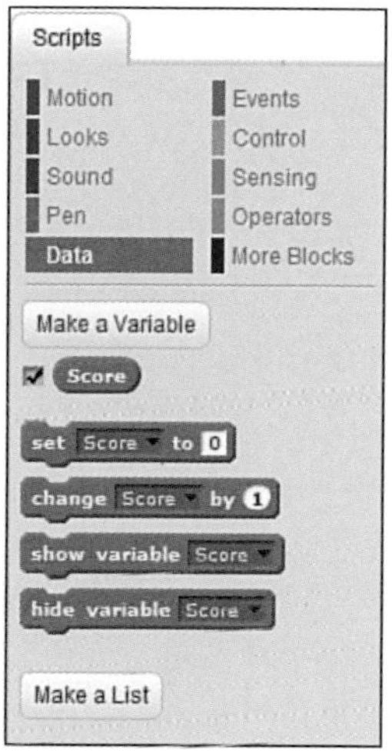

FIGURE 6.9
Creating a new variable gives you some new "toys" to play with.

TRY IT YOURSELF ▼

Contact!

In this Try It Yourself exercise, you continue to work on your current Scratch project and turn it into a fun little hand-eye coordination-based game. Study the annotated source code in Figure 6.10 as you work through the following instructions.

The name of the completed solution file is Hour06c.sb2. Work through the following steps to complete the exercise; don't forget to cross-reference your work with the annotations in Figure 6.10:

1. Focus on the Cursor code first. Select the cursor and head to the Scripts tab. In the code section labeled A in Figure 6.10, you set (or reset, as the case may be) the Score variable to zero. You also ensure that the Score reporter Stage monitor is always visible at runtime.

2. Switch to the Starfield backdrop and play the introductory audio clip you recorded earlier (see the code section labeled B in the figure). Feel free to use my 321.wav clip, if you are so inclined.

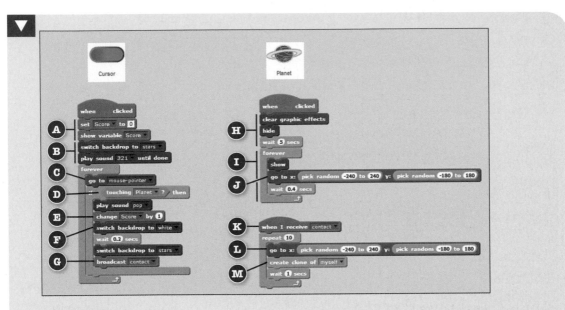

FIGURE 6.10
Source code for the Contact! Try It Yourself exercise.

3. You now start the main loop in the program, which runs forever (again, you'll learn how to formally end your projects in Hour 8). Use the `go to mouse-pointer` stack block to map the Cursor sprite to your mouse cursor (see the code section labeled C in the figure). This is a great method for putting control into the gamer's hands!

4. Set up a conditional expression such that if the Cursor sprite touches the Planet sprite, you do a bunch of stuff, including playing the pop sound, quickly toggling between two backdrops, and incrementing the score. (See the code section labeled D in the figure.)

5. Add 1 to the Score variable. Thus, each time the Cursor connects with the Planet, you bump up the Score by one. (See the code section labeled E in the figure.)

6. Create a fast visual effect by swapping backdrops on a 0.2-second delay. This creates some anticipation in your game and gives the player some incentive to hit a Planet sprite. (See the code section labeled F in the figure.)

7. Next, send out a broadcast that you'll create and name "contact." In just a minute, you'll program the Planet sprite to respond to the contact broadcast. Remember, broadcasts are how you can communicate among sprites. Here, you need to notify the Planet sprite that a collision has taken place. (See the code section labeled G in the figure.)

8. Now turn your attention to the scripts for the Planet sprite. Set up the environment such that you hide the sprite and remove any graphic effects that are leftover from previous runs of the game. (See the code section labeled H in the figure.)

9. Define the planet's pseudorandom appearances on the Stage. (See the code section labeled I in the figure.)

10. Answer the question, "How can you randomize where the Planet appears on the Stage?" The algorithm for generating pseudorandom numbers is defined with the Scratch `pick random 1 to 10` reporter block; you can embed those into a `go to x: 0 y: 0` stack block, specifying the outer borders of the Stage. (See the code section labeled J in the figure.)

11. Code some extra visual "bling" that will occur when contact is made between the Cursor and the Planet. (See the code section labeled K in the figure.)

12. Have the Planet clone itself 10 times and place those clones in random Stage locations. After a half second, hide all the clones. The reason to add this code (besides to show you how you can integrate broadcasts into the game) is that you can add some difficulty and complexity to the game, as well as surprising the player a bit when his or her Cursor makes contact with a Planet. (See the code section labeled L in the figure.)

13. Use the `create clone of myself` block. You haven't used this block yet; it's great for, well, cloning or making an exact duplicate of a given sprite. (See the code section labeled M in the figure.)

NOTE

What Is an Algorithm?

I have a friend who told me that a single word a teacher said was enough to turn him off to the idea of learning how to program; the word was *algorithm*. This word doesn't have to scare you off, believe me.

In computer programming, an *algorithm* is a step-by-step procedure for performing a calculation. For instance, in the Contact! game, you needed to find a method for making the Planet sprite respawn in a random Stage location each time you hit it with the Cursor paddle.

In this case, you didn't have to worry about defining the algorithm for generating pseudorandom numbers because the `pick random 1 to 10` reporter blocks do that for you. Instead, your algorithm involved

plugging a couple of those reporter blocks into the `go to x: 0 y: 0` stack block.

If you find that you enjoy programming, you might eventually discover that thinking up algorithms to solve problems is one of the most rewarding aspects of the work.

Summary

In this hour, you added quite a bit of cool new functionality to your Scratch project. You can greatly enhance the effectiveness of your Scratch project by adding audio effects and perhaps your own recorded narration.

In the next hour, you'll learn how to use the Pen tools.

Workshop

Quiz

1. What audio file format is used when you save a copy of a recorded audio clip from the Scratch Editor to your computer?

    A. MP3

    B. WAV

    C. OGG

2. Which of the following blocks should you use if you need to code a 10 percent reduction of the current project's volume for a playing audio clip?

    A. Set volume to 10%

    B. Change tempo by 10

    C. Change volume by −10

3. Which of the following statements correctly defines the purpose of the variable in Scratch 2.0?

    A. A variable is used to communicate messages between sprites.

    B. A variable is used for switching among drum or instrument MIDI sounds.

    C. A variable is used as a place to temporarily store data.

Answers

1. The correct answer is choice B. Audio clips that are saved to your computer from the Scratch Project Editor are saved in uncompressed WAV format.

2. The correct answer is choice C. The easiest way to reduce the volume of a playing clip by a specified percentage is to use the change volume by −10 stack block.

3. The correct answer is choice C. A variable is a named object that temporarily stores data. You can use variables in a variety of places, including as arguments for stack or Boolean blocks.

Challenge

Create a children's storybook using Scratch 2.0. Specifically, the storybook should have at least three "pages" (Stage backdrops) and include at least three narration audio clips featuring your own voice.

Add some interactivity to the storybook by requiring the player to press the spacebar to continue to the next page.

Figure 6.11 shows a screenshot of a sample solution. Also, the sample source code is provided in the file `Hour06d.sb2`.

FIGURE 6.11
A sample solution for the storybook exercise.

HOUR 7
Working with Pen Blocks

What You'll Learn in This Hour:

▶ Getting to know the Pen blocks
▶ Gaining some experience with the Pen tools
▶ Creating a simple drawing program

My three-year-old daughter Zoey loves to draw with her crayons. Give her a box of crayons and a stack of construction paper, and Zoey will happily keep herself occupied indefinitely.

Bear with me here for a moment: I want to share with you Zoey's workflow for creating drawings:

1. First, she selects an appropriate crayon based upon desired line thickness and color.

2. Second, she puts the crayon down to the paper surface.

3. Third, she draws lines and fills until she is satisfied with the result.

4. Fourth, she lifts the crayon from the paper and admires her handiwork.

5. Fifth, she grabs another sheet of paper and starts the entire process over again.

As you'll learn in a moment, drawing in Scratch 2.0 involves this very same workflow. You might find Scratch's implementation of drawing a bit wonky at first, but in time you'll come to appreciate how using the drawing tools forces you to think like a programmer—step-by-step, with methodical purpose.

This hour, you also become more familiar with Scratch's built-in Paint Editor, which allows you to draw sprites from scratch. With no further ado, let's get to work!

Getting to Know the Pen Blocks

Scratchers use the Pen blocks most commonly to accomplish the following project goals:

▶ Making a Snake-type game; Snake (http://is.gd/sVrxje) is one of the classic arcade games and is a great place to begin your own game development

▶ Creating an animated trail behind a sprite (useful in Snake!)

▶ Drawing patterns on the Stage

▶ Creating graphs

Please create a new, blank Scratch project and spend some time gaining initial familiarity with the Pen blocks. You can cross-reference the blocks you see in the Scratch Editor with the information provided in Table 7.1.

TABLE 7.1   The Pen Blocks

Block Image	Block Type	Description
clear	Stack	Removes any pen markings from the Stage
stamp	Stack	Creates a nonprogrammable duplicate of the active sprite on the Stage
pen down	Stack	Activates the pen function and prepares the pen to draw on the Stage
pen up	Stack	Stops the pen from drawing on the Stage
set pen color to	Stack	Sets the pen color by using the Eyedropper tool
change pen color by 10	Stack	Changes the pen color by using a specific integer value
set pen color to 0	Stack	Sets the pen color by using a specific integer value
change pen shade by 10	Stack	Changes the pen shade by using a specific value
set pen shade to 50	Stack	Sets the pen shade by using a specific value
change pen size by 1	Stack	Changes the pen size by using a specific value
set pen size to 1	Stack	Sets the pen size by using a specific value

The green color-coded Pen blocks are a bit unique inasmuch as every block in the Pen palette is a stack block. Also, if your experience mirrors mine, you might find the Pen Color, Shade, and Size controls to be nonintuitive (at best) upon first inspection.

To that end, you need to spend a bit of time getting to know those blocks in greater detail. Hopefully, this part of the book will save you quite a bit of unnecessary frustration!

You'll also notice a key difference between sprites and the Stage in this regard. Whereas all of the Pen blocks are available on the Scripts tab for sprites, only the [clear] stack block is available to the Stage. Although this might seem counterintuitive at first, it makes sense if you think about it this way: The Pen tools need to be "operated" by a sprite. Basically, the Stage cannot "hold" a pen, but a sprite can. Make sense?

How Pen Color Works

Notice that Scratch 2.0 gives you not one but two stack blocks with which you can set the pen color. The [set pen color to] block uses a technique called a *color picker* or *eyedropper* to pick up another color that is visible in the Scratch Editor interface. To use the Eyedropper tool, follow these steps:

1. Click your mouse once inside the [set pen color to] block's color swatch.

2. Hover your mouse over some other color that is visible on anything in the Scratch Editor interface. You should see that color appear in the block's color swatch.

3. When you find your desired color, click on the target color. This now sets the color in the block's swatch and your pen will use this color in Scratch until you change the color again.

It's a bummer, but the Eyedropper tool doesn't let you select colors from outside the Scratch Editor window. Therefore, you might need to temporarily add a sprite, Stage backdrop, or some other graphical element to your project just so you can make the correct color available to the block.

The other way to set the pen color is by using a discrete integer value. Drag out a [set pen color to 0] block and change the value. Observe how this affects the pen color.

In Scratch, the color values range from 0 to 199. Red (value 0) is the default pen color.

Unfortunately, as of this writing, neither the Scratch Team nor any other Scratch community member has published a mapping of those 200 integer values to a particular color. Perhaps you'll be inspired to do this—your work will be appreciated by many Scratchers, myself included!

How Pen Shade Works

In Scratch, pen shade refers to the relative lightness or darkness of a line. The range of values for the `set pen shade to 50` block is 50, which maps to the current set (pure) color of the pen.

The legal range of values for pen shade is 0 (completely white) to 100 (completely black).

The `change pen shade by 10` block allows you to increase or decrease the pen's shade value. Remember to use negative numbers to reduce the value and positive numbers to increase it.

Pen shade is a cool way to "fake" a transparency effect on a pen line. It's also useful to make certain lines stand out from others on the Stage.

How Pen Size Works

Pen size simply refers to the thickness or thinness of the pen. In Scratch 2.0, the legal values for pen size range from 0 (thinnest) to 255 (thickest), giving us 256 possible values.

NOTE

Pixel Perfect?

Sometimes functionality in Scratch is limited by the capabilities of its underlying architecture. Recall that Scratch 2.0 uses Adobe Flash technology as its "engine." As it happens, two Flash-related limitations yield negative pen effects for us Scratchers. First, Flash Player itself limits the number of pen size values to 256.

More significant is what's known as the *single pixel bug* where a pen size of one draws only half a pixel, while size two gives you a single pixel-width line.

As of this writing, there is no known workaround to this problem other than never programming a pen size with a value less than two.

Incidentally, a pixel (short for picture element) is the smallest unit of graphics display on a computer monitor or television screen. You can read more about pixels by visiting the Scratch Wiki at http://is.gd/Yq8I24.

Now that you have spent some time understanding how pen color, shade, and size work, add the blocks shown in Figure 7.1 to your current blank project. This mini-project will give you some practice and experience in demonstrating the effect of changing pen values.

Use Figure 7.1 and the following list as a guide as you examine the code so you understand exactly what is happening:

▶ A: Here, you reset the environment so you can replay the interaction multiple times and have a fixed starting point. No big surprises here.

▶ **B:** Here, you use the `set pen color to ■` and `set pen size to ❶` blocks to choose a color (I nabbed orange from the Scratch Cat sprite) and a decent thickness.

▶ **C:** Here, you are adding 40 to the default pen shade of 50, yielding a grand total of 90. You can see that the output is labeled above the block stack in Figure 7.1.

▶ **D:** Here, you manually reset the pen shade to the default value of 50. Next, you reduce the shade to 10 by subtracting 40 from 50. Easy enough, right?

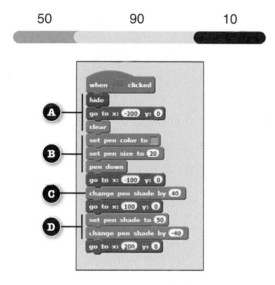

FIGURE 7.1
An experiment with pen size, color, and shade.

Gaining Some Experience with the Pen Tools

The following Try It Yourself exercise will give you some practice with using the Pen tools.

Start a new, blank project and set it up according to the following guidelines:

▶ Import the xy-grid and stars backdrops from the Backdrop Library and delete the default Stage backdrop. Remember that you cannot delete the default Stage backdrop unless you have at least one other backdrop present.

▶ Rename the default Scratch Cat sprite to Cat, and use the Shrink button on the toolbar to reduce the size of the sprite such that it is approximately 50 pixels tall.

▶ Add the zoop sound effect (found in the Electronics category of the Sound Library) to the Cat sprite.

In The Budding Artist Try It Yourself exercise, you get a chance to practice the following:

▶ Hide the Scratch Cat and reset the environment.

▶ Draw a geometric shape on the Stage.

▶ Add a cool transition effect.

▶ Draw a second geometric shape.

▶ Repeat the earlier transition.

▶ Run and duplicate the sprite around the Stage perimeter using the ⬛ stamp block.

▼ TRY IT YOURSELF

The Budding Artist

Figure 7.2 shows a representative screen from this Try It Yourself exercise (specifically a scene from midway through the animation), and you can see the annotated source code listing in Figure 7.3. As usual, you can find the completed solution file for this project in the book's supplemental resources; the filename is Hour07a.sb2. Using Figure 7.3 as you code guide, work through the following steps to complete this exercise:

1. Select the Cat sprite and navigate to the Scripts pane. In this exercise, all of your code will be attached to the Cat, even though the initial drawing isn't particularly relevant to the Cat. In Hour 16, "Documenting Your Project," you'll learn how to make your code more centralized and modular; don't worry about that for now.

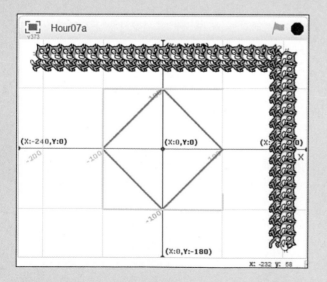

FIGURE 7.2
Screen output from The Budding Artist Try It Yourself exercise.

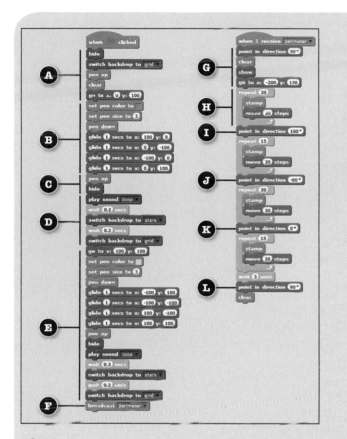

FIGURE 7.3
Source code from The Budding Artist Try It Yourself exercise.

2. Notice that you have two scripts happening here. The [when clicked] procedure handles the first (drawing) phase; the [when I receive message1] procedure defines the second (Scratch Cat perimeter run) phase. Reset the environment by hiding or showing the Cat, setting the correct Stage backdrop, and clearing graphical (pen) effects. (See the code sections labeled A and G in Figure 7.3.)

3. In the code section labeled B in the figure, you make your first drawing. This requires you to study the xy-grid backdrop to figure out which coordinates map to where you want the pen to go (which is why you imported the xy-grid).

4. Lift the pen from the Stage and hide any visible trace of the pen. (See the code section labeled C in the figure.)

5. Perform some graphical "magic" to create a quick audiovisual transition between the first drawing and the second one. (See the code section labeled D in the figure.) What's happening is that you are (a) playing the zoop sound, (b) switching to the stars backdrop, and (c) switching back to the xy-grid backdrop, all in the space of 0.4 seconds. Pretty neat, eh?

6. Draw a second geometric shape, this time using a different line color to make the shape stand out a bit from the first one. (See the code section labeled E in the figure.)

7. Link the drawing phase from the cat-perimeter phase by using a broadcast named perimeter. (See the code section labeled F in the figure.)

8. Once the perimeter broadcast goes out, it is immediately picked up by the Scratch Cat. In the code section labeled H in the figure, you can see the algorithm for "marching" the Cat around the outside boundary of the Stage. This gives you a chance to see the `stamp` block in action; this block produces an image of the current object. However, the stamped image(s) cannot be programmed in any way. You can use the `clear` block to wipe the copies off the Stage, though. By contrast, the `create clone of myself` block creates a complete, programmable copy of the current object.

9. Use the `point in direction 90` block to position the directionality of the sprite appropriately depending upon its trajectory on the Stage. (See the code sections labeled I, J, K, and L in the figure.)

NOTE

Avoiding Repetitive Code

In The Budding Artist Try It Yourself exercise, you repeated the same block sequence to accomplish some tasks. In computer programming, a function is a named, stored code sequence that can be run multiple times within a project.

Functions represent a great way that programmers use to centralize code and avoid unnecessary repetition. Remember that repetitive code procedures lend themselves to human error and are more difficult to troubleshoot and to make changes to in the future.

In Hour 15, "Creating Your Own Blocks," you'll learn how to create your own blocks from (yes, I went there) scratch. This gives you functionality as close as Scratch can get to providing functionlike behavior in your projects.

Creating a Simple Drawing Program

It's definitely a "light bulb" moment when a programming student realizes, "Hey, I'm using the Scratch Editor to create computer programs, but Scratch is, itself, a computer program!"

Going further, the operating system from which you're using Scratch is also a computer program that a team of people developed. This "meta" thinking is important for you to ponder, embrace, and accept. In terms of computer programs, nothing comes from nothing.

Enough uberabstraction—let's come back to Earth and create a new Scratch project! This one will be the most ambitious you've attempted thus far.

You've probably used paint programs, right? For instance, Microsoft Windows has included a free, built-in paint editor since version 1.0. Figure 7.4 shows the Windows 7 Paint program.

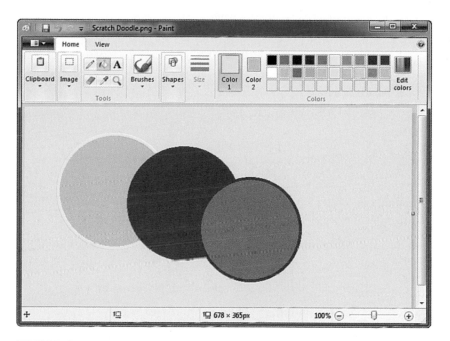

FIGURE 7.4
Windows Paint is a popular paint program.

Of course, Scratch includes its own built-in Paint Editor that you can use to create and edit sprites and Stage backdrops. Let's leave that aside for a moment and ponder, "How could we build a simple paint program in Scratch?"

Well, why don't we brainstorm a bit? For instance, in our drawing program, we could:

▶ Use a sprite as the drawing "pen" and map its movement to the player's mouse.

▶ Create some color swatch sprites and code them such that clicking them on the Stage changes the pen color.

▶ Include a Clear button sprite to remove all drawing from the Stage.

The project you are about to create owes a heavy debt to the Scratcher aleboy10, whose outstanding Scratch project "Drawing Program" (http://is.gd/2jjGzf) is the inspiration and model for the project.

Because the drawing program project is so large, it is split up into a few separate Try It Yourself exercises. To begin, fire up a new, blank project and set it up as follows:

▶ Delete the default Scratch Cat sprite.

▶ Import the Magic Wand sprite from the Things category in the Costume Library. Use the Shrink tool to make the wand about 50 percent smaller than its original size.

▶ Create four new, empty sprites by using the Paint New Sprite button in the Sprites panel. Name the sprites Red, Green, Blue, and Clear. You'll actually draw their costumes soon enough.

Now don't fret! You'll do this project piece by piece. Here's how you'll develop this particular solution:

1. First, you'll draw the sprites that will represent the program's color swatches and Reset button.

2. Second, you'll program the control logic such that the Magic Wand sprite is wired to the player's mouse and drops the pen whenever the player clicks the mouse button.

3. Third, you'll code the color swatch and reset sprites to kick out broadcasts when they are clicked.

4. Fourth and finally, you'll code the Magic Wand controller to respond to any triggered broadcasts.

You can find `Hour07b.sb2`, the completed solution file, with the rest of this book's resources. However, please don't jump to the solution file the moment you get stuck. Part of the joy of being a computer programmer is figuring out solutions to problems. Remember that a common term for computer programmer is *solution developer*.

▼ TRY IT YOURSELF

Drawing Program Phase 1: Drawing the Sprites

The following steps show you how to create the first color swatch, and then you create the second and third ones yourself. You'll learn how to create the Clear button immediately after this exercise.

1. Select the Red sprite in the Sprites panel. In the middle part of the Scratch Editor, switch to the Costumes tab. Here, you see the Paint Editor.

2. Now this is a bit tricky, so pay attention: You want to select your color first, and then create your shape. In this case, you want to create a small square that is colored red.

   In the color panel at the bottom of the Paint Editor, click the red color swatch to select it. (Label A in Figure 7.5 points to the general vicinity of the swatch.)

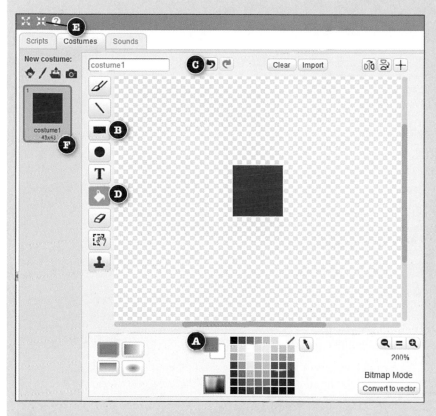

FIGURE 7.5
You can build your own sprites in the Scratch Paint Editor.

3. Next, click the Rectangle tool (labeled B in the figure). If you hold down the Shift key as you click and drag in the drawing canvas, you'll get a square instead of a rectangle. If you make a mistake, click the Undo button (labeled C in the figure). Don't get too frustrated if you make mistakes—the Paint Editor is pretty clunky.

▼

4. To fill in the rectangle, click the Paint Bucket tool (labeled D in the figure) and then click inside your square.

5. Use the Shrink tool (labeled E in the figure) to make the square approximately 43×43 pixels in size. You can check the size of the costume in the Costumes panel (labeled F in the figure).

6. On the Stage, use your mouse to position the swatch to the lower left.

7. To create the Blue and Green sprites, you have two choices. One method, which is probably best because you're a beginner who needs practice, is to follow the previous steps to create each swatch. Position them next to each other on the Stage along the bottom.

   The other method is to right-click the Red swatch in the Sprites panel and select Duplicate from the shortcut menu. Now you can simply select another color in the Paint Editor and quickly match the first square in all attributes except for color.

   If you use this second method, remember to delete the empty sprites you created for the Blue and Green colors.

For the Clear button, create a longer, flatter button that is filled in with a pink shade. What's different here is that you can use the **T** tool to add a text label to the rectangle.

To create a text label for the Clear button, follow these steps:

1. Click the Text tool.

2. Select a color from the color blocks. I suggest black.

3. Click somewhere in the paint canvas, type the word *Clear* and press the Enter key.

4. Position your mouse on the border of your new text block to reposition the text to the center of the block.

Figure 7.6 shows an annotated screenshot from the project.

A word of warning: Once you click your mouse outside the text block, you won't be able to select it again. Bummer, I know. This is one of the many weaknesses of the Scratch Paint Editor. In fact, many Scratchers simply create their art and text labels outside of Scratch and simply import the assets.

That approach is covered in Hour 21, "Creating Your Own Sprites and Backdrops." For now, reposition the new Clear button next to the color swatches, as shown in Figure 7.7.

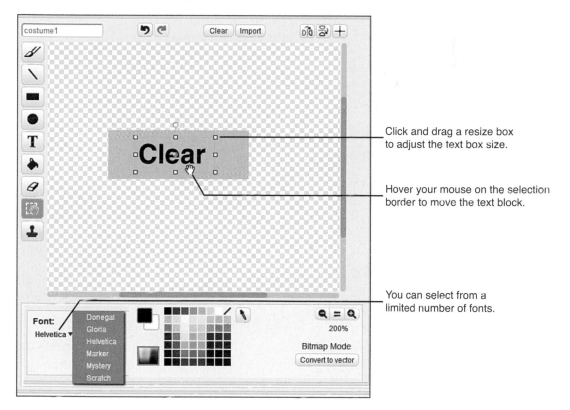

FIGURE 7.6
Adding text to sprite shapes can be both tricky and frustrating.

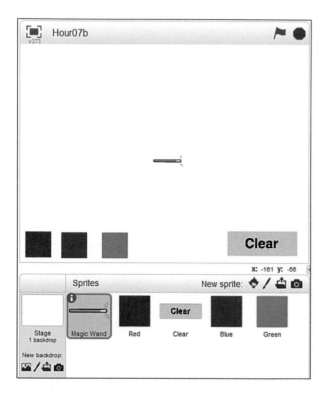

FIGURE 7.7
The state of the doodle program thus far.

▼ TRY IT YOURSELF

Drawing Program Phase 2: Adding the Logic

It's time to turn your attention to "wiring up" each sprite so that the sprites behave correctly. You begin by programming the color swatches and the Clear button. Perform the following steps to complete the exercise:

1. Select the Red sprite and navigate to its Scripts pane. The logic you use here is the sprite will issue a broadcast when it is clicked by the player. Look at Figure 7.8 to see what the code looks like for the Red, Blue, Green, and Clear sprites. Note that you need to define the broadcast messages from within the `broadcast message1 ▼` stack blocks.

2. Now finish things up by wiring up the Magic Wand. Create a `forever` loop that first clears any pen marks from previous program runs and then tests for the condition "Did the player click the mouse button?" If the player did click the mouse button, the loop maps the mouse pointer to the Magic Wand sprite, sets the pen color, and puts the pen down on the Stage. This makes sense because you want the player to draw by clicking his or her mouse button.

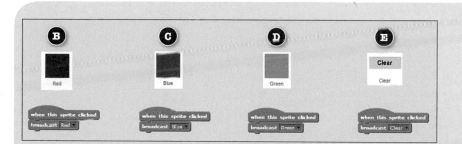

FIGURE 7.8
The code for the color swatches and Clear button is straightforward enough.

3. In the code segments labeled B, C, D, and E, you see how you can elegantly capture the broadcast messages coming from the respective color swatches and Clear button on the Stage by calling the `set pen color to` stack block. Here, the Eyedropper tool works beautifully: Simply click the color swatch in the block, and then click the appropriate sprite in the Sprites list. Voila!

Once you've finished your code, click the Green Flag and ensure that the drawing program functions as expected. For instance, run the following tasks as a unit test:

▶ Try to move the Magic Wand around the Stage prior to selecting a color. Did this work?

▶ Select a color and draw some lines. What room for improvement can you see?

▶ Click the other two color swatches and add some more lines.

▶ Click the Clear button. Did the Stage reset properly?

It is very important to become rigorous about testing your application's functionality, whether you are working in Scratch, Python, C, or whatever language.

In computer programming, unit testing refers to a systematic process of testing your code in small chunks.

Best practice dictates that you define a series of tasks (preferably automated) that test every aspect of how your Scratch program works. This way, you can run your unit tests after every significant change to your code that you make.

In fact, in enterprise software development, where programs run into the millions of lines of code and affect thousands of users, programmers turn to dedicated unit testing software suites to create, run, and manage the "exercising" of their program.

Summary

Great job so far, friend! At this point, you should have a good handle on how to draw in Scratch 2.0. As I stated earlier, neither the Pen tools nor the Paint Editor are the most user-friendly tools in the world. As you gain experience with programming, you'll probably want to use a dedicated art tool to build your sprites, backdrops, and text blocks.

Thus far, all of the programs you have created in Scratch include code that responds to particular events, such as the player clicking the Green Flag button or moving the mouse pointer over a sprite.

There is a name for this programming paradigm: event-driven programming. In the next hour, you'll delve deeply into the Scratch 2.0 Events blocks and how to structure events logically and for best program performance.

Workshop

Quiz

1. Which of the following statements best describes the difference between the `stamp` block and the `create clone of myself` block?

    A. The `create clone of myself` block creates an image of the sprite but has no code associated with it.

    B. The `stamp` block creates an image of the sprite but has no code associated with it.

    C. Both blocks are functionally identical in Scratch 2.0.

2. If you're programming a drawn line in Scratch and you use the `change pen shade by 10` block to change the shade from 60 to 30, what is the net effect on the line on the Stage?

    A. The line gets darker.

    B. The line gets lighter.

    C. The line becomes transparent.

3. In Scratch 2.0, changing the pen size by –2 has the following effect on the sprite:

    A. Makes pen smaller by 2 pixels

    B. Makes pen smaller by 2 percent

    C. Makes pen smaller by a multiple of 2

Answers

1. The answer is choice B. The  stamp block simply creates an ephemeral image of the selected sprite. By contrast, the create clone of myself block literally clones the sprite, along with any associated costumes and scripts.

2. The correct answer is choice A. Remember that with pen shade in Scratch, lower values denote darker, or more concentrated, shading.

3. The correct answer is choice C. In Scratch 2.0, the basic unit of size is the pixel. Thus, a pen size of 2 represents a 2-pixel thick line.

Challenge

For this hour's challenge, you create what's called a *splash screen* for the paint program. Look at Figure 7.9 to see an example.

FIGURE 7.9
Your first program splash screen.

Many programs use the splash screen to introduce the program to the player, as well as to provide instructions on how to play the game or work with the interaction.

Here is a list of specifications for the new splash screen addition:

▶ Make sure you work off a copy of your current project so you don't overwrite the original. In the Scratch Editor, you can click File, Save as a Copy to accomplish this goal.

▶ Create the splash screen as a new Stage backdrop. We aren't going to cheat and import a predone backdrop from the Gallery any more than we absolutely have to from now on!

▶ Use the built-in Scratch font to add the text. (Recall that the Paint Editor has a Font control that allows you to choose from a small collection of Web-safe fonts.)

▶ Program the splash screen such that it shows up by default when the player clicks the Green Flag.

▶ Program all sprites to disappear when the Green Flag is clicked.

▶ Program all project elements to (1) switch to the game (white) backdrop and (2) show all sprites when the spacebar is pressed.

Whew! This is a lot to ask, but you can handle it. *Hint*: Broadcast messages are your friend! Remember that the Stage can have scripts associated with it and the Stage can both create and respond to broadcast messages.

If you find yourself hopelessly stuck, please take comfort in the fact that the solution to this exercise is provided in the file `Hour07c.sb2`.

HOUR 8
Using Events Blocks

What You'll Learn in This Hour:

▶ Understanding Events blocks
▶ Digital versus analog events
▶ Understanding broadcasts
▶ Watch me move!

Scratch 2.0 is an example of an event-driven programming language. In event-driven programming, your computer program's flow is determined by the occurrence and handling of events.

What is an event? For the purposes of this text, an event is either a digital user action, such as a mouse click or keyboard press, or an analog sensor input, such as a volume or light change.

Events blocks in Scratch 2.0 are absolutely crucial to the success of your program. In fact, your scripts simply won't run without at least one Events block—the [when clicked] block.

Understanding Events Blocks

As you can see in Table 8.1, the Events palette in Scratch 2.0 includes six Hat blocks and two stack blocks, all color-coded brown.

TABLE 8.1 Scratch Event Blocks

Block Image	Block Type	Description
when clicked	Hat	Fires when the Green Flag is clicked
when space ▾ key pressed	Hat	Fires when a keyboard key is pressed
when this sprite clicked	Hat	Fires when the attached sprite is clicked
when backdrop switches to backdrop1 ▾	Hat	Fires when the background switches to a particular backdrop

Block Image	Block Type	Description
when loudness > 10	Hat	Fires when the detected audio signal is above a threshold value
when I receive message1	Hat	Fires when a specific broadcast is sent out
broadcast message1	Stack	Sends a broadcast and continues the script execution
broadcast message1 and wait	Stack	Sends a broadcast and halts script execution

The Events palette might not feature very many blocks, but trust me, these Events blocks will be among the most popular (and powerful) blocks in your Scratch programming arsenal.

You'll observe that the vast majority of Events blocks are Hat blocks with a smooth top and a notched bottom. The smooth top is meant as a visual clue to remind you that Hat blocks are used only to start scripts.

Because every Scratch project starts when the player clicks the Green Flag icon, the when clicked block is used universally by all Scratchers to kick off their projects.

Event Receivers and Event Handlers

Sometimes programming nomenclature can get confusing, especially when terms overlap. Take, for instance, the terms *event receiver* and *event handler.*

For the purposes of this text, these terms are synonymous; in fact, this text uses only the term event receiver.

So what the heck is an event receiver? I'm glad you asked. You know by now that when your player clicks the Green Flag to start your project, the code you assembled is set to receive (that is, act upon) a variety of user events.

For instance, perhaps you developed a 2D side-scrolling arcade game in which the player controls the avatar with the keyboard arrow keys. Any Scratch script code that you add to handle one of these key presses is referred to as event-handler code. That was easy, wasn't it? Figure 8.1 shows you some examples of event-handling code.

One of the many challenges of the software developer is anticipating all possible events that can fire over the run state of the project—and to handle them all. The attainment of this goal rests squarely on testing. Make a change, and then test. Make another change, and then test again. Once you're finished, test a third time. At times, being a programmer involves drudgery—I'm not going to lie!

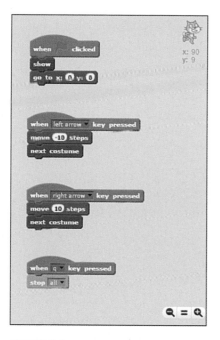

FIGURE 8.1
This event-handler code allows a user to move a sprite across the Stage by using the keyboard arrow keys.

Digital Versus Analog Events

In inspecting the Scratch event blocks, you might be puzzled by the `when loudness > 10` block, as it appears on its face to function far differently from, say, the `when this sprite clicked` or `when backdrop switches to backdrop1` blocks.

You're right—the `when loudness > 10` block is different because it relies upon an analog event instead of a digital event. The difference between digital and analog input isn't too difficult to understand.

Look at it this way: A digital input either occurs or it doesn't. It's a binary operation that can be viewed as black/white, on/off...however you want to visualize it.

In Scratch 2.0, either the user clicks the Green Flag or she doesn't. The backdrop either switches or it doesn't—there is no middle ground.

By contrast, analog input is eminently variable. For instance, the block has the following parameters that can be accessed by opening up the tiny drop-down list box control:

▶ **Loudness**: Sound intensity as measured by your computer's microphone; a value of 0 is no input, and the maximum loudness is 100.

▶ **Timer**: Elapsed time as measured as soon as you open a project and does not reset unless you use a block or you open another project. So in that sense, the timer could be considered an analog value.

▶ **Video motion**: Movement as measured by your computer's webcam. The value range here is the same as with loudness; a value of 0 represents no input, and 100 is the maximum value.

Options for Analog Input in Scratch 2.0

Scratch 1.4 had this nifty hardware device called the Scratch Sensor Board, later renamed the PicoBoard (https://www.sparkfun.com/products/10311) that provided a variety of onboard sensors for your Scratch experimentation pleasure. Figure 8.2 shows a picture of a PicoBoard. Use the figure along with the following list to explore its sensors:

▶ **A**: The slider is used to measure incremental analog input.

▶ **B**: The light sensor is used to measure raw light input.

▶ **C**: This button is used to measure tactile, binary data (pressed/unpressed).

▶ **D**: The microphone is used to measure audio input.

▶ **E**: The alligator clips are used to measure the resistance of an object.

Some good news is that Sparkfun still manufactures and sells the PicoBoard; pick one up by visiting their website at https://www.sparkfun.com/products/10311.

Although the PicoBoard was developed specifically for Scratch 1.4, it is possible to use the board with Scratch 2.0. This hour doesn't spend any more time on this subject, however, because an entire hour is devoted to working with analog inputs in Hour 23, "Connecting Scratch to the Physical World."

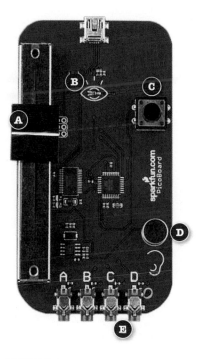

FIGURE 8.2
The PicoBoard exposes Scratch programs to the outside, analog world.

Experiment with Analog Input

In this simple Try It Yourself exercise, you create a Scratch program that reacts to the volume level in your immediate area. To complete this exercise, you need to have a microphone enabled on your computer. Most computers now include a microphone that is built directly in to the chassis or monitor.

The completed solution file can be found in the file `Hour08a.sb2`. In the meantime, work through the following steps to complete the exercise:

1. Log in to the Scratch website using your account credentials and start a new project.

2. Click the Stage and navigate to the Backdrops panel. As shown in Figure 8.3, create a total of four backdrops, each filled in with a different color and named appropriately.

   To review, you can easily fill in a backdrop with a solid color by first clicking the 🪣 icon, next selecting a color from the swatch, and then clicking anywhere inside the Backdrop window. Voila!

FIGURE 8.3
This project Stage has several backdrops that you can easily color using the Paint Editor tools.

3. Delete the Scratch Cat sprite; you don't need any sprites for this exercise.

4. Navigate to the Stage's Scripts pane. Your goal is to have the backdrop switch anytime Scratch detects a significant change in volume level. You can easily accomplish this goal by making use of the `when loudness > 10` block from the Events palette. Check out Figure 8.4 to see the code.

   In code block A, you reset the environment. Code block B contains the main program logic; when the loudness exceeds a threshold value (try 30 to start), the subsequent blocks trigger. In this case, you want to switch to the next backdrop. Code blocks C and D simply add some "spice" to the project, and code block E ends the project when the spacebar is pressed.

5. To test, click the `when / clicked` block, wait a few seconds, and then clap your hands a few times. What happened? Did the program behave as expected?

   If your immediate environment isn't quiet, you'll have to play with the Volume Level attribute to strike the right balance. If you're using the Scratch 2.0 online editor, you might be prompted to allow access to your computer's microphone. This is a good security feature, by the way.

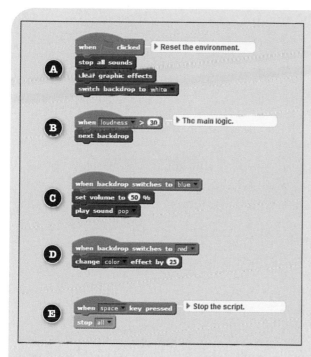

FIGURE 8.4
The source code for the Experiment with Analog Input Try It Yourself exercise.

Understanding Broadcasts

As you spend more time building programs with Scratch 2.0, you'll run into questions that never occurred to you before. "How can I get sprites to 'talk' to each other?" is a common one.

The answer to that question is—or at least *one* answer (programming usually has more than one way to solve any problem)—the use of broadcasts.

In my opinion, once you discover the power of broadcasts, you are likely to include them in almost every Scratch program that you write. Essentially, a *broadcast* is a named message that is available to all project assets, including, of course, sprites and Stage backdrops.

You can give broadcasts any name you want; my advice, of course, is to name them succinctly yet as descriptively as possible. Your goal is to instantly recognize the purpose of any broadcast in your code.

Sending out a broadcast inside your project is only one half of the equation; you also need to implement the `when I receive message1` block to "catch" specific broadcasts according to your program design.

Broadcast Use Cases

One common reason Scratchers use broadcasts is to synchronize action on the Stage. For instance, check out the code shown in Figure 8.5. You might want more than one thing to happen on the Stage simultaneously when a particular event is fired. To do this, include a broadcast in your event-handler code, and add a `when I receive message1 ▾` block for any sprites that you need to react in unison to that event.

A second reason to use broadcasts is to implement recursion. Recursion occurs in Scratch when a sprite sends out a broadcast message and also is hatted with a `when I receive message1 ▾` block that listens for that very same broadcast. This can be useful to do, but you need to be careful in implementing recursion to avoid unintentionally creating an infinite loop and hanging your program.

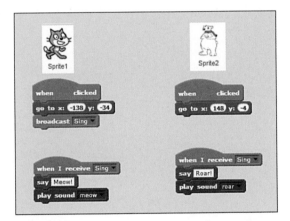

FIGURE 8.5
You can use broadcasts to synchronize and coordinate action among sprites. Note that Sprite1 responds recursively to its own broadcast.

For those of you who plan to continue using Scratch 1.4, you might want to consider Mesh (http://is.gd/6azt4C). Mesh is a Scratch 1.4 method by which you can use variables and broadcasts to link two completely different Scratch projects, even if those projects run on two different computers!

Wow—that's some cool technology! How does Mesh work under the hood? Sadly, a deeper discussion is beyond the scope of this book. The short answer is that you need to use either an early beta version of Scratch 1.4 or one of a few popular Scratch 1.4 modifications. See the Scratch Wiki article on Mesh for more information at http://is.gd/6azt4C.

How to Create a Broadcast

To create a broadcast, first drag out a `broadcast message1 ▾` or a `broadcast message1 ▾ and wait`
block to the Scripts pane. Next, open the block's drop-down list box and select New Message
from the menu.

In the New Message dialog box, type a name for the message. Do not use spaces, and as mentioned earlier, be brief yet descriptive. Click OK to complete the message.

That's all there is to it! Now drag out a `when I receive message1 ▾` block. When you open the drop-down
list control, notice that your new broadcast appears in the menu.

NOTE
_____

How to Remove a Broadcast

Removing a broadcast from your Scratch project is not an intuitively obvious process. Sadly, there is
no simple way to delete broadcasts. Instead, the recommended approach is to remove all broadcast
blocks that reference that broadcast. Once no reference to that broadcast exists in the project, it
can be considered removed from the program. Kind of clunky, but it works in theory.
_____

Wait for What?

In the Events blocks palette, you probably noticed two related stack blocks: `broadcast message1 ▾`
and `broadcast message1 ▾ and wait`. What's the difference?

I'm glad you asked! The `broadcast message1 ▾` block transmits its message and continues execution of any remaining blocks in that script. In other words, this block does not wait for any other
scripts that are "hatted" with the `when I receive message1 ▾` block to complete their execution.

If you do have a dependency between the message-sending script and the message-receiving
ones, then you'd implement the `broadcast message1 ▾ and wait` block. This block sends out the
message and pauses the rest of its script execution until all hatted blocks that are set to receive
that broadcast complete their execution.

In the next Try It Yourself exercise, you gain some experience with implementing broadcasts into
your project. Start with the same project file that you used in the previous Try It Yourself exercise
because you need those colorful Stage backdrops. Simply save a copy of the project under a different name.

This is a slightly more complicated project than those you've done thus far. The project will do the following:

▶ Green Flag starts the project.

▶ SPACE changes the Stage backdrop color.

▶ M (or m; Scratch is not case sensitive with events such as key presses) plays sound and makes a bug appear in a random location on the Stage.

▶ Q or q quits the program.

▼ TRY IT YOURSELF

Experiment with Broadcasts

In this Try It Yourself exercise you'll gain some valuable experience with creating and managing broadcasts in Scratch 2.0. You can find the completed solution file in the book's code archive under the file name Hour08b.sb2. Work through the following steps to complete the exercise:

1. Use the ✏ button to build a new sprite named **instructions** that contains the text shown in Figure 8.6. To create a text sprite, you click the Text Tool **T** button in the Paint Editor, select a color from the swatch, select a font (I am partial to the Scratch font), and start typing. When you are finished, click away from the text to commit your change.

   The bad news is that text boxes work terribly in Scratch—they are just awful in terms of the limited amount of control you have over them. In Hour 21, "Creating Your Own Sprites and Backdrops," you'll learn some important tips and tricks for creating useful text in your Scratch projects.

2. Use drag and drop along with the Zoom ⌘ and Shrink ⌘ tools to make your text block appear at the top of the screen at a reasonable size.

3. Now import a sprite from the gallery; I chose the Beetle sprite. Use the Shrink ⌘ button to reduce the size of the bug. Figure 8.6 shows what the interface for this project looks like.

4. Look at the Stage scripts in Figure 8.7. When the Green Flag is clicked, you want to reset the environment and reset the built-in timer. You also make sure the white backdrop shows up first.

   Next, you have event handlers for three main events: When the spacebar is pressed, you switch to the next backdrop as ordered on the Stage's Backdrops pane. When the M key is pressed, you play the zoop sound and send out a broadcast. Finally, when the Q key is pressed, you reset the backdrop to white, change the color effect, and then stop the program.

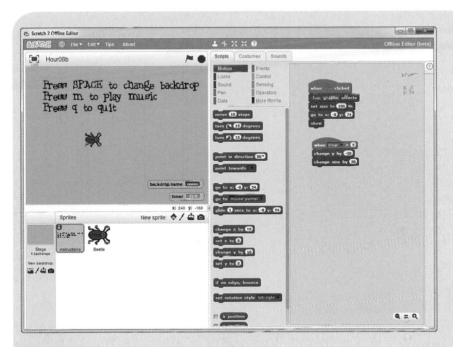

FIGURE 8.6
The Experiment with Broadcasts Try It Yourself exercise.

5. Pay particular attention to that broadcast. When the user presses the *M* key, that Stage script sends out the SpriteAppear broadcast across the entire project.

   Remember that the way you handle broadcasts is that you configure code to catch that sent message. Switch over to your Beetle sprite Scripts pane, and follow along with the code given in the solution file and in Figure 8.7.

   For the Beetle sprite, use the `when    clicked` block to reset the Beetle's physical appearance and to hide the sprite from the Stage when the program is started.

   Now for the good stuff: When the Stage transmits the SpriteAppear broadcast, the Beetle sprite is here to receive that message and take programmatic action upon it. Specifically, you're pointing the beetle in a random direction and then showing the beetle on Stage in a random location. You gotta love those `pick random 1 to 10` operator blocks!

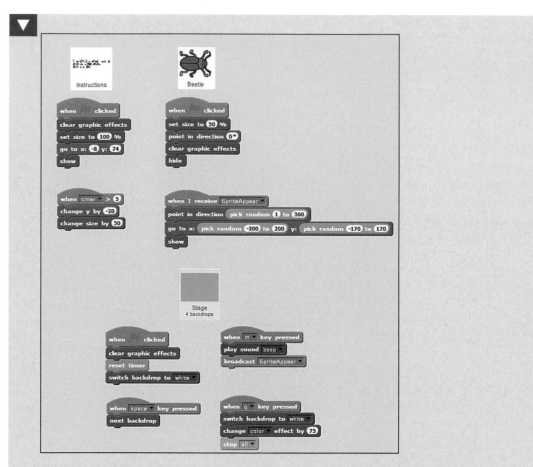

FIGURE 8.7
The source code for the Experiment with Broadcasts Try It Yourself exercise.

6. Click the Green Flag and then press the spacebar. Does the backdrop change? Now press *M*: Does this cause music to play, as well as add sprites on the screen?

   You might want to add the backdrop name and timer stage monitors to the Stage for troubleshooting purposes. For reference, the backdrop name operator block 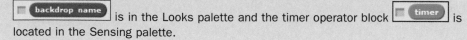 is in the Looks palette and the timer operator block is located in the Sensing palette.

Notice that the timer is included in this project, but you didn't actually use it. That was an intentional move. As a challenge, add code to your project such that additional sprites appear on your Stage in random locations when the timer reaches a certain value.

The key to using the built-in timer is to understand that you can use the `reset timer` stack block at any time to set the timer back to zero. Some Scratchers prefer to use the Scratch built-in timer as opposed to using variables and the `wait 1 secs` block because the built-in timer is so much more accurate.

Watch Me Move!

As mentioned earlier in this hour, later in this book an entire hour (Hour 23) is devoted to working specifically with analog inputs and outputs with Scratch. However, because you are already learning about events and event handling, you might find it interesting to close this hour with a discussion of the Watch Me Move! technology in Scratch 2.0.

Watch Me Move! is the name for Scratch 2.0's ability to interact with your computer's webcam. It should go without saying that in order to use these video capabilities, you must (1) have a webcam attached to your computer and (2) have the webcam driver loaded so Scratch can communicate with it.

It's one thing to have Scratch 2.0 react to the presence of a video signal; it's quite another to use video motion as a triggerable and handleable (is that a word?) event. In some ways, the Watch Me Move! functionality is similar, though far less robust, than the Kinect sensor in the Xbox 360 and Xbox One video game consoles.

Event Handling with the Video Sensor Blocks

Table 8.2 summarizes the video event-related blocks in Scratch 2.0.

TABLE 8.2 Video Sensor Blocks in Scratch 2.0

Block Image	Block Category	Block Type	Description
`turn video off ▼`	Sensing	Stack	Turns your webcam on or off
`set video transparency to 50 %`	Sensing	Stack	Makes the webcam video completely opaque (with a value of 0) or completely transparent (with a value of 100)

Block Image	Block Category	Block Type	Description
 video motion ▼ on this sprite ▼	Sensing	Reporter	Reports on either web-cam motion or movement directionality
 when loudness ▼ > 10	Events	Hat	Triggers a script when detected video motion exceeds a defined threshold value (Note that you have to select "video motion" from the drop-down menu.)

You can do some very fun things using video and audio-related events in Scratch 2.0. For instance, the code shown in Figure 8.8 does the following:

▶ **A:** Turns on your webcam and sets the image to be completely opaque.

▶ **B:** Instructs a sprite to "say" something if video motion is detected in the Sprites area on the Stage. Figure 8.9 shows what this looks like.

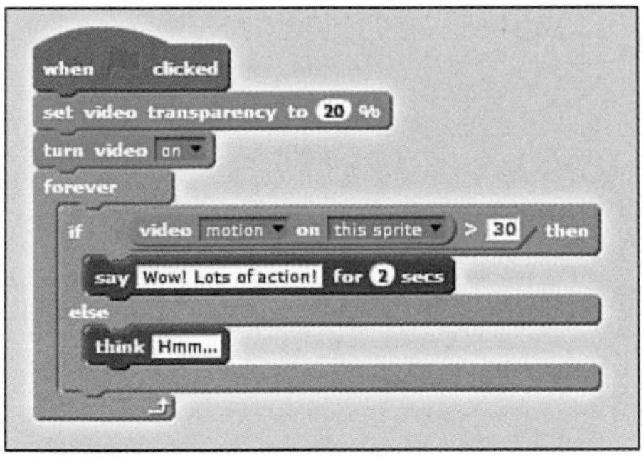

FIGURE 8.8
Scratch source code that enables the webcam and detects motion on the Stage. The script was running when the screenshot was taken; that accounts for the glow surrounding the script.

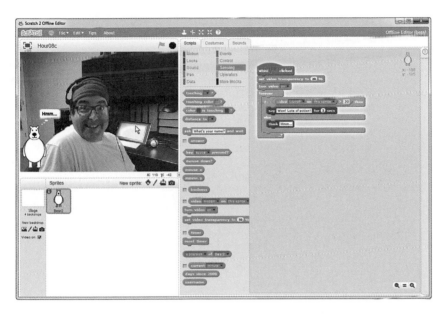

FIGURE 8.9
Programming audio and video in Scratch is a lot of fun.

Let's complete this hour with one more Try It Yourself exercise. This one ought to be a lot of fun: Let's pop some balloons!

Popping Balloons

To complete this Try It Yourself exercise, you need to nab the sprite `balloon.png` from the book's solution files. Rather than reinvent the wheel and draw balloons from scratch, I downloaded one of the assets from the fantastic Balloons project by the Scratch user SandboxProductions (http://is.gd/i9UFYq). Check it out—it's a great game! If you get stuck, you can view the solution file, which is contained in this book's code archive as `Hour08c.sb2`.

This Try It Yourself exercise gives you experience in implementing multimedia and analog detection in a Scratch project. I'm sure you'll have a lot of fun with this! Follow these steps to complete the exercise:

1. Start a new project, and use the Upload Sprite ⬆ button to import the `balloon.png` sprite from the book's solution file archive.

2. Navigate to the Stage, and change the default white background to a nice sky blue using the Paint Bucket ⬥ button in the Paint Editor. You should be an old hat at doing that by now.

3. Navigate to the Sounds pane for the Balloon sprite, and delete the meow audio file. Instead, browse the Sound Library and import the pop sound; that's more appropriate for the purposes of this exercise.

4. Using the code in Figure 8.10 as your guide, complete this project's programming logic by adding some scripts to the Balloon sprite.

   Before the Forever loop, you reset the environment by placing the balloon initially in a fixed location, explicitly showing it, and then turning on the webcam with a 50 percent transparency value.

   The Forever loop is really where the magic takes place. The embedded if loop says that if Scratch detects motion of more than 30 percent, then you'll play a popping sound and make the sprite disappear. After a 2-second delay, the balloon appears again in a random location on the Stage.

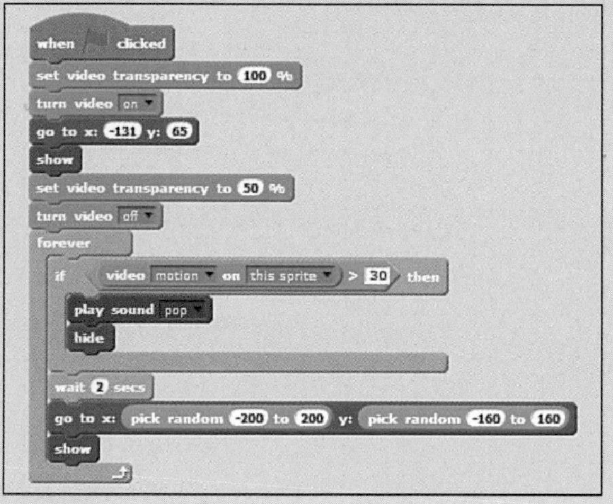

FIGURE 8.10
Source code for the Popping Balloons Try It Yourself exercise.

5. Click the Green Flag to test your project. Wave your arm, your hand, or any other stray body part over the balloon on the Stage. Does the balloon disappear? After a pause, does the balloon reappear in a random location elsewhere on the Stage?

NOTE

Giving Credit Where Credit is Due

It is important to provide attribution to the public Balloons project authors (http://is.gd/i9UFYq) if you decide to use any of their sprite assets in a Scratch project that you publish. Recall from earlier discussions how foundational the notions of (a) asking for permission and (b) providing credit are to the Scratch community. If you develop a reputation among Scratchers as one who takes without permission or credit, then at best you'll lose potential collaborators, and at worst you'll lose your Scratch account. (The MIT Scratch Team is on the lookout for this kind of behavior.)

Summary

Hopefully, you now have a greater appreciation for how powerful event-driven programming is. In my experience, some software developers get lost in the world of object-oriented programming (OOP) and forget that the user is actually in control of the program, at least from a practical standpoint.

The skills that you picked up in this hour, and the tools you use to apply them, will go a very long way toward reducing the number of errors in your code. It might be theoretically impossible to trap every possible event, but the goal is to get as close as possible, always.

In this hour, you also experimented with some fun analog sensor inputs. I hope you enjoyed getting to know how you can handle audio and video input in Scratch 2.0. Having fun Is a large part of what being a computer programmer is all about. This is one reason why job satisfaction tends to be so high among people who work in that field full-time.

Workshop

Quiz

1. You can write conditional logic code in a Scratch project that evaluates audio and video events simultaneously.

    A. True

    B. False

2. One of your players complains that a sprite on the Stage does not behave the way it is supposed to. When the player uses the arrow keys, the sprite is supposed to move, yet it does not. Which of the following best describes the likely problem?

    A. You forgot to import the sprite to the project.

    B. You forgot to include a when green flag clicked block to the project.

    C. You forgot to add an event handler to the sprite.

3. Setting the transparency value to 0 in a Scratch 2.0 project makes your webcam image_____.

   A. Opaque

   B. Invisible

   C. Blurry

Answers

1. The correct answer is choice B. You can, in fact, combine multiple events using the logical operators less than, greater than, or equal to. Audio and video are simply two of many event types that are supported by Scratch 2.0.

2. The correct answer is choice C. In this question, you must have intended for the sprite to move when the player presses certain keyboard keys, but you forgot to add the appropriate event-handling code using Hat blocks in Scratch. Don't worry—this is a common mistake, even among seasoned programmers.

3. The correct answer is choice A. A video transparency setting of 0 makes the image opaque, or nontransparent. By contrast, a video transparency setting of 100 simply shows the Stage with no video at all.

Challenge

Your challenge for this hour is to broaden and deepen the balloon popping game that you began in this hour's final Try It Yourself exercise.

Here's a punch list of to-do items you need to tackle for this challenge:

▶ Import some additional sprites from the aforementioned Balloons project on the Scratch website, and use broadcasts to show the balloon in a popped state once you wave your hand over it on the Stage.

▶ Record your own custom pop sound, and swap that audio clip into the project to make popping the balloons a little more exciting.

▶ Instead of having the balloon appear in a fixed location at the start of every game, refactor the code such that the balloon always shows up in a random location. Try to avoid the problem of having the balloon appear where your body is already present on the Stage.

Using Control Blocks

What You'll Learn in This Hour:

▶ Introducing the Control blocks

▶ Testing out control structures

▶ Working with clones

I call Scratch Control blocks *flow-control* blocks because they serve to manage the execution and progress of your Scratch program. These blocks enable you to perform iterative and conditional logic in your projects, which greatly expands the possibilities of your work.

The Control block palette also includes the clone block; this tool gives you the ability to duplicate sprites (along with their costumes and source code) quickly and easily, yielding potentially powerful results.

I find that the Control and the Events blocks are my go-to staples, and I use them extensively in every Scratch project that I create. I'm sure you'll find that you have a similar experience, so pay close attention and be sure to invest the time and effort necessary to master the use of these blocks.

Introducing the Control Blocks

Table 9.1 summarizes the 11 blocks that make up the Control block family in Scratch 2.0. As you can see, these blocks are color-coded gold for easy visual recognition.

TABLE 9.1 Scratch 2.0 Control Blocks

Block Image	Block Type	Description
wait 1 secs	Stack	Pauses the current script for the designated time interval
repeat 10	C	Repeats the enclosed actions X times

Block Image	Block Type	Description
forever	C	Repeats enclosed actions until the script is halted or the program is stopped
if then	C	Executes the enclosed script if a Boolean expression evaluates to True
if then else	C	Executes the script enclosed in the Else block if the Boolean expression evaluates to False
wait until	Stack	Pauses the current script until the Boolean condition evaluates to True
repeat until	C	Repeats the enclosed actions until the Boolean condition evaluates to True
stop all ▼	Cap	Stops either everything, the current script, or other scripts attached to the current sprite
when I start as a clone	Hat	Initiates script when the current script is cloned
create clone of myself ▼	Stack	Creates a clone of the current instance, the current sprite, or another sprite in the project
delete this clone	Cap	Deletes the current cloned instance

C Blocks and Nesting

The C blocks can be a bit tricky to use, so let's spend a bit of time doing some C block calisthenics. The good news is that "C block" does not refer to a wing in a prison!

The C Control blocks are shaped the way they are because they are intended to contain (C...get it?) additional script that fires conditionally or iteratively, as you'll see in a moment.

For now, open up a fresh Scratch project and take a look at the sample code rovided in Figure 9.1. In the code section labeled A is a nested if block. If, for instance, you need to perform a second evaluation within the same data structure, simply pop a second `if then` or `if then else` block inside of the first one.

Specifically, the code in the section labeled A will loop anything inside the `forever` loop for the entire duration of the project. Unless, of course, the current sprite makes contact with the specified color. If the sprite touches the color, then the project stops.

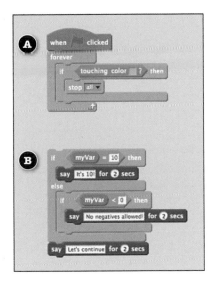

FIGURE 9.1
You can build complex data structures by using C blocks and nesting.

In the code section labeled B, you have an ⬚ block nested inside of an ⬚ block. The logic is, "If the myVar variable has a value of 10, then we say 'It's 10!' for 2 seconds. If the myVar variable has a value of less than 0, then we say 'No negatives allowed!' for 2 seconds. Finally, if myVar is neither 10 nor negative, we say 'Let's continue.'" Note that you aren't looping here, but are simply constantly asking two questions about the myVar variable.

With practice, you should be able to nest and un-nest the C blocks pretty easily. It's helpful that the Scratch Editor shows you an outline of what it expects to happen next whenever you drag one block in the vicinity of another one.

On Boolean Logic

The Operators blocks are covered in Hour 10, "Using Operators Blocks," but this section briefly covers the subject because Boolean and operator expression blocks are used so heavily with the Control blocks.

The if and wait blocks in particular have those hexagonal cutouts that are specially shaped to accommodate the so-called Boolean blocks. Technically, many of the flattened oval-shaped reporter blocks are Boolean as well.

Essentially, Boolean logic is a form of logical math in which an expression evaluates to one of two values: True or False.

NOTE

Boolean Logic: A Brief History

Boolean logic was invented by the English mathematician George Boole (1815–1864). Boolean logic has been crucial in the development of the computer and in digital information processing. Somehow I don't think that Boole envisioned iPads, however.

Look at the code section labeled A in Figure 9.2. Some of the blocks in the Sensing category operate on Boolean principles. Think of it—either the spacebar has been pressed, or it hasn't. There is no middle ground. In this case, the else condition has the sprite say either "true" or "false," depending upon whether the sprite is currently touching the mouse pointer.

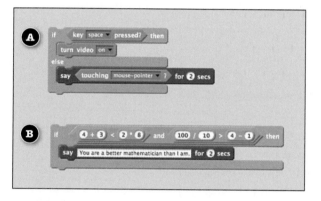

FIGURE 9.2
By using Boolean logic, you can have your Scratch program "ask" and "answer" questions, and take action upon them.

The code section labeled B goes a little crazy showing you how you can nest the oval-shaped Operations blocks inside of the hexagonal Boolean blocks to create supercomplicated expressions. In this example, if that insane expression were to evaluate to True (which it does, by the way), then the sprite says, "You are a better mathematician than I am."

Logic Structure: Looping

In programming, you use looping (also called iterative) control structures to perform some repetitive action that is based upon a condition. For instance, you might want to play an audio clip that loops from the time that the Green Flag is clicked to the time that the Scratch program ends.

Or perhaps you simply want to repeat an action a specified number of times; having the Scratch Cat move and animate across the Stage is a good example of using the C block.

Finally, if you want action to occur until a more complex expression evaluates to True, you can implement the [repeat until] C block using the previously mentioned Boolean and operations reporter blocks.

Logic Structure: Conditional

Sometimes you have script code that you don't want to simply loop in what you might call a "mindless" manner. Instead, you have a Boolean expression that controls whether or not some action happens.

As you saw earlier in this hour and elsewhere in this book, the [if then] and [if then else] C blocks are perfect for creating conditional or branching logic in your Scratch programs.

You'll probably find that the if blocks are more difficult to use and to get used to than the forever and repeat blocks; this makes sense because the if blocks require you to ask several key questions regarding your Scratch code:

▶ Under which specific circumstances do I want the code in my if block to fire?

▶ If the Boolean condition in the if block evaluates to false, do I want to test another condition (and nest another if block), do I want something specific to occur (requiring the if then else block), or do I simply want to proceed to the next block in the script outside the if block?

▶ Is the if block even necessary? How likely is it that the if condition may never occur? We programmers call having too much extraneous code in our projects *code bloat*, and it isn't a good thing under most circumstances.

Testing Out Control Structures

It's time for you to set up a new Scratch 2.0 project to lay the groundwork for the first Try It Yourself exercise in this hour.

Start a new project in the Scratch 2.0 online editor and configure the environment as follows:

1. In the Sprites list, delete the default Cat sprite by right-clicking it and selecting Delete from the shortcut menu.

2. Use the Choose Sprite from Library ⬚ button to add in the Spaceship and Earth sprites from the Space category.

3. Select the Spaceship sprite and navigate to the Costumes tab. Delete the second costume (the one with the lander feet on the bottom of the ship) by right-clicking it and selecting

Delete. Rename the first sprite spaceship1; you can see where to do this by looking at annotation A in Figure 9.3.

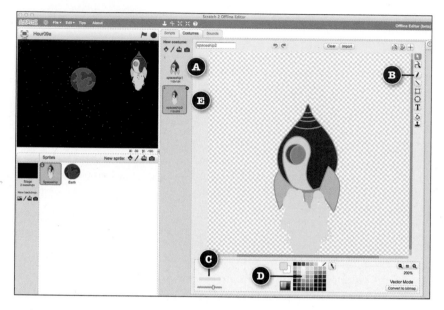

FIGURE 9.3
The Stage and sprite setup for the Looping and Conditional Logic...In Space Try It Yourself exercise.

4. Right-click the spaceship1 costume and select Duplicate from the shortcut menu. Use the Paint Editor tools, particularly the Pencil tool (annotation B), line thickness control slider (annotation C), and color swatch (annotation D), to draw flames beneath the ship. Rename the second (flame) costume spaceship2 (annotation E).

5. Whew! This is a complicated setup. Now select the Stage and go to the Backdrops tab. Import the space and stars backdrops from the Space category of the Scratch Backdrop Gallery and then delete the default backdrop. Please remember that Scratch won't let you delete the default backdrop unless you have at least one other backdrop added to the project.

6. Go to the Data blocks palette and click Make a Variable. In the New Variable dialog box, name the variable countdown, and ensure that For All Sprites is selected. Click OK to complete the action. Don't worry—you'll learn all there is to know about Scratch variables in Hour 12, "Using Data Blocks." For now, just know that you use variables to store data.

7. Finally, drag another `broadcast message1 ▼` stack block onto the Spaceship's Scripts pane. At this point, you don't have to connect it. Simply open the drop-down menu and select New Message. Create a broadcast named outerspace. Drag another `broadcast message1 ▼` block to the Spaceship's Scripts pane and define a second broadcast named finale.

Looping and Conditional Logic...In Space

In this Try It Yourself exercise, you gain some practice with using looping and conditional logic and also have some fun in an outer space environment.

First, you program the rocket ship to do a countdown to blastoff. Then, after the ship reaches outer space, you have something happen if the ship hits a planet. Finally, you turn the ship's control over to the player, allowing him or her to control the ship by using the mouse.

You can find the completed solution file in the book's solution file archive; the file name is `Hour09a.sb2`. Work through the following steps to complete this exercise:

1. One of the cool new features in Scratch 2.0 is that you can have sprites control Stage backdrops. Thus, you don't have to add any code to the Stage this time around. In Hour 16, "Documenting Your Project," you'll see how to use the Stage as a "catchall bucket" for general-purpose code that you want to centralize for the sake of convenience.

   For now, select the Spaceship sprite and follow along with the annotations in Figure 9.4.

2. In the code section labeled A, you ensure that the backdrop starts with space, that the Spaceship is "wearing" the correct costume, and that the ship is positioned correctly on the Stage. You'll find that resetting the environment is the first thing you do when you start to lay down code for your sprites.

3. In the code section labeled B, you use the set block to reset the Countdown variable to 3. You can make this 10 if you are a traditionalist.

4. Now it's time to add some looping logic. You're going to have the Spaceship perform a countdown and then launch into the night sky. In the code section labeled C, you build a Boolean expression that repeats the enclosed action until the value of the Countdown variable reaches 0.

   What is the action, you ask? As you see in the code section labeled D, you combine the Countdown reporter block with the `join hello world` block and the `say Hello!` block to have the Spaceship report the countdown value to the player.

   You'll find that when you want a sprite to "say" or "think" something that reports data, the `join hello world` block is your friend.

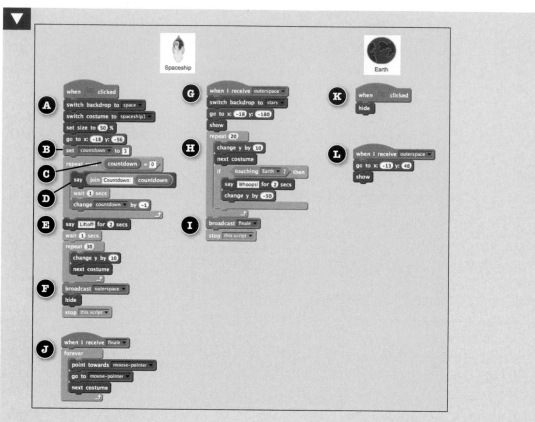

FIGURE 9.4
The source code for the Looping and Conditional Logic...In Space Try It Yourself exercise.

The rest of the repeat looping code involves waiting 1 second and decrementing the Countdown by 1. Each time you pass through the loop, in other words, Countdown goes down another integer. When it reaches 0, you move on to the next block of code.

5. In the code section labeled E, the Spaceship says "Liftoff" and, after another 1-second wait, you hit another ![repeat 10] loop block. If you change the *y* position of the ship by 10 pixels (and cycle between the two costumes by using the ![next costume] block), you can animate the Spaceship off the first screen.

6. In the code section labeled F, you trigger the outerspace broadcast. Broadcasts are excellent mechanisms for synchronizing actions within a single sprite, between multiple sprites, and between sprites and the Stage.

7. In the code section labeled G, you recursively respond, or "catch" the outerspace broadcast and perform some initial environment setup, including changing the Stage to the stars backdrop and positioning the Spaceship at the bottom of the screen.

8. In the code section labeled H, you have a relatively complicated structure with an statement embedded inside of a C block. What's going on here?

   Well, whatever it is, you want it to repeat 20 times. Specifically, the enclosed action is to change the Spaceship's y position and swap its costume, again simulating animation.

   The if statement evaluates the condition "Is the Spaceship touching the Earth sprite?" If so, then you bump the Spaceship back 50 pixels (remember you use negative values for inversion) and have it "say" a "Whoops!" message.

   Once you're finished with the repeat block, you send out a second broadcast—the finale one you created at the start of this exercise. This, and the block that I mentioned previously, serve to cap off this script and is shown in the code section labeled I.

9. In the code section labeled J, you program the Spaceship to respond to its own broadcast again, this time creating a loop that persists until you end the script. Inside the loop, you specify that the Spaceship (a) point toward the mouse, (b) follow the mouse wherever the player moves it on the Stage, and (c) cycle between the two costumes.

10. Now for the Earth sprite. This code is stunningly simple by comparison with the Spaceship's code, isn't it? In the code section labeled K, you instruct the Earth to hide when the game is started. In the code section labeled L, you explicitly show and reset the x, y position of the sprite when the outer space phase of the program is initiated.

11. Time for a test! Click the Green Flag and see how things work. Does the countdown work correctly? Does the ship animate toward the top of the first screen? How does the flame effect animation look?

    Does the screen (Stage backdrop) transition function correctly? How about the collision detection between the Spaceship and the Earth sprite? Does the Spaceship track (and animate) correctly when moved around the Stage with your mouse?

NOTE

Flipbook Animation

The primitive type of animation you employ in Scratch projects is called flipbook animation. When I was a boy, I drew tiny stick figures in the borders of thick textbooks, changing the scene ever so slightly on each page. When I flipped the pages quickly, the series of pictures appeared to animate, albeit crudely.

You do the same thing in Scratch 2.0 by creating multiple costumes for a sprite and then cycling among them with various code blocks. It's simple, but effective.

Working with Clones

In Scratch, you can make use of the clone control blocks to make a quasi-duplicate of a sprite while a project is running. I call clones *quasi*-duplicates because, as you see momentarily, there exists a key difference between a cloned sprite and a duplicated one.

To clone a sprite, all you have to do is use a `create clone of myself ▼` stack block and BAM—it's done. You then can use the `when I start as a clone` Hat block to write custom code to control the clone or clones. You can create up to 300 clones for a single sprite on the Stage.

Differentiating Sprite Clones from Duplicates

You need to remember that although a cloned sprite can be coded using the properties of its original, parent sprite, the clone does not have its own inventory of assets. For instance, your Scratch Cat sprite might have five scripts, four costumes, and three audio files attached to it.

If you create a clone of the Cat sprite, you can use the `when I start as a clone` block to switch the clone's costume to one of the parent sprite's costumes or play one of its audio clips. However, clones don't actually have their own copy of those assets.

If you have that need in your Scratch 2.0 program, you need to right-click the sprite in question and select Duplicate from the shortcut menu. Based on experience, if you need cloned sprites to do stuff like detect each other's presence and interact with each other in a meaningful way, your best bet is to use duplicates instead of clones.

So then the question arises, "What good are clones if you have limited programmatic access to them?" Clones are good for creating action in the background, for instance, creating particle effects like twinkling stars; glistening, falling rain; or snowflakes. In fact, you create a clone-based starfield simulation in the next Try It Yourself exercise.

Clone Collision Detection

In my work with Scratch, the biggest weakness of clones is that doing stuff like collision detection requires a lot of hacky workarounds. The Scratch Wiki (http://is.gd/pnuT4e) has an entire article devoted to how you can use global variables, local variables, and list variables to work around the limitation that, by default, clones are not at all aware of each other's presence.

Working with Clones in Your Projects

The final Try It Yourself exercise in this hour gives you some experience in using clones and duplicated sprites. The project presents a starfield background consisting of cloned sprites that perform a twinkling animation. You then duplicate a Spaceship sprite to demonstrate how duplicate sprites differ from cloned ones.

As usual, you need to set up the project environment. Fire up a new Scratch 2.0 project and follow these preliminary instructions:

1. Select the Stage, navigate to the Backdrops pane, and change the fill color to black by using the Paint Editor's Fill ⬛ tool and the color picker.

2. Delete the default Scratch Cat sprite.

3. In the Sprites list, use the Choose Sprite from Library 🐱 tool to import the Star1 sprite from the Things category and the Spaceship sprite from the Space category of the Sprite Library.

4. Select the Spaceship sprite, navigate to the Looks palette, and double-click the `hide` block to temporarily hide the Spaceship.

5. You need a broadcast message for this project, so bring out a `broadcast message1 ▼` block from the Events palette to the Spaceship's Scripts area, open the menu, and choose New Message. In the New Message dialog box, name the broadcast duplicate.

6. Speaking of duplication, right-click the Spaceship and select Duplicate from the shortcut menu. You should now have an exact duplicate—costumes, audio clips, scripts, and all—of the Spaceship sprite. The clone is called Spaceship2 by default.

TRY IT YOURSELF ▼

Create a Starfield Simulation

In this Try it Yourself exercise, you create an animated backdrop in a Scratch 2.0 project. You can find the completed solution file, Hour09b.sb2, in the book's solution file archive. Also, you can follow along with these instructions by cross-referencing the annotations in Figure 9.5. Figure 9.6 shows this exercise's Stage and sprite configuration. Complete the following steps to complete the exercise:

1. Let's program the Star1 sprite first. In the code section labeled A, you set an initial size for the sprite and clear any graphical effects that are residual from the last time you ran the program. In the code section labeled B, you use the `repeat 10` control block to build a field of 80 stars; feel free to tweak this number to suit your project's needs.

   Inside the C block, you create a clone and determine a random Stage position by implementing the `pick random 1 to 10` reporter block. Remember that (a) the Stage dimensions are 480 pixels wide by 360 pixels high, and (b) you use positive and negative numbers in accordance with the rules of the Cartesian coordinate system.

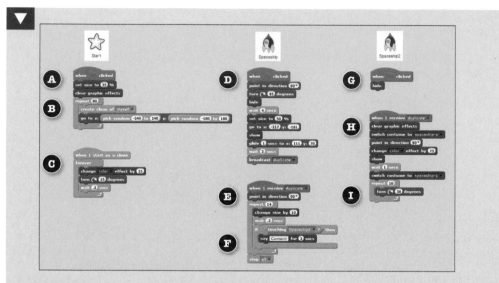

FIGURE 9.5
The source code for the Create a Starfield Simulation Try It Yourself exercise.

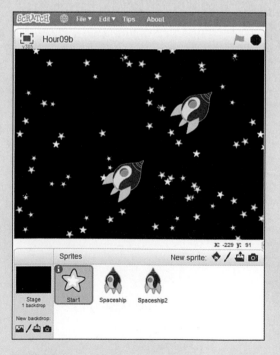

FIGURE 9.6
The Stage and sprite setup for the Create a Starfield Simulation Try It Yourself exercise.

2. In the code section labeled C, you specify what happens when the Star1 sprite is instantiated as a clone. In another Forever loop, add a color effect and turn the star 15 degrees clockwise. To slow down the animation a bit, you can drop in a `wait 1 secs` block with a low threshold value such as 0.2 seconds.

3. Click the Green Flag to test. It's a pretty stunning effect, isn't it? Play around with the `set size to 100 %` block value if you want your stars to appear larger or smaller on the Stage.

4. Now turn your attention to the Spaceship sprite. You'll have it fly in from the lower-left corner of the Stage and travel about 80 percent across the Stage. In the code section labeled D, you reorient the sprite and build in an artificial wait. After that, you position the sprite and have it glide across the Stage. After a 2-second period to admire your handiwork, you kick off the duplicate broadcast. What are you going to do with the duplicate broadcast? Hang on—you'll get to that in just a moment.

5. In the code section labeled E, you respond to the duplicate broadcast message by pointing the ship straight up (90-degree orientation) and using the `repeat 10` control block to balloon the size of the ship. Eventually, the Spaceship sprite will overlap with the Spaceship2 clone that you are getting ready to code. When that happens, in the code section labeled F, you embed an `if then` block to invoke a `say Hello! for 2 secs` speech bubble.

6. Now for the duplicate sprite action. Select the Spaceship2 sprite, which is a duplicate of Spaceship. In this case, you don't want to reuse any code from the original sprite. In the code section labeled G, you hide the clone by default.

7. In the code section labeled H, when the duplicate broadcast message is sent out by the Spaceship sprite, you reset this sprite's look, orientation, and position; show the sprite; and then perform a cool 360-degree rotation in place (see the code section labeled I). The simple math works out here—by performing a 36-degree clockwise turn a total of 10 times thanks to the `repeat 10` block, you spin the ship 360 degrees.

8. Now test the entire project by clicking the Green Flag. How do the stars appear? Are there too many or too few? Does the "twinkling" effect work? Does the first Spaceship fly across the screen, stop, and animate? How about the clone—does it appear on cue? Finally, do you get the contact indication when the sprites overlap each other?

Summary

In this hour, you delved quite deeply into traditional programming fare; namely, how you can add control structures to your Scratch 2.0 projects to manage program execution and flow.

Specifically, you now have a thorough understanding of Control blocks, and you know how to test for conditions within your project code. You should also understand the clone functionality in Scratch.

Workshop

Quiz

1. One key difference between a cloned sprite and a duplicated one is that the clone does not include its own set of costumes, scripts, or sounds.

    A. True

    B. False

2. Which of the following is an effective way of animating a sprite?

    A. Toggling between slightly different backdrops

    B. Toggling between slightly different costumes

    C. Adding a Boolean expression to a forever block

3. Which of the following is a good reason to nest one if block inside of another if block?

    A. If you need to wait a specified time interval before continuing script execution

    B. If you need to loop through a series of actions a second time

    C. If you need to perform multiple evaluations of an expression or condition

Answers

1. The correct answer is choice A. You can programmatically adjust the costumes and sounds of a clone because, after all, the clone is a representation of the parent sprite. However, only a duplicate creates an entirely separate object with its own set of costumes, scripts, and sounds.

2. The correct answer is choice B. You can perform rudimentary sprite animation by programming the sprite to rapidly shift among multiple costumes that appear slightly different from each other. As an experiment, check out the two costumes for the default Scratch Cat sprite. You'll find that if you use a Control block to quickly toggle them, the Cat appears to walk or run.

3. The correct answer is choice C. A single if block gives you one condition to evaluate. Granted, you can use logical operators such as AND or OR to make that expression pretty complex, but it's still one expression. By contrast, you can nest additional if blocks inside of the outer C block if you have more than one condition or expression to evaluate.

Challenge

For this challenge, work through the code in the "Detecting Clones" page of the Scratch Wiki at http://is gd/pnuT4e. Spend some time trying to get a second sprite to detect contact with a clone of a first sprite.

Take a look at Figure 9.7; in the solution found in the file `Hour09c.sb2` in the book's code archive, I cloned Sprite1 and then had Sprite2, a second, "real" sprite, walk a 360-degree circle. The way the code works, element1 in the touching variable list toggles between false and true depending upon whether Sprite2 makes contact with the clone of Sprite1, shown at the bottom of the figure.

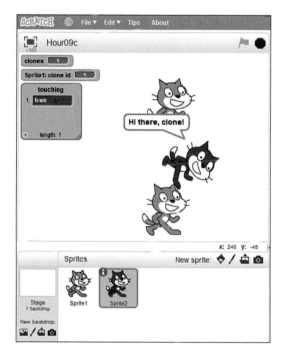

FIGURE 9.7
It's challenging, but not impossible, to perform collision detection with sprite clones.

HOUR 10
Using Operators Blocks

- ▶ Becoming familiar with the Operator blocks
- ▶ Performing more complex math
- ▶ Integrating operators into your Scratch projects

Everybody loves doing math, right? Uh...no, I guess not. In fact, math anxiety drives many people away from the thought of learning computer programming.

The bottom line is that computer programming does require that you think along formal, structured lines. And because computers think in terms of mathematical, comparison, and logical operations, you need to get a handle on how to use these numeric tools to make your Scratch 2.0 projects do what you want them to do.

By the conclusion of this hour, you'll know all you need to know about the Operator blocks. The Scratch Editor calls the block palette "Operators," but being somewhat of an English grammar stickler, I use "Operator" in the singular because it sounds better.

Let's begin!

Becoming Familiar with the Operator Blocks

Take a moment to study Table 10.1, which shows you the 17 reporter and Boolean blocks that make up the Operators suite. Non-color-blind people can see that the MIT Scratch Team color-coded these blocks light green.

TABLE 10.1   The Scratch 2.0 Operator Blocks

Block Image	Block Type	Operator Type	Description
( ) + ( )	Operator	Arithmetic	Performs addition
( ) - ( )	Operator	Arithmetic	Performs subtraction
( ) * ( )	Operator	Arithmetic	Performs multiplication
( ) / ( )	Operator	Arithmetic	Performs division
pick random (1) to (10)	Operator	Arithmetic	Chooses a pseudorandom number within a range
(<)	Boolean	Comparison	Tests for the less-than condition
(=)	Boolean	Comparison	Tests for an equality condition
(>)	Boolean	Comparison	Tests for a greater-than condition
and	Boolean	Logical	Tests for the logical AND condition
or	Boolean	Logical	Tests for the logical OR condition
not	Boolean	Logical	Tests for negation
join hello world	Operator	String Manipulation	Concatenates strings and numbers
letter (1) of world	Operator	String Manipulation	Finds an index value in a string
length of world	Operator	String Manipulation	Finds how many characters exist in a string
( ) mod ( )	Operator	Arithmetic	Calculates the modulo (remainder) from division of the first number by a second number
round ( )	Operator	Arithmetic	Rounds a number up or down to next or previous integer
sqrt ▼ of (9)	Operator	Arithmetic	Calculates a value using a list of built-in functions

Some Necessary Mathematical Terminology

In mathematics, the difference between an *expression* and an *equation* is an equal sign. For instance, this is an equation:

$2 + 7 = 9$

whereas $2 + 7$ is considered to be an expression. The addition symbol is an example of an operator; an operator is a mathematical symbol that performs some...well...operation on two quantities.

Thus, you make use of operators like +, *, <, and > all the time when you need to evaluate mathematical or logical expressions in Scratch or any other programming language.

Operator Block Arguments

Notice that the Operator blocks have "holes" or cutouts in them; reporter blocks have white circle cutouts, whereas Boolean blocks have white square cutouts.

These openings leave space for arguments, which represent data that you pass into a mathematical function or expression. Take a look at Figure 10.1 to see some ways in which you can use arguments with Operator blocks:

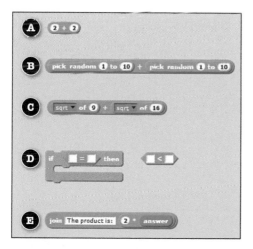

FIGURE 10.1
Scratch makes it intuitive to add arguments to expressions and functions.

> ▶ **A:** It's not programming best practice, but you can add static values as arguments.

> ▶ **B:** It's more effective to use variables or function blocks as arguments. Here, you perform addition of two pseudorandom numbers.

▶ **C:** Scratch includes support for several mathematical (mainly trigonometric) functions out of the box.

▶ **D:** The Boolean blocks are great for inclusion in [if ⬭ then] evaluations.

▶ **E:** Here, you use the [join hello world] block to perform concatenation of string data with numeric data.

Although the previous examples used integers (whole numbers), you can use decimal fractions as well. In professional programming, decimal fractions are referred to as *floating-point numbers*.

NOTE
_____

What Is a Truly Random Number?

This hour uses the term *pseudorandom numbers* instead of *random numbers* because in mathematical theory, it is extraordinarily difficult for a computer to generate a "true" random number that is not in any way deterministic. The term *deterministic* refers to the ability to predict a result in advance. For the purposes of this text, though, Scratch's ability to generate pseudorandom numbers is more than sufficient to meet our needs.
_____

Performing More Complex Math

From experience, the vast majority (over 90 percent) of mathematical algorithms don't involve anything more complex than addition, subtraction, multiplication, and division (with or without modulo).

However, if your Scratch project needs to demonstrate higher-level math, for instance demonstrating geometry and/or trigonometry, then Scratch 2.0 has you covered.

The [sqrt ▼ of 9] block performs a specified function on a given number and returns (reports) the result.

If you open the of block's drop-down menu, you see the following list of functions:

▶ **abs:** Absolute value

▶ **floor:** Rounds down to nearest integer

▶ **ceiling:** Rounds up to nearest integer

▶ **sqrt:** Square root

▶ **sin:** Sine

▶ **cos:** Cosine

▶ **tan:** Tangent

▶ **asin:** Arcsine

▶ **acos:** Arccosine

▶ **atan:** Arctangent

▶ **ln:** Logarithm

▶ **log:** Logarithm

▶ **e^:** Euler's number (2.718)

▶ **10^:** Multiplies 10 by the input value ($10^6 = 1,000,000$)

NOTE

Fun with Trigonometry

If you want to see a wonderful demonstration of how you can employ Trigonometry functions for fun, see the Scratch project "Trigonometry Cannon" (http://is.gd/udwhl5) by the Scratcher Paddle2See. To enjoy learning what sin, cos, and tan mean, check out "Operator Blocks: sin, cos, and tan" (http://is.gd/r21vqr) by scmb1.

But What About Exponentiation?

Some Scratchers have asked the MIT Scratch Team by means of the discussion forums to add a new Operator block that performs exponentiation.

So far, the Scratch Team has not made an official reply, although the request has been officially noted in the Scratch Wiki (http://is.gd/mXexjD).

The most popular workaround for solving exponents in Scratch 2.0 is to use the opposite of the exponent, or the logarithm. In fact, complete the following Try It Yourself exercise to gain some practice using Operator blocks while at the same time testing out this workaround for exponentiation.

Open up a new, blank project and get ready to learn. Here is the plan for this project:

▶ First, you'll program the Scratch Cat to ask the player for the base and store the answer in a variable named base.

▶ Second, you'll have the Scratch Cat ask the player for a power value, and pack that response into a second variable named power (in case you haven't received the memo, variables are "buckets" for storing and manipulating data).

▶ Third, you'll make use of Scratch Operator blocks to perform the calculation.

▶ Fourth, you'll use a `say Hello!` block to have the Cat give the answer to the player.

▼ TRY IT YOURSELF

Solve Exponents (Sort Of)

In this Try it Yourself exercise, you work around the limitations of Scratch 2.0 to solve for exponent problems. Please use Figure 10.2 as your guide as you follow these instructions. You can find the completed solution file, `Hour10a.sb2`, in the book's solution file/asset archive. As always, work through the following steps to complete the exercise:

1. Create the variables first. Select the Scratch Cat, navigate to the Data palette, and click Make a Variable. Create a variable for all sprites named base and click OK. Now create a second variable called power.

2. Okay, let's get this party started. Select the Cat and navigate to the Scripts pane. In the code section labeled A in Figure 10.2, you start the script as usual with the `when clicked` block, and then with the `ask What's your name? and wait` sensing block to fetch the base value from the user. You then nab the set block from the Data palette to set the base variable's value to answer (you can find the answer sensing block from the Sensing palette).

3. In the code section labeled B, you do another ask/set combination to retrieve the power value from the player.

4. In the code section labeled C, you have the centerpiece of the project. The `say Hello!` block has a cutout into which you can stick an expression or string literal. The complicated argument is exploded in the code section labeled D so you can see what blocks are required to put it together.

   What you're seeing is the workaround to calculating exponents that appears in the Scratch Wiki (http://is.gd/SlzcBF). It's beyond the scope of this book to get into a detailed discussion of the math here.

5. Now click the Green Flag and start the project. Try various positive integers for the base and power values. I like to start with ones that I already know (such as 2 to the 3rd power) so I can verify that Scratch calculated the correct answer.

6. If you want the Scratch Cat to format the answer in a more user-friendly way, then check out the code section labeled E. The `join hello world` reporter block excels at combining, or concatenating, string values with number values. In this case, you combine the string literal "The answer is: " with the result of your exponentiation expression. Pretty cool, isn't it?

7. Remember from the earlier discussion that you are undertaking a hacky workaround to get around Scratch's lack of an exponent Operator block.

   To test this, try running the project with negative or zero base and/or power values and check the results with what you get on your calculator.

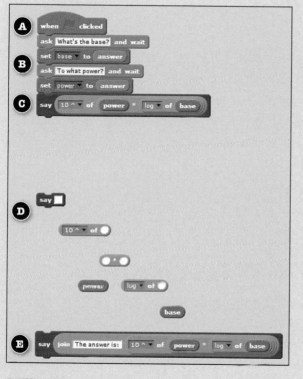

FIGURE 10.2
Source code for the Solve Exponents (Sort Of) Try It Yourself exercise.

Integrating Operators into Your Scratch Projects

Now that you have explored the Scratch Operator blocks and covered some of the mathematical operations surrounding them, it's time to get some practice in seamlessly integrating these operations into your Scratch 2.0 scripts.

"Breaking" Scratch Logic

As mentioned earlier in this hour, you use the join hello world block to combine string (character-based) data with numbers; that's true. But what happens if you try to, for instance, add a number to a string?

To investigate this question, take a look at Figure 10.3. When you work in your own instance of Scratch, remember that you can test each block by double-clicking it.

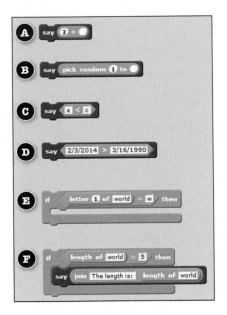

FIGURE 10.3
Programming calls it "kicking the tires" when they attempt to test the limits of a software program.

Compare the annotations in Figure 10.3 with the following descriptions:

- ▶ **A:** Try typing in "abc" in one of the arithmetic Operator blocks. You'll find that Scratch allows only numbers here.

- ▶ **B:** Try typing in text in the pick random 1 to 10 block. Again, you'll see data type enforcement here and you'll only be able to add numeric data.

- ▶ **C:** Will this expression evaluate to True or False, or will it crash Scratch? In logical operations, the letter *A* is considered lower than, and therefore less than, the letter *C*. So this expression is True.

- ▶ **D:** Likewise, you can perform logical operations with dates.

▶ **E:** Here, you use the ⟨letter ❶ of world⟩ block to evaluate whether a letter exists in a particular location in a string.

▶ **F:** Here, you combine Boolean logic with an ⟨if ___ then⟩ block, and then implement the ⟨join hello world⟩ block to give the player a more user-friendly response.

Understanding Comparison Logical Operators

Expressions like 2 + 2 or 100 / 5 are arithmetic in nature. By contrast, when you need to compare two values, you use one of the comparison operators: less than (<), equal to (=), or greater than (>).

You can compare both string and numeric data. These comparisons, and their operators, are called Boolean in their nature because in Boolean logic you have only two possible results: True or False.

This isn't a weakness; in fact, Boolean True and False results are used all the time in Scratch programs specifically and in computer programming in general.

Three additional logical operators are available in Scratch 2.0; all of them return a True or False result based on an evaluation of two conditions:

▶ **AND:** Reports True if both conditions are true

▶ **OR:** Reports True if either condition is true

▶ **NOT:** Reports True if the condition is false, and reports False if the condition is true

Working with Time and Date

Now this section doesn't say too much here because working with time and date in Scratch 2.0 involves using Sensing blocks, which are covered in the next hour.

That said, it's germane and apropos to teach you how you can work with date/time values in your Scratch projects—these are numbers after all, right?

Take a look at the labeled code sections in Figure 10.4 and use the figure as a guide as you examine the following list:

▶ **A:** This code creates a clock in the format *hour:minutes:seconds* that constantly updates. Warning: This block construction involves several (and I do mean several) nested ⟨join hello world⟩ blocks!

▶ **B:** Here, you fetch the current year (from the Sensing block palette), perform a logical evaluation, and respond to the user appropriately.

▶ **C:** Again, you embed several `join hello world` blocks to give the player a personalized message. The `username` and `days since 2000` blocks are also from the Sensing palette.

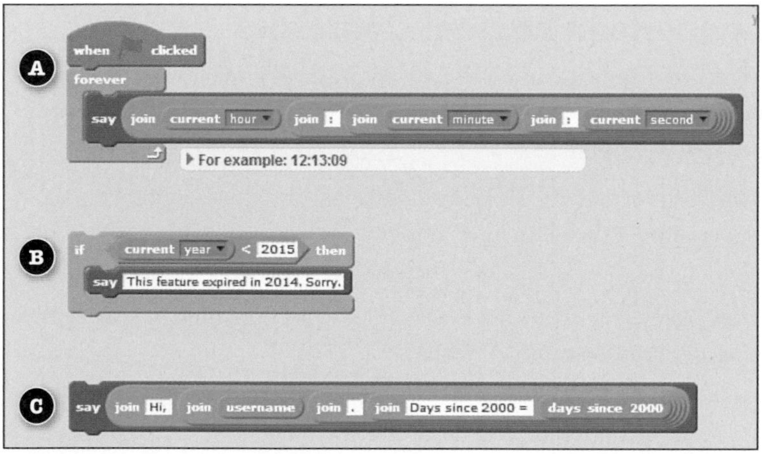

FIGURE 10.4
Playing with date and time in Scratch 2.0.

Let's wrap up this hour by doing one more Try It Yourself exercise. One of the first projects I created with Scratch was a nifty mental math trainer.

NOTE

Mental Math Rocks!

If you are interested in learning how to sharpen your ability to perform math problems in your head, check out the outstanding book *Secrets of Mental Math* (http://is.gd/kBdYo1), by Arthur Benjamin and Michael Shermer. Studying the book has helped me immensely in boosting my math confidence.

The Mental Math Trainer program will work as follows:

▶ You'll start by having the Scratch Cat give the player instructions (press the spacebar to start, etc.).

▶ The player has 10 seconds to solve as many problems as he or she can.

▶ At the end of the game, the Cat gives the player his or her score, which equals the number of problems answered correctly.

Now don't be scared when making use of programming elements like variables and broadcasts. By the end of this book, you'll have received an in-depth education on what they are and how they work in detail.

If you come across a reference to something you don't understand, trust that as you move along in this book, more will be revealed and the larger picture in Scratch 2.0 programming will certainly come into view.

As usual, start a new project and set it up according to these preliminary instructions:

► Select the Stage, navigate to Backdrops, and use the Choose Backdrop from Library button to import the brick wall1 backdrop from the Outdoors category of the Backdrop Library. Delete the white backdrop1 backdrop by right-clicking it and selecting Delete from the shortcut menu.

► Now go to the Data tab and create five (5) variables named num1, num2, Timer, CorrectAnswer, and CorrectCount. Make sure to make the variables available to all sprites in the project.

► Position the Scratch Cat on the Stage, as shown in Figure 10.5.

► Visit the Events palette and drag a `broadcast message1 ▼` stack block to the Scripts window. Open the drop-down menu and choose New Message to create a broadcast named StartGame. Do the same thing a second time, naming the second broadcast EndGame.

TRY IT YOURSELF ▼

Mental Math Trainer

In this Try It Yourself exercise, you use Operator blocks while building a mental math trainer application. Figure 10.5 shows this project's Stage and sprite setup. You can find the completed project file, `Hour10b.sb2`, in the book's solution file archive. Work through the following steps to complete the exercise:

1. You'll add all of the code in this exercise to the Scratch Cat. In the code section labeled A in Figure 10.6, initialize your Timer, CorrectCount, and CorrectAnswer variables to 0. Then place the sprite in the same Stage location every time the program is run, wait an arbitrary amount of time, and then use an ask `say Hello!` block to give the user the instructions "Hi! Answer as many two-digit addition problems as you can in 10 seconds. Press the spacebar to begin."

2. In the code section labeled B in the figure, create an event handler such that when the player presses the spacebar, it initiates the start of the actual game.

FIGURE 10.5
The Stage and sprite setup for the Mental Math Trainer Try It Yourself exercise.

3. When the StartGame broadcast is sent, it synchronizes two actions: starting the timer and starting gameplay. In the code section labeled C, create your own timer by incrementing the Timer variable by 1 every second. The `repeat until` block is handy to make sure that the timer runs only for a specified period of time.

4. The code section labeled D contains the main programming logic for this game. The repeat block puts a parameter on the gameplay; the player can answer addition questions until the value of the Timer variable reaches 10, after which it sends out the EndGame broadcast.

    To create the questions, first set num1 and num2 to two pseudorandom numbers that fall within the range 10–99. Having done that, store the sum of the two random numbers inside a third variable called CorrectAnswer.

    Implement the `ask What's your name? and wait` block and multiple nested `join hello world` blocks to form the questions. The if statement evaluates whether the user's answer is equal to the correct answer; if so, then it increments the value of the CorrectCount variable by 1 as expected.

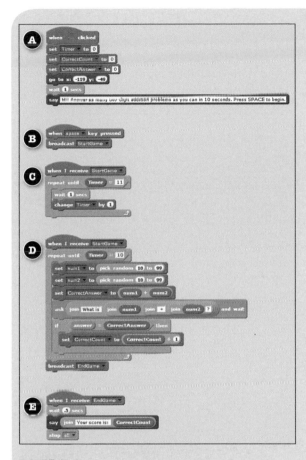

FIGURE 10.6
The source code for the Mental Math Trainer Try It Yourself exercise.

5. In the code section labeled E, set up what happens when the timer reaches its limit. Basically, you put in an artificial pause and then have the sprite say "Your score is:," feeding in the value of CorrectCount via yet another join block. I told you that you'd be using join blocks all the time in Scratch programming!

6. Test the program by clicking the Green Flag. Did you see the instructional message? Does the game start when you press the spacebar? Do the variables reset to 0 correctly, and does the timer count up the ways it is supposed to? Does the game end when you reach the time limit? Does the Cat report your score correctly?

Notice the presence of Stage monitors in Figure 10.5. You can enable or disable the Stage display of variable data by selecting or deselecting the check box control that appears to the left of your variable reporter blocks on the Data palette.

For this Try It Yourself exercise, it is helpful to display the Timer and CorrectCount variables in the end product; this is useful information for the player to have.

On the other hand, you want to make sure to hide the CorrectAnswer field in the released product or you'll give away all the answers to the player! However, during play testing and trouble-shooting, it's convenient to not have to actually perform mental math in order to increment the CorrectCount variable.

Summary

In this hour, you developed familiarity with the Scratch 2.0 Operator blocks. At this point, you know the difference between arithmetic, comparison, and Boolean (logical) operators and how you can implement each to give intelligence and flexibility to your Scratch programs.

The next hour—Hour 11, "Using Sensing Blocks"—serves as a sort of bookend to this hour because the sensing blocks all involve some sort of comparison or Boolean operator to do their work.

Workshop

Quiz

1. The `join  hello   world ` block enables you to concatenate string or numeric data with:

   A. String data only

   B. Numeric data only

   C. String or numeric data

2. The logical expression *NOT touching Sprite1* will evaluate to True if:

   A. The current sprite is not touching Sprite1.

   B. The current sprite is touching Sprite1.

   C. The current sprite is a duplicate of Sprite1.

3. What is the result of the comparison *Ben < Julie*?

   A. True

   B. False

Answers

1. The correct answer is choice C. The join reporter block has immense flexibility; with it, you can combine data from both the string and numeric data types seamlessly.

2. The correct answer is choice A. The NOT logical operator isn't as difficult as you might think. Take a look at Figure 10.7.

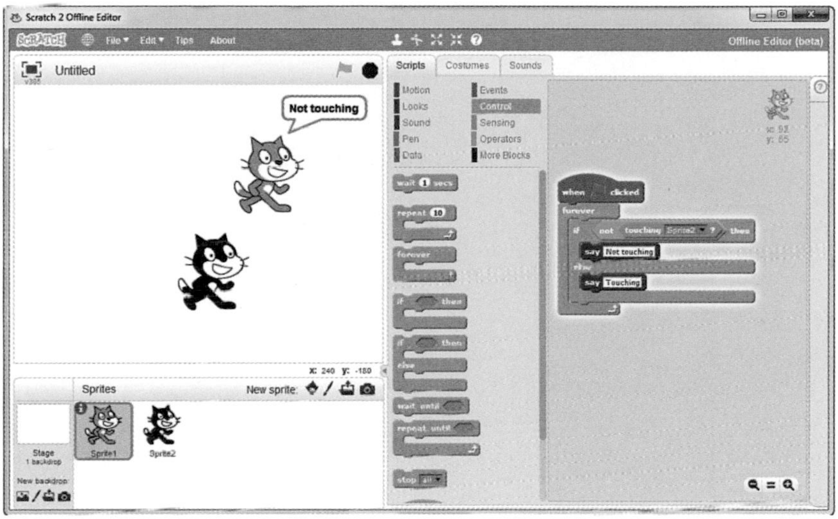

FIGURE 10.7
Using the NOT logical operator in Scratch 2.0 code.

3. The correct answer is choice A. Because the letter *B* occurs earlier in the alphabet than the letter *J*, the expression Ben < Julie evaluates to True (just as the expression *Julie > Ben* is also True).

Challenge

Your challenge for this hour is to extend the Mental Math Trainer game that you developed in the second Try It Yourself exercise in this hour. Here are your tasks:

▶ At the start of the game, allow the player to press 1 to receive addition problems, or 2 to receive subtraction problems.

▶ Refactor the main game logic to produce and track both addition and subtraction problems.

▶ Add a game option to specify the time limit during runtime, and use the new value as the timer variable threshold.

HOUR 11
Using Sensing Blocks

What You'll Learn in This Hour:

▶ Introducing sensing blocks

▶ Delving deeper into sensing

▶ Putting together everything you've learned so far

The Scratch 2.0 Sensing blocks are crucially important inasmuch as they allow us to place an interaction layer between our project and our players. For instance, we can ask the players questions and respond to their responses.

We can put game control in the players' hands by allowing them to perform keyboard, audio, and/or video input and, again, take action upon that input. This is important stuff for us us game developers, and it's an awful lot of fun to program as well!

Introducing Sensing Blocks

In the Scratch 2.0 Editor's Sensing palette, you meet the family of 20 light-blue blocks that enable Scratch to detect, or sense, various digital and analog events. Consult Table 11.1 for a detailed breakdown of each.

TABLE 11.1 Scratch 2.0 Sensing Blocks

Block Image	Block Type	Description
touching ▼ ?	Boolean	Evaluates to True if a sprite is touching another sprite, the Stage edge, or the mouse pointer
touching color ?	Boolean	Evaluates to True if the sprite is touching a specified color
color is touching ?	Boolean	Evaluates to True if a sample of the first color is touching a sample of the second color

Block Image	Block Type	Description
distance to ▼	Reporter	Reports the distance between the specified sprite and the mouse pointer
ask What's your name? and wait	Stack	Asks the player a question and stores the response in the ☐ answer block
☐ answer	Reporter	Reports the player's response from the most recent ask What's your name? and wait block
key space ▼ pressed?	Boolean	Evaluates to True if a specified key is pressed by the player
mouse down?	Boolean	Evaluates to True if the player presses the mouse button
mouse x	Reporter	Reports the mouse pointer's x position on Stage
mouse y	Reporter	Reports the mouse pointer's y position on Stage
☐ loudness	Reporter	Reports detected sound (1 to 100) from the computer's microphone
video motion ▼ on this sprite ▼	Reporter	Reports how much motion or direction is detected in the computer webcam's video image
turn video off ▼	Stack	Turns the webcam on or off
set video transparency to 50 %	Stack	Sets the webcam video transparency
☐ timer	Reporter	Reports the value of the built-in timer in seconds
reset timer	Stack	Sets the built-in timer to zero
x position ▼ of Sprite1 ▼	Reporter	Reports an attribute (x position, y position, direction, costume #, costume name, size, or volume) of the sprite or the Stage
☐ current minute ▼	Reporter	Reports a date/time attribute (year, month, date, day of week, hour, minute, or second)
days since 2000	Reporter	Reports the number of days since the year 2000
username	Reporter	Reports the Scratch username of the player

Remember that the flattened, oval-shaped blocks are called reporter blocks because they (for the most part) simply report a current value; they do not perform any evaluation in themselves. From your work in the previous hour, you know now that the Boolean blocks have the primary purpose of performing an evaluation and reporting Boolean True or False as a result.

The exception to the "Reporter blocks simply report values" is the operators blocks like addition

 that look and act like reporter blocks, but they also perform computation before reporting a value.

Picking Colors

Many Scratchers have difficulty in using the color-oriented sensing blocks:

▶ touching color ▇ ?

▶ color ▇ is touching ▇ ?

Because these blocks are definitely not intuitive, this section covers how to use them in your Scratch code. Why not kick off a Try It Yourself exercise? Here is how the program will work:

▶ You'll map the original orange Scratch Cat to the mouse pointer to give the player full control over this sprite on the Stage.

▶ You'll use the touching ▼ ? sensing block to detect when the player's sprite makes contact with the second sprite.

▶ You'll use the color ▇ is touching ▇ ? sensing block to do a color-based collision detection between the player's avatar and a rectangle you'll draw and add to the Stage.

▶ You'll do more color-based collision detection by using the touching color ▇ ? sensing block.

To get started, log in to the Scratch Editor and start a new project. Set the project up as follows:

▶ Right-click the default Scratch Cat sprite and select Duplicate from the shortcut menu. Now select Sprite2, click the Costumes tab, and use the Fill 🔲 tool and the color palette to change the Cat's primary color to something darker; you can see an example in Figure 11.1.

▶ Now import the Star2 sprite from the Things category of the Sprite Library.

▶ Click the Paint New Sprite [/] button in the Sprites list and draw a red rectangle. In the Paint Editor, you can do this by choosing red from the color palette, using the Rectangle [■] button to create the shape, and the Fill [◆] button to fill it in.

▶ Position the red box on Stage left, as shown in Figure 11.1.

That's all you need for now—let's roll!

▼ TRY IT YOURSELF

Sense Color

In this Try It Yourself exercise, you experiment with color-based collision detection in Scratch 2.0. Follow along by cross-referencing the following steps with the labeled code segments in Figure 11.2. You can find the completed solution file, `Hour11a.sb2`, in the book's solution file archive. Perform the following steps to complete this exercise:

1. You begin by coding the initial state of all four sprites. In the code sections labeled A, B, C, and D in Figure 11.2, you use the `when clicked` and `go to x: 0 y: 0` blocks to ensure that the sprite "players" on the Stage always start in the same initial positions.

2. All the rest of the logic is part of Sprite1's script. In the code section labeled E in the figure, you run a Forever loop that runs through the runtime of the project. First, you map the sprite's position to the mouse pointer so the player can move the orange cat around the Stage.

3. Next, in the code section labeled F, you demonstrate object-level collision detection by creating an `if then` expression such that if Sprite1 touches Sprite2, you use the `say Hello! for 2 secs` block to say "Touching Sprite2" for 1 second.

4. In the code section labeled G, you'll see that in order to evaluate multiple expressions, you need to nest `if then` or `if then else` blocks inside each other. For the second if statement, you come to the heart of the matter—exactly how do you use those little colored boxes in the `color ■ is touching ■ ?` block?

   Here's how it works: (a) Click in the first box in the `color ■ is touching ■ ?` block to select it. (b) Now carefully click your mouse on the thin, black border of Sprite1. You may have to try a few times before you get it because the border is only 1 pixel thick. You'll notice that the block box takes on the color that you clicked on the Stage. Note that if a script is started, you'll be unable to pick up colors. You'll need to stop the script first in order to select a color.

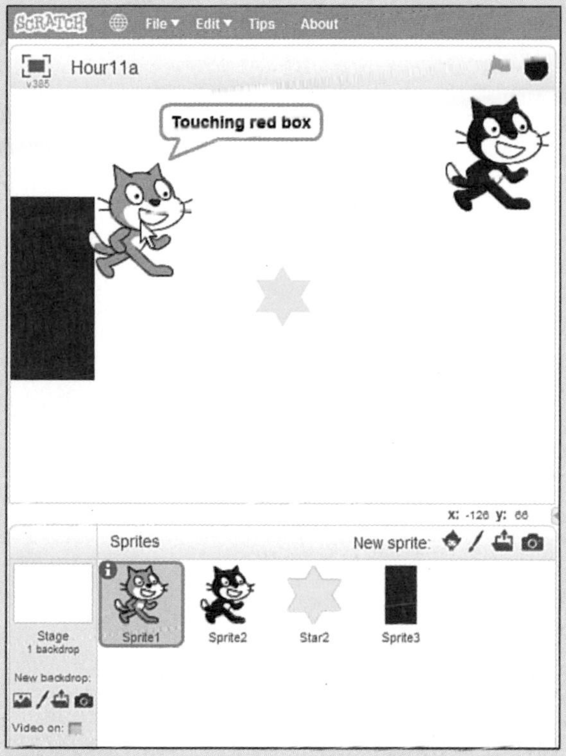

FIGURE 11.1
The Stage and sprite setup for the Sense Color Try It Yourself exercise.

Now repeat that action for the second box in the `color   is touching   ?` block. First click the block and then click the middle of Star2 to pick up the color. Great job—you know how to do it now!

5. In the code section labeled H, use the technique you just learned to map the `touching color   ?` Boolean block to detect the red color that you used to fill in the rectangle.

6. Time to test! Click the Green Flag. Did you gain mouse control over the sprite after the one-second wait? What happens when you mouse over the star? The other sprite? The rectangle?

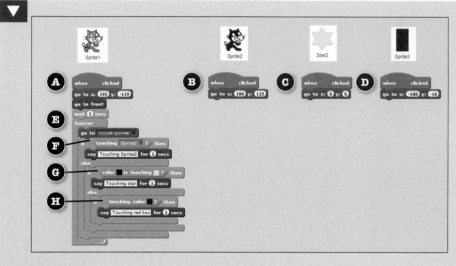

FIGURE 11.2
The source code for the Sense Color Try It Yourself exercise.

Delving Deeper into Sensing

I cut my teeth playing console video games on such classic systems as the Atari 2600, ColecoVision, and the Intellivision. Those games, while simple due to technical limitations at the time, nonetheless were addictive to play because they relied upon tried-and-true game mechanics like collision detection and auditory feedback to the player.

Let's now consider a number of "special case" sensing issues for your Scratch projects.

Sensing Location

Recall that the Scratch Stage is a panel that is 480 pixels wide (x-axis) and 360 pixels high (y-axis). You can use a couple different Sensing blocks to detect the x,y coordinate of both the mouse pointer as well as any sprite.

NOTE

Don't Forget the xy-Grid Backdrop

Please don't forget the xy-grid backdrop located in the Other category of the Backdrop Library. This backdrop is fantastic both for learning and troubleshooting purposes because it plainly reveals the Stage's underlying Cartesian coordinate system layout.

Fire up a blank project and let's play around a bit. Let's walk through the code samples shown in Figure 11.3; I encourage you to add the scripts to your new project so that you can see how they work with your own eyes.

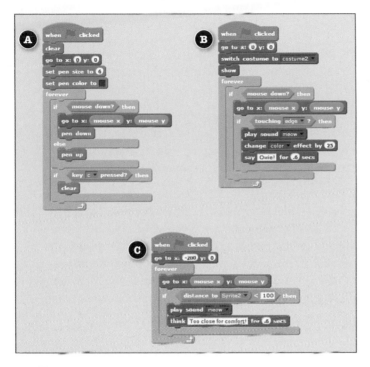

FIGURE 11.3
Practice in sensing mouse and sprite location.

The code section labeled A in Figure 11.3 has a nifty little script that allows you to draw on the Stage with your mouse. Look at the first five blocks: First, you reset the Cat's position on the Stage and set up the Pen tool. Incidentally, you now understand how to use color in Sensing blocks, so choosing a color for your pen with the set pen color to block should be a breeze for you now.

Now look inside the forever block—you test for whether the player presses the mouse button down, and, if so, you map the sprite's coordinates to the mouse's x,y coordinates on the Stage and drop the pen, creating a line of the specified color and thickness. When the mouse button is up, so is the pen. I encourage you to test this script both by clicking the mouse as well as by holding it down while moving the Scratch Cat around the Stage.

Oh, I almost forgot: You have that second if block that senses whether the C key is pressed, and, if so, you clear any drawing that you might have made on the Stage. Pretty cool, right?

Detecting Collisions

I'm sorry to bring up retro video games so much, but they are so analogous to the capabilities of Scratch that I just can't help myself. Besides, if you do have game design aspirations, you would be well-advised to study video game history, of which the classic consoles of the early 1980s are principal.

My point is that all of the classic "twitch" arcade games rely heavily on collision detection. In Scratch, you often need to detect when one sprite connects with another sprite, or when the player's mouse pointer connects with the Stage edge or a sprite. How do you do this?

Take a look at the code section labeled B in Figure 11.3. Here, you again map the Scratch Cat's movement to the mouse pointer, but only when the mouse pointer is clicked or held down. If you run the Scratch Cat into any edge of the Stage, then you play the "meow" sound clip, change its color effect, and have the Cat say "Owie!" for 0.6 seconds. Try it and see—pretty simple, yet highly effective.

Please study the location of the embedded if blocks in the code sections labeled A and B in Figure 11.3. In the code section labeled A, the two if blocks appear one above the other, at the same level. You do this when the if statements are not related to each other; consider the arrangement a logical OR operation. By contrast, in the code section labeled B, the second if statement is literally embedded in the first if C block. This is analogous to the logical AND operation; you are saying, "If the mouse is down AND is touching the edge, then take the following action." Understand?

Detecting Distance

In your Scratch projects, there may be occasions in which you need to detect not actual contact between sprites, but instead simply proximity. Add a second sprite to your testing project and take a look at the code section labeled C in Figure 11.3.

Here, you program Sprite1 such that the sprite follows your mouse pointer all the time, regardless of the state of the mouse button. Next, you employ the `distance to ▼` Sensing block along with an `if  then` C block and a less than `< ` Operator block to set up a condition; the condition says, in plain English, "If Sprite1 comes within 100 steps of Sprite2, play the meow sound and say 'Too close for comfort!' for 0.6 seconds."

Sensing Multimedia

You are probably wondering, "Tim, aren't you going to teach me how to use the cool multimedia Sensing blocks so I can incorporate microphone audio and webcam video into my projects?!"

My answer to that astute and relevant query is, "Yes, gentle reader. I plan to show you those features in exhaustive detail." In fact, you'll devote an entire hour of training (Hour 14, "Adding Multimedia to Your Project") to the subject of audio and video.

Moreover, the use of the PicoBoard and MaKey MaKey devices are covered in Hour 23, "Connecting Scratch to the Physical World." You'll really love that hour—the idea of playing a piano made entirely of bananas (!) tends to spark most peoples' imaginations.

Putting Together Everything You've Learned So Far

You'll wrap up this hour by doing a fun Try It Yourself exercise that wraps up everything you've discovered about Scratch and Sensing blocks. Specifically, you'll create a cool little racing game in which you see how many laps you can complete in 10 seconds.

To save yourself time and art skills (although you'll learn all about drawing your own sprites and backdrops in Hour 21, "Creating Your Own Sprites and Backdrops"), you'll borrow a sprite and a backdrop from the Scratcher Cartercon's fun project "race track" (http://is.gd/hHfiPo).

If you decide to publish your game, please give attribution to Cartercon if you use his or her assets, okay? Thanks.

Open up a new Scratch project and set it up according to the following parameters:

- ▶ Access the book's code archive and import the `vehicle.sprite2` sprite and the `racetrack2.png` backdrop. Recall that you can import external assets by clicking the Upload button in the Sprites list and Stage Costumes pane, respectively.

- ▶ Delete the default Scratch Cat sprite and the original white backdrop.

- ▶ Create two variables, one named, imaginatively enough, Timer, and the other one named LapCount.

- ▶ Create two broadcasts, one named StartGame and the other named EndGame.

Racing Game

In this Try It Yourself exercise, you create a game with the purpose of seeing how many laps around the racetrack you can accomplish in 10 seconds. Controlling the vehicle with the mouse is okay, but could be improved—that's your job as a budding Scratch game developer. All assets for this project, including the completed file named `Hour11b.sb2`, can be found in the book's code archive. You can see the Stage and sprite setup for the game in Figure 11.4 and the source code is shown in Figure 11.5. Please complete the following steps to complete the exercise:

▼

1. Go to the Data palette and enable the Stage monitors for the LapCount and Timer variables. Arrange the Stage monitors as you see in Figure 11.4.

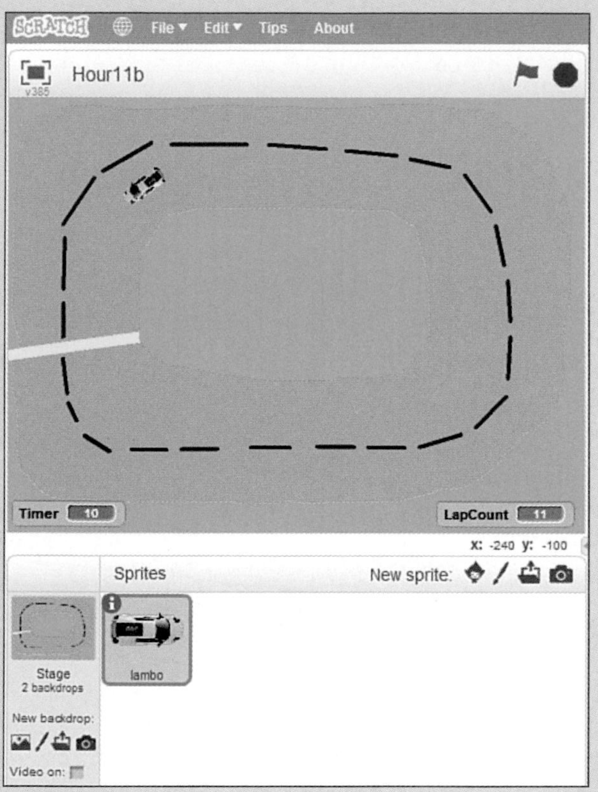

FIGURE 11.4
Stage and sprite setup for the Racing Game Try It Yourself exercise.

2. Let's start with the Lambo sprite. In the code section labeled A in Figure 11.5, set up the initial size and position of the sprite, and then broadcast the StartGame message after a 1-second delay. The reason a few delays are included in the game is to give the player the opportunity to get the car sprite under control before the timer starts. Unfortunately, the animation is a bit jerky.

   The ◻️ block orients the Lambo car sprite toward the mouse pointer, and then glides the sprite to follow the mouse pointer.

3. Now jump over to the Stage's Scripts pane. In the code section labeled B in the figure, ensure that the proper backdrop is displayed and reset the Timer and LapCount variables every time the game is started.

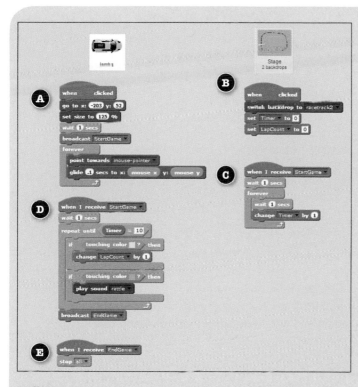

FIGURE 11.5
The source code for the Racing Game Try It Yourself exercise.

4. In the code section labeled C, have the Stage respond to the StartGame sprite by running the timer. Remember that you can use either Scratch's built-in timer, or you can use a variable. In general, you'll get more granular control over time in your Scratch projects by using the variable method.

5. In the code section labeled D, you have the main "plumbing" of the game. When the car sprite receives its own StartGame broadcast, wait 1 second (again, to give the player time to get his or her bearings), and then run two forms of collision detection until the Timer reaches a threshold value (I chose 10 seconds, but you are free to choose another value, of course).

   You use two `touching color ■ ?` blocks to detect (a) when the car sprite crosses the yellow lap marker and (b) if the car makes contact with the green track edge. When you cross the lap marker, you increment the LapCount variable. The challenge for the player is to see how many laps he or she can complete before the timer runs out.

▼

When the player's car hits the green field, you can play the rattle sound from the built-in library. However, you might want to substitute your own custom, cooler sound clips. When the timer reaches the threshold value, send out the EndGame broadcast to bring the game session to a close.

6. In the code section labeled E, you use the `stop all ▼` cap block to end the game.

7. Testing time. Can you control the vehicle sprite okay? Does the timer increment properly? Does the game end when the timer expires? What happens when you cross the lap marker—does the LapCount variable increment? What happens when your car hits the green field? Do you hear the audio clip?

Summary

In this hour, you developed some skills that will greatly enhance your ability to create quality projects in Scratch. After all, how often do you need sprites to be aware of each other in some way, shape, or manner? The combination of broadcast messages, variables, and Sensing blocks represents an extraordinarily powerful kit of tools to make projects that engage the players and keep them clicking the Green Flag again and again. And as a game designer, that's exactly what you want.

Workshop

Quiz

1. Which of the following statements accurately describes how to use the `color ■ is touching ■ ?` block in Scratch 2.0?

    A. Click a target color on the Stage, and then click the color box on the block.

    B. Click a color in the Paint Editor color palette, and then click the color box on the block.

    C. Click the color box on the block, and then click a target color on the Stage.

2. Suppose you use two `ask What's your name? and wait` blocks in a row in your script, one right after the other. If you use the `■ answer` block in the next line of code, what data is retrieved?

    A. The answer to the first ask block question

    B. The answer to the second ask block question

    C. The answers to both ask block questions

3. You can use the  reporter block in a Boolean expression.

   A. True

   B. False

Answers

1. The correct answer is choice C. Using a color block in Scratch 2.0 involves first clicking the block's color block, and then clicking the target color on the Stage to "pick up" that color, transferring it to the block.

2. The correct answer is choice B. You have to be careful when you use multiple ask blocks because the answer block picks up only the most recently asked question. If you need to store a player's response for later retrieval, create a variable and set the variable's value to the desired answer.

3. The correct answer is choice A. You absolutely can use reporter blocks in Boolean expressions. For instance, consider the expression shown in Figure 11.6, in which you take action on what the player gives to the ask `What's your name?` and `wait` block question.

FIGURE 11.6
Reporter blocks are excellent for inclusion in conditional logic.

Challenge

There are myriad ways in which you can improve the rudimentary racing game that you developed in the second Try It Yourself exercise. Your challenge for this hour is to (a) implement as many of the following suggestions for improvement as possible and (b) think of and implement more suggestions for improvement on your own:

▶ Code the game to prevent players from cheating by hovering their mouse over the yellow lap indicator strip.

▶ Code the project so that the player's lap count is displayed in a speech bubble at the end of the game.

▶ Code the project so the player can press the spacebar to begin the race instead of having it automatically start.

- ▶ Make the transition to player mouse control less jerky and more accurate.
- ▶ Add some more cool sound effects to the game; the built-in library doesn't have anything good for, say, engine noise or collision "bangs."
- ▶ Add some additional obstacles to the course and code collision detection for them.
- ▶ Add a visual effect when the car makes contact with the green field.
- ▶ Add another penalty when you hit the green field—perhaps make the timer jump ahead 2 seconds per collision.
- ▶ Consider adding cloud high scores to better include the Scratch community in your game—cloud data is covered in Hour 13, "Using Cloud Data."

HOUR 12
Using Data Blocks

What You'll Learn in This Hour:

▶ What are variables?

▶ What are lists?

▶ Combining variables and lists

The skills you learn in this hour go a long way toward making your program more personal and dynamic. Suppose you are developing a game—how do you plan to track the player's score?

Or perhaps you're using Scratch to make a role-playing game (RPG)—how do you intend to keep track of the player's backpack inventory? The answers are simple: variables and lists, respectively.

Mastering variables is key not only because you'll wind up using them all the time in your projects, but also because variables form the basis of almost every single programming language in the world.

In this hour, you learn how variables and lists work; you'll learn about cloud variables in the next hour.

What Are Variables?

The dictionary definition of the noun *variable* is "An element, feature, or factor that is liable to vary or change." In programming, a variable is essentially the same thing: a named element that can store data.

I tend to visualize programming variables as data buckets that are shaped to the specific type of data that they contain. In more formal programming languages such as JavaScript or Python, variables have *data types* that are associated with them that constrain the type of data they can contain.

For instance, a string variable can contain only alphanumeric or nonalphanumeric data characters. A numeric variable can contain only numbers and is typically used to perform mathematical operations.

In Scratch 2.0, variables don't have explicit data types; you can define a variable by giving it a name and store any data you need for future use in your project. For example, you can have a sprite gather input from the user by using a `ask What's your name? and wait` block, and then access the response by means of a variable.

It's important to keep in mind that variables are persistent in your computer's memory only for so long as the project is running. That is, variable data is purged every time the project stops. You'll learn in the next hour that cloud variables can persist data across project executions, which is pretty darned cool, in my opinion.

Rules Governing Variables in Scratch 2.0

Variables in Scratch 2.0 can have three types of scope, also called visibility:

- ▶ **Local:** The variable is attached to a single sprite and is accessible only to that sprite.

- ▶ **Global:** The variable is freestanding inasmuch as its value can be accessed or modified by any sprite (or the Stage) in the project.

- ▶ **Cloud:** The variable is stored publicly on the MIT Scratch servers and is accessible by multiple users; you'll delve deeply into cloud variables in Hour 13, "Using Cloud Data."

You might wonder when you would create a local variable versus a global variable. From experience, local variables are helpful when you plan to duplicate or clone a given sprite. Unless you make any of that template sprite's variables local (also called private), you'll run into variable name collisions as multiple instances of the sprite are instantiated on the Stage.

Most of the time, however, you will find that global variables represent the most flexible approach to storing data in your Scratch projects.

Getting to Know the Data Blocks

Okay, enough preliminary theory. Let's fire up the Scratch 2.0 online editor, select a sprite, and check out the contents of the Data tab, where the variable blocks exist.

Right away you should notice that the Data palette is empty save for the Make a Variable and Make a List buttons. Therefore, click the Make a Variable button and create a new global variable named myVar. Figure 12.1 shows the "before and after" in the interface.

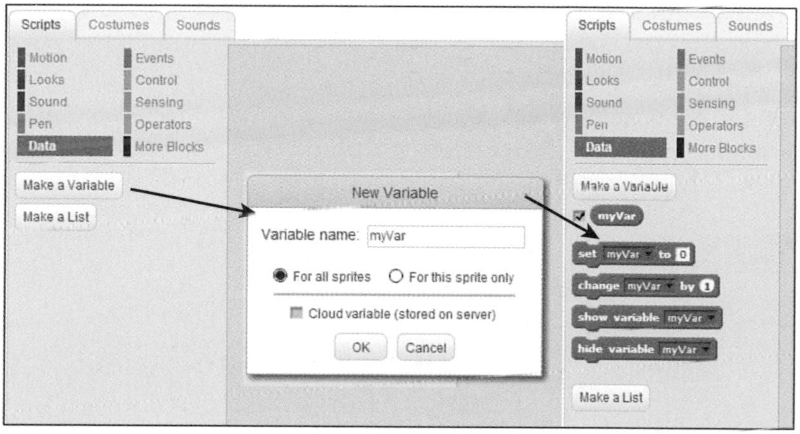

FIGURE 12.1
Creating a variable in Scratch 2.0.

Once you have your variable defined, the Data tab fills in with five blocks per variable, as described in Table 12.1.

TABLE 12.1 The Scratch 2.0 Data Blocks

Block Image	Block Type	Description
 myVar	Reporter	Signifies the current value of a variable
 set myVar to 0	Stack	Assigns a discrete value to the variable
 change myVar by 1	Stack	Changes the data that is assigned to a variable
 show variable myVar	Stack	Explicitly shows the variable Stage monitor
 hide variable myVar	Stack	Explicitly hides the variable Stage monitor

About Variable Stage Monitors

You can display the variable as a Stage monitor by selecting the check box that appears immediately to the left of the variable reporter block in the Data palette (shown in Figure 12.2). Click the Stage monitor to toggle the variable among three different views:

▶ **Normal readout:** This view displays the variable name and current value.

▶ **Large readout:** This view displays only the variable value in a larger font.

▶ **Slider:** This view includes the variable name, its value, and a slider with which you can dynamically adjust the variable's value on the fly.

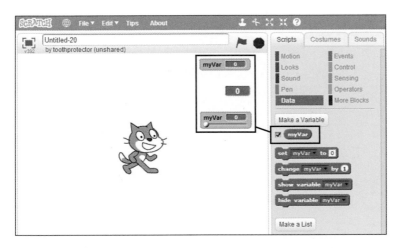

FIGURE 12.2
Variable Stage monitors have three display types.

At this point, the next logical step is for you to play with global and local variables in a Try It Yourself exercise. Open up a new project in the Scratch 2.0 online editor and set it up according to the following parameters:

▶ Select the Stage and import the beach malibu backdrop from the Nature category of the Backdrop Library.

▶ Delete the default Scratch Cat sprite.

▶ Use the Choose Sprite from Library ⬚ button in the Sprites list to import three sprites from the Underwater category of the Sprite Library: Crab, Starfish, and Octopus, as shown in Figure 12.3.

Here's what your first test project will do: First, the Crab sprite will ask the player for his or her name and age and store the responses in two global variables. Second, the Starfish will retrieve and display the variable data to prove that global variables are accessible to all sprites in the project. Third and finally, the Octopus will ask the player to give it a name and then store that data in a local variable. Let's get started!

FIGURE 12.3
The Stage and sprite setup for the Try Variables on for Size Try It Yourself exercise.

TRY IT YOURSELF ▼

Try Variables on for Size

You can find the completed solution file in the book's code archive; the filename is `Hour12a.sb2`. Work though the following steps to complete the exercise:

1. Let's begin by creating two public (global) variables. Select any sprite in the list; global variables aren't attached to any single sprite. Navigate to the Data palette and click Make a Variable. Create one variable named age, and another variable named name. As always, the source code is shown in Figure 12.4.

2. Now you code the Crab. Select this sprite and add the code that you see in Figure 12.4. In the code section labeled A in the figure, reset the age and name variables and lock in the sprite's position on Stage when the project is started.

   In the code section labeled B, use the `ask What's your name? and wait` blocks to fetch two pieces of information from the player. Then use the set blocks to pack the player's answer (stored initially in the answer reporter block) into the name and age variables. Finally, create a broadcast named starfish that initiates phase 2 of your project.

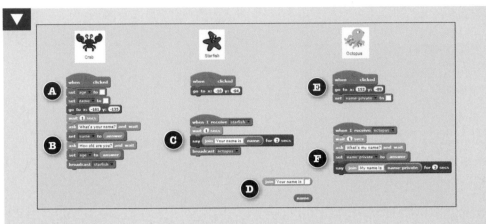

FIGURE 12.4
The source code for the Try Variables on for Size Try It Yourself exercise.

3. Select the Starfish sprite; let's wire up that guy. In the code section labeled C, specify that when the Starfish receives the starfish broadcast, it echoes the content of the name global variable. Check out the code section labeled D: The `join hello world` block is useful when you need to combine (also called *concatenate*) string data with variable data.

Finally, have the Starfish send a second broadcast, this one called octopus, which initiates phase 3 of the project.

4. Now code the Octopus. Start by creating a private variable called name-private. Notice that private variables are accessible only to that sprite. To test this, select another sprite and open up a set block. You won't see the name-private variable in the list!

In the code section labeled E, reset the environment for the Octopus, including clearing out any stored content in the name-private variable. In the code section labeled F, respond to the octopus broadcast message by asking the player for his or her name, and then storing the `answer` in the name-private variable and echoing it on the Stage.

5. On the Data palette, enable the Stage monitor for all three variables so you can see their values on the Stage as they are populated. Click the Green Flag and test the project. Does the project behave as expected? When you reset the project, are the variables reset as well?

More Information on Private Variables

Thus far, you have learned that if you create a variable specifying the For This Sprite Only option, then that variable is private, or personal, to the currently active sprite. As an experiment, select another sprite in the project and navigate to the Data tab—what actions can the second sprite undertake on the first sprite's personal variable?

That's correct—none. It's as if the private variable is invisible. Of course, you can add the private variable to the Stage as a monitor and its value will be visible to the player. But how can other sprites in the project read the private variable's data?

Actually, this is possible by using the [answer] block from the Sensing category.

For instance, you can combine the [say Hello! for 2 secs] and [join hello world] blocks to have one sprite echo the contents of a private variable that is owned by a second sprite. That's a pretty cool trick, isn't it?

What Are Lists?

Sometimes in your software development, you'll need to pack more than one discrete piece of data into a variable. For example, what if you want to manage multiple data elements as a set? Sure, you could create separate variables, but the administration of those separate variables yields bigger-than-desired projects and increased complexity.

In the professional programming world, there is a special variable type called an *array*. An array is nothing more than a single variable that contains more than one data element. The great news for you as a beginning programmer is that you can work with arrays as well, but in a much more user-friendly context. Gentle reader, I give you the Scratch 2.0 *list*.

A list in Scratch 2.0 enables you to easily add, sort, and delete more than one item in a single, named variable. As of this writing, lists are available only within Scratch projects. However, the MIT Scratch Team reports that, eventually, list variables will be enabled to be stored in the cloud, like regular variables can be.

Getting to Know the List Blocks

As you saw with ordinary variables, you need to actually create a list before you see any blocks in the Data palette. Study Table 12.2 to get a feel for the Scratch 2.0 list blocks.

TABLE 12.2   The Scratch 2.0 List Blocks

Block Image	Block Type	Description
myList	Reporter	Reports the active list value
add thing to myList	Stack	Adds a value to the end of a list
delete 1 of myList	Stack	Removes an element from a list
insert thing at 1 of myList	Stack	Adds an element to a specific position in a list

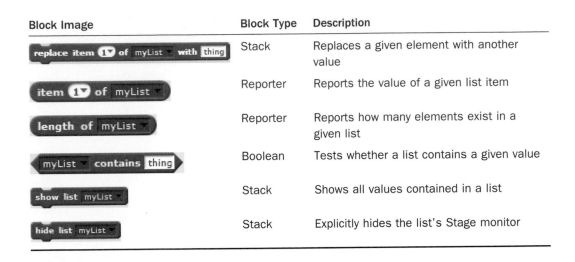

Block Image	Block Type	Description
replace item 1▼ of myList ▼ with thing	Stack	Replaces a given element with another value
item 1▼ of myList ▼	Reporter	Reports the value of a given list item
length of myList ▼	Reporter	Reports how many elements exist in a given list
myList ▼ contains thing	Boolean	Tests whether a list contains a given value
show list myList ▼	Stack	Shows all values contained in a list
hide list myList ▼	Stack	Explicitly hides the list's Stage monitor

About the List Stage Monitor

It's fun to play with the List Stage monitor! Recall that standard variables have three different Stage monitor views. Lists, by contrast, have a single view, but you can do some novel things with the Stage monitor.

Check out Figure 12.5 and the following list to see the high points:

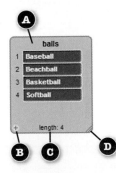

FIGURE 12.5
The List Stage monitor is quite customizable.

► **A:** The Stage monitor displays list items in an ordered (numbered) manner for easy identification.

► **B:** Here, you can add new items to the end of the list on the fly.

► **C:** The length refers to the total number of items in the list.

▶ **D:** You can drag this resize handle to make the Stage monitor larger or smaller. You can drag the entire monitor to another location on the Stage as well.

List Methods

In professional programming, methods describe the actions that an object is capable of doing inside a project. Accordingly, in Scratch 2.0, lists have a number of methods (also called functions) that enable you to control the list membership.

You'll now do a second Try It Yourself exercise to give you some exposure to controlling Scratch 2.0 lists. Fire up a new project; this exercise keeps things simple to focus tightly on learning the concepts.

Set up your project environment as follows:

▶ Swap in the brick wall 1 backdrop from the Outdoors category of the Backdrop Library.

▶ Reposition the Scratch Cat sprite, as shown in Figure 12.6.

Create and Control Lists

In this Try It Yourself exercise, you create a list and get some practice in controlling its contents. The solution file is named Hour12b.sb2 and can be found in the book's solution files archive. Complete the following steps to finish the exercise:

1. Select the Cat sprite, navigate to the Data tab, and click Make a List. Define a list for all sprites that's named myList. Click OK to create the list.

2. On the Stage, click the little plus sign to add the values apple, pear, and banana to the list. Notice that the Add button adds each new list element to the top and not the bottom of the list.

3. Let's force the apple entry to position 1 in the list by using a replace item stack block and the item reporter block (see the code section labeled A in Figure 12.6).

4. Now, you can add mango to the list by using the add stack block (see the code section labeled B in the figure). Interestingly, this stack block adds new items to the end of the list instead of the beginning.

5. Let's remove apple, which should be at position 1, from the list. To do this, invoke the delete block (see the code section labeled C).

6. Insert peach specifically in list position 2 by invoking the insert block (see the code section labeled D).

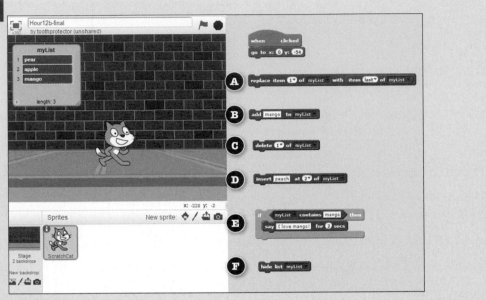

FIGURE 12.6
The sprite and Stage setup for the Create and Control Lists Try It Yourself exercise.

7. It's time to try some conditional logic. In the code section labeled E, evaluate whether the list contains *mango*, and, if so, instruct the Scratch Cat sprite to say, "I love mango!"

8. Finally, hide the list programmatically by using the list's hide stack block (see the code section labeled F).

NOTE

Test-Driving Scratch Blocks

As a reminder, you can test out individual Scratch 2.0 blocks by double-clicking them either from their original location in the blocks palettes, or from the Scripts pane. If you double-click the first block in a stack, all the blocks in that stack fire. By contrast, if you double-click an individual, unconnected blvock, only that block's code is triggered.

While you have this momentum built up, let's undertake another Try It Yourself exercise so you can both practice more with lists as well as integrate a lot of other Scratch 2.0 knowledge that you've amassed thus far.

Start a new project and set it up according to the following specifications:

- Use the Paint Editor and the Fill tool to make the Stage a neutral, solid color.

- Delete the default Scratch Cat sprite.

- Add three sprites from the Things category of the Sprite Library: Baseball, Basketball, and Beachball. Rename them as appropriate.

- Go back to the Things category of the Sprite Library and add in the Button4 and Button5 sprites. Rename the sprites to Add and Delete, respectively. Position all the sprites on the Stage, as shown in Figure 12.7.

TRY IT YOURSELF ▼

Take Lists to the Next Level

In this Try It Yourself exercise, the player can click the ball sprites to add instances of each to a list. You also include Stage controls that allow the player to add his or her own list items or remove them. The solution file for this exercise is called `Hour12c.sb2` and can be found in the book's code archive. Figure 12.7 shows the Stage and sprite setup for this project, and Figure 12.8 shows the source code.

1. In your new project, navigate to the Data palette and create a new global list named balls. Position the Stage monitor in the upper-left corner of the Stage and resize as appropriate.

2. Start by coding the Stage. In the code section labeled A in Figure 12.8, use the delete block to nuke the balls list contents every time the project is started.

3. To populate the balls list, use the add stack block for the Baseball, Basketball, and Beachball sprites, as shown in the figure in code sections labeled B, C, and D, respectively.

4. Click the Green Flag to perform some initial testing. Notice that clicking each sprite multiple times adds multiple instances into the list. How would you prevent more than one instance from appearing in the list?

5. Now wire up the Delete sprite. Select the sprite and add the block code shown in the code section labeled E. Because you've already used the delete block, you should understand what's going on now instantly.

6. Finally, select the Add sprite and implement the `ask What's your name? and wait` block, the `answer` reporter block, and the insert block to add the player's response to the end of the list (see the code section labeled F).

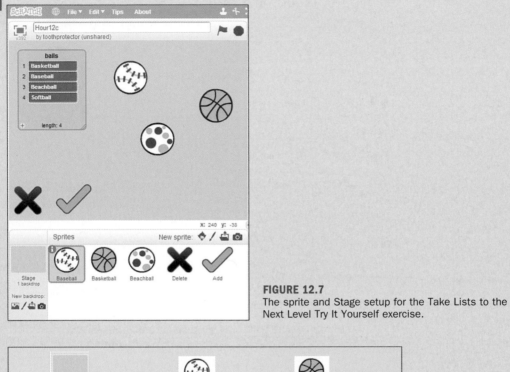

FIGURE 12.7
The sprite and Stage setup for the Take Lists to the Next Level Try It Yourself exercise.

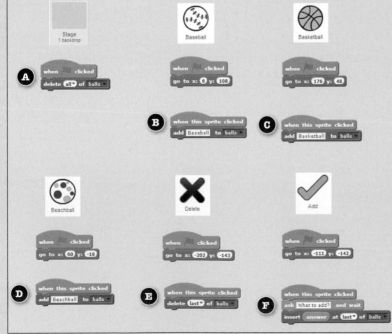

FIGURE 12.8
The source code for the Take Lists to the Next Level Try It Yourself exercise.

Combining Variables and Lists

The old aphorism "and never the twain shall meet" does not apply to Scratch 2.0 variables and lists. In fact, you can combine their functionality to good effect. For instance, you may be working on a project in which you need to reuse a variable, but you still want to store previous values for future use. Why not use a list as a "catchall" bucket for variable data?

A Little Experiment

Start a new, blank project in the Scratch Editor. Next, create a variable for all sprites called movies. Continue the experiment by creating a list for all sprites called movie-list. You can see where you're headed with this test by looking at Figure 12.9.

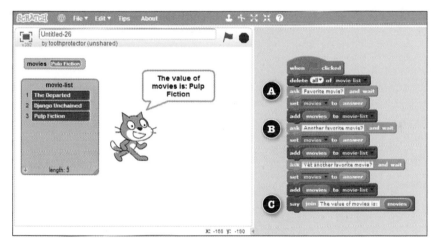

FIGURE 12.9
Combining variables and lists in Scratch 2.0 can yield very powerful data storage and retrieval possibilities.

Here's the workflow that you can see in the code section labeled A in Figure 12.9:

▶ First, you ask the player for an answer.

▶ Second, you store the answer in the movies variable.

▶ Third, you add the variable's value in the movie-list list for "permanent" storage.

The importance of popping the current value for movies is important because, as you see in the code section labeled B, the original value is overwritten when the player answers the second question. Finally, in the code section labeled C, you use the join hello world reporter block to combine, or concatenate, the static text "The value of movies is: " with the current value of the movies variable.

Summary

How do you feel about variables? In my experience with programming Scratch, variables and lists rank right up there in importance with broadcasts—in terms of tools with which you can make your project do what you want it to do. Recall that the MIT Scratch Team uses the room metaphor to describe how Scratch works as a "learn to program" environment that does real work:

▶ **Low floor:** Scratch makes it easy for newcomers to get comfortable in the environment and unleash their creativity.

▶ **High ceiling:** Stuff like variables and lists empower you to create real programs that accomplish real goals.

▶ **Wide walls:** Scratch's open source nature means you can extend the program's functionality in new, uncharted ways.

At this point, you should be comfortable with differentiating variables and lists, as well as how you can combine them in your Scratch 2.0 projects. The next hour follows hot on the heels of this hour; in Hour 13, you'll learn how to use cloud variables, which are a kind of "super" public variable that are actually readable by other Scratchers all around the world! Hang on to your hat for that upcoming stuff—it's powerful stuff indeed.

Workshop

Quiz

1. Suppose you have one global variable defined in your two-sprite project. You then attach a private variable named priv to spriteA. Which of the following actions is possible on priv by spriteB?

   A. Set

   B. Change

   C. None

2. What is the maximum number of members you can add to a list in Scratch 2.0? (To answer this question, you might need to perform some research on the Scratch Wiki at http://is.gd/zi2pLU.)

   A. 10

   B. 50

   C. No limit

3. Which list method would you use to include a new item in a specific position in the list?

   A. Insert

   B. Add

   C. Replace

Answers

1. The correct answer is choice C. If you created a variable that is private to spriteB, then spriteA cannot change the private variable in any way. However, you can read the value of the private variable by using the [x position ▼ of Sprite1 ▼] reporter block from the Sensing category. Figure 12.10 shows you what this looks like.

FIGURE 12.10
You can apply some creative use of reporter blocks to give sprites read-only access to other sprites' private variable data.

2. The correct answer is choice C. According to the Scratch Wiki (http://is.gd/fr3ias), "There is no limit to the length of an item or the amount of items a list can hold, apart from an amount sufficient to crash Scratch."

3. The correct answer is choice A. The insert block adds a new item to a specific position in a list. By contrast, the replace block deletes an item in the list, which is not what is specified in this quiz question.

Challenge

Your challenge in this hour is to extend the functionality of the balls list project you undertook in the Take Lists to the Next Level Try It Yourself exercise. First, add programmatic logic that prevents more than one instance of the Baseball, Basketball, and Beachball sprites from being added to the list when they are clicked.

Next, use the create clone ⬛ block to duplicate the Basketball sprite and see how this affects your project in general and the list in particular. See the file `Hour12d.sb2` in the book's code archive to see one possible solution of how to attack this curious problem.

HOUR 13
Using Cloud Data

What You'll Learn in This Hour:

▶ What is a new Scratcher?

▶ Creating cloud variables

▶ How to post high scores using cloud data

▶ More about username

Cloud computing is all the rage nowadays, that's for sure. Contrary to popular opinion, however, cloud services aren't difficult to understand. You already know, for instance, that Scratch 2.0 is a cloud-based application. This means that all of your Scratch project data is stored not on your own laptop or desktop computer, but instead is located on a server computer (several of them, actually) owned by the MIT Media Lab people.

Cloud services are cool because they are so convenient. You could start a Scratch project from your home in Nashville, and resume work on the project seamlessly from your relative's home in Los Angeles, assuming that you had a Web browser and an Internet connection.

In the previous hour, you learned how to store and access data by using variables and lists. Those data objects were "trapped" inside your Scratch program. But what if you want to publish a global high scores list for your nifty new Scratch 2.0 arcade game? Or what if you want to conduct a survey and display the worldwide results on your Scratch project page?

Happily, cloud variables in Scratch 2.0 allow you to accomplish both of those goals, and more. However, pay attention because, unfortunately, accessing cloud variables in Scratch 2.0 isn't as user-friendly as it could be.

Fasten your seat belt, put on your thinking cap, and enjoy the ride!

What Is a New Scratcher?

Whoa—you might be thinking, "What is this 'new Scratcher' business, Tim? I thought you were going to teach me about cloud variables." Hold your horses; that's exactly what I'm preparing to do. However, you first need to define what a *new Scratcher* is and why that information is important to know.

When you create a new user account at the Scratch website, you are considered to be a new Scratcher. To prevent spam and the abuse of the cloud resources, the MIT Scratch Team specifies that your Scratch user account attain "Scratcher" status before you can use cloud data in your projects.

This idea is great in theory—sadly, many people take advantage of websites like Scratch to automatically create spam accounts to bombard message boards with advertising and abuse cloud storage services—but is a little more tricky in practice.

You can see at a glance whether you are a new or "full" Scratcher by logging in to the Scratch website and viewing your profile page. Figure 13.1 shows two accounts, one still considered new and another considered to be a veteran.

FIGURE 13.1
Two Scratch accounts: one is considered new, and the other has full Scratcher status.

Limitations of a New Scratch Account

According to the Scratch Wiki (http://is.gd/oGLWKS), accounts with the New Scratcher designation have the following account restrictions on the Scratch websites:

- ▶ Can't use cloud data
- ▶ Can't post images
- ▶ Can't delete their posts
- ▶ Have to wait 30 seconds before leaving comments
- ▶ Can't post hyperlinks in comments to sites outside of scratch.mit.edu

If you're a new Scratcher, you can try to create a cloud variable in the Scratch Editor, but nothing will happen. By contrast, if you try to run another Scratcher's project that implements cloud data, you'll be stopped with the error message shown in Figure 13.2.

> Because you have a new Scratch account, any changes to cloud data won't be saved yet. Keep participating on the site you'll be able to use cloud data soon!

FIGURE 13.2
New Scratchers are barred from using cloud data...period.

Of course, the most significant limitation for the purposes of this text is the inability to access cloud data. This restriction not only bars new Scratchers from creating cloud variables in their own projects, but also prevents them from accessing cloud data in other Scratchers' projects.

How Do You Become a Scratcher?

Many Scratchers find it mildly infuriating that the MIT Scratch Team does not outline the requirements to have your account promoted from New Scratcher to Scratcher. Clearly, the length of time that the account has been active on the site is not one of the metrics that is considered.

Again according to the Scratch Wiki, Scratchers need to be "active on the main site" to gain Scratcher status. In other words, you'll want to make sure that you perform the following actions at the very least to maximize your chance of account promotion:

- ▶ Publish at least three projects.
- ▶ Create at least two studios.
- ▶ Favorite several projects.
- ▶ Follow several other Scratchers.
- ▶ Leave comments on other Scratchers' project pages.
- ▶ Participate in the Scratch Discussion Forums.

If and when you qualify for promotion, you'll receive an invitation in your Messages list. Click a confirmation link, and you'll observe that your rank has shifted from New Scratcher to Scratcher on all Scratch websites, including the Scratch Discussion Forums.

In any event, the remainder of this hour assumes that your account has reached the vaunted Scratcher status—because otherwise, you won't be able to access cloud data at all.

Creating Cloud Variables

Recall from the previous hour's training that variables' data typically persists only so long as the host project is running. When a player clicks the Green Flag again to have another run at your project, especially in a different web browsing session, you cannot reliably access previously stored variable data. In other words, variable data is ordinarily volatile.

By contrast, cloud data represents data persistently across project executions and even browsing/ computing sessions. In other words, you could set a cloud variable to a value 10 today, and six months later, you could return to the project, run it again, and observe that the value of 10 still exists in the cloud (that is, unless the project is shared and another Scratcher modified the variable's value).

Let's look at the process of creating a cloud variable by cross-referencing Figure 13.3 with the following list:

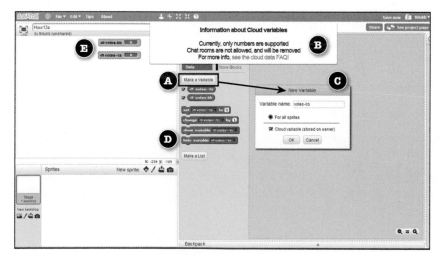

FIGURE 13.3
The process of creating a cloud variable is pretty much the same as that of creating a normal public variable.

▶ **A:** On the Data tab in the Blocks palette, click Make a Variable as usual.

▶ **B:** When you create a cloud variable, this text box appears, letting you know that only numeric values are supported, and that you should not create cloud-based chat rooms. These points are discussed in more detail momentarily.

▶ **C:** In the New Variable dialog box, be sure to select the Cloud Variable (Stored on Server) check box; notice that the For This Sprite Only option disappears (as well it should, as it defeats the purpose of the cloud variable). Click OK to complete the cloud variable creation process.

▶ **D:** In addition to a reporter block, you also have set, change, show, and hide method (function) stack blocks.

▶ **E:** You can display or hide cloud variable Stage monitors just as you can with other variable types.

Notice that cloud variable blocks have a small cloud icon printed on them to make it easy to distinguish cloud variables from traditional variables.

About Numeric Data and Chat Rooms

Recall that in all programming languages, variables can have a data type that constrains the type of data (string, numeric, datetime, and so forth) that variable can store. As you saw in Figure 13.3, as of this writing, you can store only numeric data in a cloud variable; this means no text is allowed.

If you do try to store string data in a cloud variable, then the string data is replaced by 0 and you get an error message, as shown in Figure 13.4.

Remember that the MIT Scratch Team is a nonprofit enterprise, so the rate at which Scratch features are corrected, broadened, and deepened isn't driven by a market economy. Perhaps the Scratch Team wants to keep the cloud data scope as narrow as possible for now as it gauges (1) interest in the technology, (2) the capacity of its network infrastructure, and (3) the system load generated by storing string and list data on the servers. Only time will tell what will develop in the coming weeks and months.

The Username Reporter Block

The **username** reporter block is significant inasmuch as it stores the username of the Scratcher who is currently running the project. Hopefully, you can see immediately how useful having this information available is—perhaps you want to keep a "High Scores" list for your Scratch game, and you want to identify the Scratchers who posted their high scores.

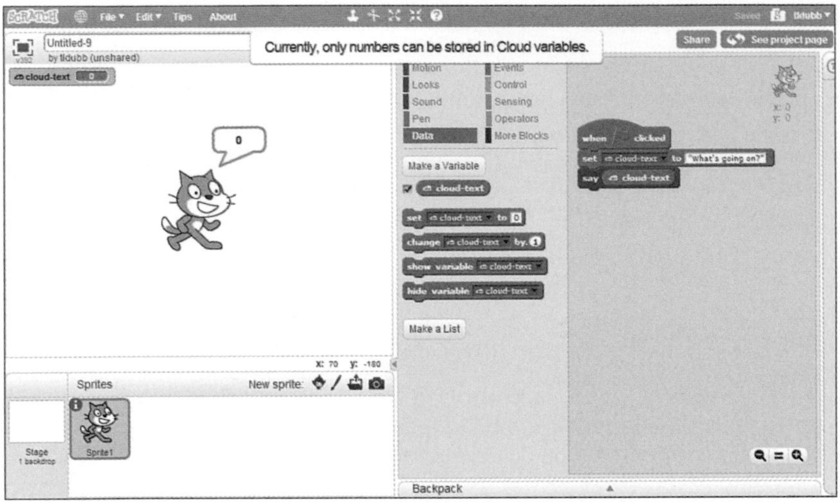

FIGURE 13.4
Scratch 2.0 stops you if you try to pack string data into a cloud variable.

Another cool idea that many Scratchers had was using cloud data and the username block to create chat programs. Although this is a cool idea, the Scratch Wiki is very clear that chat programs will be flagged and removed by the Scratch Team.

Eventually, once cloud variables can contain string data, the Scratch Team may allow Scratchers to build chat and chatlike programs because (at least in my humble opinion) there is much powerful technology to be mined and important skills to be learned.

Just as an intellectual exercise, check out Figure 13.5, which shows you the sample chat project that appears in the "Cloud Data" article on the Scratch Wiki (http://is.gd/ERWIif). As usual, use the figure as a guide while you examine the following list:

▶ **A:** Here, you create a standard global variable named localuser, and initialize its value with the username (identity) of the Scratch user who runs that instance of the project.

▶ **B:** The main  loop in this project prompts the user for input and then posts it to a cloud list.

▶ **C:** The add and join blocks work together to create the user interface that's shown at the bottom of Figure 13.5 (labeled as F); you specify the standard chat format *username*: *message*.

▶ **D:** Simultaneously, this second  loop adds a sound effect whenever a user posts a chat message to the cloud list.

▶ **E:** First, you create a standard variable named templength and pack it with the length (number of messages in) of the Chat cloud list. Second, you wait until a new message shows up (which causes that logical expression to evaluate to True), and third, you play the pop sound.

▶ **F:** The main user interface of the Scratch application is just the Chat cloud list Stage monitor.

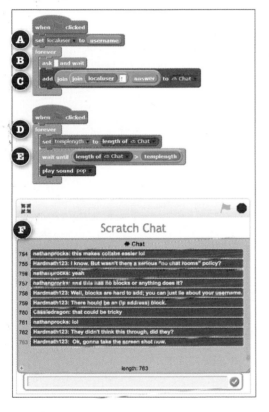

FIGURE 13.5
The sample (and forbidden to try yourself) online chat project from the Scratch Wiki (http://is.gd/ERWlif).

Let's Create a Poll Using Cloud Data!

Polls or informal surveys are a great way to get your feet wet with using cloud data in Scratch 2.0. For example, my two favorite TV series of all time are *Breaking Bad* and *The Shield*. It struck me as a good idea to create a simple Scratch 2.0 poll to ask other Scratchers which show they preferred.

▼ TRY IT YOURSELF

Create a Poll

In this Try It Yourself exercise, you ask the player to vote on which TV show he or she likes better. To make data input as simple as possible (and in keeping with the numeric restriction of cloud data), you have them type 1 or 2 to signify their vote. The solution file is named `Hour13a.sb2` and is located in the book's solution file archive. Work through the following steps to complete the exercise:

1. Fire up a new, blank project and use the Paint New Backdrop 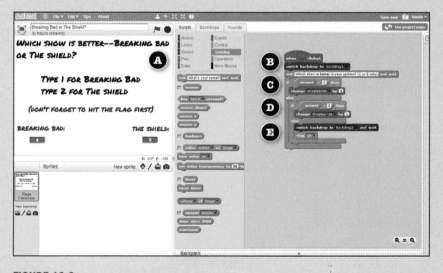 button to create a second backdrop. Use the Fill tool in the Paint Editor to change the color of the second screen, as shown in Figure 13.6. You'll have one screen for voting instructions and a second screen to trap data input errors.

FIGURE 13.6
The user interface and source code for the Create a Poll Try It Yourself exercise.

2. For backdrop1, use the Paint Editor's Text **T** tool to type out the poll instructions; you can see an example in Figure 13.7. Be sure to select a font and choose a font color. Once you're finished, click away from the text box once, and then use the text box controls to resize and reposition the text box.

    Unfortunately, the text, once committed, becomes noneditable, so be prepared to click Undo and start over if you make a mistake.

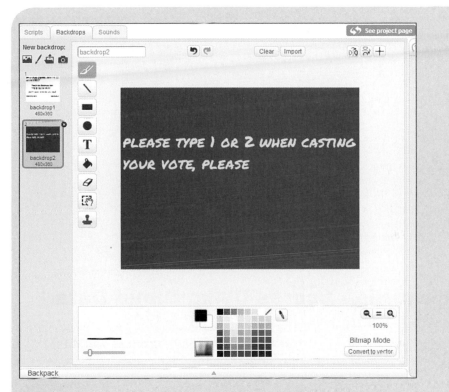

FIGURE 13.7
For a poll, it's important to create error-handling code to handle invalid user input.

3. Now navigate to the Data palette and create cloud variables to store votes. In the example, there are two choices, so you need two variables. Click Make a Variable and be sure to select the Cloud Variable (Stored on Server) check box to make them cloud-based and not locally stored. You should name the cloud variables as descriptively as possible because you may show the variable text to your users on the Stage.

4. Now go to the Scripts pane for the Stage and create the vote input and counting code. In the code section labeled B in Figure 13.6, reset the environment and use an `ask What's your name? and wait` block to solicit a vote from the user. It is imperative to be clear with your instructions. For example, notice in the figure that "use only 1 and 2" is mentioned not only in the `ask What's your name? and wait` block, but also on the Stage.

5. In the code section labeled C, you use two nested `then` blocks to perform the main program logic. If the `answer` block fetched from the user equals 1, then you increment the appropriate cloud variable by 1. If the answer block contains a value of 2, then you increment the other variable (code section D).

▼

6. In the code section labeled E, you see an important consideration that many Scratchers forget about—trapping error conditions. What if the user typed "The Shield" in the ask box instead of 2? You need to handle those exceptions so the program doesn't screech to a halt.

   One solution is to switch to the red backdrop, which contains a pointed reminder that the user should type only numeric values to signify his or her vote, and then stop script execution.

7. Go back to the Data tab and enable the Stage monitors for both of your choices. On the Stage, click each monitor to display the "big number" view. In the example, there are labels for each counter added directly to the Stage backdrop for convenience.

8. Run the project and cast a valid vote. Did the vote counter increment properly on Stage? Now rerun the project, this time typing in an invalid value, such as 3 or "Breaking Bad." What happens? Did your exception-handling code fire correctly?

How to Post High Scores Using Cloud Data

Another way that we can show off the capability of cloud data in Scratch 2.0 is the high scores list. In the next Try It Yourself exercise, you remix one of my published projects, Timed Target Practice, and modify the code such that you display the high score of the previous player.

NOTE

High Scores in Scratch 2.0

If you want to see three examples of an exceptionally cool implementation of high scores, check out the projects Saving Usernames on the Cloud by sonicfan12p (http://is.gd/es84FA), SDP (Star Destroyer Program) v10 by SFollis (http://is.gd/fqJK14), and How to Set High Score Username v2 by tacoswami (http://is.gd/czBKIQ).

Challenges

I grew up with the quarter arcades of the 1980s, where all the stand-up arcade cabinets displayed each game's list of high scores along with the initials of each player. At the time of this writing, Scratch 2.0 suffers from two architectural limitations that make it extraordinarily difficult to post username/high score combinations by using cloud variables:

▶ **Cloud variables can contain only numeric data:** The MIT Scratch Team says that this limitation exists "for security reasons." Although you can fetch the Scratch username of each player trivially by means of the username block, the username itself is string data and, therefore, cannot be displayed to the world by means of a cloud variable.

▶ **Cloud lists are not implemented yet:** The MIT Scratch Team promises that it will have cloud lists someday, but right now lists are local to the project. Therefore, your challenge is trifold when you set out to create a traditional global high score list:

  ▶ You need to code a mechanism for encoding the string username into numeric values that can be stored in cloud variables.

  ▶ You need to code a way to decode the now-numeric username back into readable string data for inclusion in the high score list.

  ▶ You need to build and display the decoded username and high score data in a list that is persistent across browsing sessions and different Scratchers' sessions.

Sadly, this encoding/reencoding process is long, cumbersome, and complex—far outside the scope of this book. If you want to pursue this topic on your own, start with the Scratch Wiki article, "Global High Scores" (http://is.gd/RsyCCO), which includes (somewhat of) a tutorial.

TRY IT YOURSELF ▼

Post an Anonymous High Score

In this Try It Yourself exercise, you use a cloud variable to store the highest score ever achieved in your game. This exercise gives you some advance experience with project remixing, which is a subject that is covered in detail in Hour 20, "Remixing a Project." The completed solution file is located in the book's code archive and is named Hour13b.sb2. As always, work through the following steps to complete this exercise:

1. Locate my project Timed Target Practice (http://is.gd/Hscu5U) and click See Inside to enter its source code.

2. Click Remix in the Scratch 2.0 Editor to create a copy of the project and add it to your My Stuff project list. Notice that the MIT Scratch Team adds "remix" to the project title to help you with attribution.

3. In this game, I centralized as much global code as I could on the Stage. First, though, navigate to the Data tab and create a global variable named HighScore (shown in the code section labeled A in Figure 13.8). Second, navigate to the Scripts tab for the Stage and let's see what's going on.

4. In the code section labeled B in the figure, you see that the EndGame broadcast initiates the conclusion of the game. This is the key event from a score-gathering standpoint.

5. In the code section labeled C, you add an block to include your high score logic. Here's what's happening: First, you evaluate whether the current score (stored in the previously created Score global variable) is higher in value than what is currently stored in the HighScore cloud variable.

▼

If so, then you update the value of HighScore and show its Stage monitor on screen (feel free to use your mouse to reposition that Stage monitor, by the way).

If the current game score is less than the cloud HighScore, then the current HighScore value is retained.

6. Click the Green Flag and play several rounds of the Timed Target Practice game. Does the cloud HighScore variable update properly when you beat its value?

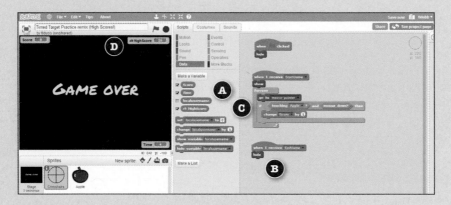

FIGURE 13.8
The Stage, sprite, and source code setup for the Post an Anonymous High Score Try It Yourself exercise.

More About Username

In this hour, you've been hamstrung by learning that it is very difficult to work around current Scratch 2.0 capability limitations to store string data such as a username in a cloud variable.

The **username** block has an interesting history, so you'll learn more about it in the remainder of this hour.

According to the Scratch Wiki (http://is.gd/rUBkY8; http://is.gd/rUBkY8), the username block was once called user id and stored a globally unique identifier (GUID) number for every Scratcher. The idea behind the user id is that you could reference other Scratchers while preserving their identities.

However, due to popular demand, the Scratch Team relented and provided the username block instead, which reports the friendly Scratch username as a string value.

Let's buzz through some sample use cases of the username block by cross-referencing the source code in Figure 13.9:

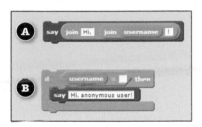

FIGURE 13.9
You can implement the username block creatively to add personalization features to your projects.

▶ **A:** Here, you use two nested [join hello world] blocks and a [say Hello!] block to create a personalized welcome message.

▶ **B:** Here, you test for whether the user is logged in to the Scratch site (if not, then this expression will evaluate to True) and you welcome the anonymous user.

As you can see in Figure 13.10, the online Scratch player lets you know if a project contains a reference to the [username] block. If the player wants to hide his or her identity, then he or she should sign out of his or her Scratch account before playing that game.

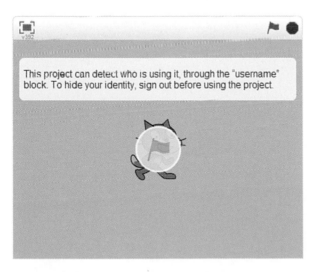

FIGURE 13.10
The Scratch player warns you that your username will be captured by a project that implements the username block, and that you should sign out if you want to preserve your identity.

Summary

I realize that some of the content you learned in this hour was a letdown for you. I hear you! Perhaps by the time you're reading this, the MIT Scratch Team will have implemented cloud lists and string content for cloud variables; that would be awesome.

In the meantime, however, there are still lots of cool things you can do with numeric cloud variables that persist across user sessions. The next hour takes you back into the world of multimedia. In Hour 14, "Adding Multimedia to Your Project," you'll find out the answer to the question, "Is it possible to play my own video and audio clips in a Scratch project?"

Workshop

Quiz

1. The term *cloud* in *cloud data* refers to data being stored:

   A. On the user's computer

   B. In the user's web browser cache

   C. On a service provider's computer

2. Which of the following is *not* a valid cloud variable block method?

   A. Rename

   B. Set

   C. Change

3. What do the processes of encoding and decoding accomplish when you want to use string data in a cloud variable?

   A. Translating numeric data to string data, and then back again to numeric

   B. Translating string data to numeric data, and then back again to string

   C. Translating string or numeric data to pseudocode

Answers

1. The correct answer is choice C. In cloud computing, user data (and sometimes entire applications) run remotely in a service provider's infrastructure instead of on the user's own equipment. For example, Scratch 2.0 cloud variable data "lives" in Cambridge, Massachusetts, on the Scratch Team's content servers.

2. The correct answer is choice A. Cloud variables in Scratch 2.0 have four basic methods, or actions represented by blocks: set, change, show, and hide.

3. The correct answer is choice B. Remember that, as of this writing, you cannot store string data in cloud variables, so the hacky workaround to this problem is (a) encoding string data to a numeric representation, typically by using mapping lists, and (b) decoding the numeric data back to a human-readable format for display in a third Stage list.

Challenge

Your challenge for this hour is perhaps the most difficult challenge in the book. Work through the "Global High Scores" tutorial on the Scratch Wiki (http://is.gd/RsyCCO). The purpose of this tutorial is to walk you through the basics of storing usernames and high scores by using cloud variables in a Scratch 2.0 project. To save time and effort, search the Scratch project gallery for related projects. Some helpful search phrases include the following:

- ▶ Global high scores
- ▶ Username high score cloud
- ▶ High score cloud data
- ▶ Username cloud variable

Adding Multimedia to Your Project

What You'll Learn in This Hour:

▶ Adding photos to your project

▶ Adding audio to your project

▶ Adding video to your project

▶ What about hyperlinks and interactivity?

Our good friend Wikipedia defines the noun multimedia as "content that uses a combination of different content forms." These content forms take the, well, form of the following types at the minimum:

▶ Text

▶ Still images

▶ Audio

▶ Animation

▶ Video

▶ Interactivity

In this hour, you pay close attention to the still image, audio, and video content types. This hour gives lesser emphasis on the animation and interactivity types, as these are more difficult to add to your Scratch 2.0 projects.

By the end of this hour, you'll have the knowledge under your belt to make Scratch projects much more dynamic and less "cookie cutter." After all, let's face it—Scratch projects that use and reuse the same shared assets (particularly from the Scratch libraries, which all Scratchers have access to) are straight-up boring.

By contrast, you can add your own photographs, audio clips, and even video streams to your projects, making them unique and engaging. Let's get to work!

Adding Photos to Your Project

Suppose you visited Greece this past summer and you want to use Scratch to create an educational slideshow featuring the pictures that you've taken. How can you get this great idea off the ground with a minimum of muss, fuss, or greasy aftertaste?

You learn how to upload your own Stage backdrops in Hour 21, "Creating Your Own Sprites and Backdrops"; that procedure works just as well for your photo files. In this section, you learn how you can add your photos as sprites; this gives you much greater control over their animation within the project.

Before getting to the specific click-through procedure, let's quickly review the popular image formats that Scratch supports.

Image Formats That Are Supported by Scratch

Because Scratch 2.0 is an Adobe Flash-based web application, the environment supports all of the contemporary image formats, including the following:

▶ `.jpg`: This bitmap format, pronounced *JAY-peg*, yields small files, but with the caveat that you lose resolution and clarity heavily as you zoom the image.

▶ `.gif`: This bitmap format, pronounced *GIHf*, has a low color saturation (256 colors maximum, actually), but is useful for small black-and-white line art as well as for animated GIF "movies."

▶ `.png`: This bitmap format, pronounced *PING*, gives you the flexibility of `.jpg` with the lossless resolution of `.gif`. This is the preferred still image format for the Web.

▶ `.svg`: This format, pronounced *ess-vee-gee*, actually uses vector lines instead of a bitmap, yielding great clarity at any magnification. As of this writing, `.svg` is not a good format for photos, but only for relatively low-color line art.

Performing Pre-Upload Surgery on Your Pictures

Before you upload your photos to Scratch, you need to undertake a bit of surgery on your files. Why? Well, number one, the smaller the external assets that you include in your Scratch project, the faster it will run and the happier your users will be. Number two, the Stage is of limited dimension (480×360, you'll recall). Thus, it's pointless uploading an image file that is larger than those dimensions.

The following laundry list of image-processing tips has been used to good effect:

▶ **If you plan to do a lot of image processing, consider buying a dedicated tool**: You don't need to spend hundreds of dollars on Adobe Photoshop Lightroom (http://is.gd/1Q2OhK) to get good image-processing performance. The GIMP tool (http://is.gd/q8Axq1) discussed in Hour 21 is a wonderful image-processing Swiss Army Knife.

▶ **Resize your images proportionally to be at or below 480×360 resolution**: Remember that Scratch 2.0 isn't the place to display high-fidelity artwork or images. If you want to show off your beautiful photos and do them justice, consider putting them on Flickr (http://is.gd/F1u71Q) or another service.

▶ **Consider cropping if you can't resize too much**: If resizing an image results in either distortion or too low a detail, then consider using a tool like GIMP and cropping the image instead. Cropping refers to removing parts of an image that you don't want, thereby implicitly focusing on the areas of the photograph that are most important.

▶ **Compression matters**: Although scaling down your photo to smaller dimensions will necessarily reduce the overall file size, you should use your image-editing software to compress the image as much as acceptable. Remember—the larger your Scratch projects assets are, the slower the project will function, both behind the scenes at design time and on the public project page at runtime.

In the following Try It Yourself exercise, you practice uploading and working with an imported image file.

TRY IT YOURSELF ▼

Use Your Own Photos in a Scratch Project

In this Try It Yourself exercise, you upload your own image to a new Scratch project. While you're here, you also use the built-in Camera Capture tool to snap a webcam picture on the fly and add that to the project. If you are stuck for a picture, you can use my `zoeycat.jpg` file from the book's code archive. The completed file is located there under the filename `Hour14a.sb2`.

As always, I encourage you to work through the following steps to complete the exercise.

1. In a new Scratch project, select the Stage and use the Paint New Backdrop ⁄ and Fill 🖌 tools to create two additional backdrops. Fill all three backdrops with a different solid color, and leave the default backdrop names: backdrop1, backdrop2, and backdrop3.

2. In the Sprites list, delete the default Cat sprite by right-clicking it and selecting Delete from the shortcut menu. Next, click Upload Sprite from File 📤 and browse your computer to locate your desired photo. After you click OK in the Open dialog box and wait a moment, you should see your new photo in the list as a new sprite.

3. Now click the New Sprite from Camera  button so you can take a webcam snapshot. You may (and hopefully will) be prompted for access in the dialog box shown in Figure 14.1. This dialog box is a security measure that is intended to protect you against web-based programs accessing your webcam and/or microphone remotely without your express permission.

FIGURE 14.1
Adobe Flash includes built-in security to prevent unauthorized access to your webcam and microphone.

After you give Adobe Flash permission to access your webcam, you can pose, smile, and click Save to take the snapshot. Your snapshot shows up in the Sprites list right alongside your uploaded picture file.

4. Now that you have your images uploaded and your Stage backdrops filled in, you'll write some simple Scratch block code to walk the player through them. As you complete the remaining steps in this exercise, you can use Figure 14.2 as a guide to help explain the process.

5. Start with the uploaded pic. Select that sprite and navigate to its Scripts pane. In the code section labeled A in Figure 14.2, the **show** block is used to ensure that the image is visible when the user starts the project. After a 1-second pause, you ask the user a simple question and wait for his or her response.

The block includes a Boolean expression that tests "Did the player answer 'yes' to the question?" If yes, then you proceed to the next phase of the project by sending a broadcast named NextScreen. If the player types any other response, you end the project.

Finally, in the code section labeled B in the figure, the picture responds to its own broadcast by turning invisible. You'll see why this is necessary in just a moment.

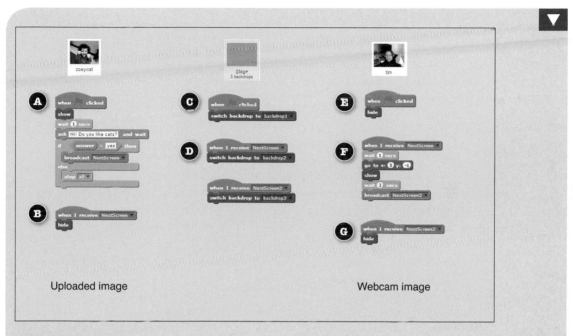

FIGURE 14.2
Source code for the Use Your Own Photos in a Scratch Project Try It Yourself exercise.

6. Code the Stage second. Select the Stage and navigate to its Scripts pane. In the code section labeled C in the figure, you force backdrop1 to appear as your starting sprite. In the code section labeled D, you respond to the NextScreen message that was sent out by your uploaded pic; when this happens, you switch to Stage backdrop2. In the next step, you create one more broadcast named NextScreen2. After doing that, return here and add the

   `when I receive message1` Hat block that switches to the final backdrop.

7. Finally, code the webcam pic. In the code section labeled E in the figure, you hide the sprite by default when the interaction is started with the Green Flag. In the code section labeled F, you respond to the first broadcast, NextScreen, by waiting a second and then showing the snapshot in a specific location on the Stage. After another pause, you send out your second broadcast, this one named NextScreen2. In the code section labeled G, you respond to your own NextScreen2 broadcast by hiding from the project.

8. Test the project by clicking the Green Flag. Does the Stage backdrop change as you move through the two broadcasts? Do the two images show up properly? Does the first image process user input correctly?

Adding Audio to Your Project

Off the top of my head, I can think of many applications for audio in my Scratch projects. Perhaps you want a long-running instrumental clip to play in the background throughout the run cycle of your project. Or maybe you want individual sprites to emit a sound effect when particular events happen on the Stage.

Recall that sprites as well as the Stage have a Sounds tab where you can attach audio to a sprite. In terms of audio clip possibilities, you can add audio to the project in one of three ways:

▶ **Choose Sound from Library** ◀ button: Here, you can import an audio clip from the built-in Scratch Asset Library. Although the library consists of several dozen clips of various lengths, they get old fast because all Scratchers in the world have simultaneous access to them.

▶ **Record New Sound** ◀ button: Here, you can access your webcam microphone to record your own audio directly into the Scratch Editor.

▶ **Upload Sound from File** ◀ button: Here, you can upload an audio clip that is stored on your computer.

About Fair Use

I'm not an attorney, but my understanding of copyright law is fairly sharp because I am a content provider myself and, I'm sad to say, I've had my work pirated all over the world for a number of years now. Please avoid using audio clips that are under copyright protection.

Yes, the United States has "fair use" laws that allow you to borrow clips from copyright-protected audio of up to 30 seconds. However, in my humble opinion, the safest way to go is either to (1) use royalty-free audio assets, (2) ask the content owner for permission and give proper attribution in your project, or (3) record your own audio.

I'm a fan of the third option because I'm a creative person and any assets that you build from scratch are globally unique. Unique is compelling—highly compelling—in the software development world.

Audio File Formats

Like graphic files, audio files also embrace many formats and file types. However, for Internet use, let's focus on the most common ones:

▶ `.mp3`: This format is ubiquitous and popular because it yields good quality audio at a small file size. Moreover, MP3s are playable by almost every platform in the world.

- ► **.wav:** This format is popular for small sound clips. Its disadvantage is that the audio is uncompressed, resulting in bigger-than-desired file sizes. Remember that you want to keep your Scratch projects as "lean and mean" as possible.

- ► **.wma:** This format is proprietary to Microsoft, which limits the contexts in which the clips can be played back.

- ► **.mid:** This format is excellent for small, simple audio clips and jingles. Its audio fidelity can't match the other formats, but any computer system in the world can typically play .mid files.

The preceding list of audio formats is far from comprehensive; you can read about other popular formats, such as .aac, .ogg, .aiff, .flac, and others, at the Scratch Wiki (http://is.gd/FQ4U82).

Friends, I have some good or bad news for you, depending upon your perspective. Scratch 2.0 supports only the .mp3 and .wav audio formats, primarily due to architectural limitations with Adobe Flash. What this means for you, practically speaking, is that you need to convert your .wma or .mid files to the .mp3 or .wav format before the clips are usable within Scratch 2.0.

NOTE
Converting MIDI Audio to MP3

The obvious question is "How can I convert my .mid files to .mp3 so I can use them in my Scratch 2.0 projects?" The answer is that you can use an online or offline service to perform this action for you. For online converters, I've had good luck with Sol Me Re (http://is.gd/Q2n1cH). As far as desktop applications go to perform .mid to .mp3 conversion, you can't go wrong with Audacity (http://is.gd/BgKPrZ).

Besides the file type issue, when you want to include audio in your projects, you are always faced with counterbalancing audio quality on one hand with file size and performance on the other. Get used to resolving these balancing acts; they are the daily task of the computer programmer.

It is also important that you know that the MIT Scratch Team imposes a 50MB limit on Scratch projects and a 10MB limit on individual uploaded assets. So in case you were wondering, yes, there are indeed hard limits on resources, even in the ethereal world of cloud-based storage!

Uploading and Editing an Audio Clip

To set the stage (as it were) for your next Try It Yourself exercise, fire up a new blank project, give it a name, and import the Jay sprite from the People category of the Sprite Library. Now select the Stage and nab the bench with view backdrop. Oh, you might want to delete the default Scratch Cat sprite as well.

You need to obtain an audio clip for use in this exercise; you can find some cool royalty-free .mp3 clips at Sound Jay (http://is.gd/b0Qkar). As always, work through the following steps and cross-reference the exhibit to complete the exercise.

▼ TRY IT YOURSELF

Integrate Audio into a Scratch Project

In this Try It Yourself exercise, you experiment with uploaded and recorded audio. You also get a handle on the basic audio editing tools that are built in to Scratch 2.0. If you want to use my assets, then that's wonderful: You can find `barn-beat-01.mp3` (which I downloaded from Sound Jay at http://is.gd/6wKBln) and `tim-voice.mp3` in the book's code archive. The completed project file is named (as if you couldn't guess by now) `Hour14b.sb2`.

1. Use the Shrink ⊠ tool to resize the Jay sprite so that he fits more appropriately in the bench with view Stage backdrop, as shown in Figure 14.3.

FIGURE 14.3
Stage and sprite setup for the Integrate Audio into a Scratch Project Try It Yourself exercise.

2. You'll now upload a clip to run in the background as a sort of soundtrack. Click the Stage and navigate to the Sounds panel. Use the Upload Sound from File 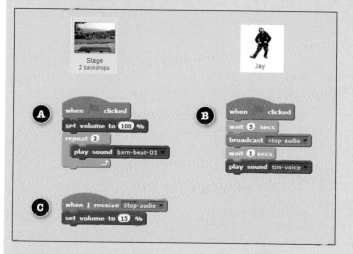 button to locate either my barn beat `.mp3` clip or one of your jingles. You might see a Converting MP3 message box appear depending upon the size of the uploaded audio file.

3. Look at Figure 14.4 to see this project's source code. In the code section labeled A, code the Stage to play the audio clip twice by using a `repeat 10` block from the Control palette and the `play sound meow ▼` stack block from the Sounds panel. Of course, you could use the `forever` block if you wanted the clip to loop throughout the entire run of the project; it's up to you.

FIGURE 14.4
Source code for the Integrate Audio into a Scratch Project Try It Yourself exercise.

4. Now select the Jay sprite and navigate to the Sounds panel. Click Record New Sound 🎤 to connect to your computer's microphone; if you are prompted by Adobe Flash to give permission to access your webcam and microphone, approve the request. The Sound Editor appears.

5. Adjust the Microphone volume slider and, when you're ready, click Record ⏺ to start your recording. Click Stop ⏹ when you're finished.

As you can see in Figure 14.5, your recorded audio shows up in the editor as what is called a waveform; this is a digital representation of your analog audio wave.

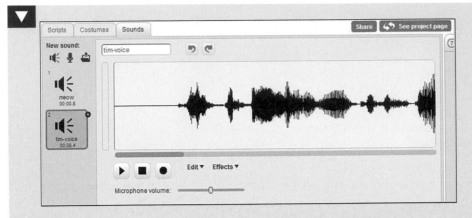

FIGURE 14.5
The Scratch 2.0 audio editor gives you basic control over the clip's waveform.

   6. Before coding the clip, let's see what's possible in terms of editing. Using your mouse, click and drag within the waveform to make a selection. For instance, select a long pause if one exists in your audio. Notice that the highlighted area turns blue.

   Open the Edit and Effects menus in the Audio Editor to see what audio editing options are available. For instance, click Edit, Cut to remove the selection from the audio clip. Next, make another selection and click Effects, Louder. This is pretty cool stuff, isn't it?

   7. Now let's go to the sprite's Scripts pane and wire in the audio. Check out the code section labeled B in Figure 14.4; here, you wait 5 seconds while the background sound plays at 100 percent volume, and then you send out a broadcast named stop-audio. Remember that to create a broadcast, you pick up a **broadcast** message1 Stack block from the Events palette, open its drop-down list, and select New Message.

   What does the stop-audio message do? In the code section labeled C in Figure 14.4, you can see that the Stage lowers the background audio volume so you can hear your recorded clip better.

   8. Click the Green Flag to test. Does the background audio clip start playing at 100 percent volume? Does it fade appropriately into the background so you can hear your recorded clip?

NOTE

Taking the Next Step with Your Audio Editing

If you want greater control over audio recording and editing, then I enthusiastically recommend Audacity (http://is.gd/BgKPrZ) to you. Audacity is free, is open source, runs on Windows and Mac, and has the same audio tools found in expensive commercial software. What's more is that Audacity is richly documented; you can find tutorials on YouTube, in the blogosphere, and beyond. While we're on the subject, we at Pearson published a compact eBook called *Podcasting with Audacity* that you may like (http://is.gd/M7M5yd).

Adding Video to Your Project

I'm sure that you aren't the first Scratcher who thought of integrating a video clip into a project. Is this possible? Yes and no. What a reply, right?

The truth is that you can, in fact, import content from videos into your Scratch projects, so long as you keep the following limitations in mind:

- ▶ 10MB file size limit for all uploaded project assets
- ▶ No sound capability in video clips

However, the reason why I answered "no" to the previous question is because you cannot natively display video files in your Scratch project. Instead, you must import the video as a multicostumed sprite.

Common Video Formats

Let's buzz through the most common video formats on the Web today:

- ▶ `.mov`: This is the Apple QuickTime movie format.
- ▶ `.mp4`: This is the vendor-neutral version of the `.mov` format.
- ▶ `.avi`: This is a video format that is supported by Microsoft Windows, but not so much by Macs, Linux computers, and mobile devices.
- ▶ `.mpg`: This is a vendor-neutral format that is often used for downloadable movies.
- ▶ `.flv`: This is Adobe Flash video; its highly proprietary nature limits its usability.

Of course, this list is not comprehensive; hit the Web (a nice summary can be found at http://is.gd/0qW3QU) to learn about additional video file formats.

So How Does This Work?

Suppose you used your cell phone to record a cute video of your cat and you want to include the clip in your current Scratch project. As mentioned earlier, you cannot import the movie directly but instead must import the clip as a multicostumed sprite. How the heck does this suggestion work in practice?

In practice, you need to convert your video clip to an animated GIF format. You've seen animated GIFs all over the place on the Web, I'm sure. Animated GIFs need to be relatively brief (10 seconds or so) to keep file size and complexity down, and they have a limited color palette (256 colors) and absolutely no audio. However, beggars can't be choosers, am I right?

Because so many people in the world, much less Scratchers, have need to convert their video clips to animated GIF format, quite a market has sprung up to meet this demand. For instance, you can use any of the following free online services to make your animated GIFs:

▶ GIFMaker.me (http://is.gd/ORDn0y)

▶ imgflip (http://is.gd/Bw6HhN)

▶ Picasion (http://is.gd/3FrIQt)

By contrast, if you are more comfortable using a desktop application to make the conversion instead of sharing your source video clip with some random website, you can investigate any of the following software products:

▶ GIMP (Windows and Mac, http://is.gd/q8Axq1)

▶ Easy GIF Animator (Windows, http://is.gd/Yxnu6U)

▶ Microsoft GIF Animator (Windows, http://is.gd/LQbXh2)

▶ GIF Brewery (Mac, http://is.gd/QX9PGm)

▶ GIFfun (Mac, http://is.gd/oCLO7N)

Complete the following Try It Yourself exercise to see how this process works. Start a new, blank project and set it up with the following parameters:

▶ Delete the Scratch Cat sprite.

▶ Use the Fill [⬧] tool in the Paint Editor to change the default Stage backdrop to a darker, more neutral (and eye-friendly) color. This will be your video backdrop, so even black is appropriate.

▶ Obtain an animated GIF image—if you are absolutely stuck, feel free to use my `tim-video.gif` from the book's code archive. By the way, you can see my original video clip with sound in the archive as well; the filename is `tim-video.mp4`.

Add Video to a Scratch Project

This Try It Yourself exercise is pretty self-explanatory; you add an animated GIF file as a sprite, and then play back the content on the Stage. The completed solution file is named `Hour14c.sb2`. Try to complete the following steps without relying on the solution file, though. The feeling of accomplishment you'll get by doing so can't be beat!

1. In the Sprites list, click the Upload Sprite from File button and browse to your target animated GIF. After a moment's pause, you should see the sprite appear, as shown in Figure 14.6.

   Navigate to the sprite's Costumes panel and observe that every frame in the animated GIF file is now a separate costume.

FIGURE 14.6
Notice that Scratch split up the animated GIF file into multiple costume frames.

2. Click the Green Flag. Does the animated GIF sprite play? No? Why not? Well, you need to code the costume change yourself, that's why. Check out Figure 14.7, then position the sprite on Stage and then loop through the costumes with a `forever` block and a `next costume` block.

FIGURE 14.7
Source code for the Add Video to a Scratch Project Try It Yourself exercise.

3. Why do you think that I added a .2 second delay with a `wait 1 secs` block? Try changing the .2 to 0, and then rerun the project. I think you'll figure out why the delay is necessary pretty quickly. Experiment with different delay values to see how this affects the video clip.

NOTE

Hacking Scratch

If you don't mind working in Scratch 1.4, you can play around with the Scratch Movie Player Morph to play honest-to-goodness movie clips inside your Scratch projects. Read more about this hack at the Scratch Wiki at http://is.gd/yliRlh.

What About Hyperlinks and Interactivity?

Speaking for myself, I wasn't a Scratcher for very long before I discovered that I wanted to add hyperlinks to my project. For instance, I might want to point the player to another Scratch project from within my project. Or perhaps I developed my own Adobe Flash interaction and wanted to pop that into my Scratch project?

Sadly, neither clickable hyperlinks nor embedded Flash content are supported by Scratch 2.0. Nevertheless, if you browse the project gallery you'll find Scratchers attempting both of these actions (for instance, see this project for a hacky workaround to the hyperlink problem: http://is.gd/xioFSh). The trouble with these projects is that very few (if any) of the hacks actually work in practice.

Summary

You've learned in this hour that audio clips are much easier to implement in Scratch projects than are video clips. To be sure, you now know how to upload your own audio clips, as well as record and edit your own sounds from within the Scratch 2.0 audio editor interface.

You are well armed with the facts regarding project and asset size limitations. You also know how to convert video clips to animated GIF format, and then import and play those GIFs in your projects.

Workshop

Quiz

1. Which of the following audio formats is *not* supported by Scratch 2.0?

    A. `.wav`

    B. `.mp3`

    C. `.wma`

2. In which format does your video clip need to be in before you can add it to your Scratch 2.0 project?

    A. `.gif`

    B. `.mp4`

    C. `.avi`

3. Which of the following blocks can be used to control the playback speed of an imported animated GIF?

    A.

    B.

    C.

Answers

1. The correct answer is choice C. The only audio file formats that are directly supported by Scratch 2.0 are `.mp3` and `.wav`. If you have an audio clip in another format, then you need to convert it before you upload it into the Scratch 2.0 Editor.

2. The correct answer is choice A. The only video-type format that is supported by Scratch 2.0 is the animated GIF, which Scratch separates into frames.

3. The correct answer is choice C. Of the three choices given, the ⬚`wait ① secs` block is best for controlling the rate at which your animated GIF sprite costumes rotate.

Challenge

Your challenge for this hour is an interesting one: Create a Scratch project that includes an animated GIF sprite, but that has an audio track that plays simultaneously and tracks with the video as closely as possible! For instance, you can try to accomplish this goal by using the `tim-video.gif` and `tim-voice.mp3` assets if you want. You can find my attempt at solving this programming challenge in file `Hour14d.sb2`.

Creating Your Own Blocks

What You'll Learn in This Hour:

▶ Spending some time with layers

▶ Understanding custom blocks

▶ Creating custom blocks in Scratch 2.0

▶ Building your own blocks in Snap!

A common phrase that is used by teachers to describe the Scratch programming environment is that it has "a low floor, a high ceiling, and wide walls." What the heck does that "teacher-speak" room metaphor mean? Let me tell you:

▶ **Low floor:** Beginners can get up and running in Scratch quickly and easily.

▶ **High ceiling:** Scratch supports enough features to give Scratchers a challenge no matter what their programming skill level is.

▶ **Wide walls:** Scratch is extensible, which means that Scratchers can extend the functionality and application of Scratch in novel ways.

This hour focuses on the "wide walls" aspect of the room metaphor. You learn all about the "build your own blocks" functionality in Scratch 2.0, as well as an important Scratch extension called Snap! Before doing that, however, now is as good a time as ever to learn about another awesome extension to Scratch—creating simulated 3D environments by using layers. Let's get started.

Spending Some Time with Layers

For all intents and purposes, Scratch 2.0 is a two-dimensional development environment. Have you ever heard of Alice? Alice (http://is.gd/53sbC3) is a free, beginner's programming toolkit that focuses specifically on creating three-dimensional environments. It's pretty cool—check out the interface screenshot shown in Figure 15.1.

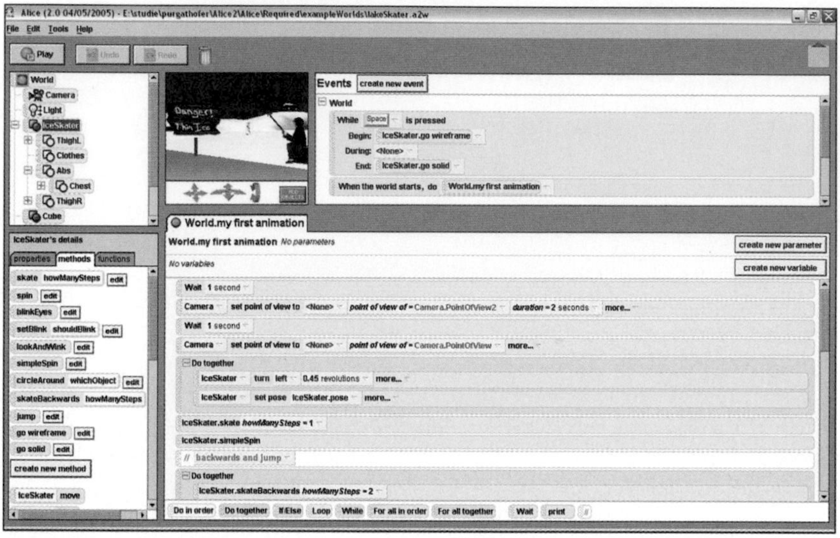

FIGURE 15.1
Alice can teach you a lot about 3D game programming. Interface screenshot courtesy of Wikipedia (http://is.gd/lpM55v).

Programmers often use the term *hack* to describe a creative workaround to a problem. The adjectival version of the word is hacky. Thus, you are about to learn a somewhat hacky method for simulating a 3D environment in Scratch 2.0.

How Layers Work in Scratch

Have you ever used transparency sheets? When I was in college (early 90s, before the ubiquitous nature of laptops and LCD projectors), all my professors wrote their notes on transparency sheets and put them up for the class to see by using an overhead projector.

Layers in Scratch work very much like stacked transparency sheets (or stacked sheets of paper, for that matter). The sprite on top of the stack is said to occupy layer 1. Check out Figure 15.2, in which you can see that if you move a sprite back from layer 1, it's at layer 2, and so forth.

NOTE

Viewing Sprite Layer Information

Sadly, it is not possible to view a sprite's current layer value through the Scratch Editor interface. The Scratch Wiki (http://is.gd/w5xeBO) describes a method where you can download your project and read the layer assignments for all sprites by examining the `.json` manifest file in a project archive.

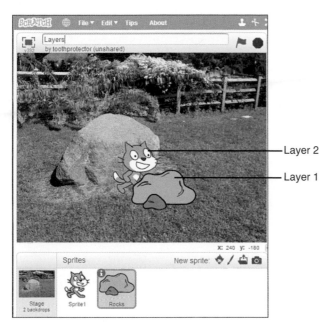

Layer 2

Layer 1

FIGURE 15.2
Here, you can see how layers are ordered in Scratch 2.0.

Layer Blocks

Four Scratch blocks provide (limited) control over layers; Table 15.1 summarizes those blocks.

TABLE 15.1 Layer-Oriented Blocks in Scratch 2.0

Block Image	Block Type	Block Category	Description
go to front	Stack	Looks	Places the sprite at layer 1, in front of all other sprites
go back ❶ layers	Stack	Looks	Changes a sprite's layer value by a specified amount
show variable	Stack	Data	Shows a variable's Stage monitor and places the object at layer 1
show list	Stack	Data	Shows a list's Stage monitor and places the object at layer 1

Perhaps the best way for you to get a handle on using layers in Scratch 2.0 is to take on a Try It Yourself exercise. Are you ready?

▼ TRY IT YOURSELF

Use Layers

In this Try It Yourself exercise, you create a simple project that does nothing else but shows you how layers work in Scratch 2.0. If you want to see a project that truly shows off the power of layers in a Scratch game, then check out Robot_man's project Realistic Jump Test (http://is.gd/TM9X6t). That game, in my humble opinion, contains the seeds of a truly great Scratch-based side-scrolling arcade game!

In any event, you can find the completed file in the book's code archive; the filename is `Hour15a.sb2`. Work through the following steps to complete the exercise:

1. Fire up a new project, select the Stage, and change the backdrop to something more appropriate to the purposes of this exercise. For example, choose the boardwalk backdrop from the Outdoors section of the Backdrop Library.

2. Keep the Scratch Cat sprite, but click the Paint New Sprite button to create a new sprite in the Paint Editor. Use the Rectangle tool to draw a rectangle; click elsewhere to see the sprite on Stage.

   If the rectangle is too big or too small, click Undo and try again. When you're happy, select the Fill tool, choose a color, and then click inside the rectangle shape to fill it in.

3. Now go to the Sprites list, right-click the first rectangle, and select Duplicate from the shortcut menu. In the Paint Editor, use the Fill tool to apply a different fill color.

4. Rename the sprites Cat, Rect1, and Rect2, respectively. Position the three sprites on Stage, as shown in Figure 15.3. Note that the Cat sprite is directly behind Rect2.

5. Now let's have some fun with the code (follow along with Figure 15.4). First, program the project such that after a 3-second delay after clicking the Green Flag, the Cat pops to the front of both rectangles.

   How can you do that? Look at the code section labeled A in Figure 15.4; when the Green Flag is clicked, you reset the Cat's position, move to the top of the layer stack, and then move back two layers. After a 1-second delay, you go to the front, delay for 2 seconds, and then send out a broadcast you can call switch1.

6. Now let's add some code to Rect1. In the code section labeled B, you reset the sprite's position on Stage and set it back just one layer, so that the sprite is in front of the Cat in the stack. When Rect1 receives the switch1 broadcast message (see the code section labeled C), you move to layer 1 and glide in front of the Cat, totally eclipsing the Cat in the project. You then send out the switch2 broadcast. Note that in the code section labeled D, Rect1 responds to its own switch2 broadcast, moves to layer 2 (remember that layer 1 is the front), and glides out of the way on Stage to the left.

7. Look at Rect2's script now. In the code section labeled E, you reset the sprite at the run of the project, but, more important, you put the sprite in layer 2 and glide to the right when it receives the switch2 broadcast event (see the code section labeled F).

8. Finally, return to the Cat sprite. In the code section labeled G, you put the Cat on layer 1 and position it between the two rectangles so you can clearly see the layer overlap. You've done some interesting choreography in this exercise; shouldn't you receive some sort of award or something?

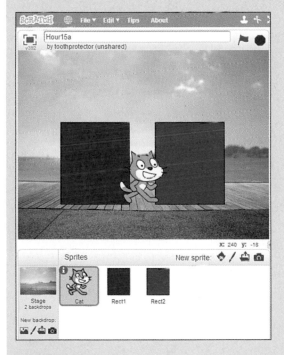

FIGURE 15.3
The sprite setup for the Use Layers Try It Yourself exercise.

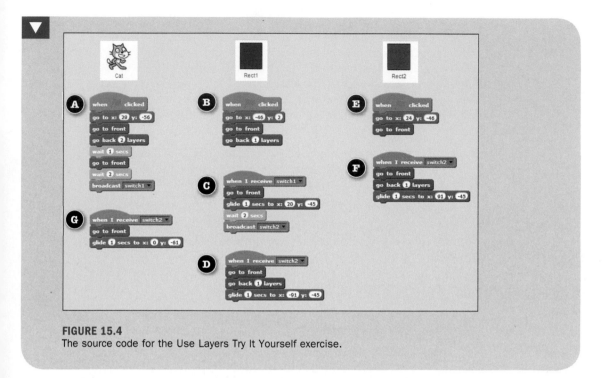

FIGURE 15.4
The source code for the Use Layers Try It Yourself exercise.

Understanding Custom Blocks

Now, turn your attention to the concept of creating your own blocks in Scratch 2.0. This was certainly a highly anticipated feature among Scratchers when the MIT Scratch Team first announced that it planned to include this capability in version 2.0 of the software.

However, I must confess that the initial iteration of the "build your own blocks" idea falls a little flat, as you'll see more clearly as you proceed through the rest of this hour.

First of all, Scratch 2.0 custom blocks cannot, by themselves, extend the functionality of Scratch. Blocks that you create yourself in the Scratch Editor can encapsulate existing functionality, but you cannot add any features or functions that aren't already a part of the Scratch 2.0 toolset.

Second, custom blocks cannot be shared (easily) among sprites in a project. This is the biggest disadvantage of Scratch's custom blocks functionality. After all, doesn't it stand to reason that you would want your custom code to be accessible to all sprites at once?

But Is There a Silver Lining?

Enough negativity—is there any advantage to the "create your own blocks" feature? Yes, and its name is *encapsulation*. This fancy term refers to taking a potentially long procedure and packaging it up for easy reuse.

As a programmer, you want to avoid repetitive tasks as much as possible. After all, isn't grinding through boring tasks one of the reasons to use computer programs in the first place?

The cool thing about custom blocks is that instead of having to re-create or clone a script over and over again, you can define the procedure once in a custom block, and then invoke that function in the future by using a single block.

Let's look at a concrete example so the concept is clearer: Imagine you created a script that simulates a realistic jump action that includes the effect of gravity. Suppose that script involved a stack of 50 blocks.

Now suppose you want a sprite to make that gravity-enabled jump several times at various points throughout the runtime of your project. Are you going to clone or retype that 50-block script over and over again as needed?

No—instead, you encapsulate all the jump function code into a single stack block. Whenever you need the function, you drop in the single custom block and you're done. That's pretty handy, isn't it? It's called *code reuse*, and it is one of the guiding principles of any professional coder.

Anatomy and Physiology of a Custom Block

In the Scratch Editor, mosey on over to the More Blocks palette and click Make a Block. The New Block dialog box appears, as shown in Figure 15.5.

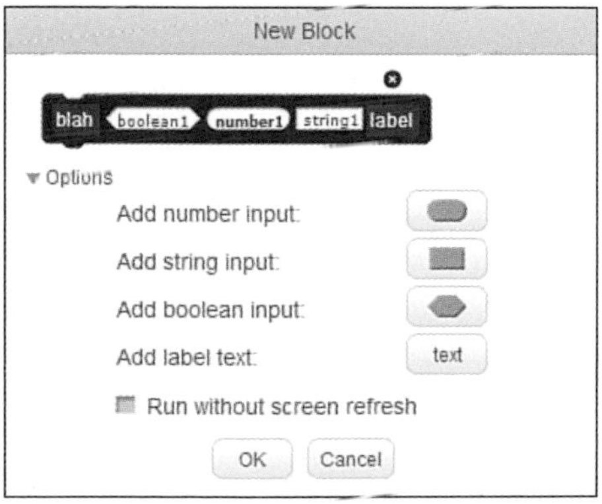

FIGURE 15.5
The New Block dialog box. Clicking Options expands the dialog box to show the various input and data refresh parameters.

Type *My New Block* in the purple block and click OK. Notice that you are presented with a Hat block that appears on the current sprite's Scripts panel and a new stack block; these are shown in Figure 15.6 and described in the following list. Don't be put off by my "blah" placeholder text in Figure 15.6—I suppose I wasn't feeling particularly imaginative that day.

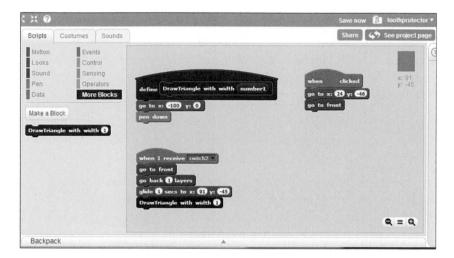

FIGURE 15.6
When you create your own custom block, the new block is attached to the currently selected sprite, and actually consists of at least two blocks.

▶ **Define block:** This Hat block is where you add your custom code that describes the actual functionality of your custom block.

▶ **Stack block:** This stack block is used when you want to insert the code you created in your Define block into the current sprite's script.

If you decide to add one or more input parameters to your custom block, you have additional Boolean and reporter blocks to work with. You'll learn how to use inputs later in this chapter.

NOTE

What Is a Function?

The custom block is an analog to what professional programmers call a function. A function is a named block of code that performs one or more actions, returns a specific result, and can be reused at various levels within a project. The custom stack block is analogous to what professional programmers call a function call, in which a function is invoked in code.

Creating Custom Blocks in Scratch 2.0

Let's get this party started! In the next Try It Yourself exercise, you create a custom block named Jump that makes the sprite leap skyward with a realistic velocity. I borrowed the algorithm for this jump function from the previously mentioned project Realistic Jump Test (http://is.gd/TM9X6t).

As you know, all the source code for the projects is provided with labels in the figures and descriptions in the text. Because the Jump algorithm is such a long block, this section just explains the logic and, later in the chapter, Figure 15.9 shows a truncated version of the block.

Basically, you're going to use the `change y by 10` and `wait 1 secs` blocks to move the sprite up and then down in very small, stepwise increments. Check out Figure 15.7, which shows you a smaller-scale example.

FIGURE 15.7
The algorithm you use to make your sprites jump realistically.

It's Time to Practice

In the upcoming Try It Yourself exercise, you want the sprite to jump pretty high, so you give the first `change y by 10` block an initial value of 18 pixels, and then count down from there. Now imagine if you copied and pasted this Jump routine 10 times in a sprite's script! This is where the custom Define and stack blocks can truly help.

To set up for the Jumping Sprites Try It Yourself exercise, fire up a new project in the online Scratch Editor (as you'll see, you need to use the online editor for this because you need the Backpack, and as of this writing, the Backpack has not made it into the Scratch 2.0 Offline Editor).

Next, use the Paint Editor to edit the default Stage backdrop and sprites cast to look something like what is shown in Figure 15.8:

▶ Use the Rectangle ▬ tool to draw a "land" shape at the bottom of the Stage.

▶ Use the Fill ◆ tool to fill in the land shape with green or brown.

▶ Use the Fill ◆ tool to fill in the sky with a blue shade.

▶ Use the Paint New Sprite ✏ tool to draw a cloud. I drew the cloud by using the Paint Editor's Brush 🖌 tool, and set the line and fill color to white.

▶ Use the Choose Sprite from Library ◆ tool to bring in the Sun sprite from the Things category of the Sprite Library.

▶ Bring in the Crab sprite from the Animals category of the Sprite Library.

▶ Rename the sprites to Cat, Crab, Cloud, and Sun, as appropriate.

FIGURE 15.8
The sprite setup for the Jumping Sprites Try It Yourself exercise.

Jumping Sprites

This Try It Yourself exercise gives you the opportunity to experiment with the "build your own blocks" functionality in Scratch 2.0. Here, you program the Cat sprite such that pressing the up arrow key makes him jump. You program the Crab such that she jumps when you press the U key. You include layers in this project to tie in what you learned earlier in this hour with what you're doing now.

Make sure that you set up your project like what you see in Figure 15.8. You can find the sample version of the completed project in the book's code archive; the filename is `Hour15b.sb2`. As has become your habit, work through the following steps to complete the exercise:

1. Begin by coding the Cat sprite. In the code section labeled A in Figure 15.9, you start the Cat's runtime environment by resetting its position on stage. The main ![forever] loop puts the Cat on the top layer (layer 1), and then responds if the player presses the up arrow key. You can create the custom Jump block by navigating to the More Blocks palette, clicking Make a Block, typing *Jump* in the block placeholder, clicking OK, and then dragging the new stack block into place. Easy as pie, right?

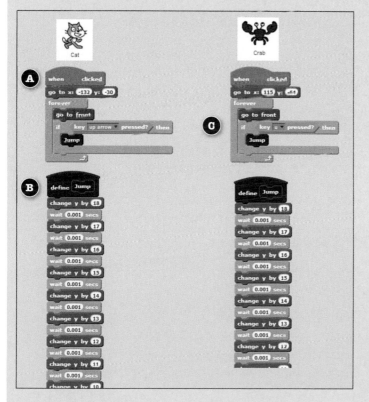

FIGURE 15.9
The source code for the Jumping Sprites Try It Yourself exercise.

2. In the code section labeled B in the figure, you see the source code for your custom Jump procedure. You can save yourself a lot of block dragging by creating one `change y by 10` / `wait 1 secs` couplet, clicking the Duplicate button from the top toolbar, and then clicking the top block in the stack. This tool makes short work out of repeating block stacks multiple times. In this example, the change Y values range from 18 to –18 because the sprite needs to return to the ground.

3. Now select the Crab and wire up that guy. Hmm—you need the same jump code for the Crab, but if you go to the More Blocks palette, you won't see the Jump block you defined for the Cat. Here, you bump against the aforementioned weakness of custom blocks—they are not shared among sprites.

   Go back to the Cat and drag the `when clicked` and Define scripts to the Backpack. Next, select the Crab and drag the scripts into its Scripts pane. If you see the Jump stack block show up as "Undefined," simply remove that block by dragging it into the Blocks palette, navigate to the More Blocks pane, and redrag a fresh Jump stack block into the script. In the code section labeled C, you can see that the only difference in the Crab's script is that you trigger on the U key instead of the spacebar. The reason you do this should be obvious; you need to avoid key binding collisions.

4. Now test the project by clicking the Green Flag and pressing the spacebar. Does the Cat jump realistically? Now press the U key; does the Crab move appropriately as well? The reason you implemented layers here is that you should see the sprites jump in front of the Cloud and Sun sprites instead of behind them. If the sprites jump behind the other sprites, you have a code problem to troubleshoot and resolve.

NOTE

What Is an Algorithm?

The term *algorithm* scares many of those who are new to computer programming. There is no reason to be intimidated! An algorithm is simply a step-by-step procedure intended to perform some calculation. The calculation does not necessarily have to be mathematical. For instance, a common Scratch algorithm is, in pseudocode, "When the player clicks the Green Flag, have the sprite say 'Hello' and wait for user input."

Implementing Custom Block Inputs

In programming, you define functions to easily reuse code blocks. Professional programmers can extend functions even further by including what are called input parameters. This is a string (alphanumeric) or numeric value that is passed to the function just before it executes.

Did you know that you can do the same basic thing with custom Scratch blocks? Yep—go back and reexamine Figure 15.5. If you expand Options in the New Block dialog box, you can include the following types of input parameters:

- ▶ **Add number Input:** Here, you can accept a numeric (integer or decimal fraction) value for runtime processing.

- ▶ **Add string input:** Here, you can accept an alphanumeric or nonalphanumeric character sequence as input.

- ▶ **Add Boolean input:** Here, you can include an expression that evaluates to a Boolean True or False value.

- ▶ **Add label text:** This isn't really an input parameter, but instead it's a way to make your custom block more descriptive.

The Run Without Screen Refresh option is useful when you want to improve project performance by instructing Scratch to run all code in your custom block all at once before refreshing the screen again. You might have noticed that sometimes the screen flickers when your code includes long control structures that loop (or iterate) over several values. Enabling this option reduces the screen flicker at the expense of some CPU cycles on your computer.

Let's do one final Try It Yourself exercise in this hour that gives you some practice with using string input with custom Scratch blocks. Start with the project you worked on in the previous Try It Yourself exercise; simply use the command File, Save as a Copy in the Scratch Editor to preserve the original file.

TRY IT YOURSELF ▼

Add Input to Custom Blocks

In this Try It Yourself exercise, you create a custom block to dynamically control what and for how long your Crab sprite says something in the project. The completed file can be found in the book's code archive under the name `Hour15c.sb2`. Work through the following steps to complete the exercise:

1. Select the Crab and navigate to its Scripts pane. From the More Blocks palette, click Make a Block as usual.

2. In the New Block dialog box, click Options to expand the input parameters choices. Type *say* in the custom block, and then click the Add String Input icon. Next, double-click in the white box in the custom block and type *text*. Finally, click the Add Label Text icon, and change the text to read *until SPACE is pressed*. Finally, click OK to complete the new block creation. You can see this in action in Figure 15.10.

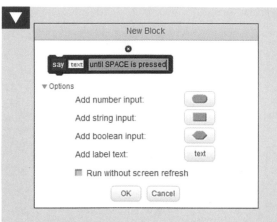

FIGURE 15.10
The New Block dialog box for the Add Input to Custom Blocks Try It Yourself exercise.

3. In Figure 15.10, you can see the procedure for the new Define block; essentially what's going on here is that any text you pass into the say until S is pressed stack block is "said" by the Crab sprite. The text balloon remains on the Stage unless and until the player presses the S key, after which the text balloon empties out. This is an ultrasimple example, but hopefully you get the idea of how you can parameterize your custom blocks. Figure 15.11 shows the Stage for this exercise.

FIGURE 15.11
The Stage and sprite setup for the Add Input to Custom Blocks Try It Yourself exercise.

4. When you run the project, what happens if you press the U key to instruct the Crab to jump? Does it work? If not, how can you refactor the code such that you can make the sprite jump before you press the S key to dismiss the **say Hello!** block? You might observe that your "Hello there" text appears behind the cloud. My challenge to you is to apply what you've learned about layers thus far to correct this minor glitch.

Many Scratchers find it as confusing that their inputs show up in the Define Hat block as reporter blocks. That isn't the confusing part, though. The befuddling part is that *the custom reporter blocks are not available anywhere in the Blocks palettes!*

This means that you need to take the nonintuitive action of dragging the reporter block, again and again, from the Define block into whatever other targets you have in your scripts. Annoying, isn't it? Hopefully, the MIT Scratch Team will correct this oversight in a future Scratch release.

Building Your Own Blocks in Snap!

Snap! (http://is.gd/s26Lr1), previously called Build Your Own Blocks (BYOB), is a Scratch 1.4 modification (mod) that uses JavaScript to render the Scratch 1.4 Editor interface in a web browser window. This means, among other things, that you can build Scratch projects on your iPad and other devices that don't play well with Adobe Flash.

NOTE

Investigating Scratch Mods

If you are interested in discovering more Scratch mods to see what's possible, please read the "List of Scratch Modifications" article in the Scratch Wiki (http://is.gd/PFEoVt).

This book draws your attention to the Snap! project at several points throughout the text. This is because the MIT Scratch Team actually takes some development queues from what the University of California at Berkeley group (that makes Snap!) does with its projects. Custom blocks are a good example of this, actually.

As you can see in Figure 15.12, Snap! gives you much, much greater control in your custom code than does Scratch 2.0. The primary downside to Snap! is that the project is a clone of Scratch 1.4 and not Scratch 2.0. Regardless, you should study Snap! because it will certainly broaden and deepen your understanding of what is possible in the "high ceiling" aspect of Scratch programming.

FIGURE 15.12
Snap! gives you great experience in building your own custom Scratch blocks.

Summary

In this hour, you learned how to extend the functionality of Scratch (to an extent) by implementing layers and custom blocks. If you are a fan of retro 2D side-scrolling action games, then you'll get a lot of mileage out of using layers in your Scratch projects. Moving backgrounds, anyone?

Although the implementation of custom blocks in Scratch 2.0 feels unfinished and is maddening in places, it's cool that you can make your projects smaller and potentially more efficient by encapsulating repetitive procedures into a custom code block.

As you learned, you cannot make custom blocks that are global to the project. However, you can leverage the Backpack functionality in the Scratch 2.0 online editor to share the Define code with other sprites. That's better than nothing, for sure!

Workshop

Quiz

1. If you have three sprites "stacked" on top of each other on the Stage, on which layer does the middle sprite reside?

    A. 0

    B. 1

    C. 2

2. When you create a custom block, on which Blocks palette does your new custom block appear?

    A. Data

    B. More Blocks

    C. Operators

3. Which custom block input evaluates an expression to a True or False value?

    A. Number

    B. String

    C. Boolean

Answers

1. The correct answer is choice C. The top layer in Scratch is called layer 1, and as you move back in the stack, each subsequent layer is labeled 2, 3, and so forth. What's confusing is that Scratch 2.0 has no onscreen way for determining to which layer a particular sprite belongs.

2. The correct answer is choice B. Your custom blocks always appear on the More Blocks palette in Scratch 2.0. By contrast, in Snap! you can have your custom block appear on the Blocks palette of your choosing, which makes more sense intuitively.

3. The correct answer is choice C. The Boolean input type allows you to build a mathematical or logical expression that evaluates to Boolean True or False into your custom block's code.

Challenge

Your challenge for this hour, should you choose to accept it (and I hope dearly that you do), involves you creating a custom block that creates a square. Here are the design parameters:

▶ Use the Pencil sprite to do the "drawing," and ensure that the drawing starts at the pencil's tip instead of in the center of the sprite.

▶ Program the custom block to create a 100 pixel × 100 pixel square shape.

▶ Create a numeric input for the custom block that determines the thickness of the square.

You can see a sample solution to this challenge by examining the file `Hour15e.sb2` in the book's code archive.

Documenting Your Project

What You'll Learn in This Hour:

▶ Commenting your code
▶ Working with pseudocode
▶ Wireframing and storyboarding
▶ Publicly documenting your Scratch project

This hour marks a change from what you've been doing in the book thus far. Rather than learn about specific Scratch commands, you'll now focus on documenting your Scratch project both privately and publicly.

What exactly does documentation mean from a software development standpoint? Why would you do it? Why is it important? By the end of this hour, you'll know answers to all three of these questions.

In this hour, you also tackle some related metaprogramming topics as they relate to Scratch 2.0. You examine the concepts of pseudocode and wireframing, two techniques that experienced programmers around the world use every day in software development.

Don't be afraid: Although you learn skills in this hour that are used by full-time computer programmers—and you might think of yourself as a new beginner—you are in the right place. You can handle this information, and it will make you a better programmer.

With that, let's get started by learning about documentation through code commenting.

Commenting Your Code

In general terms, a *comment* is simply an observation. In Scratch programming, or programming in general, a comment works basically the same way, with the exception that the comment persists indefinitely in the project source code (unless you delete it, of course).

You'll use comments in code for two main reasons:

▶ **For yourself**: As your projects become larger and more comprehensive, over time it can be difficult to remember your thinking when you developed certain procedures.

▶ **For others**: You know that Scratch is an open source software. Therefore, your code is available for others to see and understand. Leaving comments in your code provides signposts for others to learn from.

Some programmers feel more evangelistic about comments than others do. Yes, it's possible to go overboard with comments and clutter up your code with them; you want to avoid that, of course. In my own professional experience, I use comments both to explain my thinking when developing certain routines and also as a sort of to-do list.

That second point is an especially good one: As you code, you're likely to have ideas on how to improve the program in the future. Leave yourself a comment! That way, when the time comes, you can implement those changes and make your program that much better.

Adding Comments to Your Scratch Project

In Scratch 2.0, comments are implemented in two ways. You can leave standalone comments that are not attached to any particular script or block. This type of comment is ideal for more general remarks, to-do items, and so forth.

The other kind of comment is called a linked comment and is attached to a particular script block. It's important to note that Scratch ignores all comments when it runs your program. Comments are intended only for those human beings who examine the underlying Scratch code.

Before you undertake the first Try It Yourself exercise, log in to the Scratch website and create a new, blank project.

In the Scratch Editor, ensure that the default Scratch Cat is selected and navigate to the Scripts area. Next, build a simple script; it doesn't matter what the script does, that's not the point of this exercise.

▼ TRY IT YOURSELF

Add Comments to Your Scratch Project

In this Try It Yourself exercise, you'll gain some experience with documenting your Scratch project. Believe me, this is time well spent because, once you solidify your habit of annotating and explaining your code, you'll find other programmers flocking to your projects because they know that you're offering value. Follow these steps to complete the exercise:

1. Right-click an empty area of the Scripts window. In the shortcut menu that appears, click Add Comment.

2. A yellow comment block appears that bears a striking resemblance to a 3M Post-it Note. Add whatever text you want inside the note to complete your comment.

3. Note the resize handle in the lower-right corner of the comment block. Click and drag that to resize the comment.

4. Point your mouse at the upper-left corner of the comment block, and click the disclosure triangle. You'll find that comments exist in one of two states: either collapsed or expanded. Collapsing comments is useful to save space in the Scripts area.

5. Create another comment, and add some generic text again. Collapse the comment. Now drag the comment on top of one of your script blocks, and watch what happens.

   You should see that the comment is now attached to that particular block. The thin connector line could be thicker, in my humble opinion. You'll find that the comment connection line is painfully difficult to discern against some color backgrounds.

6. Now try moving around the script block. You should find that the comment travels along with its block no matter where you place it in the project. You can see an image of all these goings-on in Figure 16.1.

   You can detach an anchored comment from a block simply by dragging it away from its connected block.

7. To delete a comment, right-click the target comment and select Delete from the shortcut menu. Note that this is a permanent action; there is no Undo for this.

FIGURE 16.1
Comments can bring clarity to your Scratch projects.

NOTE
_____

Which Scratch Scripts Are the Most Popular?

In an interesting bit of trivia, the MIT Scratch Team conducted a survey of its users to identify the top scripts used by Scratchers. As it turns out, the comment block ranked 10th in the survey. The members of the Scratch Team were evidently very happy and surprised with these results, because code commenting is considered to be a programming best practice, and many Scratchers are first-time programmers.
_____

Comments Can Improve Your Project's Popularity

In my opinion, one of the "secret sauces" of Scratch project popularity is the judicious use of code comments. You should always remember that Scratch is an educational programming language and that many people will use your project as a springboard to help them learn programming themselves.

To that end, any effort that you put in to educating other Scratchers in how you designed your project will go a long way toward improving the popularity of your project and adding to the Scratch community ecosystem.

This idea speaks to one of the principal aspects of software development in general and in game design in particular: Always keep your user in the forefront of your mind. Always.

Working with Pseudocode

Have you ever been struck by a good idea, so much so that it sent you racing for the nearest pencil and paper so you could capture your thoughts before you forgot them?

As you gain experience with computer programming and Scratch, you'll have similar "light bulb" moments. Many programmers use a technique called *pseudocoding* as a way of documenting their ideas in a way that's fast and does not bog them down with having to remember arcane programming syntax.

As you probably know, the word *pseudo* comes from the Greek, meaning *fake* or *false*. Consequently, pseudocode is fake code that is not intelligible by Scratch or any other code interpreter. Instead, you use pseudocode to make your ideas clear, so that you (and perhaps other Scratchers) can understand what you were thinking when you return to it in the future.

For example, I've been at coffee shops, quietly sipping my espresso, when a great program idea jumps into my head. Because I carry around a notepad and a pen, I can seize the proverbial moment and write out the skeletal code for my idea by using plain English pseudocode.

You're probably wondering how to actually use pseudocode. Good question! Let's tackle that subject right away.

How to Use Pseudocode for Scratch Projects

Honestly, there is no one single tool that is preferred for writing pseudocode. You can use a pencil and paper, a text editor or word processor on your computer—the proverbial sky is the limit.

The main idea here is that you want to capture your code thoughts as quickly and efficiently as possible. You want to be able to take your pseudocode and use it in the future to create real, live Scratch scripts.

Although pseudocode doesn't use real programming syntax, the underlying logic and data structures do tend to mimic their real-life counterparts.

For instance, check out the following bit of pseudocode that I've come up with just now off the top of my head:

```
when green flag clicked
       go to x:0 y:0
       set volume to 100
       play drum 1 for 5 beats
```

That's some pretty simple code, but you get the general idea. Note that pseudocode isn't necessarily intended only for your consumption. One great place for you to share your pseudocode (or any Scratch scripts with which you're having problems) is the Scratch Forums at http://is.gd/S4ZeId.

As you browse the Scratch Forums, you're likely to observe the presence of realistic-looking Scratch scripts and blocks. What is that? How is that done?

What you're seeing is a web browser plug-in called the Block Plugin, or scratchblocks2 (http://is.gd/o3y9gB). This is an excellent web browser add-on developed by a Scratcher named blob8108 that allows Scratch block images to be rendered on a web page in a highly realistic manner.

The good news is that you don't need to know the underlying Block Plugin syntax to create pseudocode in Scratch discussion forum posts. In time, you'll greatly appreciate the convenience that the Block Plugin gives you when you post to the Scratch Forums.

One of these days, you'll hit a stumbling block with your Scratch code, and you'll want to enlist the help of other experienced Scratchers from around the world on the forums. To get the help, you'll need to share your code with them as accurately as possible.

Visit the Scratch Forums, navigate to the appropriate subforum and start a new discussion. In the body of your post, use the toolbar controls (that you'll learn to use in just a second; be patient) to build pseudo Scratch code scripts in full, glorious color, exactly as they appear in your own Scratch Editor.

Try the following Try It Yourself exercise to underscore this point.

▼ TRY IT YOURSELF

Experiment with the Scratch Block Plugin

To begin, point your web browser to the Scratch Discussion Forums website (http://is.gd/S4Zeld) and make sure you're logged in with your Scratch user account. Find the New Scratchers forum, and then enter the Introduce Yourself Here! subforum. Please work through the following steps to complete this exercise and gain some practical experience with the Scratch Discussion Forums:

1. Scroll to the bottom of the Introduce Yourself Here! subforum until you see the New Reply box. Hover your mouse over the toolbar button that resembles a Scratch block; this interface is shown in Figure 16.2.

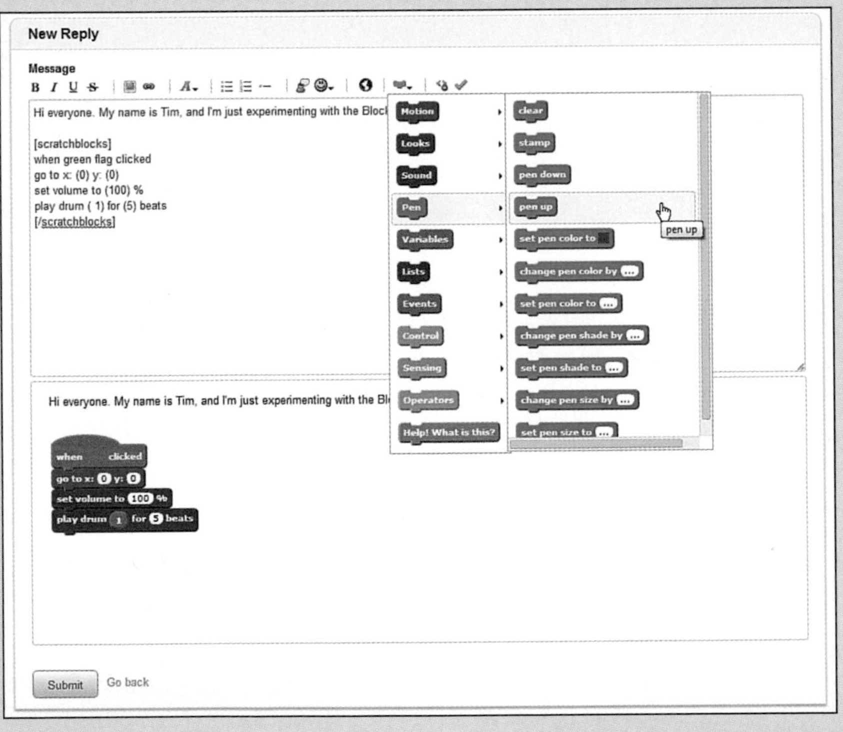

FIGURE 16.2
You can easily share realistic pseudocode with fellow Scratchers on the Scratch Forums.

2. Using the same toolbar button, create a simple script. You'll see that the toolbar button has a flyout submenu for each block category. If your imagination fails you, feel free to use the code shown in Figure 16.2. Note that as you work, the message box in the New Reply area fills in with the underlying Block Plugin code syntax.

If you've done any HTML programming, then the underlying scratchblocks2 markup should look instantly familiar.

3. The rightmost button on the toolbar (the check mark icon) is useful to get a live preview of what your Block Plugin code will look like in the published forum post.

4. If you plan to actually publish your post, add a paragraph explaining that you're just learning Scratch and you're playing around with Block Plugin syntax. The other Scratchers will certainly appreciate and support your motivation.

5. Click Submit to add your post into the subforum. Alternatively, you can simply browse to another page to discard your changes.

NOTE

How to Participate in the Scratch Wiki

Another place where you'll see a lot of Scratch block pseudocode is the Scratch Wiki (http://is.gd/zi2pLU). Unlike at the Scratch Forums, the Wiki does not allow anyone to add or modify content. Instead, you are required to request access to become a contributor. If you're interested in doing that, then you can request a Wiki editor account by visiting the Request Account page at http://is.gd/IXUXha.

One final note about pseudocode and the Scratch Block Plugin: You can visit blob 8108's Scratch Block sandbox page at http://is.gd/uijpWS to experiment with Block Plugin code. The Scratch Wiki (http://is.gd/dM8rhY) provides detailed instructions for understanding Block Plugin syntax. One cool thing about the sandbox page, besides the fact that it helps you to learn the underlying markup syntax, is that you can then paste this code into a Scratch Forums post.

Commenting Pseudocode

Believe it or not, you can add comments to your Scratch blocks that are based in Block Plugin pseudocode. As you can see in Figure 16.3, the Block Plugin supports both standalone comments as well as linked comments.

To create a Scratch comment, simply place two forward slash (/) characters immediately before your comment text. This syntax choice is an interesting choice by the Scratch Team because the double-slash syntax is how comments are created in many popular full-scale programming languages.

As you can see in Figure 16.3, adding a double-slash comment after a block creates a linked comment, and putting your double-slash text on its own line creates a standalone comment. It's as simple as that!

Please note that double-slash comments work only with Block Plugin pseudocode and not in the online or offline Scratch Editors.

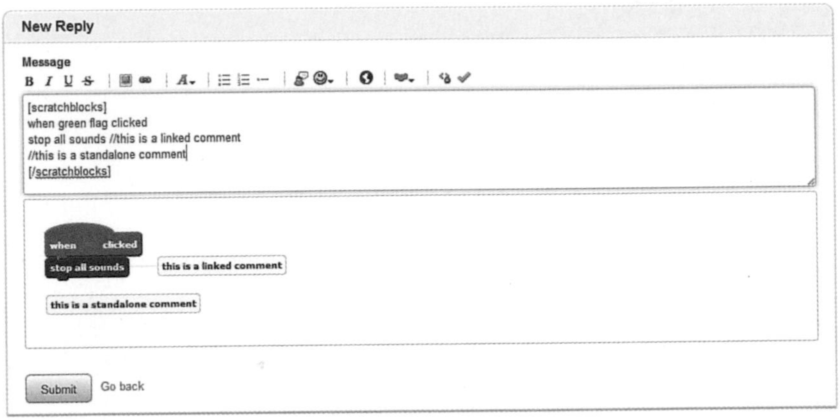

FIGURE 16.3
Block Plugin syntax supports comments, too!

Wireframing and Storyboarding

Let's move outward toward a more macro level, shall we? Whereas pseudocode deals with more of the low-to-the-ground concerns of your code (how the program actually works), wireframing and storyboarding are more global, general approaches to software project planning.

Don't be alarmed: I'm going to throw several software industry buzzwords at you in the next several paragraphs. The good news is that, as your teacher and guide, I'll explain everything as we go along.

First is the concept of the prototype. A *prototype* is a representation of all or part of a software project. The prototype may be limited in some way (and most of the time it is) but is used for evaluation purposes nonetheless.

The goal of the prototype isn't to demonstrate a finished product, but is instead to show proof of concept.

Today, many software developers are required to produce a proof-of-concept prototype before their client or customer will sign off on a work-for-hire contract. Thus, prototypes are useful not only for the developer himself or herself, but also for the customer—it's dollars and cents, as are most things in the business world.

Let's consider an example: You have a great idea for a new Scratch-based adventure game. From a high level, you know what you want to accomplish in terms of plot and general game story arcs.

You know that the project will likely take many hours, and possibly many days or weeks, to complete. Therefore, you develop a prototype so you have an initial blueprint to work from. The prototype then serves as a model as you begin to actually build the project in the Scratch Editor.

A software project prototype typically consists of the following two elements:

▶ **Wireframe**: This is a blueprint of the single screen of your Scratch project.

▶ **Storyboard**: This is a series of wireframes that are placed next to each other in sequence, and gives you and anybody else an idea as to the flow of your Scratch project.

Creating a Wireframe and Storyboard for Your Scratch Project

As you saw earlier in this hour when discussing pseudocode, a myriad of methods exist for creating wireframes and storyboards. One tool that I like a lot, although you're certainly not required to use it, is Balsamiq Mockups (http://is.gd/gZstLx).

I like Balsamiq for a number of reasons. First, the program is operating system neutral, running equally well on Microsoft Windows or Apple OS X systems. Second, the interface is easy to use and understand. You can see an example of Balsamic Mockups in action in Figure 16.4.

In Figure 16.4, notice that the arrows graphically show you how the three game screens interrelate to each other. Trust me: These storyboards go a long way in making your Scratch project more user-friendly and logical.

Incidentally, this simple storyboard is included in the book's exercise files archive; look for a file named `storyboard.bmml`.

Balsamiq Mockups uses the same underlying technology as does Scratch 2.0, namely Adobe AIR. You can visit the Balsamiq website to learn about purchase details if you like the program after enjoying the fully functional free trial.

One word of advice as you build your storyboards is not to get too bogged down with details. Remember that the purpose of your prototype is to remind you how your Scratch project will flow from end to end.

As a software developer, you need to remain flexible. Software projects can and do change their form over time. Therefore, you will update your wireframes and storyboard as the project proceeds and as you actually develop your live project by using the Scratch Editor.

As you're learning during this hour, you might think to yourself, "Tim, isn't this going overboard? After all, I'm new to programming, and I just want to have fun with Scratch!"

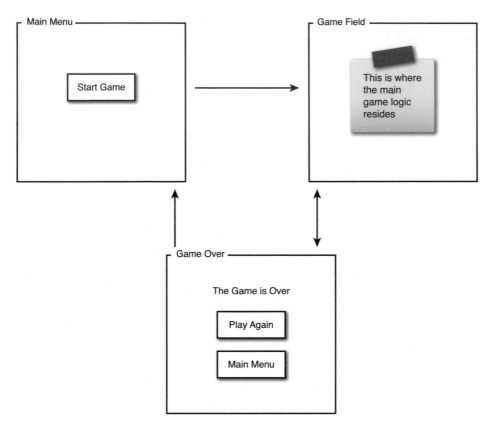

FIGURE 16.4
Balsamiq Mockups is great for quickly prototyping Scratch projects.

Well, if you truly are a mere tourist to the world of Scratch development, then perhaps the concepts of pseudocode, wireframing, and storyboarding are a bit much. On the other hand, if you find that Scratch programming lights a fire deep within you and encourages you to move forward with learning as much as you can about software development, then these topics are absolutely cogent.

In this hour, you are learning about software development best practices. They are the rough equivalent of having excellent manners in public discourse.

How Reverse Engineering Can Help You

In computer software development nomenclature, *reverse engineering* refers to the process of transforming a finished software project back into its source components. Certainly, hackers and other illicit users attempt to do this to steal intellectual property. However, reverse engineering has an entirely different purpose in the open source world, which of course is where we live in the Scratch 2.0 ecosystem.

In the following Try It Yourself exercise, you pick a project from the Scratch online gallery and build a simple storyboard based on the flow of that project. This exercise will give you valuable experience in prototyping.

TRY IT YOURSELF ▼

Use Reverse Engineering to Build a Storyboard

This Try It Yourself exercise gives you experience in building a storyboard from a completed project. It's a useful experiment because it forces you to look at storyboarding in the reverse direction. Work through the following steps and think about what each action you take means:

1. Point your web browser to the Scratch gallery (http://is.gd/tsr9gM) and explore several published projects until you find one that interests you.

2. Spend time both playing the game as an ordinary player, as well as analyzing the project's underlying code. Remember that you can do this by clicking the Look Inside button on the project's home page.

3. Using whatever tool or tools that you feel most comfortable with, construct a storyboard that reveals the project's structure. Create a wireframe of each significant screen in the project.

4. When you're finished with your work, step back and compare your prototype with the published project. Does your prototype accurately represent the program flow of that project? If someone were to study only your storyboard, could they instantly recognize the associated project if they were to play it?

Publicly Documenting Your Scratch Project

The probability is high that no other Scratcher will ever see your project storyboards. Furthermore, not all Scratchers are even aware of what comments are, much less actively read them in project code.

On the other hand, the documentation fields that are present on your Scratch project page are viewable to the public. To that end, it is of crucial importance that you fully document your project at this level so that users know exactly what they're in for when they click the Green Flag.

As a reminder, you can see your project page from within the Scratch Editor by clicking the See Project Page button in the upper-right corner of the Editor interface. You can use Figure 16.5 as your guide to examine the main editable fields on the public project page:

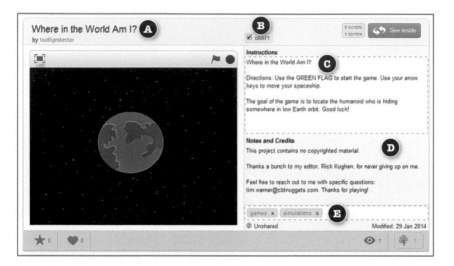

FIGURE 16.5
Good documentation is a critical success factor for your Scratch project.

NOTE

Limitations of the Scratch Offline Editor

The Scratch Offline Editor does *not* allow you to interact with the project's public web page at the MIT Scratch site. The logic behind this should be clear; namely, you may be using the Scratch Offline Editor to build a project that has not yet been uploaded to the Scratch website.

▶ **A:** Click in this field to edit the public title for your project. Your title should be snappy and memorable, but it also should be easy to pronounce and contain rich keywords. Besides being a good game or project developer, you need to think of things like search engine optimization (SEO) and project discoverability.

▶ **B:** The Draft check box is used to let other Scratchers know that your project is not in a completed state. In a sense, you're telling other Scratchers "Pardon the dust. I want you to play my game, but also know in advance that it's not finished and should be evaluated accordingly."

▶ **C:** Click and type in the Instructions field to tell people how to use your project. I can't overstate the importance of populating this field completely. As a gamer, I find it exquisitely frustrating to try somebody's Scratch project only to find myself bumbling around with the keyboard and mouse, not having any earthly idea how the project works.

The best practice to writing good project documentation is to use descriptive language. Unfortunately, the Page fields support only plain, unformatted text, so you don't have the ability to add rich text formatting. Bummer, right?

▶ **D**: The Notes and Credits field is useful both to provide supplemental information to other Scratchers, and also to give credit where credit is due. For example, if you obtain permission to use someone else's intellectual property, you can add the appropriate attribution here.

If, by contrast, you've remixed someone else's project, it is considered good Scratch etiquette to thank that Scratcher publicly in this space.

▶ **E**: Tags, also called taxonomic tags, are keywords used to describe the gist of a Scratch project. When you click your mouse in the Tags field, you can choose from a number of built-in tags. However, you're not limited to these, and you can add any tags that you feel describe your project.

Tags are designed to make it easier for other Scratchers to discover your project. For instance, suppose you developed a retro arcade game. By adding the tag *retro*, Scratchers can search the Scratch gallery by using that keyword to find your Scratch game quickly and easily.

To avoid so-called tag spam, the Scratch Team limits you to a maximum of three tags, so choose them carefully.

The old Scratch 1.4 website had a tag cloud on the front page that made using tags a lot easier. A tag cloud is a graphical representation of cloud keywords, with more frequently used tags showing up in a larger font. This way, you could see tag trends conveniently. You can see an example of this shown in Figure 16.6.

FIGURE 16.6
I wish that the Scratch 2.0 website still used the tag cloud. Image source: Scratch Wiki (http://is.gd/cjknTh).

In any event, you can use tag names in the Search box on the Scratch website to find projects that include those names; the Scratch search engine parses all Project fields, including the Title, Description, and Tag fields, when finding search results.

Summary

This hour represented a departure from what you've done in this book thus far. In this hour, you learned a lot of best-practice programming theory, which you'll use to good effect as you continue gaining more experience with Scratch programming.

Some Scratchers are motivated by a desire for project popularity—even eventual profit. These are noble and understandable aspirations, to be sure. The skills that that you've gained in this hour, from comments to pseudocode to storyboarding to richly documenting your project's public page, will all have a definite positive impact on the number of Scratchers who visit your project page. It's then up to you to wow the Scratchers with the quality of the project itself.

Workshop

Quiz

1. Which of the following terms represents an individual screen in your Scratch project?

    A. Wireframe

    B. Prototype

    C. Storyboard

2. Which of the following comment types is most appropriate for a general to-do item in your Scratch project?

    A. A linked comment

    B. A standalone comment

    C. A Block Plugin comment

3. Which of the following methods is used to delete a comment in a Scratch project?

    A. Pressing the Delete key on the keyboard

    B. Right-clicking the comment and selecting Delete

    C. Double-clicking the comment

Answers

1. The correct answer is choice A. A wireframe represents an individual screen in a storyboard. The storyboard is a sequence of wireframes that tells the story of your Scratch project. A prototype represents the complete project; this could consist of one or more storyboards.

2. The correct answer is choice B. A standalone comment in Scratch is a comment that is not attached to any particular script block. By contrast, linked comments are connected to individual blocks and travel with them as you move the block around the Scripts area. Block Plugin comments are used at the Wiki and discussion forum sites.

3. The correct answer is choice B. To delete a comment, right-click the comment and select Delete from the shortcut menu. Neither of the other answer choices given will work in the Scratch 2.0 Editor.

Challenge

Your challenge, should you choose to accept it, is as follows:

Create a simple Scratch 2.0 game, from prototype to finished product. The depth and complexity of the game aren't the main points here. Instead, practice conceptualizing a project in advance, building wireframes and a storyboard, implementing pseudocode, and then ultimately translating all of those raw materials into a real, live Scratch project.

Although this might seem like a lot of work now, you'll thank me for asking you to exert the effort eventually, I promise.

HOUR 17
Publishing Your Project

What You'll Learn in This Hour:

▶ Sharing your project
▶ Project documentation, revisited
▶ Interacting with your viewers through comments
▶ Interacting with other Scratchers on the forums
▶ Improving your project's visibility

So, after much fanfare and hard work, the moment of truth has arrived: You are ready to share your Scratch 2.0 project with the world. How do you go about this?

Well, by the end of this hour, you'll know everything you need to know to put your Scratch project on the World Wide Web, making it available for play to anyone who has an Internet connection, a web browser, and the Adobe Flash Player plug-in installed in that browser.

In addition to learning the actual click-through procedures for sharing and unsharing your project, you'll also spend time understanding and implementing the basics of Netiquette, the online variety of traditional etiquette.

You must always remember that the Scratch community is just that: a community. That is, the success of your projects is directly proportional to the time and effort that you put in to building connections with other Scratchers and potential players.

Sharing Your Project

Assuming that your project already exists on the Scratch website, it is trivially easy to flip the proverbial switch, publishing your project to the rest of the world.

Simply connect to the Scratch website, log in if you're not already logged in, navigate to your My Stuff page, find the project in question in the list, and click the Share button.

You might be surprised to observe that Scratch immediately shares your project with no additional confirmation prompts. As you can see in Figure 17.1, you can click the Unshare link to pull the project out of public view and back into your private unshared project collection.

Note also, as shown in Figure 17.1, that your private projects can be filtered by clicking the Unshared Projects tab in the My Stuff interface. By contrast, shared projects can also be viewed easily by clicking the Shared Projects tab.

FIGURE 17.1
Sharing (and unsharing) a Scratch project is easy. Note that you can filter your project lists by status: unshared (above) and shared (below).

When you share your Scratch project, you'll notice an abundance of strange-looking icons that appear in miniature on the My Stuff page and as full-sized, clickable buttons on the project's public page.

Using Figure 17.2 as a guide, examine the function of each of those funny-looking icons:

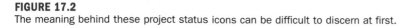

FIGURE 17.2
The meaning behind these project status icons can be difficult to discern at first.

▶ **A**: The Total Views icon shows the number of people who have viewed the project page. This number does not necessarily represent the number of people who have actually played your game, however. You'll note that project view counts always start with one; this makes sense because the creator counts for the initial view.

▶ **B**: The Loves icon shows the number of people who've chosen to "love" your Scratch project. The love index relates directly to the visibility of your project on the Scratch website.

▶ **C**: The Comments icon shows the number of people who have left a comment on your project page. As you learn later, comments represent a valuable way for you to interact with your players.

▶ **D**: The Remixes icon shows the number of people who formally remixed your project. Scratch does a good job at preserving project attribution and limiting intellectual property theft. You'll learn about remixing in greater detail in Hour 20, "Remixing a Project."

▶ **E**: The Favorites icon shows the number of people who've chosen to "favorite" your project. Favorites function rather like web browser bookmarks, but they also have an effect on the visibility of your project throughout the Scratch community.

▶ **F**: The Studios icon shows the number of studios in which your project appears. You can take it as a high compliment when another Scratcher decides to include your project in a studio that he or she creates.

As you can see, those so-called funny icons on your project page and your My Stuff page represent exceedingly valuable metadata concerning the status and relative popularity of your project.

Project Documentation, Revisited

You spent a great deal of time in the previous hour learning how to richly document your project's public page. Consequently, it's not necessary to review all of that ground here in great detail.

Remember, however, to invest significant planning and execution time in populating the Instructions and Notes and Credits fields (at the very least) on your project page, so that you offer other gamers a complete experience with your project.

In my mind, it's a true weakness that those are plaintext fields and do not currently allow you to add rich text formatting, such as alternate fonts, italic, or underlining. Nonetheless, we have to work within the confines of what we are given and make the best of things.

Remember, also, to make use of the three tags that the MIT Scratch Team allows you to attach to your project. Feel free to go beyond the default tag names and think of some of your own.

As you explore other Scratchers' projects, take note of the tags that those authors have selected to describe their games. Remember that tags are additive; the more Scratchers who use the same tags, the easier it is for site visitors to find projects that are directly attached or related to those tags.

Avoiding Spam Creation and Propagation

In computer technology, *spam* refers to electronic content that appears in front of you in both an unwanted and unasked-for way. To that end, you need to take pains not to get too enthusiastic in your Scratch project development and spam the community.

For example, as much as you might want to tell everyone at the Scratch discussion forums how cool and awesome your new Scratch project is, I strongly advise you against taking that action. The truth of the matter is that most Scratchers are proud of their work and want as many eyeballs as possible on their project pages.

The purpose of the Scratch discussion forum is to learn, ask questions, and share new information, not to self-promote.

On the other hand, I see nothing at all wrong with announcing your Scratch project through the usual social media channels, such as the following:

▶ Facebook

▶ Twitter

▶ LinkedIn

▶ Google+

▶ Tumblr

Interacting with Your Viewers Through Comments

This section shows you how to use the Comments feature that the MIT Scratch Team provides and attaches to each and every one of your project pages. It is extremely important to master how to leave and respond to comments; the comment system represents the nexus, or connection point, between you and the people who play and enjoy your Scratch projects.

From experience, interacting with commenters results in the following distinct advantages:

▶ **Constructive criticism leads to a better product**: Some commenters can point out flaws that you haven't noticed or found in your own software. Other commenters may have feature suggestions that you determine are especially valuable.

▶ **You can make some good online friendships this way**: By definition, someone leaving a comment on your project page shares at least one important commonality with you: namely, a shared interest in your project.

▶ **Fostering good rapport with your commenters adds value to your Scratch project page**: If nothing else, it signifies that people are talking about your project, which is always a good thing. Moreover, the more comments that appear on your project page, the more words there are for search engines to scrape, and the more likely your project will appear in users' search results.

The Basics of Netiquette

According to Wikipedia (http://is.gd/Na27YK), "*etiquette* is a code of behavior that delineates expectations for social behavior according to contemporary conventional norms within a society, social class, or group."

Wikipedia then goes on to define etiquette in technology, or so-called *netiquette*, as "a social code of network communication, or that which governs what conduct is socially acceptable in an online or digital situation."

What makes netiquette especially challenging is that those social norms vary from Internet domain to Internet domain, much less from country to country.

For example, what is socially acceptable at your favorite video gaming community forum may be considered way over the line at the Scratch community forum site, or vice versa. Thus, it is crucial that you spend time simply browsing whichever online community interests you and learn the local culture before you jump in and begin interacting with other users yourself.

One source (http://is.gd/9jqwsb) that seeks to define the core rules of netiquette uses a 10-point list, most of which is summarized here:

▶ **Remember the human**: You must always keep in mind when you communicate with people electronically that those individuals are living, breathing human beings—and not electronic circuit boards.

▶ **Online behavior versus real-life behavior**: Don't do or say anything online that you wouldn't do or say to someone face-to-face in the real world.

▶ **Know where you are in cyberspace**: Remember that netiquette and cultural norms vary from web community to web community, with people from all over the world coexisting in each one of those virtual communities.

▶ **Respect other people**: In particular, respect the fact that those whom you communicate with online probably lead busy lives and value their time. Moreover, some of your communication partners may have limited Internet bandwidth to work with. This respect for others must also extend to respecting the privacy of your online communication partners as well.

▶ **Be forgiving of others' mistakes**: Everyone who uses a computer and the Internet has to go through a learning curve; it is useful to remember that you, too, were once a newbie at technology.

Working with Comments on Your Project Page

This section focuses on precisely how you can work with comments on the Scratch website. To begin, make sure you're logged in to the Scratch website with your Scratch username.

If you want the following Try It Yourself exercise to have special relevance, then perhaps you can create a second Scratch account. Don't worry: There is nothing formally wrong or illicit about this action.

By having two Scratch accounts, you can practice both leaving comments as well as responding to those comments. As you learn, you can easily delete comments—and even delete your second Scratch account after you're finished with the exercise—if you decide that you no longer want to keep that account.

▼ TRY IT YOURSELF

Leave and Respond to Comments

In this Try It Yourself exercise, you gain some experience in leaving a comment on another Scratcher's project. Work through the following steps to complete the exercise:

1. Browse the Scratch gallery until you find a project that you genuinely like. After all, you don't want to be disingenuous here; I want you to leave a positive comment because that's how you truly feel about someone's work.

2. Below the Stage, notice that the Comments field always reserves a place for you, at the top of the list. Isn't that great? Place your cursor within the Leave a Comment box, and record your thoughts. You have a maximum of 500 plain text characters to work with.

   When you've completed your comment, click Post to make it public.

3. Hover your mouse over another Scratcher's comment in the list. Observe the Report link. If you find a comment that you find to be inappropriate, you can report that Scratcher's comment directly to the MIT Scratch Team.

4. You should make a habit of regularly examining the status of the Messages icon on the Scratch navigation bar. The icon looks like an envelope and displays a number letting you know how many site messages pertain to you. You can see this interface in Figure 17.3.

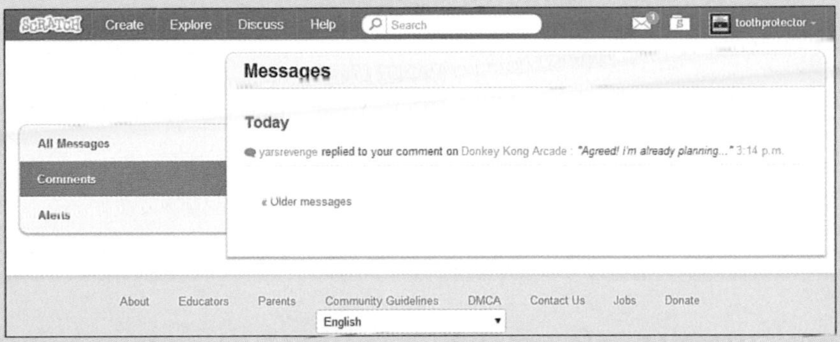

FIGURE 17.3
Check the Messages icon periodically; it shows a badge indicating how many new notifications you have.

> Click the Messages icon, and you can see hyperlinked references that point to any comments or replies that other Scratchers have directed at you.

5. Speaking of replies, let's do that now. If you're comfortable, create a second Scratch account to work with. Using your first, or primary Scratch account, leave yourself a comment on one of your project pages.

6. Now log out of your primary account, and log in to the site using your secondary account. Use the Search box at the top of the navigation bar to locate the project you commented on in step 5. Finally, click Reply and leave a reply message to your primary Scratch user. Figures 17.4 and 17.5 show the interface.

> If you're uncomfortable with this "phony baloney" commenting, make sure to pick a project that you can temporarily share and then unshare once you've completed your experimentation.

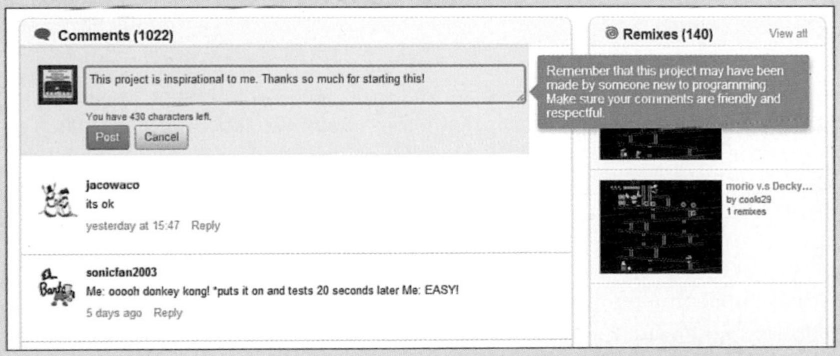

FIGURE 17.4
When you make a comment, a pop-up balloon reminds you to be respectful of other Scratchers and the community as a whole.

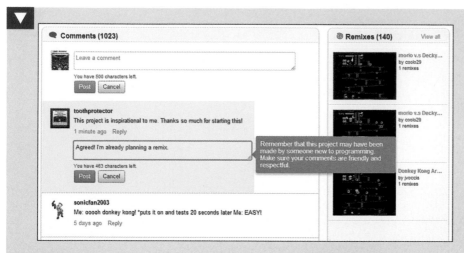

FIGURE 17.5
Replying to a comment is an excellent way to learn from your players as well as to get to know them better.

NOTE

Scratch Comments Are Forever

The Scratch Team enforces personal responsibility in its comment system, both on the project pages as well as in the forums. Namely, you are unable to delete your own comments after you've left them. The onus is on you to make sure what you're typing is positive because once you've posted the comment, it's there forever.

NOTE

Don't Be Negative—Be Happy!

Leaving a strongly negative comment is referred to in Internet lore as flaming. Sometimes the person(s) to whom you direct the comments may become "inflamed" enough to respond in kind, resulting in a flame war on that project page or discussion forum thread. The good news is that flaming is not tolerated on the Scratch site, and MIT Scratch Team members are likely to delete any inflammatory remarks.

You can see in Figure 17.6 that by the end of the Try It Yourself exercise, there is an indented, threaded comment string happening on the project page. This motif of commenting and replying should be immediately familiar to those of you who use social media systems, such as Facebook or Twitter.

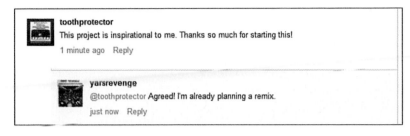

FIGURE 17.6
The finished, "threaded" comment string.

Interacting with Other Scratchers on the Forums

The terms *discussion forum*, *Internet forum*, and *message board* are all synonyms that refer to an online discussion site where people can hold conversations in the form of persistent messages.

To be sure, discussion forums can be a bit daunting at first, what with the proliferation of specialized jargon and various levels of welcome offered to new members.

The good news is that the Scratch Discussion Forums (http://is.gd/S4ZeId) are all about welcoming, learning, and collaboration. To participate in the discussion forums, you need to be logged in with your Scratch user account.

A common bit of Internet forum jargon is "lurk more." This means that is it advisable, at least when you're starting out, to read through several discussion forum threads to get a feel for how the community works, as well as to figure out what questions have already been asked and what questions have already been answered.

The Scratch discussion forums are divided into the five following categories:

▶ **Welcome to Scratch**: Here, you have the Announcements and New Scratchers forums. These forums are a great place to begin if you're new to using Internet forums in general and Scratch Forums in particular.

▶ **Making Scratch Projects**: Here, you have five forums that pertain to getting help with scripts, sharing project ideas, and lodging Scratch feature requests.

▶ **About Scratch**: In these five forums, you can notify the MIT Scratch Team about any bugs or glitches that you feel you have found in the Scratch program. You can also learn about so-called advanced topics, such as integrating Scratch with the analog world, "Sensor boards, Lego, and so forth."

▶ **Interests Beyond Scratch**: These are the off-topic forums, where you can post on anything that's generally related to Scratch, or potentially completely random. This is a great opportunity to get to know other Scratchers on a more personal level.

▶ **Scratch in Other Languages**: Remember that Scratch, by definition, is not limited to any one particular language or culture. If your primary language is other than English, you can go into the appropriate localized forum and share with other Scratchers by using the language that's most comfortable for you.

A little bit more about jargon: Within each forum is a list of topics. The topic is a new subject for discussion; when one or more other Scratchers make a reply in that topic, you have what is referred to as a discussion thread.

Complete the following Try It Yourself exercise to help you get a feel for how the Scratch discussion forums work in a safe context.

▼ TRY IT YOURSELF

Step into the Scratch Discussion Forums

First, navigate to the Scratch discussion forums website, and ensure that you're logged in with your Scratch username. Second, under the category Welcome to Scratch, click New Scratcher's Forum. Follow these steps to work through the rest of this exercise:

1. Notice that the first several topics are marked with a pushpin icon and labeled "sticky." When the MIT Scratch Team feels that a topic is of particular importance, they will "sticky" that topic, which pins it to the very top of that discussion forum. This makes it very easy for other Scratchers to locate those important topics.

   Speaking of topics, click the New Topic button to create a new topic in the New Scratchers forum. By the way, all of these interface elements are shown in Figure 17.7.

2. Type a subject into the Subject box (you want to be as descriptive as possible here, using the fewest possible words), and then include a short message.

3. Spend time playing with the rich text formatting controls above the Message box. Pay particular attention to the Block Plugin extension, which enables you to create realistic-looking Scratch scripts in your discussion forum post.

   Click the Preview button on the toolbar (this is the check mark icon at the far right of the toolbar), to see your Block Plugin code appear in the preview pane.

4. When you're ready to publish your post, read it one more time (there's no Undo here, so be careful), and then click Submit.

5. Now let's get some experience with replying to topics. Browse the New Scratchers forum until you find a topic that intrigues you, and then click to enter that conversational thread.

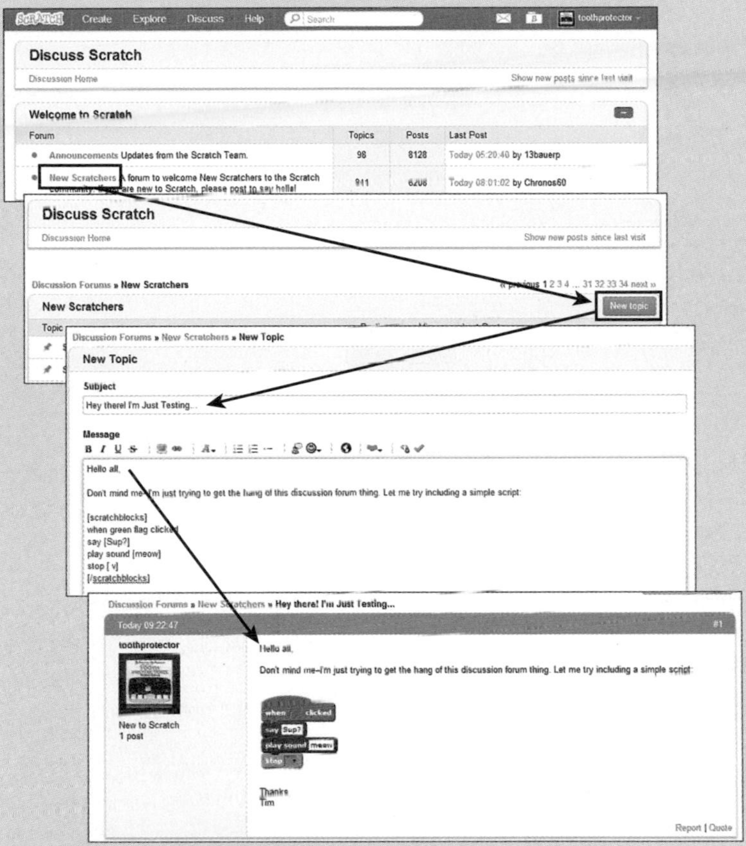

FIGURE 17.7
The Scratch discussion forums behave like any other Internet message board.

6. Scroll to the bottom of the page to the New Reply box. Note that you have the same rich text controls that you had when you started a forum topic.

Fill in a constructive reply, and then click Submit to publish your reply.

It bears stating one more time that, like comments left on a project page, there is no delete functionality. I believe the rationale behind this is to force Scratchers to take full accountability for everything they say on the website.

Notice that, after you've submitted a new topic to the discussion forum, an Unfollow Discussion button appears. By default, you'll be notified in your Messages area when another Scratcher replies to your post. This interface is shown in Figure 17.8.

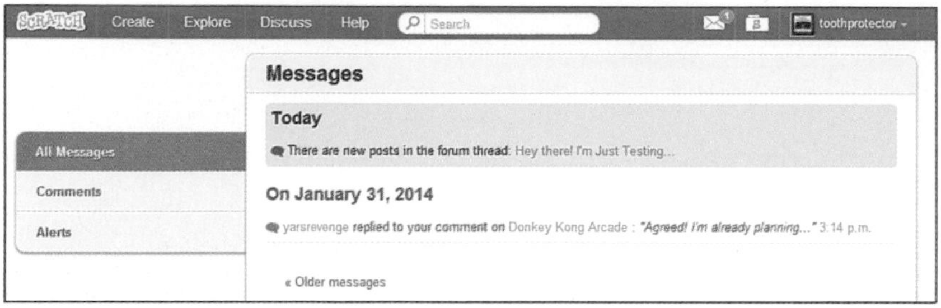

FIGURE 17.8
A handy notification of a follow-up message to my new forum post.

NOTE
Completeness Counts

You may get a better response on the discussion forums if you fill out your user profile, in particular, adding an avatar picture. To do this, click your username in the upper-right corner of the Scratch web page, and select Profile. Here, you can upload an avatar image, as well as fill in information about yourself and the projects that you're working on.

Improving Your Project's Visibility

You may very well have authored the greatest Scratch project that ever existed. However, that fact is rendered meaningless if other Scratchers are unable to find your project.

Therefore, it is incumbent upon you to practice some general principles of search engine optimization (SEO) to improve your project's visibility, both within the Scratch website ecosystem and within the entire World Wide Web.

How the Scratch Search Works

According to the Scratch Wiki, the Scratch website uses a custom Google search engine to scrape its own content and make it easily findable. As you know, the Scratch website includes a Search box at the top of the page.

However, many Scratchers don't know that, with Google being Google, the public Google search engine scrapes the Scratch project gallery, just as it does any other public website.

I challenge you to visit Google.com and run a search for one of your project titles. If you don't yet have any project titles, try searching for "Dodgeball Challenge." This is one of my projects, and I was very pleased to see that it has a relatively high Google search page rank. Figure 17.9 shows this example.

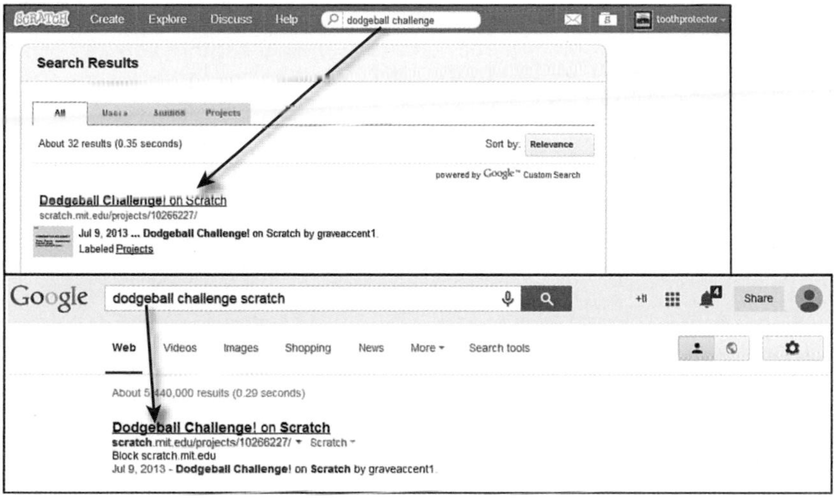

FIGURE 17.9
Exerting a little effort in optimizing your Scratch project for search goes a long way toward improving its visibility to your potential players.

SEO Tips

The process of optimizing a web page or entire website for inclusion in the Google search corpus is referred to as search engine optimization, or SEO. Of course, other search engines besides Google actually do exist, but this section focuses on Google for two reasons:

▶ Google is the technology embraced by the MIT Scratch Team in its own website.

▶ Having used Internet search engines since the beginning of the World Wide Web, I choose Google as the best one of them all!

A detailed discussion of SEO is certainly beyond the scope of this book; however, if you're interested in learning more about the subject, check out the following great books:

▶ *SEO Made Easy*, by Evan Bailyn (http://is.gd/rcZWW4)

▶ *Google Power Search*, by Stephan Spencer (http://is.gd/AEUZD8)

In any event, the following is a quick laundry list of SEO tips that you can implement right now to have a net positive effect on the visibility of your Scratch project:

▶ **Populate every possible field on your Scratch project page**: Google can index words only when those words are present on a web page. Therefore, it is critically important that you spend time completely populating your Scratch project page with metadata.

▶ **Be terse, yet be descriptive**: No one wants to spend days reading through a Leo Tolstoy-ish exposition or description of your project. Your goal is to strike a balance between being terse, or brief, while at the same time conveying accurately and crisply what your Scratch project is all about.

Google search algorithms are only semipublicly known; the algorithm is much smarter than you might think, though. Avoid using "filler" words. You want every word to have meaning when describing your project, both on the project page as well as at the Scratch discussion forums.

▶ **Promote your project, yet don't propagate spam**: If you have a Twitter feed, it is certainly appropriate for you to make periodic tweets advertising the presence of your Scratch project to your followers. Likewise, it's acceptable in most cases to create Internet forum posts that offer other people the opportunity to come to your page and play through your Scratch project and leave feedback.

If you have a blog, that might be a good opportunity to more fully describe the purpose of your project, how you came to code it, and so forth. As you probably know, many free blogging platforms exist, including Google's own blogger (http://is.gd/fxOKpS).

If you want to notify friends and family via email, then so much the better. The caveat here is to be judicious: Remember that nobody likes spam, and propagating spam on the Internet will most certainly have a negative impact on your Scratch project's popularity.

According to the Scratch Wiki (http://is.gd/mOHTjV), if the MIT Scratch Team determines that you're spamming either its website or the discussion forums (or, heaven forbid, both), this could lead to a ban. A *ban* occurs when a website owner blocks connection attempts from your computer. This is obviously a bad thing and should be avoided.

Summary

A common complaint I hear from my students who are spending time learning a new technology is, "I feel so vulnerable because I feel that I'm doing it wrong and will receive blowback from other community members." I'm grateful to say that if you understand everything you've learned in this hour, you'll successfully manage to avoid unintentionally committing a breach of Scratch community netiquette.

By now, you understand how to publish a project to the Scratch website. You know how to leave comments, reply to comments, and, of course, read them. You're also familiar with the Scratch discussion forums, including browsing, creating topics, and replying inside conversational threads.

This hour concluded with a brief discussion of search engine optimization: Use these tips to bring as many possible players to your project pages as possible.

Workshop

Quiz

1. The Scratch 2.0 website allows commenters to edit their comments.

    A. True

    B. False

2. Once you share your project on the Scratch website, it is permanently shared.

    A. True

    B. False

3. A pattern of spamming behavior on the Scratch website may result in your user account being banned, temporarily or permanently.

    A. True

    B. False

Answers

1. The correct answer is choice B. You need to be very careful when you make comments or participate in the Scratch discussion forums because you are accountable for those remarks forever. That is, as of this writing, there is no delete functionality for Scratch comments or discussion forum posts.

2. The correct answer is choice B. You can take a Scratch project offline with a single click of the mouse from the My Stuff page. In addition, you can mark a published project in Draft status to let other Scratchers know that the project is currently incomplete and should not be judged as such.

3. The correct answer is choice A. The MIT Scratch Team may, in fact, ban your user account if it feels that you're abusing the Scratch discussion forums and/or the Scratch website for your own benefit.

Challenge

Your challenge for this hour consists of the following three discrete tasks:

1. Browse the Scratch project gallery until you find a project that you genuinely admire. Leave a constructive comment for the author on the project page.

2. Visit the Scratch discussion forums, find an appropriate forum, and start a new discussion topic. Periodically check back to see if anyone has replied in your conversational thread, and, if so, reply to that reply to keep the conversation going!

3. While you're at the Scratch discussion forums, navigate into a conversational thread in which you feel you can provide positive input. Add a reply to include your voice in the discussion.

HOUR 18
Using the Scratch Offline Editor

What You'll Learn in This Hour:

▶ A bit of Scratch version history
▶ Introducing the Scratch 2.0 Offline Editor
▶ Uploading and downloading assets
▶ Understanding the Scratch file format
▶ Integrating Scratch 1.4 with Scratch 2.0
▶ Converting Scratch projects into other formats

For me, the biggest change between Scratch 2.0 and Scratch 1.4 (the previous major version) is that Scratch 2.0 is a cloud-based application. As you know by now, this means that you work on your projects by using an Internet connection and a web browser, and your projects are stored not on your local computer, but on the MIT Scratch website.

As convenient as the schema is, there is one Achilles' heel: If you lose your Internet connection, you lose access to your Scratch projects. Along the same lines, if the MIT Scratch web servers go down for any reason, you lose access as well. What can you do about this?

The good news is that the Scratch Team provided the Scratch 2.0 Offline Editor. You'll learn all about it in this hour; it represents a method for you to create and edit Scratch projects in a completely offline manner.

By the end of this hour, you'll not only know all there is to know about the Offline Editor, but you'll also greatly improve your knowledge of the Scratch file formats, as well as how to upload and download assets to and from the Scratch website.

Let's get started!

A Bit of Scratch Version History

Scratch 1.4 was the previous major version of the Scratch application, and was released officially on July 19, 2009. Scratch 1.4 is a completely offline application, which means that you need to download the app from the Scratch website and install it locally on your computer.

The software is still available on the Scratch website (http://is.gd/iIuIQK). Under the hood, Scratch 1.4 was built using the ancient Smalltalk programming language, specifically a dialect called squeak. The software is available for all three major operating system platforms: Windows, OS X, and Debian/Ubuntu Linux.

As you'll learn later in this hour, you can still use Scratch 1.4 and even upload version 1.4 projects to the Scratch website. The old Scratch 1.4 version of the website used a Java-based web player to render projects. However, you're not able to open Scratch 2.0 projects in the Scratch 1.4 editor. This should make sense to you intuitively. If not, you'll learn more about that subject later in this hour.

Scratch 2.0 was released officially on May 9, 2013. Under the hood, the underlying programming technology was completely revamped. Instead of squeak and Smalltalk, the MIT Scratch Team chose Adobe technologies, which many professional programmers find to be a highly controversial choice.

Instead of Java, the industry-standard Adobe Flash Player is used in the web browser to render Scratch 2.0 projects.

You might wonder why Adobe technologies are controversial. First, Adobe Flash historically does not run on Apple mobile devices. This means that Scratch never has been, and probably never will, run on iPhones, iPads, or iPod touches. That's unfortunate, for sure.

NOTE

Scratch and HTML5

There is a persistent rumor that the MIT Scratch Team is rewriting the Scratch application in the vendor-neutral, industry-standard HTML5 markup language. This would make Scratch finally completely platform neutral and allow Scratch projects to run on Apple mobile devices. Before you get your hopes up too high, however, you should know that what little the Scratch Team has had to say on the subject points to them not performing the code rewrite themselves.

As far as features are concerned, Scratch 2.0 represents a great advance over Scratch 1.4. The major new features are summarized here in an unordered list:

- ▶ The ability to create your own blocks

- ▶ Sprite cloning

- ▶ Cloud-based data variables

- ▶ A Backpack that makes your code portable

- ▶ A sound editor

- ▶ Vector graphics

Without any further ado, let's download and get to know the Scratch 2.0 Offline Editor.

Introducing the Scratch 2.0 Offline Editor

The Scratch Team released the Scratch 2.0 Offline Editor on August 26, 2013. For those who care about such geeky technical details, the Scratch 2.0 Offline Editor is an Adobe AIR application. Adobe AIR is a runtime environment that supports the deployment and running of desktop applications.

The cool thing that Adobe AIR brings to the table is a seamless, integrated installation and maintenance routine. You'll see this in action in just a second. The good news is that you don't have to install Adobe AIR separately; initiating a download of the Offline Editor automatically invokes the Adobe AIR installer if you don't have it on your system.

System Requirements

Like the Scratch 1.4 editor, the Scratch 2.0 Offline Editor is a cross-platform application. This means that it runs on Windows, OS X, and Linux machines. You need at least Adobe AIR version 2.6, but this isn't a problem in any case, as previously discussed.

The hard disk space footprint is remarkably small. You need only 23MB of free hard drive space to install the editor.

Installing the Editor

You'll be surprised how easy it is to install and update the Scratch 2.0 Offline Editor. Simply visit the download page (http://is.gd/sB2h1k), click Install Now, and follow all prompts, accepting all defaults. This workflow is shown in Figure 18.1.

FIGURE 18.1
To install the Offline Editor, (A) click the Install Now button, (B) install Adobe AIR if it isn't already on your computer, (C) approve the installation, and (D) sit back and wait for the installation to complete.

Getting to Know the Editor User Interface

Use Figure 18.2 and the following list as a guide while you examine the interface of the Scratch 2.0 Offline Editor. You'll find that the interface is almost identical, but not quite, to the online Scratch 2.0 editor. To that end, this section focuses only on the features that are unique to the Offline Editor:

▶ **A:** Clicking the Scratch icon opens your default web browser and points to the Scratch website.

▶ **B:** Besides the expected New, Open, Save, and Save As commands, the File menu includes Share to Website and Check for Updates options. You'll learn about both of those options in a moment.

▶ C: The Edit menu includes a command to set the Small Stage layout, as well as an option to set Turbo mode.

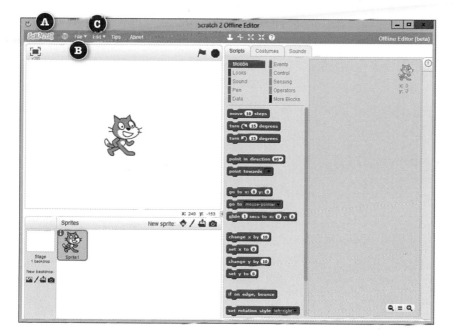

FIGURE 18.2
The Scratch 2.0 Offline Editor interface.

NOTE

Putting Scratch in Turbo Mode

In Turbo mode, Scratch executes your scripts at an accelerated speed. This is useful both for troubleshooting Scratch projects as well as for speeding up projects that include quite a bit of math-ematical heavy lifting. However, Turbo mode should only be used during diagnostic periods because graphics rendering in particular causes the sprites to lag an unacceptable amount.

Updating the Software

Take a close look at Figure 18.3. Beneath the Full Screen button, you'll see an identifier that begins with a *v*. This integer value represents the Scratch version number. Specifically, I believe this is a build number, given that, as of this writing, the Offline Editor is up to v385.

Keeping track of product versions is a key principle of software development. Over time, bugs get fixed, new features get added, and so forth. By printing the version number prominently in the editor interface, both the Scratch Team as well as the end user instantly know which version they're dealing with.

You never have to worry about keeping the Scratch 2.0 online editor up to date; because this is a cloud-based application, all updates are handled by the MIT Scratch Team.

Frankly, you don't have to worry about keeping the Offline Editor up to date either: You'll find that if a new version of the editor is available, you'll be asked to update during the next time you launch the application. The update dialog box is shown in Figure 18.3 as well.

Of course, you can always perform a manual update check by clicking File, Check for Updates in the editor.

FIGURE 18.3
Above, you can see the version number for my Scratch 2.0 online editor is v392. Below, you can see that my Offline Editor is outdated and I'm prompted to update to v385. (Yes, the Offline Editor tends to lag behind its online counterpart.)

The following section focuses on actually using the Offline Editor specifically. You'll learn how to do a project offline and then add it to the Scratch website.

Uploading and Downloading Assets

Personally, I prefer to use the Offline Editor rather than the web browser-based editor. Why? Well, I never liked being tied to an Internet connection. When traveling with my laptop, I do have Wi-Fi access most of the time. Nonetheless, I can always fire up my Scratch 2.0 Offline Editor to work on my projects in complete freedom.

Uploading an Offline Project to the Scratch Website

To lay the groundwork for the following Try It Yourself exercise, open the Offline Editor on your computer and save the file locally to your system by clicking File, Save, and selecting a save location on your system.

Use the Offline Editor

This Try It Yourself exercise gives you some valuable experience with the Scratch 2.0 Offline Editor. For grins, if you're interested, you can find a simple AgeCalc project in the book's solution files archive; the filename is `AgeCalc.sb2`. Follow these steps to complete the exercise:

1. Once you're finished with your project and the Scratch 2.0 Offline Editor, click File, Share to Website.

2. As you can see in Figure 18.4, you're prompted to specify a project name as well as your Scratch username and password.

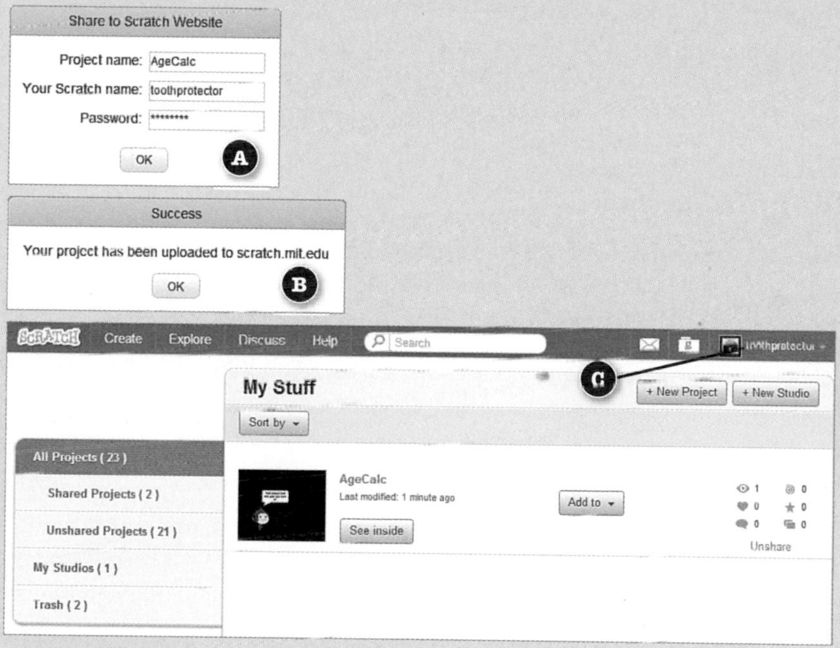

FIGURE 18.4
When you upload an offline Scratch project, you (A) provide a title and login details, (B) receive a Success status notification, and (C) can browse the published project on the Scratch website.

3. If all goes well, you're presented with the Success dialog box, which is also shown in the figure.

4. Unfortunately, the Offline Editor does not automatically invoke a connection to the Scratch website. Consequently, open your favorite web browser and navigate to your My Stuff page on the Scratch website. You'll see your project in your My Stuff list, and you'll observe that it is, in fact, shared to the public.

▼

5. If you decide to leave the project in a published state, don't forget to fully populate all of the description fields on your project web page. If you've decided to take the project offline, simply click the Unshare link on your My Stuff page.

Downloading an Online Scratch Project to the Offline Editor

Suppose you've invested some time in building a project at the Scratch website, using the online editor. Now you want to take a copy of that file offline, to work on with your Offline Editor. How you do this?

Well, the download question is a little bit more complicated than the upload question. The reason for this is that the MIT Scratch Team actually allows you to download the entire project to your local computer, or, if you want to, you can download individual assets.

That's right—you can download individual sprites, sound clips, Stage backgrounds, and so forth, from the MIT web servers to your local system.

You already know that you can upload your own assets to the online editor for inclusion in your project. However, many Scratchers are unaware of the rich download capabilities that they have at their disposal.

For instance, you could browse the Scratch gallery until you find a project that you really enjoy. You can then download individual components from that project for inclusion in your own project. Keep in mind, though, that it's absolutely imperative that you understand the importance of respecting intellectual property and ask for permissions when appropriate.

If you want to use someone's sprite from his or her project in your own project, and do not want to remix the entire thing, you need to reach out to that Scratcher to obtain explicit permission. Not doing this is a violation of the open source community guidelines and potentially represents a breach of legal intellectual property law.

With that said, complete the following Try It Yourself exercise, this time focusing on pulling down project assets from the cloud to your local computer for offline use.

▼ TRY IT YOURSELF

Download Online Assets to the Offline Scratch Editor

For this Try It Yourself exercise, use the `Hour18a.sb2` project file so you can work with the same assets as listed in the exercise. To do this, you need to upload the offline project to your online Scratch profile. When you do this, be sure to unshare the project on the website. To complete this exercise, follow these steps:

▼

1. Open the AgeCalc project from your My Stuff page on the Scratch website. Start with the Pico sprite: On the Stage, right-click the sprite and click Save to Local File. Leave the default filename, `pico.sprite2`. Use your operating system commands to create a folder on your local computer called AgeCalc, and use that folder to save all related downloaded project assets.

2. Next, download the backdrop. Click the Stage sprite, and navigate to the Backdrops tab. Next, right-click the stars backdrop thumbnail icon and click Save to Local File. Leave the default filename, `stars.png`, and save to the AgeCalc folder.

3. There's a sound clip in the project, stored on the Stage script page. Once there, navigate to the Sounds tab and download the techno sound clip to the AgeCalc folder on your local system. You should know how the general procedure works by now. The default filename for the sound clip is `techno.wav`.

4. Now, for the coup de grace, download the entire project to your computer. In the Scratch online editor, click File, Download to Your Computer. Leave the default filename and extension: `agecalc.sb2`.

   Congratulations! You now know how to pull down individual project components, as well as entire Scratch projects, from the Web to your local computer for use with the Scratch 2.0 Offline Editor. That's a very valuable skill to have.

NOTE

Viewing File Extensions

To see the three-character file extension that is typically appended to filenames, you might need to configure your computer specifically to show these extensions. If you run a Windows computer, see the following tutorial: http://is.gd/Qhnt6V. If you run a Mac computer, see this tutorial: http://is.gd/NwPGa4.

Understanding the Scratch File Format

In the previous exercise, you pull down various assets from an online Scratch project. Depending upon how your computer is set up, these filenames may have shown a three-character file extension after the filename.

Specifically, a file extension, also called a file type, is the way that your operating system knows what to do with a particular file. For instance, a Windows user who double-clicks a file with the .html extension will see that file open up in the computer's configured default web browser.

In Scratch 2.0, project files have the extension .sb2. In Scratch 1.4, the file project extension .sb is in a binary format that cannot be cracked open and viewed.

What's really cool about Scratch 2.0 is that the .sb2 file format is essentially an archive, or suitcase file for lack of a better word. You can actually add the .zip extension manually to your downloaded project file, and then double-click the file to extract its contents just as you would any other ZIP archive you might've downloaded from the Internet.

Take a look at Figure 18.5 to see what I'm talking about. Notice that the .sb2 file is not a binary, monolithic blob, but instead acts like a sort of suitcase, as mentioned earlier.

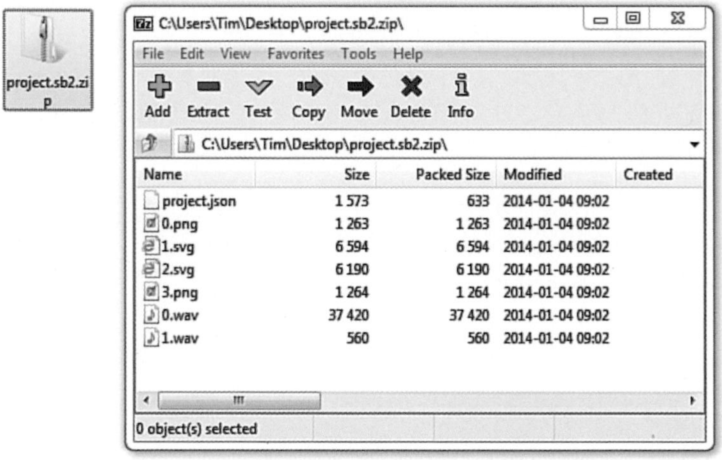

FIGURE 18.5
On the left is an .sb2 project file renamed to .zip; on the right is the .zip file contents, revealing the "innards" of a Scratch 2.0 project file.

The graphical assets in the project are represented as SVG or PNG graphics files. Sound clips are represented as .wav audio files. Finally, all of the specific project metadata (that is, data that describes data) is stored in a file with the extension .json.

JSON, which stands for JavaScript Object Notation and is typically pronounced *JAY-sahn*, is an industry-standard method for representing data.

The contents of a typical JSON manifest file are shown in Figure 18.6. What's so interesting here is how the manifest file is able to describe every parameter of the project, every asset, in such a nice, compact way. The manifest file is negligible in size, as well.

Do you need to know all of this technical stuff to become proficient in Scratch? No, but it certainly doesn't hurt for you to understand some of the architectural underpinnings of the technology.

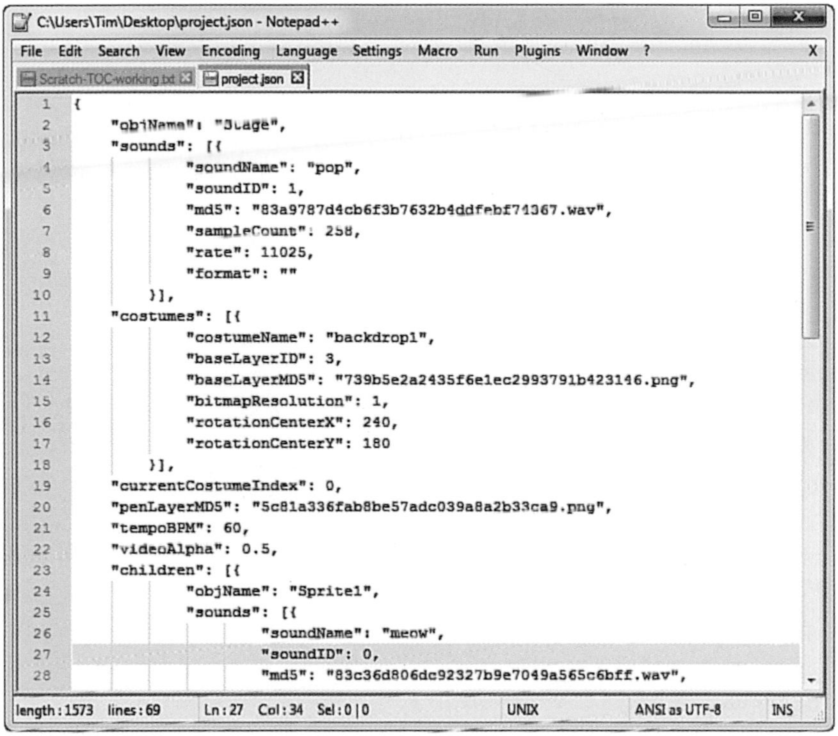

FIGURE 18.6
The JSON manifest contains all of your Scratch project's contents, all described in meticulous, standardized detail.

Given the discussion of the Scratch 2.0 and Scratch 1.4 file formats, hopefully you can see that a fundamental incompatibility exists between the two project versions.

Generally speaking, with software, you can open up documents from earlier versions in more recent versions. For instance, I can open up old Microsoft Word files that were authored 10 years ago in my copy of Microsoft Word 2013.

However, if I try to open a Word 2013 document in, for example, Word 2003, then I'm going to find myself in big trouble—it simply is not going to work.

The same rules apply with Scratch. You can use the Scratch 2.0 Offline Editor to open Scratch 1.4 projects that use the .sb extension, period. Conversely, you cannot use the Scratch 1.4 editor to open .sb2 Scratch 2.0 projects.

In the next section, you'll spend a little more time integrating the two Scratch versions. It is good to have at least an introductory familiarity with Scratch 1.4 because many people around the world still use that product version.

Integrating Scratch 1.4 with Scratch 2.0

Let's get some practice working with projects from both the old as well as the new Scratch project versions. By the time you complete the following Try It Yourself exercise, you'll have a very clear grasp on what's possible in mixing Scratch 1.4 projects with Scratch 2.0 projects.

▼ TRY IT YOURSELF

Integrate Scratch 1.4 with Scratch 2.0

Start this Try It Yourself exercise by opening the Scratch 1.4 project in the Scratch 2.0 Offline Editor. You then upload the project to the website, and then go from there. To complete the exercise, work through the following steps:

1. From the book's solution file archive, locate the practice file `scratch1.4.sb`. This is a very simple Scratch 1.4 project that I created. Open the project in the Scratch 2.0 Offline Editor by opening the editor, then clicking File, Open, and browsing to `scratch1.4.sb`.

2. Using the skills you gleaned in the previous Try It Yourself exercises in this hour, upload the project to the Scratch website. Be sure to give it a unique name. You'll need to keep the project shared for the duration of this exercise, but you should unshare it when you're finished.

3. From your My Stuff page on the Scratch website, click See Inside to go inside the Scratch 1.4 project. Click the Green Flag and run the project to verify that it runs the same way it did from the Scratch 2.0 Offline Editor.

4. For grins, click File, Download to Your Computer and notice how the file appears on your system. You'll see that saving a Scratch 1.4 project from the Web to your local system results in a Scratch 2.0 `.sb2` file.

5. To download a Scratch 1.4 project as a Scratch 1.4 project, navigate to the project web page and click Share To, as shown in Figure 18.7. Click the Download Code button, and you'll see the `.sb` file materialize on your computer.

FIGURE 18.7
You can download published Scratch 1.4 projects either in 1.4 or 2.0 format.

NOTE

What Is a Studio?

In Scratch nomenclature, a *studio* is a page on the Scratch website that consists of a group of related projects. Several studios exist that are focused on so-called legacy Scratch 1.4 projects. Here is one that I enjoy quite a bit: http://is.gd/hVn2Cr.

Converting Scratch Projects into Other Formats

I mentioned in the introduction to this hour that the MIT Scratch Team's decision to write Scratch 2.0 using Adobe technologies was controversial due to the proprietary nature of those technologies and the fact that they tend to not play nicely with other platforms, particularly mobile platforms.

After you spend a considerable amount of time in coding a Scratch project, you'll obviously want to know what other options exist for getting your project in front of people using different technologies. That subject is covered next.

An HTML5 Player?

According to the Scratch Wiki (http://is.gd/Xu0FFf), the Scratch Team was at one point designing an HTML5 player that would enable Scratch projects to be played on any platform. For those who don't know, Hypertext Markup Language, called HTML for short, is the principal programming (technically, a markup) language used on World Wide Web pages.

HTML5 is the latest and greatest generation of HTML, including many advances over the previous HTML 4 specification. We don't need to get into the specifics here—the take-home message for the purposes of this text is that an HTML5 player for Scratch would be a godsend.

The sad news is that, again according to the Scratch Wiki, the Scratch Team is not designing the HTML5 player anymore. Instead, the team has released the project to the Scratch community, putting the onus on them to complete the project.

Speaking candidly, an HTML5-based Scratch player might not be quite all it's cracked up to be when you run Scratch projects on mobile devices. The reason for this is simple: What about the keyboard? Keyboard-based control from mobile devices occupies quite a bit of screen real estate, for one thing. Second, even the best tablet soft keyboards tend to be a bit on the twitchy side. That reduces a Scratch game's fun factor.

An Android Scratch Player?

Anybody who uses iOS devices, such as iPhones or iPads, is aware of the fact that you cannot play Adobe Flash content on those devices.

On the other hand, those who use Google Android tablets or smartphones can, in fact, take advantage of the (surprisingly discontinued) Adobe Flash Player Lite.

Because the Android mobile operating system supports Adobe Flash, albeit in a sluggish, uneven, and now unsupported way, it is technically possible to play Scratch projects on Android devices. For those who are interested, there does exist an Android Scratch player under development by a Scratcher named ZeroLuck: Here is a link to his or her public Scratch profile: http://is.gd/pvxDce.

The Build Your Own Blocks (BYOB) Scratch Modification

Some very intelligent folks at the University of California at Berkeley have developed a Scratch clone called Snap! (http://is.gd/s26Lr1) that greatly expands the capabilities of Scratch.

This JavaScript-based web application, which was formerly called Build Your Own Blocks or BYOB, is a browser-based, visual, drag-and-drop programming language that represents a reimplementation or reenvisioning of Scratch 1.4. The nifty user interface is shown in Figure 18.8.

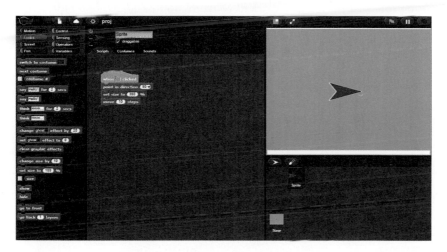

FIGURE 18.8
The JavaScript-based Snap! editor (Scratch 1.4 clone).

You should definitely visit the project website and play around with the tool (http://is.gd/ 5u7UHn); it looks and feels much like the Scratch 1.4 online editor. Yes, you read that correctly. Snap! is a clone of Scratch 1.4, not Scratch 2.0.

Unfortunately, we don't have the whitespace in this book to give Snap! the attention that it deserves. You can do things in Snap! that are impossible in Scratch 1.4 or even Scratch 2.0, including building your own custom blocks from...well...scratch.

For the purposes of this text, I want to point out that it's possible to export a Snap! project as an executable program file that runs independently of any offline player.

NOTE

On Scratch File Extensions

On Windows computers, executable program files typically use the file extension `.exe`. Mac systems use the file extension `.app` for program files.

Sadly, the latest version of the product, Snap 4.0! appears to be missing the ability to compile projects into a locally executable format. However, as a workaround, I discovered that you can still download a previous version and go about project compilation that way. To complete this exercise, follow these steps:

1. Download BYOB from the website. For the Windows version, use this link: http://is.gd/4ArTMk. For the Mac version, use this link: http://is.gd/jYLKcW.

2. Double-click the downloaded ZIP file to unpack its contents. Both Windows and Mac should be able to do this action transparently and automatically.

3. In the extracted folder, double-click the BYOB executable program file. The BYOB interface is shown in Figure 18.9. If you have Scratch 1.4 already installed on your system (incidentally, Scratch 1.4 and the Scratch 2.0 Offline Editor coexist just fine when installed on the same computer), then compare the similarities and differences between BYOB and Scratch 1.4.

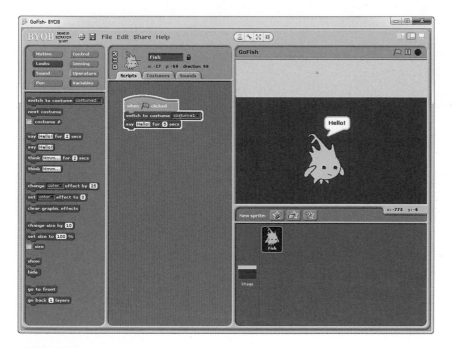

FIGURE 18.9
The BYOB v3 offline editor.

4. Spend some time creating a simple, sample project. This is a good exercise for you because it gives you some experience using Scratch 1.4. Make sure to save your work to your local computer before proceeding to the next step.

5. In BYOB, click Share, Compile This Project. The Windows version notifies that the project compiled successfully; the Mac version does not. Such is the sometimes inscrutable nature of open source software.

6. On Windows systems, check your Documents folder for an `.exe` file that matches the BYOB project name. On Mac systems, BYOB saves the .app executable program file on the Finder Desktop. Either way, double-click the compiled file to run the project. On my systems, the projects ran in Full-Screen mode.

Although you are limited to the Scratch 1.4 feature set, I think it's a good thing that there is a workaround method for creating compiled Scratch projects. The freedom here is that you can share those executable files with other users who might not know anything about Scratch, much less have an editor installed on their system. At the end of the proverbial day, you want as many people as possible playing with your Scratch project, right?

Summary

This was an important hour for those of you who had no previous experience with Scratch, in particular Scratch 1.4. By this time, you are fully apprised as to how Scratch 1.4 and Scratch 2.0 interoperate with each other.

You also understand the mechanics of uploading and downloading Scratch project assets to and from the Scratch website. Finally, you learned some methods for sharing Scratch projects completely independently from the online or offline official Scratch players.

Workshop

Quiz

1. What programming technology underlies Scratch 2.0?

   A. HTML5

   B. Smalltalk

   C. Adobe Flash

2. Which of the following statements is false?

   A. You can open up Scratch 2.0 projects by using Scratch 1.4.

   B. You can open up Scratch 1.4 projects by using the Scratch 2.0 Offline Editor.

   C. You can open up any Scratch project by using the Scratch 2.0 online editor.

3. Imagine that you created a Scratch 2.0 project on the Scratch website. How can you download a Scratch 1.4 version of that project to your computer?

   A. From the project web page, click Share To, and then click Download Code.

   B. From the Scratch online editor, click File, Download to Your Computer.

   C. This action is not possible.

Answers

1. The correct answer is choice C. Scratch 2.0 makes use of a variety of Adobe technologies, including Adobe Flash in the Flash Player. An HTML5 Scratch project player is in development but not by the Scratch Team itself. Smalltalk is the ancient programming language that underlies Scratch 1.4.

2. The correct answer is choice A. The general rule holds that you can open earlier-version projects from later-version software, but the reverse is untrue in all cases.

3. The correct answer is choice C. If you uploaded a Scratch 1.4 project to the Scratch website, that project is considered to be a 1.4 project, and you can use the technique described in answer choice A to accomplish that task. However, downloading the Scratch 1.4 project from the website using the File menu results in a Scratch 2.0 project.

Challenge

Your challenge for this hour is as follows: Create a simple Scratch project that is playable in as many different formats as possible. Make sure that your project runs at full, 100% fidelity in the following situations:

▶ Scratch 1.4 offline player

▶ Scratch 2.0 offline player

▶ Scratch website

▶ Standalone executable code

To accomplish this goal, you need all of the tools discussed in this hour. They are all included in this book's solution file archive, to save you some clicking and some Internet bandwidth. Have fun!

Troubleshooting Your Project

What You'll Learn in This Hour:

▶ Learning the basics of debugging

▶ Resolving common Scratch script errors

▶ Accessing code block help

I once worked for a guy whose favorite expression was GIGO: garbage in, garbage out. Have you heard that expression before?

You must always remember that in computing, there are three processes: input, processing, and output. What my boss referred to is the fact that a computer is only as effective as the instructions it receives from a human being.

If you feed garbage to the computer, then you can expect nothing less than garbage in the output.

This hour of content is particularly important because these skills will help you troubleshoot and debug your program code. You learn a lot of important terminology in this hour, starting with the term *bug*, as a matter of fact.

These software best practices, although sometimes tedious, pay off huge dividends in the end because your players will appreciate the care and effort you put in to making sure that your programs run error free.

You begin this hour by learning the foundational concepts behind troubleshooting software projects.

Learning the Basics of Debugging

I'm sure that you've heard the term *software bug* before. According to Wikipedia (http://is.gd/ZXF662), it was actually the great American inventor, Thomas Edison, who first used the term *bug* in 1878 to describe a problem that lay within a process. You should read that Wikipedia article, actually; it contains a humorous etymology of the term bug.

So if a bug represents a particular problem in your software project, then the practice of debugging refers to your methodology of identifying and removing those errors.

Understanding the Bug Types

Speaking in the broadest terms, a software project may contain errors from one of the following three categories:

▶ **Syntax errors:** These are errors that occur because you structure your code in a way that is inconsistent with the way the programming language works. The good news is that Scratch, with its visual block motif, all but eliminates syntax errors.

▶ **Logical errors:** A logical error occurs due to faulty programming logic that you've included in your project. You'll examine some specific examples of this type of error, as well as how to overcome them, later on in this hour.

▶ **Runtime errors:** These errors make themselves manifest only during the running of your Scratch program—that is, when the Green Flag is clicked. Again, the reasons behind this type of error are myriad, and you'll learn more about this later in this hour.

Color-Coded Script Execution

Have you noticed that when you run a Scratch project, script code that's currently firing on the Stage becomes highlighted, or appears to glow? You can see an example in Figure 19.1.

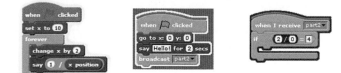

FIGURE 19.1
At left, a running, error-free Scratch 2.0 script. In the middle, a running, error-free Scratch 1.4 script. At right, an unfortunate Scratch 1.4 script that contains a runtime error.

In Scratch 1.4, scripts that are working correctly are highlighted in white, whereas script code that contains one or more errors gets highlighted in a very easy-to-see red. This is also shown in Figure 19.1.

Frankly, it's a mystery why the MIT Scratch Team removed so much troubleshooting functionality with Scratch 2.0. That is, you'll find that if you try to execute a script that contains a definite error, the Scratch interpreter simply ignores that script—and doesn't visually let you know that there's a problem.

I highly suggest that you download and install Scratch 1.4 on your computer (http://is.gd/iluIQK), so you can take advantage of the troubleshooting goodness that the Scratch Team included in that project version. In fact, you'll use Scratch 1.4 during the first Try It Yourself exercises in this hour.

What Is Unit Testing?

In software development, unit testing describes the method by which a programmer systematically tests all code modules that are included in a project, to make sure that the project runs correctly.

It is considered sloppy programming practice to put your project together as quickly as possible and release it to the public without performing rigorous unit testing along the way.

Unit testing is an iterative process, which means that you need to practice it over and over again, especially once you've made a change somewhere in your Scratch project code.

The good news is that you can easily perform unit testing with Scratch by simply double-clicking each script throughout your project. Is this tedious? Yes. Nevertheless, your players will thank you for it as your project grows in stature and popularity.

NOTE

Get Used to Unit Testing

Unit testing is a big deal in professional software development. To that end, some vendors sell entire software suites that enable programmer groups to automate unit testing for large-scale enterprise projects. The bottom line is that if you're interested in entering programming as a career, you'd better get used to unit testing, and quickly.

Differentiating Single Stepping Mode from Turbo Mode

Scratchers like me who cut their proverbial teeth on Scratch 1.4 were doubly disappointed to observe the MIT Scratch Team's excision of Single Stepping mode from Scratch 2.0. What do I mean?

In Scratch 1.4, you can instruct the Scratch interpreter to execute each script one block at a time, slowly. Believe me, once you get used to single stepping, it's very difficult to adapt to not having it in Scratch 2.0.

For example, you may have a fairly complicated Scratch project that you're working on, and you're not exactly sure which script block is causing a runtime error. You can enable single stepping, and carefully watch what happens as each block in each script stack is executed. It's good stuff!

By contrast, Turbo mode runs the scripts in your Scratch project at an accelerated speed. This feature is advantageous if you, for instance, want to closely examine events that occur later in your project's runtime cycle, and don't want to sit around waiting for long pauses. The downside to Turbo mode is that enabling it can make some of your graphics appear and move sluggishly.

Either way, it is important to understand that both Single Stepping mode and Turbo mode are diagnostic modes that should not be enabled when you publish your project to the public. These are internal development tools only.

NOTE

What Are Breakpoints?

Single Stepping mode in Scratch is redolent of yet another enterprise software development principle. In the professional software world, your programming tools ordinarily include a rich debugging environment, including the ability to set breakpoints in your code. With a breakpoint, your code executes up to the breakpoint and then script execution stops. Working in slow motion like this makes it much easier to isolate bugs that otherwise would be remarkably difficult to find.

▼ TRY IT YOURSELF

Work with Scratch 1.4 Troubleshooting Tools and Unit Testing

This Try It Yourself exercise assumes that you have Scratch 1.4 downloaded and installed on your computer. From the book's solution files archive, open the file `Hour19a.sb`. Note that this is a Scratch 1.4, and not a Scratch 2.0, project file.

In this exercise you gain some experience with troubleshooting and testing a Scratch 2.0 project. Work through the following steps to complete the exercise:

1. Open the project file, and click the Green Flag icon to run it. Watch the two scripts in the Scripts pane very carefully. What color was the `when   clicked` script highlighted when it ran? How about the `when I receive message1` script?

2. For a bit of experience with unit testing, try double-clicking the `when   clicked` block. Now do the same thing with the `when I receive message1` block. This is, in fact, unit testing, albeit on a more simplified, smaller scale.

3. Now disconnect the `if   then` block from the `when I receive message1` block and connect the longer script that is included below it in the Scripts pane.

   Click Edit, Start Single Stepping, then click the Green Flag icon and watch as the two scripts are slowly executed, block by block. Do you see how much easier single stepping makes understanding your script's execution? When you're finished, click Edit, Stop Single Stepping to turn the function off.

You might have noticed the option Set Single Stepping in the Edit menu. The Scratch 1.4 single stepper allows you to set one of four possible values for script block execution:

▶ **Turbo Speed**: Runs the project at an accelerated speed, with no block highlighting

▶ **Normal**: Runs the project as it normally does, with no block highlighting

▶ **Flash Blocks (Fast)**: Runs a project at normal speed, but highlights active blocks yellow

▶ **Flash Blocks (Slow)**: Runs the project slowly, and turns blocks yellow as they become active

As mentioned earlier, the only stepping feature that the Scratch Team included in Scratch 2.0 is Turbo mode. In the Scratch 2.0 Editor, click Edit, Turbo Mode to enable or disable this function.

Centralizing Your Code

One method to make tasks like unit testing and stepping through your scripts granularly a lot easier is to organize your scripts throughout your project in a logical manner.

In the computer software industry, poorly designed and written programs are called *spaghetti code*.

The general rule is simply this: For each sprite included in your project, make sure that all scripts attached to each sprite are pertinent only to that sprite.

You should store general, program-wide assets, such as background sounds, variable definitions, and the like, on the script page for the Stage. This methodology has the advantage of centralizing general-purpose code, which makes the rest of your code easier to understand—both for you and anyone else who examines your Scratch project source code.

As you can see in Figure 19.2, you can add a great deal of generic programming logic to the Stage. The only type of code that the Stage cannot handle is speech; you'll see far fewer blocks on the Looks palette for the Stage than for any other sprite. This makes sense because we typically don't envision the Stage as a speaking part (unless discussing the *Wizard of Oz*, but that's a discussion for another time).

Remembering to Use Stage Monitors

In Hours 12 and 13, "Using Data Blocks" and "Using Cloud Data," respectively, you gained a lot of valuable experience in creating and using variables. Those hours stressed how useful Stage monitors can be for presenting data to your end users.

However, for the purposes of this hour and debugging Scratch projects, temporarily and selectively enabling Stage monitors can prove invaluable. Complete the following Try It Yourself exercise to underscore that point.

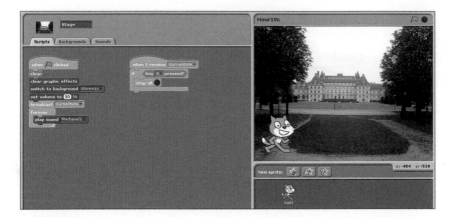

FIGURE 19.2
Centralizing generic code on the Stage is a nice way to keep your scripts organized and clutter free.

▼ TRY IT YOURSELF

Debug Scratch by Using Stage Monitors

For this Try It Yourself exercise, open up the file `Hour19b.sb` from the book's solution files archive. In this exercise, you continue your journey with Scratch 1.4; hopefully you're enjoying comparing and contrasting the two Scratch Editor versions. Work through the following steps to complete the exercise:

1. Once you have the practice file open, click the Green Flag to start the project. There is an intentional logical error in the code; can you spot what it is?

2. It might be helpful for you to see the value of the This Year variable on the Stage, as well as the answer provided by the player. Turn on the Stage monitor for the This Year variable by visiting the Variables palette. Enable the answer Stage monitor by navigating to the Sensing palette.

3. A hint to solving this logical problem is that you need to replace the Operator block that is nested inside the `say Hello! for 2 secs` block.

Resolving Common Scratch Script Errors

This section walks you through a brief "rogues gallery" of common Scratch script errors—and how you can fix them or, even better, prevent them from occurring in the first place.

Obsolete Blocks

Throughout this book, you've seen in stark color that later versions of Scratch, besides adding nifty new features, also remove functionality that was present in Scratch 1.4.

For example, you may have a Scratch 1.4 project that works fine in the Scratch 1.4 environment, but trying to run that code in Scratch 2.0 produces unexpected results. To wit, the following Scratch 1.4 blocks were removed in the official release of Scratch 2.0:

> ▶ **Forever If ()**: This block was removed because the Scratch Team felt that you can replicate the same functionality by placing an ![if then] block into a ![forever] block.

> ▶ **Stop All**: This block was removed because the Scratch 2.0 ![stop all ▼] block expands upon the ability to simply stop all scripts in the project at once.

> ▶ **Stop Script**: This block was removed for the same reason as was the Stop All block.

Figure 19.3 shows an example of what you'll see if you run a Scratch 1.4 project with an obsolete block in the Scratch 2.0 Editor.

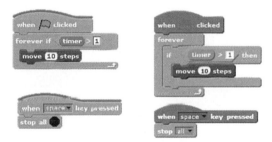

FIGURE 19.3
Scratch 2.0 does a great job of transforming obsolete blocks. At left, you see the Scratch 1.4 code containing obsolete blocks; at right, you see how Scratch 2.0 made dynamic substitution to make the code continue to work.

NOTE

The Debug It Studio

The MIT Scratch Team also publishes a number of educational Scratch projects at the gallery; the Scratch Team's username is ScratchEdTeam. In particular, pay attention to the Debug It Studio (http://is.gd/IKQ29w), from which many of the debugging ideas in this hour were derived.

Logic Errors

A logic error is a cognitive mistake that is manifested in your program code and that prevents your program from doing what you intended it to do.

Logic errors are differentiated from syntax errors; as mentioned at the beginning of this hour, a syntax error is almost impossible to make in Scratch because Scratch uses blocks instead of requiring you to memorize arcane keywords and mathematical operators.

Normally, a logic error in code that results in division by zero generates an error at best and crashes the program at worst. Luckily, Scratch 2.0 saves you from this particular error. You'll find that division by zero in Scratch scripts results in an answer of Infinity, which is both mathematically sound and continues your script running, albeit with potentially unexpected results.

As you know, computers can perform mathematical operations with 100 percent accuracy. However, in accordance with the aforementioned GIGO rule, if your algorithm is off the mark, then the end result in code (and the program's runtime) will be correspondingly off the mark.

NOTE

What Is an Algorithm?

Algorithm is a five-dollar word that's used in computer programming as a way to scare off newcomers to the field.... Just joking! An algorithm, in terms of computer science, is simply a step-by-step procedure for performing a particular calculation or data-processing task. An algorithm does not need to involve higher-level mathematics and intense, lateral thinking. For example, a simple Scratch script that determines whether one sprite is touching another sprite, and if so, a particular action occurs, is a perfectly valid programming algorithm.

Managing Timing

Have you run into the problem with one of your Scratch projects where you need more than one sprite to act in conjunction with each other, and the timing is simply off?

Don't worry; this is a common problem. The good news is that it's quite simple to fix. My preferred method for synchronizing or otherwise coordinating scripts is to use broadcasts.

You've used broadcasts quite a bit in the book thus far, so I won't belabor the point any further than that. For my money, the sending and receiving of broadcasts provides the best possible way for sprites to interact with each other on the Stage.

Another method you can try is to manipulate the built-in Scratch timer. According to the Scratch Wiki (http://is.gd/vfvM5d), the built-in timer is extraordinarily accurate, accumulating only one full day of error after approximately 185 years.

As discussed previously, the timer denotes how long each project has been open; the two ways to reset the timer are to (1) open a new project in the editor or (2) use the `reset timer` block from the Sensing category.

You gain some experience with mastering the timer in the forthcoming Try It Yourself exercise.

Orphaned Assets

Sometimes in Scratch development, it's easy to get caught up in the excitement of things and inadvertently remove assets from your project, without performing immediate unit testing.

For example, suppose you added a particular sound file to your project, and you hinged some conditional logic upon that sound file itself. If you later removed that sound file from the project, you might be unpleasantly surprised the next time you click the Green Flag.

NOTE

What Is Smoke Testing?

Professional software developers have a name for testing the execution of your project quickly after performing any significant change to the code: *smoke testing*. This somewhat tongue-in-cheek term arises from the world of electronics and electrical engineering, where, when you turn on a test circuit, the presence or absence of smoke from the materials lets you know immediately whether or not there's a problem.

The bottom line, friends, is that developing software, even in the hand-holding confines of Scratch 2.0, requires rigorous testing. Checking and rechecking your code needs to be the rule— *not* the exception.

TRY IT YOURSELF ▼

Smoke Testing with Sprites and the Scratch Timer

For this Try It Yourself exercise, you return to the world of Scratch 2.0 and gain some experience with smoke testing and using the timer. Using your Scratch 2 Offline Editor, open the practice file `Hour19c.sb2` from your solution files archive. Work through the following steps to complete the exercise:

1. After you have the project open, click the Green Flag to get a general feel for what's going on. Essentially what's happening is this: The centralized code on the Stage, among other things, resets the timer back to zero.

   Make sure that you're showing the timer as a Stage monitor.

▼

2. Now it's time for some experimentation. First, click File, Save As to save a copy of the file under a different name; you don't want to destroy the original copy of the file. Second, delete the Cat2 sprite and rerun the program, observing how the Scratch interpreter handled the change of the missing asset.

3. As a challenge, rework the code (the technical term for this is *refactor*) so that you use only broadcasts and variables instead of the built-in timer. Before you do this, use Undo or reopen the original file to bring back the Cat2 sprite. If you're stuck, check out the solution file in the code archives; the filename is `Hour19d.sb2`.

NOTE

What Is Refactoring?

Code refactoring is a big deal in the professional programming world. The main point of refactoring is that you want to restructure your existing computer code to make it smaller, more compact, and more sensible, but without changing its external behavior one iota. Now more than ever before, things like code readability and reduced complexity are valued highly in the software development world. You must develop these habits early if you plan to take your Scratch programming to the next level with more complicated programming languages and frameworks.

Accessing Code Block Help

For the remainder of this hour, you work with the Scratch 2.0 Editor. The MIT Scratch Team did a good job of documenting the editor itself, both the online and offline varieties.

Open up a representative project on the Scratch website, and go inside to see the source code. Click the Tips menu on the top navigation bar. This item is actually a button—a toggle switch as it were—that opens and closes an online help panel, as shown in Figure 19.4.

The Tips panel is broken down into the following three general categories:

▶ **Getting Started**: The links here take you to tutorials of various depths. The first is for beginners, the second is for more intermediate users, and the third and fourth provide in-depth help for the Project Editor and Paint Editor, respectively.

▶ **How To**: The help here is divided into five subcategories: Effects, Animation, Games, Stories, and Music. Not coincidentally, these are the main Scratch project types that you'll find in the Scratch gallery.

▶ **Blocks**: The help here is divided by the Scratch block pallet designations, such as Motion, Looks, Sound, and so forth.

FIGURE 19.4
The Tips panel on the Scratch 2.0 Editor provides a convenient way to obtain online help.

To use the Tips panel, click a hyperlink to go directly to that topic. By contrast, the little + denotes a disclosure; click the + to expand that category into a number of options. You can see what I mean by studying Figure 19.4.

One advantage of the Tips panel is that the help is visual—and not simply a sea of dense text, as you see with some other vendors' help systems. In fact, you should check out Scratch Cards (http://is.gd/Ydl8MZ), which are freely downloadable Adobe Portable Document Format (PDF) files that graphically show you how to accomplish a number of common tasks in Scratch 2.0.

Getting Help with Specific Scratch Blocks

If you find yourself at a loss as to remembering the purpose of a particular Scratch block, fear not. In the center of the top toolbar in the Scratch Editor, click the question mark icon .

When block help is active, your mouse pointer appears as a small question mark itself. Next, click on a block you want to know more about from the middle Scripts pane. After a moment's pause, the Tips drawer opens (unless it was open already) and displays a graphical online Help screen for that particular block.

Therefore, accessing block help via the Tips drawer directly and accessing block help using the question mark icon are simply two equivalent means of performing the same task. Figure 19.5 shows the relevant interface.

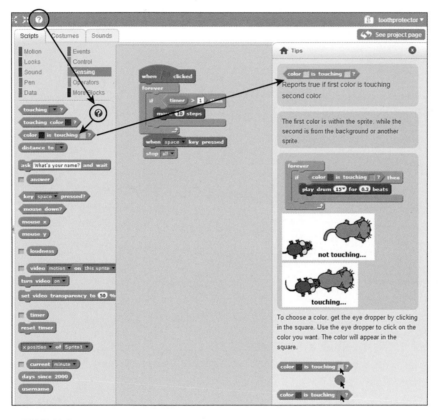

FIGURE 19.5
Scratch block help is context sensitive, which offers convenience to the busy Scratcher who does not want to lose momentum.

Summary

In this hour, you learned the basics of software debugging. Hopefully, you found the material presented here and the associated opportunities for practice were less fear-inducing than you might've thought at the outset. To be sure, many of the subjects discussed in this hour—especially those that relate to mathematics and logical thinking—tend to be the main fear areas for those who have trepidation about learning to program.

In the next hour, you'll be back to the "fun stuff." That is, you'll learn how to use other Scratchers' work as a springboard in creating and publishing a remix. Stay tuned!

Workshop

Quiz

1. Which of the following expressions will likely result in a logic error in your Scratch project code?

   A. (2 + 3) / 8 – 2

   B. (2 / 3) + 8 – 2

   C. 2 + 3 / 8 – 2

2. Which of the following statements best describes the purpose of single stepping in Scratch 1.4?

   A. You use single stepping as a way to speed up a project.

   B. You use single stepping as a way to slow down a project.

   C. You use single stepping as a way to convert your project.

3. Which of the following methods is an example of performing unit testing in Scratch?

   A. Double-clicking each script in turn

   B. Resetting the timer

   C. Creating a custom block

Answers

1. The correct answer is choice C, although perhaps not for the reason that you would expect. Any computer programmer worth his or her salt needs to be fully aware of and a master of the arithmetic order of operations. (Here's a reference: http://is.gd/cV6wUu.) Choices A and B are much more explicit in terms of how those arithmetic operations relate to the order of operations. By contrast, the expression in choice C is highly ambiguous, and can result in a number of different solutions.

2. The correct answer is choice B. By enabling single stepping in a Scratch 1.4 project, you can carefully watch the execution of every block within every script as the project runs. This makes debugging the project much easier. It is unfortunate that Scratch 2.0 does not include single stepping, at least as of this writing.

3. The correct answer is choice A. Although Scratch includes no automated user-testing tools, you can manually unit test by double-clicking each script in turn and watching for unexpected results, abnormal behavior, and so forth.

Challenge

Your challenge for this hour is to work through all of the MIT Scratch Team's Debug-It projects published at http://is.gd/IKQ29w.

Now this is important, so listen up: Read the Instructions field before you enter the project and use your newfound troubleshooting skills to determine where the problems lie. However, do not under any circumstances read the comments because doing so will ruin your challenge. (Many Scratchers explained the rationale for solving the problems in the comments.)

I think you'll find these projects to be interesting and educational in addition to being challenging. In fact, you can also choose to remix any of these debug projects; you'll learn all about remixing in the following hour in this book.

HOUR 20
Remixing a Project

What You'll Learn in This Hour:

▶ The importance of attribution

▶ Understanding the remix tree

▶ How to remix a Scratch project

▶ Remixing part of another Scratcher's project

▶ Improving the visibility of your remix

As you'll recall, the MIT Scratch Team named its product after the disc jockey (DJ) technique of moving a vinyl record back and forth on a turntable with the goal of producing unique sounds.

The Scratch Team, if nothing else, has a sense of humor because what you'll learn about in this hour, remixing, also dates back to my generation—the 1980s.

According to Wikipedia, a *remix* is a song that has been edited or completely redone such that it sounds different from the original version. In case you're not of my generation and have no idea what a vinyl record or remix cassette tape looks like, check out Figure 20.1.

FIGURE 20.1
A vintage turntable (left) and a remix cassette tape (right).

The Importance of Attribution

While browsing the Scratch gallery, you're sure to find projects that you strongly admire. Perhaps you'll see a project and think to yourself, "Wow. I could really improve upon this project." That's fine—that's what the open source Scratch community is all about.

In the closed source software development world, you must always ask for permission before using anyone else's intellectual property. These rules are relaxed somewhat in the open source world, which is where the Scratch project lives.

Nonetheless, you need to understand how important it is to give attribution, or credit, whenever you borrow another Scratcher's ideas, no matter how insignificant the "borrowing" you might perceive it to be.

You might wonder, "Okay, then. How *do* I contact another Scratcher to ask permission to use some of his or her project assets for a Scratch game I'm working on?"

Actually, answering this question isn't as straightforward as it might appear. You see, the MIT Scratch Team feels strongly that all communications (and I mean *all* communications) should occur in public.

To that end, you'll see a decided lack of instant message (IM) functionality on the Scratch website. From experience, the best way to reach out to another Scratcher is either to leave a comment on his or her profile page, or to participate in a discussion forum thread in which that user has posted.

To its credit, the MIT Scratch Team has done a great job in preserving the privacy of all of its members. You would be hard-pressed to "mine" personal information such as an email address given simply a Scratch username. It's a good system, even if it is a bit counterintuitive at times, like when you're actually seeking attribution.

What Not to Do: Project Copying

If you download another Scratcher's project, and then upload the unmodified project to your own account and publish it with no attribution, then you've undertaken a big no-no in the Scratch community called *project copying*.

Project copying is a bad idea for many reasons, not the least of which is that you are claiming someone else's work as an original creation where no original creation exists.

If you, by contrast, download another Scratcher's product and make any change to it before reuploading and republishing that project, this is considered a remix, and not a project copy. In this case, you need to provide clear documentation that you've remixed that Scratcher's project, and that you are giving him or her proper attribution.

The good news is that Scratch 2.0 makes the process of remixing very easy, and therefore the process of project copying or inappropriately claiming credit much more difficult. That's what you learn about in this hour,

What If Someone Copies Your Work?

If you discover that another Scratcher has copied your work without providing proper attribution and/or a remix notification, you can report that project.

As you can see in Figure 20.2, the project page has a Report This button that, when clicked, exposes a message pane where you can clearly explain to the MIT Scratch Team why you're reporting that project.

FIGURE 20.2
You can easily report a project to the Scratch Team if you feel, for example, that the author is using your work without providing due credit.

Every Scratcher should be aware of the Scratch Community Guidelines, posted on the website at http://is.gd/N1wwTw. The following is a brief version of the guidelines for your convenience and reference:

▶ Be respectful.

▶ Be constructive.

▶ Share.

▶ Keep personal information private.

▶ Help keep the Scratch website friendly.

The other place in the Scratch website hierarchy where you can report content that you feel to be inappropriate is the Scratch Discussion Forums. Every single post has a Report link that you can click to call out that post to the MIT Scratch Team for whatever reason you choose. Be descriptive, but also don't go overboard with the complaints. Instead, be judicious if at all possible. After all, we are all human, and we all make mistakes.

Now, then: I guess I'll get off my soapbox and we can continue... ;-)

Understanding the Remix Tree

Remember earlier when I told you that Scratch 2.0 includes technology that makes remixing easier and stealing other people's work more difficult? Well, you might've noticed the small tree icon that appears on every Scratch project page.

This button links to the remix tree, which is a graphical representation and history (call it a chronology) of the remix history for a particular project.

The remix tree serves several benefits, some of which include the following points:

▶ The tree lets project authors know who has remixed their project.

▶ The tree gives attribution both to the original creator of the project as well as those who have remixed the project.

▶ The tree serves as a measure of relative popularity of the project; the more remixes a project has, the higher that project's visibility across the Scratch website.

NOTE

Behind the Scenes with the Remix Tree

In contrast to the online Scratch project player, which as you know by now was written using Adobe Flash, the remix tree animation is a combination of two web standards: HTML5 and JavaScript. Eventually, you'll outgrow Scratch and seek to learn more powerful programming languages. You will discover that in web development, HTML5 and JavaScript represent the "bread-and-butter" programming languages.

Get to Know the Scratch Remix Tree

In this Try It Yourself exercise, you visit a popular Scratch project and spend some time in understanding its remix history. Make sure you're logged in to the Scratch website with your user account prior to starting this exercise; follow those steps to complete all required tasks:

1. Point your web browser to the Super Mushroom Bowl! project by Broguy (http://is.gd/ E6x4B8). If, for whatever reason, this project does not exist by the time you undertake this practice exercise, simply search the Scratch online gallery for a popular project.

2. Click the Remix Tree button in the lower-right corner of the Scratch player interface. Before you do that, though, look at the view count immediately to the left of the remix tree. That's a pretty impressive number, isn't it?

3. Figure 20.3 shows a screen capture of the remix tree as it appeared during this writing. Notice that the original project shows up in the trunk of this metaphorical tree. Hover your mouse over that project and a pop-up window appears, providing metadata.

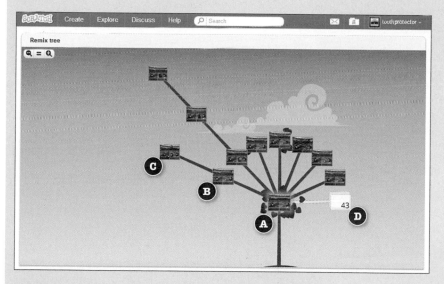

FIGURE 20.3
Scratch remix tree: (A) The original project, (B) a remix, (C) a remix of a remix, and (D) links to additional remixes of this project.

4. Now work your way outward in the tree. Notice that the tree graphically represents not only direct remixes, but also remixes that are based on remixes. Thus, the tree metaphor for Scratch project remixing is especially apt.

5. Click your mouse on one of the remix or re-remix projects to jump to that project page. As shown in Figure 20.4, you can see clear attribution, all having been added automatically (or "automagically" depending upon your perspective) by the Scratch Team.

6. Finally, notice the Remixes box that appears on the project page. In Figure 20.4, you can easily view any directly linked remixed projects by clicking their thumbnail icons here.

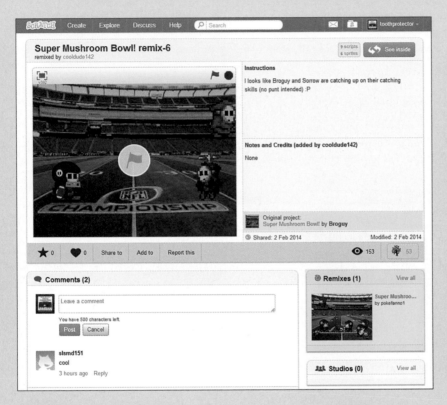

FIGURE 20.4
Remixed projects have automatically generated attribution links that make it easier to trace the development history of a Scratch project.

How to Remix a Scratch Project

Okay—you have finally reached where the proverbial rubber meets the road. You understand what remixing is and you see how the remix tree provides many benefits to all Scratchers involved in the process.

The question remains, though: How can you remix a project that you really love? Try the following Try It Yourself exercise to see how easy that is.

Remix a Project

In this Try It Yourself exercise, you pick out a project that you admire and initiate a remix of that project in Scratch 2.0. As always, make sure that you are at the Scratch website and logged in to the site with your Scratch account. To complete this exercise, work through the following steps:

1. Browse the Scratch project gallery until you find a project that inspires you. Take a look at the number of people who have favorited, loved, viewed, and remixed that project. For myself, I chose the cool Asteroids game by RadthorDax (http://is.gd/hRUNpT).

2. Click the See Inside button, as you've grown accustomed to doing seemingly countless times as you've worked your way through this book.

3. Here is where things get different: Click the orange Remix button in the upper-right corner of the Scratch 2.0 online editor. You'll find that the following two things have happened automatically:

   ▶ The project title has "remix" appended to it.

   ▶ A copy of the project has been saved to your My Stuff page.

4. Click See Your Project Page In the Scratch Editor; observe that the instructions from the original game have been carried over to your remixed copy. However, this is a read/write field, and you can edit this text if you want to.

5. In the Notes and Credits box, read the encouragement text provided by the MIT Scratch Team.

6. Notice the link to the original project on the page. Attribution made easy!

7. Share your remixed project, at least temporarily, and click the View the Remix Tree icon on your project page. You should be able to find your project in that tree. Congratulations! By now, you are a true member of the Scratch community. All of this is shown in the interface in Figure 20.5.

FIGURE 20.5
Here, you can see the entire Scratch 2.0 remixing process in one figure.

Remixing Part of Another Scratcher's Project

What if you are inspired by bits and pieces of another Scratcher's project, but you do not want to remix the entire thing? What are your options in this regard?

Well, you can certainly cherry-pick bits and pieces from other Scratchers' work, with the caveat that it is your responsibility to provide attribution once you've reuploaded those assets into your project. There exist two primary workflows for remixing individual components from another Scratcher's project:

▶ Use the Backpack.

▶ Manually download and upload the assets.

Using the Scratch 2.0 Backpack

Personally, I find the Backpack functionality in Scratch 2.0 to be a godsend. The Backpack enables you to transport assets (sprites, code blocks, and so forth) between projects in the Scratch 2.0 online editor.

As of this writing, the MIT Scratch Team has not yet implemented Backpack functionality in the Scratch 2.0 Offline Editor. Maybe someday!

To reuse assets between Scratch projects, follow these general steps:

1. In the source project, drag the asset (for instance, a sprite) from the editor's main interface down on top of the Backpack. The Backpack is docked to the bottom of the Scratch 2.0 online editor interface, as shown in Figure 20.6.

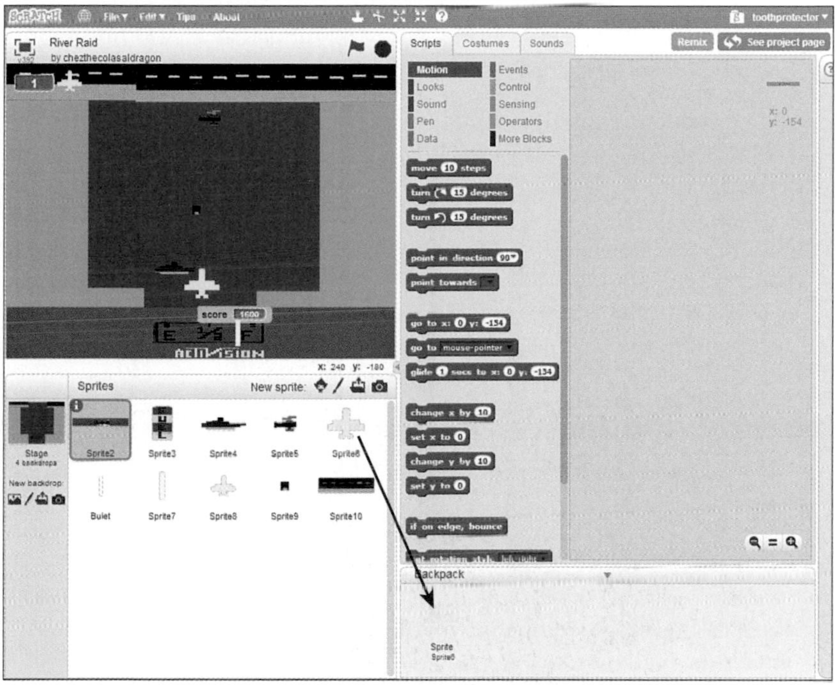

FIGURE 20.6
To add an asset to the Backpack, simply drag it into the Backpack pane.

2. In the target project, click on the Backpack pane to expand the Backpack.

3. Drag the asset from the Backpack into the Scratch online editor interface. That's all there is to it!

NOTE

How Long Do Assets Stick Around in the Backpack?

The Scratch 2.0 Backpack has a feature that can be simultaneously considered an advantage and a disadvantage. That is, objects that are included in your Backpack persist indefinitely. It is up to you to remove them by right-clicking on the unwanted Backpack assets and selecting Delete from the shortcut menu. Otherwise, the assets will remain in your account's Backpack (theoretically) forever.

Another point to ponder is that the items in the Backpack are difficult to preview because they are represented with tiny icons. Therefore, over time you might find yourself dragging Backpack items into the Scripts pane of your current project simply to remind yourself of what they are and what they do.

So you see that you can use the Scratch 2.0 Backpack to shuttle assets around. This feature is much more powerful than you might think. For instance, not only will the Backpack transmit a sprite, but it will also transmit all associated costumes in script code along with it!

Now about the question of attribution. Unlike the remix model, which automatically credits those from whom you borrow assets, the Backpack method and the manual method you are about to learn do not do this.

Therefore, it is incumbent upon you to add attribution manually on your project's public web page. You might also want to leave a comment on the original project's page, thanking the author for making his or her assets available. As you'll learn in the next hour, you can invest quite a bit of time and effort in drawing your own sprites and Stage backdrops.

Manually Exporting and Importing Scratch Assets

Given how easy it is to use the Scratch 2.0 Backpack, you might wonder why you would ever manually download an asset from another Scratcher's project.

Actually, there are some very good reasons for doing so. For example, you might like a particular Stage backdrop that another Scratcher added to a project, but you feel it would be just perfect if you added a couple tweaks to the image. To do this, you need a local copy of the file on your computer, so you can load it into your favorite image editor.

The same goes for audio files, other media files, sprites, and the like.

To manually download and upload assets in Scratch 2.0, follow the general workflow in the following steps:

1. In the source project, save the sprite or media asset from the online editor to a local file on your computer.

2. Use tools on your local computer to modify that downloaded asset, until it is satisfactory to you.

3. Start a new project in the Scratch online editor.

4. Use the Scratch Editor's upload functionality to transfer your locally stored copy of the asset to your new project.

Complete the following Try It Yourself exercise to gain some practice in both manual asset transfer and in the use of the Scratch 2.0 Backpack.

Work with the Backpack

Suppose you've become enamored with the River Raid Atari 2600 clone published on the Scratch gallery by the Scratch user chezthecolasaldragon (http://is.gd/XRCSOr). Specifically, you determined that you don't want to do a remix of the game, but instead want to make use of particular sprite and Stage assets for your own new project. To complete the exercise, perform the following steps:

1. Once you're at the project page, click See Inside to enter the Scratch 2.0 online editor.

2. Click the Stage and navigate to the Backdrops panel. Download background1 by right-clicking its thumbnail icon and selecting Save to Local File from the shortcut menu. Make a note of where you saved the file on your local computer.

3. Once you've downloaded the file, open it up in your favorite paint program, and make some modifications to the file. The specific changes are not important here; the general procedure is the learning opportunity.

4. Back in the Scratch 2.0 online editor, drag the Sprite6 sprite (the plane, if you are using the River Raid game) on top of the Backpack to add the asset to the Backpack.

5. Click File, New to start a new project. Give the file a unique name, and click File, Save to add the project permanently to your My Stuff project list.

6. Expand the Backpack, and drag and drop the Plane sprite into your new project's Sprites list. Look in the Scripts area, and verify that the script code from the original project came along for the proverbial ride. Isn't that cool? The interface is shown in Figure 20.7. The figure doesn't to show the default Scratch Cat sprite. However, as you know, any new project includes an instance of this sprite to get you started.

7. Click the Stage, and navigate to the Backdrops tab in your new project. Click the button and select your previously downloaded backdrop image.

8. Click See Project Page to navigate to the project's public web page. Make sure that you populate the Notes and Credits field, giving credit to the original project author. The best practice is to include the web address of that project page; this is particularly important because of the lack of a remix chain when using this method.

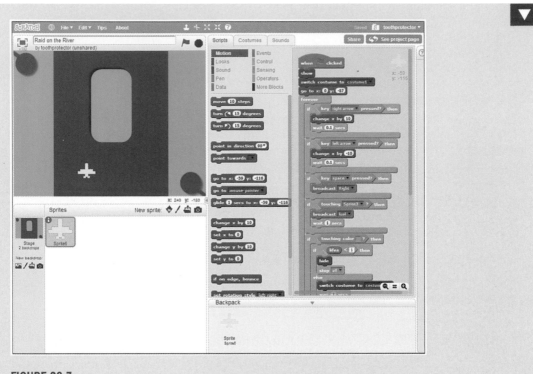

FIGURE 20.7
A new project that includes selected assets from another project.

Improving the Visibility of Your Remix

One of the many cool things about Scratch remixes is that everyone in that remix tree wins in terms of benefitting from project popularity on the Scratch website. What do I mean by this?

On the Scratch home page, also called the front page (http://is.gd/V68DV9), you'll see a section called What the Community Is Remixing. This mini gallery shows the most remixed projects over the past 10 days. An edited version of the front page is shown in Figure 20.8.

Hopefully, it stands to reason that if you remixed a project that gets picked up by the What the Community Is Remixing feature, you are going to get more "eyeballs" on your project as well. That's what is meant by "everybody wins in a remix chain."

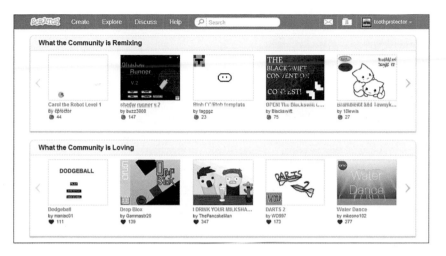

FIGURE 20.8
The What the Community Is Remixing feature on the Scratch home page.

About Studios

Studios were called *galleries* in Scratch 1.4. A studio is a container web page where Scratchers can place links to multiple projects. For example, you might want to create a studio that aggregates other Scratchers' projects that you are considering remixing.

Using Figure 20.9 as a guide, examine the following main interface elements of a typical Scratch studio. For instance, check out the Atari Collection studio at http://is.gd/UQqp5v.

- ▶ **A:** The cover image is an image that the project owner uploads as a way to visually describe the purpose of the studio.

- ▶ **B:** The Projects tab provides links to all Scratch projects that are included in the studio.

- ▶ **C:** The Comments tab provides a way for Scratchers to communicate with each other in the context of the entire studio.

- ▶ **D:** The Curators tab lists managers and curators, who represent the two chief administrative roles in a studio. You'll learn more about them in a moment.

- ▶ **E:** The Activity tab lists metadata related to projects being added to the studio, comments, and so forth.

I'd like to talk a little bit more about the delegated administration model used in Scratch studios. When you create your own studio, you are, by definition, the manager for that studio. This means you can do whatever you want with the studio, including deleting it.

FIGURE 20.9
Components of a Scratch studio.

In a brilliant move, the MIT Scratch Team also allows studio managers to designate one or more curators, who have some, but not all, administrative ability within the studio. The main action the curators can take is to add new content (that is, projects) to the studio.

In the following Try It Yourself exercise, you gain the experience of creating your own studio.

▼ TRY IT YOURSELF

Create a Studio

Imagine that you want to create a studio to house those projects from which you might want to harvest assets or create complete remixes of. Log in to the Scratch website prior to starting this exercise. Work through the following steps to complete the exercise:

1. Navigate to your My Stuff list. At the top of the page, click the New Studio button. The Untitled Studio page appears.

2. Click the Add Projects button. Observe that you'll need the uniform resource locator (called URL, or more commonly a web address) of each project that you want to add to the studio.

▼

3. In your web browser, open up another browser tab, navigate to the Scratch website, and locate a project that you want to add to your studio. On that project's page, for example, a typical project URL looks like the following:

   http://scratch.mit.edu/projects/16497682/

4. Switch your browser tab back to your studio, paste in the previously copied URL, and click the Add by URL button. The project will be added to your studio.

5. Hover your mouse over the newly added project; clicking the X icon in the upper-right corner removes that project from your studio. Don't worry—you're not deleting the project.

6. In your studio interface, navigate to the Curators tab. Click the Invite Curators button and observe that you need another Scratcher's username to send an invitation message to that Scratcher, asking him or her to become a curator of your studio.

7. Before leaving the studio interface, hover your mouse over the studio image placeholder, and notice the Change button. Clicking the thumbnail allows you to upload a custom studio image from your computer. Also, be sure to use the Description field to describe to other Scratchers what your studio is all about.

8. Navigate back to your My Stuff page, and click the My Studios filter. This is where you can quickly and easily find all of your own studios.

NOTE

The Power of the Web Browser Refresh

There might be times when you make a change in Scratch 2.0 (for example, adding a project to a studio), and the change doesn't appear to take place. When this happens, your best corrective method is to reload the browser web page. You can do that by clicking the Reload or Refresh button on your web browser toolbar. Also, you can press F5 on your computer keyboard. Performing a refresh fetches a new copy of the page from the Scratch web servers in Cambridge, Massachusetts.

Summary

In this hour, you learned quite a bit more about collaboration from the perspective of Scratch software development. You now understand how the remix process works, how to perform remixes, and how to ensure that all attribution guidelines have been correctly implemented.

You also learned about some of the Scratch 2.0 technologies that surround the remix, namely, the What the Community Is Remixing feature on the front page and the concept of the project studio.

Workshop

Quiz

1. Which of the following is *not* directly one of the Scratch Community Guidelines?

   A. Keep personal info private.

   B. Give credit where credit is due.

   C. Help keep the site friendly.

2. What is the first step toward remixing a project that you are interested in?

   A. Click the Remix button in the Scratch 2.0 online editor.

   B. Click New Project in your My Stuff list.

   C. Click See Inside to expose the project source code.

3. A Scratch studio can contain links only to your own projects or those projects remixed by you.

   A. True

   B. False

Answers

1. The correct answer is choice B. The concept of giving credit where credit is due is indirectly part of the Scratch Community Guidelines as part of the Share guideline. However, this question asked you which one of those statements is *not directly* one of the Scratch Community Guidelines. (Incidentally, you can read the guidelines at http://is.gd/N1wwTw.)

2. The correct answer is choice C. Your first step in remixing a project is clicking the See Inside button to expose the project source code. Your second step is to click the Remix button.

3. The correct answer is choice B. The studio can contain links to any Scratch project, regardless of its ownership status. The only requirement is that the project must be shared.

Challenge

Your challenge for this hour is to create a new studio named My Remixed Projects that contains at least two project remixes created by you. Be sure to "dress up" your studio by including a detailed description as well as a colorful cover image.

Creating Your Own Sprites and Backdrops

What You'll Learn in This Hour:

▶ Introducing GIMP

▶ Understanding bitmap and vector graphics modes

▶ Creating a new Stage backdrop

▶ Creating a custom sprite—the easy way

▶ Creating a custom sprite—the difficult way

As nice as the built-in library of Scratch assets is, sometimes you simply feel that you can do a better job by creating those assets yourself. In this hour, you learn how to draw your own sprites and Stage backdrops from (again, pardon the pun) scratch.

No, this hour is not an art class. To be sure, my own creative outlet takes the form of making music with my guitar—I can't draw to save my life. Nonetheless, by the end of this hour, you'll have the tools and skills with which, should you need or want to, you can build your own, one-of-a-kind graphic assets to share with the Scratch community at large. Let's get to work!

Introducing GIMP

You can always use the built-in Paint Editor in Scratch to draw your own sprite costumes and Stage backdrops. However, I feel that the tool set has the following fatal flaws, at least as of this writing:

▶ **Weak text tools**: As you've seen in previous hours, once you commit a text block to a Stage backdrop, the text becomes a permanent, noneditable part of the Stage.

▶ **Limited Undo levels**: In my experience, the multilevel Undo is inconsistent. Sometimes, it appears to track over 20 previous actions in the Paint Editor; just as often, though, the Undo button is grayed out, causing me to lose access to previous actions.

▶ **Clunky line and shape tools:** If you've ever worked with lines and shapes in a dedicated paint program, you'll immediately observe how limited these commands are in the Scratch Paint Editor.

▶ **Restricted font set:** The Paint Editor supports only six font choices. If you have another font that you want to include in your Scratch project, you must compose the backdrop offline on your computer and then import the asset into your project.

What Is GIMP?

GIMP (pronounced *gimp*, not *gee-eye-emm-pee*) is a free, open source bitmap graphics program. Don't worry—the next section explains the difference between bitmap and vector graphics. If you've ever used a member of the Adobe Creative Suite, you'll probably feel right at home with GIMP.

The reasons I suggest GIMP is that I'm assuming that you use either a Windows, Mac, or Linux computer (GIMP runs on all three operating systems) and that you aren't willing to spend money on a premium product like Adobe Photoshop. That having been said, Adobe made a good decision lately by making its Creative Suite applications cloud-based and selling yearly or monthly subscriptions. Learn more about the Adobe Creative Cloud by visiting the Adobe Web site at http://is.gd/IfFkf1.

NOTE

Learning More About GIMP

GIMP is a complex program, and a detailed tutorial on its use is beyond the scope of this book. For a comprehensive walk-through of how to use GIMP to create and edit bitmap images, please check out the book *Using Gimp* by James Pyles (http://is.gd/qMJlOM).

For the purposes of this text, GIMP allows you to create and/or edit Stage backdrops and sprite costumes. You can invoke multiple layers and add text—the proverbial sky is the limit with the GIMP tool. Before going any further, you can download and install GIMP by visiting the GIMP website: http://is.gd/q8Axq1.

More Information About Open Source

To be sure, I throw around the phrase *open source* quite a bit in this volume. I've described Scratch as an open source project, and just now I introduced the GIMP image editor as an open source project. Let's make sure you understand the term.

First of all, open source refers both to a certain kind of software as well as a philosophy. With open source projects, anybody is free to examine and modify the underlying source code of a given application. You can even re-release your customized version of the project with the proviso that you release your project's source code under the open source license.

The Scratch application itself (that is, the online and offline editors) is indeed open source; in other words, the MIT Scratch Team allows the general public to view the application's underlying source code and release alternate versions (called mods) of Scratch.

Take, for instance, the Snap! project out of the University of California at Berkeley (http://is.gd/s26Lr1). This is a mod of the Scratch 1.4 code base. If you're interested, you can download the Scratch 1.4 source code from the Scratch Wiki at http://is.gd/zWRzbi.

As of this writing, the MIT Scratch Team has not released the Scratch 2.0 source code. However, they have stated on the discussion forums that they will do so "in the near future."

The other aspect of open source as it relates to Scratch is the principle that the action of sharing your Scratch project implies that other Scratchers can examine your source code, remix the project, and/or borrow individual assets (scripts, sprites, backdrops, etc.) from that project.

A Quick Tour of the GIMP User Interface

You use GIMP throughout this hour when you create your own custom Scratch graphic assets. To that point, I think it prudent for you to open GIMP on your system and learn the most fundamental user interface elements.

As you can see in Figure 21.1, GIMP has two main user interface elements: the application window, where your image resides, and the Toolbox palette, which gives you access to tools in the same way that the Blocks palette gives you access to blocks in Scratch 2.0.

Using Figure 21.1 and the following list as a guide, examine the GIMP user interface:

- ▶ **A:** Use the Select tools in GIMP to select part of an image for manipulation.
- ▶ **B:** Use the Text tool to add and edit text in your image.
- ▶ **C:** Use the Bucket Fill tool to add color fills to your image.
- ▶ **D:** Use the painting and drawing tools to draw artwork.
- ▶ **E:** Use the color picker control to set foreground and background colors.
- ▶ **F:** Use the File menu to create new files, open, save, and so forth.
- ▶ **G:** Use the Select menu options to control the selection. These tools are important to learn—and can save you much frustration as you proceed through your GIMP learning curve.
- ▶ **H:** From the Image menu, use the Flatten command to collapse all the layers in your image. In time, you may learn how to use layers, but they are well beyond the scope of this book.

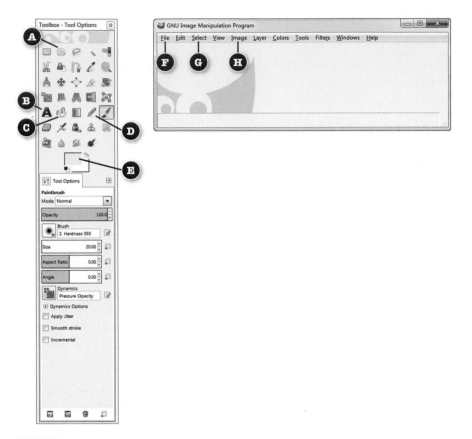

FIGURE 21.1
The GIMP user interface attempts to be friendly and intuitive, but there is much complexity lurking just beneath the surface.

NOTE

Where Did the Name "GIMP" Come From?

You might have wondered where GIMP got its name. Many open source developers have a wacky sense of humor—GIMP is actually a recursive acronym that stands for GNU Image Manipulation Program. The acronym GNU is itself recursive, meaning "GNU's Not UNIX!" Sigh...if you aren't at least moderately familiar with UNIX and Linux history, much of this open source/free software stuff might be lost on you. Wikipedia has a good overview of the GNU Project; read it if you are so inclined at http://is.gd/tKnubr.

Understanding Bitmap and Vector Graphics Modes

In your work with sprite costumes and Stage backdrops thus far, you might have noticed an interface element in the Paint Editor called Bitmap Mode. If you aren't sure what I'm talking about, look at Figure 21.2.

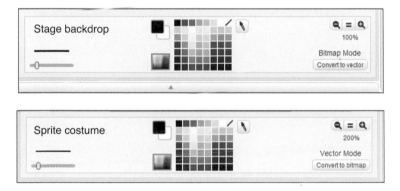

FIGURE 21.2
One of the many new features in Scratch 2.0 is support for both bitmap and vector graphics. Most built-in Stage backdrops are bitmap images by default, and most built-in sprites are vector images by default.

Here's the deal, friends: Bitmap graphics, which are also sometimes called raster graphics, are graphics that are stored as an array (or map) of pixels. You can consider pixels to be the "little blocks" you see when you view a bitmap image at high magnification. For instance, look at the Beetle sprite costume that is magnified in Figure 21.3; do you see how blocky it looks close-up?

FIGURE 21.3
A comparison of bitmap and vector sprite costume images. The vector version is on the left, and the bitmap version is on the right.

For this reason, the bitmap format is not a good candidate for line art, which is the art type used for Scratch sprites. You'll find that, besides application in line art, the bitmap format is also used for digital photos that you take with your webcam or digital camera. As you increasingly magnify a bitmap image, the image gradually pixelates, or loses detail as you see the underlying structure of pixel blocks take form.

By contrast, vector graphics are not composed of a field of bits, but instead are made up of lines created by using mathematical formulas. The upside to vector graphics is that you can scale the images up and down and lose absolutely no detail. The downside is that you can use the vector format only for line art illustrations; digital photographs do not lend themselves very well to being represented as only mathematically formulated lines.

To see the clarity difference between vector and bitmap images at close magnification, look again at the Beetle sprite in Figure 21.3.

Thus, you can summarize when to use bitmap versus vector in this way:

▶ If it's a Stage backdrop, then a bitmap image format such as `.png` or `.jpg` is the way to go.

▶ If it's a sprite costume, then the vector format is preferred. In Scratch 2.0, sprites have the file type `.sprite2`.

How Scratch Handles Format Conversions

In the Scratch 2.0 Paint Editor, you see a button labeled Convert to Bitmap if the current image is a vector; vice versa if the current image is a bitmap. Here are some guiding principles for you to follow concerning Scratch-based image format conversions:

▶ **Conversion is a one-way process**: Once you make the switch, you've permanently altered the image. If you convert a vector image to bitmap and then try to convert the bitmap back to vector, the image will remain blocky—you're out of luck.

▶ **The Undo tool is limited**: You can use the Undo tool to revert the change immediately, but after you've navigated away from the Paint Editor, forget about it (or as we say in New York: *fughetaboutit*).

The take-home message here is that you should stick with one image format. If you do need to perform a conversion, download a local copy of the art asset first to use as a backup. Even better, use GIMP or another image-editing tool to convert the file offline; you'll have more power over the process in any event.

Now that you've covered the preliminaries, it's time to create your own Stage backdrop!

Creating a New Stage Backdrop

From experience, the best first step to the process of creating a new Stage backdrop is to download a copy of the default backdrop1 backdrop from the Scratch Editor. This way, you can ensure that (1) you have the correct file type and format and (2) you have the proper backdrop dimensions and aspect ratio.

Start a new project at the Scratch website, select the Stage, and navigate to the Backdrops tab. Right-click backdrop1 and select Save to Local File from the shortcut menu. Make a note of where you save the file on your local system.

One observation you might make is that the downloaded blank backdrop is larger than the dimensions shown in the Scratch 2.0 Editor. In the editor, the backdrop image size is 480 pixels wide by 360 pixels high. If you check out the properties of the downloaded backdrop, the image size is 960×720.

Don't worry, though—the downloaded image file is exactly double the size of the Scratch Stage, so the aspect ratio is preserved. Actually, having a larger file to work with on your computer is to your advantage because you can make use of a bigger canvas.

TRY IT YOURSELF ▼

Create a New Stage Backdrop

In this Try It Yourself exercise, you use GIMP to open your downloaded blank Stage backdrop and draw a custom screen. Remember, I'm not an artist, so my custom Stage backdrop won't win any awards. The solution graphic, backdrop1a.png, can be found in the book's code archive. Please work through the following steps to complete this Try It Yourself exercise:

1. Open up GIMP, click File, Open, and browse to the blank backdrop you downloaded from the Scratch 2.0 online editor.

2. Start by drawing a rectangle. In the Toolbox, click the Rectangle Select tool and draw a rectangle on the loaded image.

3. Now fill in the rectangle with another color. Click the Foreground Color box and choose a color from the list. You can select among five different methods for choosing a color, actually. The color picker is shown in Figure 21.4.

   Once your color is chosen, click the Bucket Fill tool and then click within your rectangle to complete the fill. If you make a mistake, click Edit, Undo.

4. Click Select, None to reset your selection (I told you this command would be helpful!). Next, add an oval to the image. Click the Ellipse Select tool and draw an oval beneath the rectangle in the blank image. Again, use the color picker and the Bucket Fill tool to fill in the oval.

Use these controls to resize and reposition your text.

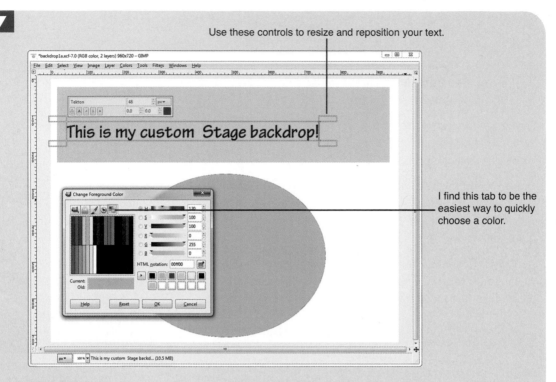

I find this tab to be the easiest way to quickly choose a color.

FIGURE 21.4
GIMP gives you complete control over color and text; what a welcome relief from the Scratch Paint Editor!

5. Click File, Save to save your project. Note that GIMP will save your image project under a different extension (`.xcf`). The reason GIMP does this is to allow you to preserve your original image—pretty cool, isn't it?

6. To add text to your rectangle, select the Text tool from the Toolbox and then click within the rectangle you added to the backdrop earlier in this exercise. As you can see in Figure 21.4, you can use the Text control tools to choose any font that is available on your computer, change the size, color, and so forth. Note that to change the color and font, the text must be selected first. Play around with these tools until your text looks good.

   Note also that you can use the resize controls in the text box to control precisely where your text appears in the backdrop.

7. Finally, close this exercise by doing some honest-to-goodness drawing. First click Image, Flatten Image to compress all of the layers into one. As mentioned earlier, layers are an advanced-level topic that you can't be bothered with at this time. Next, select the Paintbrush tool, choose a color, and then start painting! Have fun—that's what this is all about.

8. Okay—you're done for now. Do another Image, Flatten Image, and a File, Save for good measure.

9. Click File, Export and save the modified image under a different name. For instance, perhaps you can name it `custombd.png` to stand for "custom backdrop." Click Export, and then click Export again in the Export Image as PNG dialog box that appears. You can close GIMP now.

   Notice on your computer that you still have your original, blank backdrop file in its pristine condition. This is one of so many reasons why you should use GIMP or a tool like it to perform what is called nondestructive image editing.

10. In Scratch, click the Upload button to import your new graphic as a Stage backdrop. You can observe the finished product in Figure 21.5.

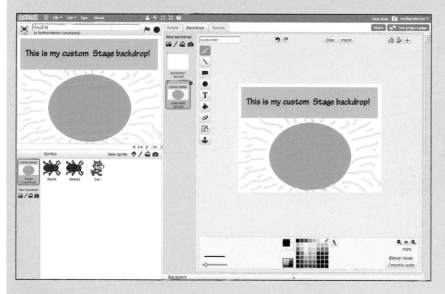

FIGURE 21.5
The custom Stage backdrop as it appears in the Scratch 2.0 project.

NOTE

GIMP on the Go

You don't need to actually install GIMP on your computer to make use of the tool. Instead, if you use Windows, you can download a standalone, portable version of the software from PortableApps. com (http://is.gd/We2faL). You can pop the portable GIMP on your USB flash drive and have image-editing goodness with you on the go!

Resolving Image Size Concerns

Suppose, for instance, that you have a preexisting bitmap image that you'd like to use as a custom Stage backdrop. However, that image uses a different aspect ratio than what Scratch uses.

As a test, try uploading a fairly large-dimension image (perhaps 1024×768 or larger) into a Scratch project and assign that image as a Stage backdrop. What happens if you try to import this image into Scratch with no modification?

As you can see in Figure 21.6, Scratch 2.0 respects the geometry of your source image, but in doing so the imported image may not fill the entire Stage area.

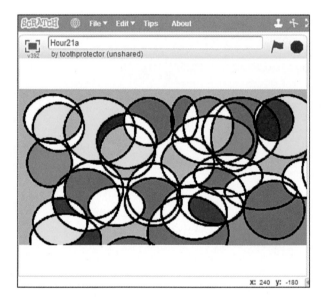

FIGURE 21.6
If your source image geometry isn't directly compatible with Scratch, then Scratch will do its best to accommodate the disparity.

One option you have for addressing this issue is to scale your image. Open up the file in GIMP and select Image, Scale Image. In the resulting Scale Image dialog box, adjust the Width and Height attributes, being careful to leave the Aspect Ratio (chain link) icon enabled. This is shown in Figure 21.7.

What you'll find is that GIMP can gracefully scale your image such that it much more closely matches the aspect ratio or dimensions expected by Scratch 2.0 (specifically, a multiple of 480 pixels wide by 360 pixels high). The difference is that GIMP's image scaling does so without warping or distorting your image. Great stuff!

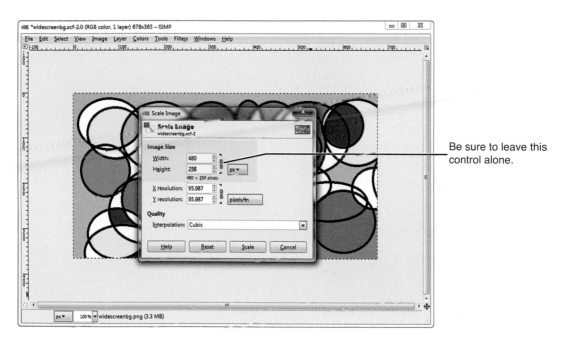

Be sure to leave this control alone.

FIGURE 21.7
GIMP gracefully scales image dimensions without distortion.

Creating a Custom Sprite—The Easy Way

By far, the easiest way to add a custom, multicostume sprite in Scratch Is to leverage an art asset that already exists. If you don't absolutely have to draw the sprite yourself, why do so?

Here are some of your options:

▶ Borrow a sprite from another Scratcher's project (be sure to give attribution).

▶ Download a sprite from the Scratch Resources website (http://is.gd/0zQFvW).

▶ Use a free animated GIF.

The first two bullet points are covered extensively throughout multiple hours of this book, so the following section shows you how to add an animated Graphics Interchange Format (GIF, pronounced *ghiff* more commonly than *jif*).

What Is an Animated GIF Image?

An animated GIF image is essentially a container that consists of a number of separate image frames. When these frames are shown in rapid succession, the illusion of animation is produced.

Although many tools exist that will stitch multiple images together for you to make animated GIFs from scratch, for the purposes of this text today, you can just as easily download a pre-made animated GIF from any number of freeware websites. A good one is Amazing Animations (http://is.gd/setwT8).

Once you've downloaded an animated GIF image, open your Scratch project and import the GIF by using the Upload 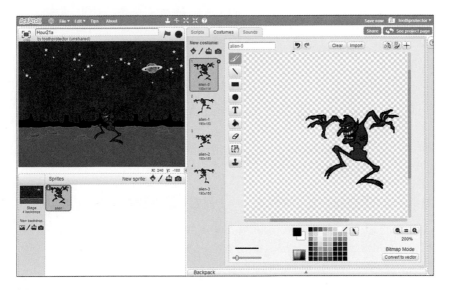 button in the Sprites list. Here's the magic: Scratch detects that the image you are importing is an animated GIF and actually breaks apart the GIF into frames and creates a separate costume out of each one! Isn't that convenient? The `alien.gif` animated GIF file is included in the book's code archive; you can see what it looks like in Scratch 2.0 by viewing Figure 21.8.

FIGURE 21.8
This alien sprite started its life as an ordinary animated GIF image on my computer.

NOTE
_____

How to Create Your Own Animated GIF Images

Some of you might be interested enough in this topic to wonder what tools I recommend for creating your own animated GIFs from your preexisting images. For Windows, I suggest the Microsoft GIF Animator because the program is small and simple (http://is.gd/LQbXh2). For Mac, I recommend GIFQuickMaker (http://is.gd/HDI8ZQ), although the app does cost 99 cents as of this writing. If, by contrast, you're looking for an online GIF animator, then I advise that you investigate Picasion (http://is.gd/3FrIQt). Believe it or not, GIMP can actually make animated GIF images as well; check out this handy online tutorial: http://is.gd/wHFbqA.

Creating a Custom Sprite—The Difficult Way

Native Scratch 2.0 sprites, when they are downloaded to your computer (by right-clicking the sprite in the Sprites list and selecting Save to Local File from the shortcut menu), have the extension `.sprite2` and are actually archive files.

For instance, you can open `.sprite2` files by using a ZIP file management tool such as 7-Zip (http://is.gd/ZLIeVb) to view their contents. Take a gander at Figure 21.9.

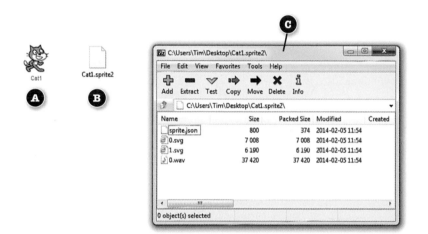

FIGURE 21.9
The Scratch Cat sprite (A) as it appears in the Scratch Editor, (B) as it appears on the computer, and (C) as its contents appear in a ZIP file management tool.

When you create a sprite on your own, outside of Scratch, and then upload the file into the Editor, Scratch creates the `.sprite2` archive as if the sprite were part of its built-in library.

As a final Try It Yourself exercise for this hour, you use GIMP to create a new sprite image, and then import the image into your project.

TRY IT YOURSELF ▼

Build Your Own Sprite

In this Try It Yourself exercise, you open GIMP and make an extremely simple "smiley face" sprite. What's cool here is that you're going to learn how to add transparency to the image so the sprite has no ugly white border. Work through the following steps to complete the exercise. Let's do this!

1. Open GIMP and click File, New to invoke the Create a New Image dialog box. On my system, the default canvas size is 640×400 pixels; that's fine for these purposes.

▼

Here's an important point: Before you click OK, expand Advanced Options, open up the Fill With: drop-down control, and select Transparency from the list. You can always add transparency to an image later in your workflow (check out a great tutorial here: http://is.gd/Xxphl4), but it's best to add the transparency during image creation, in my humble opinion.

Click OK to make the image and continue.

2. Click File, Save to save the project. For reference, the project and resulting sprite image can be found in the book's code archive as `customsprite.xcf` and `customsprite.png`.

3. Draw a perfect circle on your canvas by selecting the Ellipse Select tool from the Toolbox, choosing a color from the color picker, holding down the Shift key, and clicking and dragging on the canvas. In most drawing programs, holding down the Shift key as you create the ellipse makes a perfect circle instead of an oval. Don't be shocked to see that the circle didn't pick up your color; you handle that in the next step.

4. Choose the Bucket Fill tool and click within your circle to fill in the color. The sample image uses the traditional "smiley face" yellow.

5. Click Select, None to reset your image selection. Next, draw an eye for your smiley face. To do this, choose black from the color picker, click the Ellipse Select tool again, and draw an eye-sized perfect circle or oval on the canvas. Resize the eye as appropriate, and then use the Bucket Fill tool as previously discussed to fill in the eye with the black color. Remember to remove the selection and save your work when you're finished with this step.

6. There are myriad ways to clone areas of an image; this example chooses the path of least resistance. First, select the Ellipse Select tool and draw a selection outline around the first black eye. Second, click Edit, Copy to save the selection. Third, click Edit, Paste to actually duplicate the selection. Fourth, place your mouse cursor inside the selection and drag the second eye to its rightful place on the smiley face.

7. To draw the mouth, click the Paintbrush tool, select a brush type from the Brush drop-down in the Toolbox (shown in Figure 21.10), and then go ahead and draw!

8. Now that you're finished with your sprite, the rest of the process mirrors what you did earlier in the previous Try It Yourself exercise. That is, export the image as a `.png` image, open your project, and import the sprite into your Sprites list. Figure 21.11 shows the results.

You have complete control over all aspects of your paintbrush in GIMP.

FIGURE 21.10
Once you get the hang of it, drawing sprites in GIMP is actually quite fun. Yes, I added a little "extra" to this smiley face image.

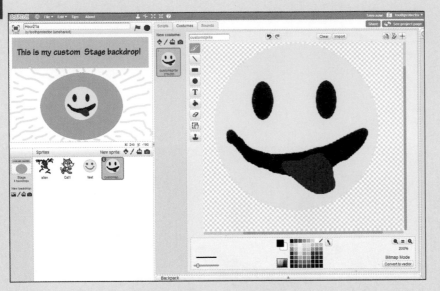

FIGURE 21.11
The finished product.

Summary

You covered quite a bit of ground in this hour. By now, you hopefully have a deeper appreciation of how graphic assets work in Scratch projects. For one thing, you know the difference
between bitmap and vector images. You understand how to create custom Stage backdrops and
sprite costumes offline by using the nifty open source GIMP editor, and you can integrate them
easily into your Scratch 2.0 projects.

Workshop

Quiz

1. Which of the following terms describes an image that is composed of mathematically generated lines and curves?

    A. Vector

    B. Bitmap

    C. Raster

2. In the Scratch Paint Editor, you can convert a vector image to bitmap and then back to vector again without losing image clarity.

    A. True

    B. False

3. Which of the following methods allows you to create a multicostume sprite easily?

    A. Adjusting the transparency of the sprite image

    B. Creating a sprite from an animated GIF image

    C. Using GIMP to create a `.jpg` image

Answers

1. The correct answer is choice A. Vector images are line art images that are composed of mathematically generated lines and curves; these images scale well without losing resolution. By contrast, bitmap images are composed of a bit field. Although its resolution is fine at its native size, scaling the image up or down in size adversely affects the image's appearance.

2. The correct answer is choice B. In the Scratch Paint Editor, you are free to convert a vector image to a bitmap, and vice versa. However, this conversion is both one-way and permanent.

3. The correct answer is choice B. You can import an animated GIF image into Scratch and Scratch automatically separates the GIF frames into individual costumes. Answer choice C bears a bit more discussion: Image transparency can be used only with `.gif` and `.png` images, not `.jpg` images. Although `.gif` is the de facto image type for animated GIF files, you can actually create animated `.png` files, though the standard here isn't universally agreed upon. Read more about animated PNG (APNG) files at Wikipedia at http://is.gd/R7KFtD.

Challenge

Your challenge for this hour is to use GIMP to create a skeleton project that consists of two Stage backdrops that you create offline by using GIMP.

Next, build a multicostume sprite in GIMP. For instance, try creating a standing figure with its arms down as the first costume, and put the figure's arms up in the second costume.

Finally, add the sprite to the project and add some script code to animate it. You can see one possible solution by checking out the project `Hour21a.sb2` from the book's code archive.

HOUR 22

Implementing Buttons and Multiple Screens

What You'll Learn in This Hour:

▶ Working with multiple screens in Scratch

▶ Creating multistate buttons

▶ Wiring up buttons to your screens

I am a child of the 1980s, and as such I spent a great amount of time during my preadolescence and early adolescence sinking quarters into arcade games at my local shopping mall. You know the games I'm talking about, right? *Moon Patrol, Robotron, Defender, Asteroids, Gyruss*—all of the classic retro arcade games that now are available for play on your smartphone.

All of these games involved player control using a joystick and one or more button switches. Sure, there were some anomalies, such as games that used steering wheels or trackballs, but the vast majority used the good old-fashioned joystick and button.

Moreover, the classic games of my youth typically involved at least five distinct screens:

▶ A splash screen that served as an initial navigation menu

▶ One or more helper tutorial screens

▶ The actual gameplay screen or screens

▶ Game over screen

▶ High scores screen

For that matter, even the games I play today on my Xbox One home video game console involve the same basic multiscreen motif. In this hour, you learn how to implement multiple screens in your Scratch 2.0 projects. You also learn how to create multistate buttons, which give players easy navigational control from the time they click the Green Flag to the time the project stops.

Working with Multiple Screens in Scratch

In Hour 16, "Documenting Your Project," you learned all about project storyboarding. In that hour, I told you that I use a nifty cross-platform desktop application named Balsamiq Mockups (http://is.gd/gZstLx) to create my storyboards, and I suggested that you give it a try.

When the Scratch project you envision will involve more than one screen, it is highly advisable to storyboard it out using Balsamic or some similar tool (heck, you can use good old-fashioned pencil and paper if you are so inclined).

As an example, let's look at designing a simple Scratch arcade game project. Examine the storyboard I've created for this project in Figure 22.1, and cross-reference the storyboard with the following descriptions:

▶ When the player clicks the Green Flag, he or she is greeted with the splash screen. Here, the player can use the Start button to start the game, or click the Help button to see online help.

▶ The actual game and gameplay are not relevant to what you're learning in this hour, so what is shown here is a single, blank playfield screen.

▶ The Help screen is a great opportunity for you to instruct players on things like controls, objectives, and tips/tricks. The player can click the Back button to return to the splash screen.

▶ Finally, the End screen is used when the game is over. For convenience, you can include a Play Again button that returns the player to the splash screen.

Creating the Screens

The smoke and mirrors behind creating multiple screens in Scratch is the fact that you can have only one Stage in the project, but the Stage can include any number of backdrops. Consequently, your screens are all encapsulated within the Stage.

As you know by now, I'm not a big fan of the Paint Editor tool included in Scratch. Its text handling is particularly inaccurate. In short, you have the following options for creating Scratch game screens that you can be proud of:

▶ **You can draw them yourself:** If, for whatever reason, you have developed a comfortable ability with the Scratch 2.0 Paint Editor, then by all means, knock yourself out. Draw your next Stage background masterpiece!

▶ **You can buy them:** My wife has worked as a graphic designer for several years, so I'm familiar with the importance of staying legal when it comes to using publicly available line art, photographs, clip art, and so forth.

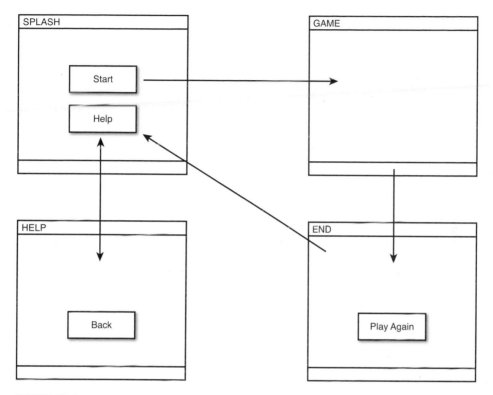

FIGURE 22.1
Storyboarding is essential when you are designing a multiscreen computer program.

A detailed description of where to find and how to buy royalty-free artwork is beyond the scope of this book. The best advice I have for you is to hit your favorite search engine and run search queries for strings such as *royalty-free line art* or *royalty-free images*. The term *royalty-free* is of particular importance here; if you're not careful, then you might have the owner of an art asset coming after you for royalty payments to compensate him or her for your use of his or her work.

▶ **You can "open source" them**: Remember that Scratch is an open source online community. By definition, any Stage backdrop assets included in any Scratcher's public projects are available for remixing by other Scratchers. The only catch, if you want to call it that, is that you must provide attribution for all Stage backdrops that you borrow from other Scratchers' projects.

As a point of review, the workflow for borrowing Stage backdrops in the Scratch website works as follows:

▶ Expose the source code of the Scratch project from which you want to borrow a backdrop. You can do this by clicking See Inside on that project's web page.

▶ Once you are inside that project, select the Stage and navigate to the Backdrops tab.

▶ Right-click the backdrop in question and select Save to Local File from the shortcut menu. The backdrop will arrive on your computer as a .png graphic image.

▶ In your target project, use the Upload Backdrop from File  button to include the borrowed asset in your project.

As fail-safe as this "borrowing" method is, it requires a fair amount of tedium to complete. A great Scratch community website you should be aware of is the Scratch Resources site at http:// is.gd/0zQFvW. Figure 22.2 shows this page.

FIGURE 22.2
You can save yourself a lot of time, money, and effort by downloading art assets from the Scratch Resources site.

NOTE

The ScratchEd Site

The ScratchEd (http://is.gd/Ciw37B) site is a resource site that is aimed primarily at educators rather than Scratch end users. However, you can take advantage of their projects and assets in the same open source way that you can at the Scratch Resources site or the Scratch portal site.

As of this writing, fellow Scratchers uploaded 515 Stage backgrounds, 128 script blocks, 687 sound files, and 486 sprites to the Scratch Resources site at http://is.gd/0zQFvW. This is invaluable information, friends. For example, would you rather spend 4 hours drawing a backdrop for a pirate ship game you're developing, or downloading the work of some other Scratcher that probably looks better than you could have done by yourself anyway?

Complete the following Try It Yourself exercise to lay the groundwork for this hour's project. In this exercise, you build your four Stage backdrops, and in so doing, you learn some tips and tricks concerning Scratch's Paint Editor.

TRY IT YOURSELF ▼

Lay Out Your Game Screens

This Try It Yourself exercise gives you some experience in building multiple screens for a Scratch project. You can find the assets for this hour's work in the book's solution files archive. Specifically, the solution project file is named Hour22a.sb2. Work through the following steps to complete this exercise:

1. Log in to the Scratch website and fire up a new project. Make sure to give it a name and click File, Save to be reassured that your work is saved to the cloud.

2. Navigate to the Stage and then navigate to the Backdrops tab. Rename the backdrop1 backdrop as SPLASH; here you'll go ahead and draw the splash screen by using the Scratch tools.

3. Select the Line [icon] tool, and then click to select a color from the swatch at the bottom of the Paint Editor. Holding down the Shift key to ensure a straight line (this tip works in most paint programs), put a horizontal line about one third of the way down the backdrop from the top. You can see the finished splash screen in Figure 22.3.

4. Keep it simple, here: Select the Fill [icon] tool, select a light color shade, and click within the Stage to fill in that color. Notice that you can choose a different color above and below your horizontal line so long as your horizontal line stretches completely across the Stage.

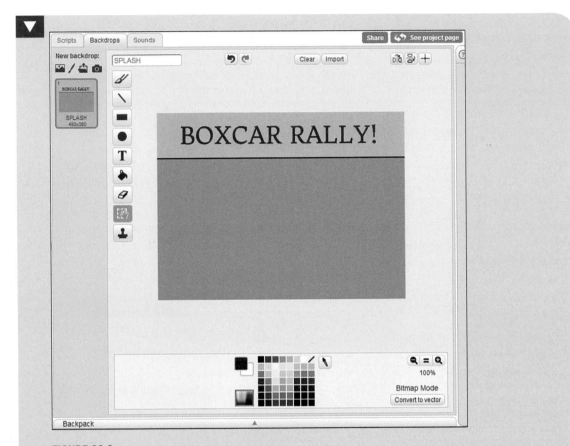

FIGURE 22.3
We drew this splash screen by using Scratch 2.0's limited painting tools.

5. Now for the stuff I struggle with—adding text directly to the Stage by using the built-in tools. Click the Text 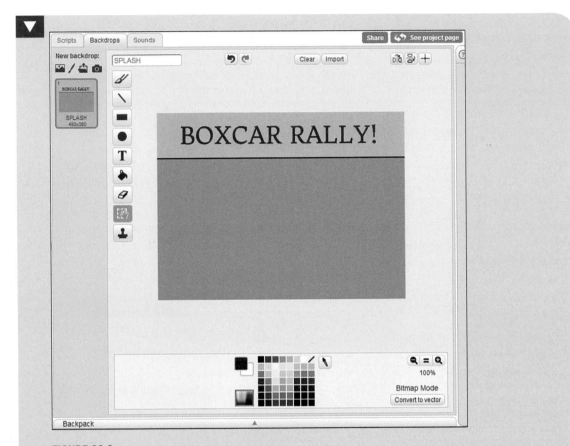 tool, and then choose a font from the drop-down list at the bottom of the Paint Editor. Next, choose a color, and then click in the top third of the back-drop. I called my project "Boxcar Rally," but feel free to choose any name that your imagi-nation inspires you with.

Notice that there are no font controls—you cannot change the font size, weight, and so forth. Instead, click once elsewhere on the Stage and the text will be surrounded by resize handles. You only get one chance at this, so be accurate. Drag a corner resize handle until you are happy with the text size.

Move the text box with your mouse to position, and then click elsewhere. Boom! The text gets "absorbed" into the Stage, and you'll never be able to edit it again. Isn't that a bummer?

6. For the other three screens you need (HELP, GAME, and END), use the Upload ⬆ button to import three images that you created, downloaded from the Web, or accessed from the solution files archive (the files are named HELP.png, GAME.png, and END.png, respectively).

7. I want you to "dress up" the GAME backdrop a little bit by drawing a border around the perimeter of the screen. Select the GAME backdrop, click the Rectangle ▭ tool, and then choose a color. Notice in the lower-left corner of the Paint Editor you can control the fill and the line color. Leave the fill at the default (unfilled), and adjust the line so that it is slightly thicker.

NOTE
How to Create Your Own Backdrops

You might wonder what paint program I recommend that you use if you want to be able to create your own backdrops on your computer. If you use a Mac, I suggest the free Paintbrush (http://is.gd/4d12fd), especially if you have previous experience with Microsoft Paint in Windows. Actually, I use Microsoft Paint a lot on my Windows systems; if you prefer a more powerful paint program that works in both Windows and OS X, I suggest GIMP, or the GNU Image Manipulation Program (http://is.gd/q8Axq1).

Creating Multistate Buttons

The button is one of the most popular and functional user controls in any graphical computer program. The button is immediately and intuitively obvious to most people because software buttons behave the same basic way as hardware buttons that you interact with in daily life.

You know how when you press a real, hardware button, the button itself depresses a bit and clicks? You can actually simulate this button-pressing behavior in Scratch by creating what are called multistate buttons.

Multistate Buttons: Behind the Curtain

Underneath the technological covers, a multistate button is really just two graphic images that are nearly identical to each other. One image represents the "up" or "not pressed" state of the button, and the second image, typically shaded a bit, signifies the "down" or "pressed" state of the button.

As you saw with Stage backdrops, your options for creating or otherwise obtaining button images are limited only by your imagination. For this hour's project, you leverage button images that are included in the Scratch 2.0 Sprite Library.

For example, the Button3 sprite can be found in the Things category of the Scratch 2.0 Sprite Library. Take a close look at Figure 22.4; you can clearly see that the button3-a and button3-b backdrops represent either the "up" or "down" states of a multistate software button. You'll learn how to "wire up" a button to a project screen later on in this hour.

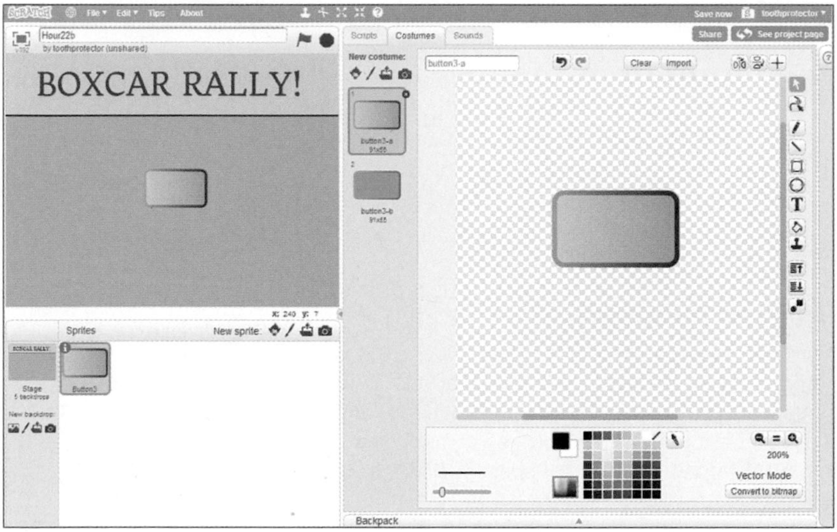

FIGURE 22.4
Contrary to popular belief, there is no "magic" involved in multistate buttons in computer programs. You simply quickly swap Stage backdrops to simulate a button press event.

Understanding Duplication

Another skill you should have under your belt before completing the second Try It Yourself exercise in this hour is that of object duplication. In a project, you may have several buttons. For this project, you have a total of four buttons. That isn't a humongous number, but it's more buttons than I want to hand-create or hand-edit.

To that end, right-click a sprite in the Sprites list of your project and select Duplicate from the shortcut menu. This is a powerful command because when you duplicate a sprite, all sprite assets are duplicated, including costumes and script code.

Two other tools for quickly duplicating assets (including Scratch scripts) are the Duplicate button on the Scratch Editor toolbar and the Select and Duplicate tool in the Paint Editor.

All that having been said, go ahead and create your buttons for this hour's Try It Yourself exercises.

Create Multistate Buttons

In this Try It Yourself exercise, you build a multistate button. From experience, it works best to spend time getting your first button perfect, and then duplicate it as many times as you need to. The solution file archive contains a finished file for this exercise named `Hour22b.sb2`. Work through the following steps to complete this exercise:

1. Open the project file that you started in the previous Try It Yourself exercise and add in a single instance of the Button3 sprite from the Sprite Library.

2. Navigate to the Costumes tab and make any color adjustments to the two backdrops as necessary. Rename the button3-a backdrop to UP and the button3-b backdrop to DOWN for your reference convenience.

3. Referring to the storyboard shown in Figure 22.1, you need two buttons on the splash screen. To that end, click the Stage and make sure that the SPLASH screen is visible.

4. Click the Button3 sprite in the Sprites list, and then click the sprite image in the Paint Editor to expose the resize handles. If you want, use the resize handles to resize the sprite. However, be advised that you need to do this separately for each costume; they are not linked in any way. This is a major pain in the butt, in my humble opinion. For my purposes, I left the buttons at their default size and color.

5. Placement of the Button3 sprite on the Stage is problematic because, again, the costumes move independently if you move them within the Paint Editor. So don't do that! Instead, drag the Button3 sprite on the Stage to position it properly.

6. Now for the fun stuff: Duplicate the Button3 sprite, and arrange it below the first button, as shown in Figure 22.5.

7. Now select the Stage, bring up the HELP backdrop, duplicate the Button3 sprite again, and position it in the lower-right corner of the HELP backdrop.

8. Although I included a button on the END screen in Figure 22.1, for simplicity's sake you'll leave that feature for a future project version.

9. Finally, rename the two sprites on the SPLASH screen Start and Help, and rename the Help screen sprite Return. You'll worry about labeling the text on the buttons themselves next.

FIGURE 22.5
Our buttons are coming right along!

Labeling and "Lighting Up" the Buttons

In completing the previous Try It Yourself exercise and looking at Figure 22.5, you probably thought, "Tim, how did you create those cool button labels?" Well, that's what you get to learn now.

First, I decided that you need to add labels only to the UP costume. When the user clicks one of your buttons, the button switches to the second, darker costume, and gives the appearance of being "pressed." You don't need the label to show for the button's Down state. That saves you some extra work right off the top.

Second, you use the same Paint Editor Text tool that you used earlier when you added text to your splash screen. In fact, complete the following Try It Yourself exercise and add text to the Help screen.

Label the Buttons

In this Try It Yourself exercise, you work to create labels for your multistate buttons. The solution file for this exercise is `Hour22c.sb2`. As has become our habit, work through the following steps to complete this exercise.

1. In your project, select the Start sprite, navigate to the Costumes tab, and select the UP costume. In the Paint Editor, select the Text 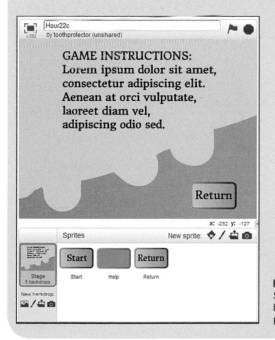 tool, which is confusingly located on the right side of the Paint Editor instead of the left side as it is with Stage backdrops.

2. Choose a color and a font (I used Donegal in black), and then click within the UP costume image. Add the text *Start*. Click away to get your resize handles, place your mouse inside the text block, and reposition on the button. Click away again; you'll be surprised to discover that you can actually edit the text that you attach to a sprite. Who wouldda thunk it?!

3. Repeat this action to label the Help button on the splash screen and the Return button on the Help screen.

4. Once you're finished, navigate back to the Help Stage backdrop; it's time to fill in some boilerplate text. As you did earlier, use the Text tool to add your generic placeholder text to the Help screen. Resize the text box and reposition as appropriate. Remember to click Undo if you make a mistake, but don't expect Scratch to give you too many levels of Undo. You can see boilerplate text in action by viewing Figure 22.6.

FIGURE 22.6
Sometimes it's appropriate to add "Lorum Ipsum" boilerplate text to your project to serve as a temporary placeholder.

NOTE

What Is Boilerplate Text?

Boilerplate text, also called "Lorum Ipsum" text, is nonsensical text data that programmers use to serve as a placeholder for production copy. Whenever I need boilerplate text fast, I go to http://lipsum.com; they can generate as much boilerplate copy as you need.

Wiring Up Buttons to Your Screens

So far, so good. At this point, all that remains in creating your game skeleton is to wire up the buttons to the game screens. We programmers use terms like *wire up* a lot because many computer programmers (myself certainly included) are also electronics nerds.

Anyway, here are the major design considerations you have as you set about integrating your multistate buttons with the screens:

▶ You need to selectively show and hide the buttons depending upon context.

▶ You need to program the buttons to "switch" to the appropriate screen when they are clicked.

▶ You might need to consider auditory feedback; perhaps a recorded "click" sound can fire whenever a user clicks a button with his or her mouse.

Right now, your program is a big, fat mess. Try clicking the Green Flag and let me know if anything useful happens. Of course it doesn't. Do you remember the garbage in, garbage out (GIGO) rule?

▼ TRY IT YOURSELF

Activate Your Multistate Buttons

In this Try It Yourself exercise, you leverage the Backpack feature of the Scratch 2.0 Editor to avoid having to redo script code for each button in your project. The completed solution, which can be found in the book's solution files archive, is named `Hour22d.sb2`. Work through the following steps to complete the exercise.

1. You start with the Start button, appropriately enough. Follow along with the labeled code sections in Figure 22.7.

In the code section labeled A, ensure that the button starts in the "up" state and is visible on the splash screen.

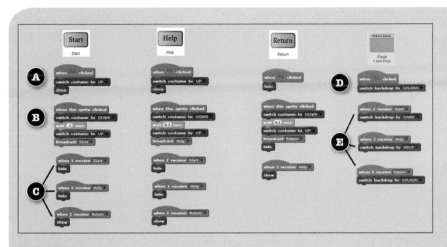

FIGURE 22.7
Source code in the Activate Your Multistate Buttons Try It Yourself exercise.

2. In the code section labeled B, program the click logic. Basically, you respond such that when the sprite is clicked, you switch to the "down" state costume, wait a third of a second, reinstate the "up" costume (giving the illusion of the button having physically been pressed), and then broadcast a new message called "Start."

3. While you are here, create two additional broadcasts with the names Help and Return by opening up the drop-down menu in the ⬛ broadcast message1 ▾ block and choosing New Message from the shortcut menu.

4. Finally, in the code section labeled C, create event handlers for the Start, Help, and Return events. When the user starts the game or goes to the Help screen, you want the Start button to disappear. When the user returns to the splash screen from the Help screen, you want the Start button to reappear.

5. Now save yourself some drudge work by dragging the Start sprite's code blocks one-by-one into the Backpack that is docked to the bottom of the Scratch 2.0 online editor interface. You then can select the Help button and copy the Backpack scripts to its Scripts pane.

6. Check out the code in Figure 22.7 and observe that the code for the Help and Return buttons is largely identical to that of the Start button. You just need to apply logical thinking and iterative testing by rerunning the project to determine when you want to show or hide each button.

7. Finally, switch to the Stage and go to the Scripts pane. As seen in the code section labeled D in the figure, ensure that the game always starts by displaying the SPLASH backdrop.

8. As shown in the code section labeled E in the figure, simply program a backdrop change to correspond to the broadcast of the Start, Help, and Return messages. You can see the completed project in Figure 22.8.

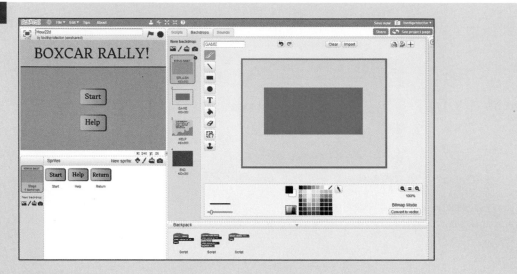

FIGURE 22.8
The finished project...for now.

Next Steps

As you transition out of this hour and into the final two hours of the book, you know that you need to add at least the following functionality to this project before you can call it complete:

▶ You need to create and flesh out the game logic; right now, all you have is a skeleton.

▶ You need to format the END screen and decide whether you want the game simply to end or offer the user a button to return to the SPLASH screen.

▶ You need to prepare the project for sharing by filling in the game's project page on the Scratch website.

You finish this game in Hour 24, "Capstone Project: Arcade Game." Before doing that, though, I want to devote an hour to broaden and deepen the discussion concerning analog inputs by giving you Hour 23, "Connecting Scratch to the Physical World."

Summary

The stuff you did in this hour is a watershed moment for many new programmers. "Wow—making a multiscreen program in Scratch wasn't nearly as complicated as I thought it would be!" Yeah, that's true, with the caveat that you have spent a considerable amount of time prior to this point in mastering all the basics.

You also learned how to create multistate buttons and integrate them into your project. Hopefully you now see that you can scale your Scratch project only to the limit of your imagination and how much work you're willing to put into wiring all of the various and sundry assets together.

Workshop

Quiz

1. What does *multistate* mean when speaking of multistate buttons in Scratch 2.0?

   A. The buttons appear differently to the player depending upon whether their sprite has been clicked.

   B. The buttons consist of one costume but multiple sprites.

   C. The buttons can appear anywhere in the project.

2. Suppose you need to add some instructional text to one of your Stage backdrops. Which of the following methods gives you the most control over the text placement and formatting?

   A. Creating the backdrop using the Scratch Paint Editor

   B. Creating the backdrop from the Backdrop Library

   C. Creating the backdrop on your computer using a paint program

3. The Scratch Resources and ScratchEd sites are good places to find cool Stage backdrops, button sprites, and sound clips.

   A. True

   B. False

Answers

1. The correct answer is choice A. With computer program buttons, *state* refers to whether the button is in an inactive or active, well, state. In Scratch, a multistate button consists of a single sprite but different costumes that denote each state, typically *up* and *down*.

2. The correct answer is choice C. I know that I've been hard on the Scratch Paint Editor in this book. Perhaps the MIT Scratch Team will add functionality to the Paint Editor in future versions of Scratch. In the meantime, the only way to gain complete control over text in your Scratch projects is to compose the backdrop offline by using a paint program on your computer, and then importing the backdrop into your project.

3. The correct answer is choice A. The Scratch Resources (http://is.gd/hRfOyN) and ScratchEd (http://is.gd/Ciw37B) sites are just two of many sites on the Web where you can source content for your Scratch projects.

Challenge

As mentioned earlier, you'll create the game logic in the final hour of the course. In the meantime, your challenge is to program the game such that clicking the Start button puts you in the GAME screen for 5 seconds, and then switches automatically to the END screen and stops all script execution.

Another task you can try is to attach click sounds to the multistate buttons in the project. See if you can find good audio assets at the Scratch Resources (http://is.gd/0zQFvW) website.

Finally, think about how you'd like the game to end. Once the gameplay is over and the user is shuttled to the END screen, do you want to stop all scripts, or present the user with a button that enables him or her to restart the game? Try this out by working on a copy of your project file and see what you can come up with.

You can check out my implementation of these challenges by examining the solution file named Hour22e.sb2.

HOUR 23
Connecting Scratch to the Physical World

What You'll Learn In This Hour:

▶ Setting up Scratch 1.4

▶ Introducing the PicoBoard

▶ Introducing the MaKey MaKey

This is my favorite chapter in this book to write because (1) my four-year-old daughter Zoey loves Scratch, and these projects put programming into her reach, and (2) these projects have a big "wow factor" that is sure to impress you, your family, your students—whomever.

In this hour, you learn how to leverage third-party hardware to connect your Scratch projects to the outside world. Instead of dealing with binary, internal events such as keystrokes, sprite movements, and the like, you can now have your Scratch project react to analog stimuli that occur in the real world.

For example, how about playing a piano that is composed of bananas? (Really.) Perhaps playing a video game with a physical slider and hardware button controls? So much is possible in this space—you'll love learning about it all.

Now before this hour gets started, I have a disclaimer to you, so be prepared for it:

As of this writing, the hardware we use in this hour is compatible only with Scratch 1.4.

There—I said it. For those of you whose knee-jerk reaction is anger, à la "Hey! I bought this book seeking to learn Scratch 2.0, not Scratch 1.4!" please don't be alarmed.

First, what you learn to do with Scratch 1.4 in this hour relates 100 percent, functionality-wise, to what you have in Scratch 2.0. In other words, this hour isn't dealing with any version-specific skills, necessarily.

Second, in time, the PicoBoard and MaKey MaKey, which are the two pieces of hardware you use in this hour, may eventually become Scratch 2.0 compatible. You'll have a leg up if and when that happens because of the time you expended having fun in this hour of the book.

Ready to rock? Good. Let's roll!

Setting Up Scratch 1.4

As stated in the introduction to this hour, you need to install Scratch 1.4 to make use of the sensing hardware you'll be using. Recall that Scratch 1.4 is a desktop application and not a web application like the Scratch 2.0 online editor is.

If you have the Scratch 2.0 Offline Editor installed on your computer already, don't worry; you can have Scratch 1.4 and the Scratch 2.0 Offline Editor installed side by side with no conflicts.

Visit the Scratch 1.4 download page (http://is.gd/iIuIQK) and download the Scratch 1.4 installer for your target operating system. Once the package is downloaded, double-click the installer to load the program on your computer.

Nothing to Fear

As you can see in Figure 23.1, the Scratch 1.4 user interface is basically the same as the Scratch 2.0 interface. Sure, some of the blocks have been rearranged somewhat, but the basic development workflow is identical.

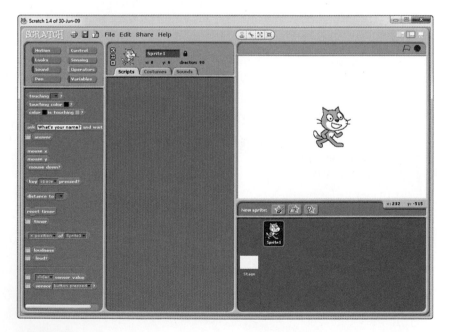

FIGURE 23.1
The Scratch 1.4 user interface is basically the same as the Scratch 2.0 interface.

Hardware That Can Connect to Scratch

Remember that Scratch 1.4 has been around since 2009, while Scratch 2.0 was introduced in late 2013. Therefore, at this point, all third-party hardware that can interoperate with Scratch does so with version 1.4 as previously described.

According to the Scratch Wiki (http://ls.gd/qYxfVs), the following hardware can be used to connect Scratch to the outside world:

▶ **PicoBoard** (http://is.gd/gpeXbm): This is a small circuit board that contains various hardware sensors.

▶ **MaKey MaKey** (http://is.gd/qYxfVs): This is a small circuit board that can create circuits by just about any physical object found in nature. You can then program Scratch to interact with those physical objects.

▶ **LEGO WeDo** (http://is.gd/HIquiE): This is a small robotics kit that uses LEGO bricks.

▶ **LEGO Mindstorms NXT** (http://is.gd/e2hc9f): You can use the Enchanting Scratch modification to control LEGO Mindstorms NXT robots with Scratch.

▶ **Microphone, Webcam:** As we covered in Hour 14, "Adding Multimedia to Your Project," Scratch 1.4 and 2.0 can both take advantage of audio and video from your webcam and/or computer microphone.

▶ **Joystick** (http://is.gd/9Hrxmv): With the JoyTail Scratch extension, you can connect Scratch to your hardware gamepad or joystick.

▶ **Arduino** (http://is.gd/dWXfBv): This is a single-board microcontroller that is very popular among hardware hobbyists. You can use the Catenary program to interoperate between an Arduino board and Scratch.

In this hour, you learn how to use the PicoBoard and MaKey MaKey devices.

Introducing the PicoBoard

The PicoBoard (pronounced *PEE-koh Board*), originally called the Scratch Sensor Board, is a Universal Serial Bus (USB)–powered hardware device that gives Scratchers the ability to measure various analog inputs, involving a slider position, button presses, light, sound, and object resistance. Figure 23.2 shows the PicoBoard. You can use this labeled figure along with the following list as you explore the PicoBoard:

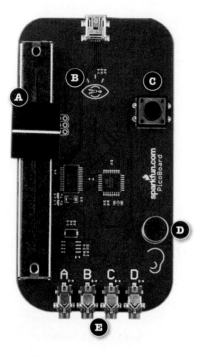

FIGURE 23.2
The PicoBoard, formerly known as the Scratch Sensor Board.

▶ **A:** Slider sensor

▶ **B:** Light sensor

▶ **C:** Button sensor

▶ **D:** Sound sensor

▶ **E:** Resistance sensors (4)

An electronics hobbyist company named SparkFun (http://is.gd/WyVO4D) manufactures and sells the PicoBoard; you can buy one at their website for $44.95 USD as of this writing. One caveat: The device does not ship with an A to Mini-B USB cable, so you'll need to either find one or purchase one. SparkFun sells these cables for $4.95 if you're interested (http://is.gd/Rxprg1).

Setting Up the PicoBoard

After you have your PicoBoard and USB cable plugged in (the bigger A connector goes into your computer, and the smaller B connector goes into the power supply plug on one end of the PicoBoard), it's time to load the device driver.

A device driver is software that enables your operating system (Windows, OS X, or Linux) to recognize and work with a hardware device. You can download the PicoBoard device drivers by visiting the PicoCricket website (http://is.gd/GTkHm7). For convenience, a copy of the driver packages can be found in the book's solution files archive. The Windows filename is `Windows_CDM_2_06_00.zip`, and the OS X filename is `FTDIUSBSerialDriver_v2_2_14.dmg`.

NOTE

A Bit of PicoBoard History

Unfortunately, the documentation for the PicoBoard is a bit convoluted. For the record, the PicoBoard was originally manufactured, sold, and supported by PicoCricket. Eventually, PicoCricket sold the intellectual property to SparkFun, who is the current custodian of the device technology.

When you have the driver, run the installer and then reboot your computer, leaving the PicoBoard plugged in. Once your computer is back up from the reboot, fire up Scratch 1.4—you are ready to start integrating Scratch with the outside world!

Creating a PicoBoard Project

A quick "smoke test" to see if the PicoBoard is initialized in Scratch 1.4 is to navigate to the Sensing palette, enable the sensor value reporter block Stage monitor, and then move the PicoBoard slider back and forth. If the slider sensor Stage monitor value changes between 0 and 100, then you're in luck. If you get no reading, try one of the following troubleshooting techniques:

▶ Restart Scratch 1.4.

▶ Restart the computer.

▶ Unplug the PicoBoard, wait 1 minute, and plug it back in.

▶ Plug the PicoBoard into a different USB port on your computer.

The following Try It Yourself exercise gives you some experience with using every onboard sensor on the PicoBoard. As usual, you need to set up your project environment. Please take the following steps:

▶ Select the Stage and import the underwater backdrop from the Nature category. Note that in Scratch 1.4, all included assets are contained locally in the Scratch 1.4 installation folder.

▶ Click Copy to duplicate the backdrop, and name the duplicate underwater1. Next, use the Fill tool in the Paint Editor, select black from the color palette, and click the blue water to turn it black. There is a method to my madness, I assure you!

▶ Delete the default Scratch Cat sprite, and instead import the fish3 sprite from the Animals category. Rename the sprite to Fish.

▼ TRY IT YOURSELF

Use the PicoBoard

In this Try It Yourself exercise, you wire up your Scratch project to respond to various analog inputs from the PicoBoard. The completed solution file can be found in the book's solution file archive; the filename is `Hour23a.sb`. As always, cross-reference the following steps with the labeled code segments in Figure 23.3. Please follow these steps to complete this exercise:

1. In this exercise, you ping-pong between coding the Fish sprite and the Stage. In the code section labeled A in Figure 23.3, you set the initial position, size, and orientation of the fish, and then send out a new broadcast you'll call sensors. Each sensor is separated into its own function here, triggering them all simultaneously on the sensors broadcast message.

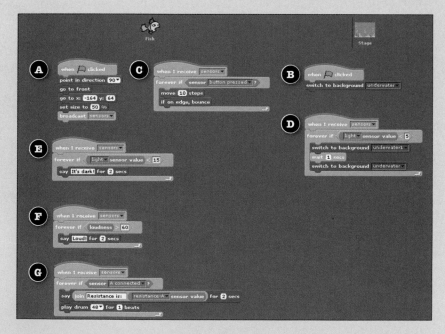

FIGURE 23.3
The source code for the Use the PicoBoard Try It Yourself exercise.

2. In the code section labeled B in the figure, you make sure that the Stage displays the blue underwater backdrop by default when the Green Flag is clicked.

3. In the code section labeled C, you make use of the PicoBoard's hardware button switch. A forever if C block constantly checks for whether you press the PicoBoard button. If you do, then you move the Fish sprite 10 steps. If and when you reach a Stage edge, you bounce the sprite so it can continue in the opposite direction automatically (or "automagically," as my former mentor Jeff Kane used to say).

4. In the code section labeled D, you return to the Stage. Here, you pull in the sensor value reporter block from the Sensing palette and set it up in a forever if block. The evaluation checks whether the light sensor's value falls below 5 and, if so, you switch to the black underwater1 backdrop, wait 1 second, and then go back to the original backdrop.

5. In the code section labeled E, your if expression also tests for the light sensor value. If the light reading falls to below 15, then the Fish sprite says "It's dark!" for 2 seconds.

6. In the code section labeled F, you turn your attention to the PicoBoard's onboard microphone. If the detected sound level exceeds a value of 60, then you have the Fish sprite say "It's loud!" for 2 seconds.

7. Finally, in the code section labeled G, you make use of one of the PicoBoard's four resistance sensors. First, the if expression evaluates whether sensor A is connected. If so, then you instruct the Fish to say "Resistance is:" and echo the resistance value, given in kiloohms.

NOTE

The Longevity of PicoCricket

Even though PicoCricket no longer manufactures, sells, or supports the PicoBoard, the company still hosts a lot of useful PicoBoard resources on its website (http://is.gd/k4yZlS). In particular, I encourage you to read their "Getting Started with PicoBoards" tutorial (http://is.gd/984gdk), which includes excellent examples of how you can experiment with the PicoBoard and Scratch.

PicoBoard-Friendly Blocks

PicoBoard-related blocks can be viewed in the Scratch 1.4 editor interface at any time, but they can be used only when the PicoBoard is connected and initialized, which should make sense to you intuitively.

You saw in the previous Try It Yourself exercise that Scratch 1.4 uses the following Sensing blocks for sensing analog input from the PicoBoard:

▶ **Sensor Value (reporter block):** Possible input options are slider, light, sound, resistance-A, resistance-B, resistance-C, resistance-D, tilt, and distance.

▶ **Sensor (Boolean block):** Possible input options are button pressed, A connected, B connected, C connected, and D connected.

▶ **Loudness (reporter block):** This reporter block reports on the current detected volume level.

▶ **Loud? (Boolean block):** This Boolean block detects the presence of sound (Boolean values evaluate only to True and False).

The integer range for these Sensing blocks ranges from 0 on the minimum end to 100 on the maximum end. By contrast, the PicoBoard button is either clicked (binary 1) or not clicked (binary 0). Please don't forget how important Stage monitors are to running and troubleshooting Scratch projects. You can see in Figure 23.4 that Stage monitors are deployed big-time to check at-a-glance how the PicoBoard sensors are behaving.

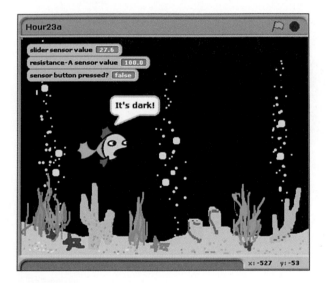

FIGURE 23.4
Stage monitors are especially helpful when you use the PicoBoard.

Next Steps

So now you know how the PicoBoard works—where do you go from here? Well, as always, you are limited only by your own imagination! Be sure to browse the online Scratch project gallery to help you gather ideas. As discussed previously, you can download Scratch 1.4 projects from the website by using the Share To button on the project page. However, this works only for projects that were in fact created and uploaded with the Scratch 1.4 editor.

Introducing the MaKey MaKey

The MaKey Makey (pronounced *MAKE-ey MaKE-ey*) is an ingenious, small form-factor printed circuit board that can be used to turn everyday objects into input keys for use with Scratch or another programming environment.

Check out the images of the MaKey MaKey shown in Figure 23.5—it's really a simple device. You connect one alligator clip to ground, and then connect the other alligator clips to any other object (a banana, a piece of paper—the list of possibilities is literally almost endless).

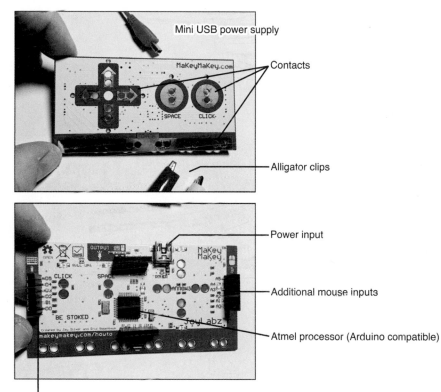

FIGURE 23.5
MaKey MaKey front view on top, and bottom view on bottom (the gnarled hand is property of your valiant author).

The MaKey MaKey detects a change in resistance across an alligator clip and reports that event to your computer as a key press—either a mouse click, a tap of the spacebar, or an up, down, left, or right arrow key press.

So in a sense, the MaKey MaKey is an extensible, imagination-driven joystick controller!

What Can I Do with the MaKey MaKey?

Oh, the things you can do with a MaKey MaKey. Be sure to visit the MaKey MaKey Gallery (http://is.gd/9i1XRX) to watch brief videos showing off hundreds of ways people are using the MaKey to make music, play games, teach kids, and so forth.

Here are some cool ideas as seen online, some of which I've tested myself to good effect:

- ▶ Draw a joystick with a pencil on a piece of paper and use the paper controller to play a game.

- ▶ Hook up various fruits and vegetables and play them like a piano.

- ▶ Create a keyboard out of alphabet soup letters.

- ▶ Bounce a real beach ball to make a sprite dance on screen.

- ▶ Create a working switch by using a lump of Play-Doh.

- ▶ Make a "beat box" machine by hooking leads up to people and then drumming on them.

- ▶ Create a webcam that snaps a picture every time your cat drinks from her water bowl.

- ▶ Use pillows as foot pads in a "Dance Dance Revolution" type game.

OK, How and Where Can I Get One?

You can purchase a MaKey MaKey kit for $49.95 USD directly from the Joylabz website (http://is.gd/ia3usI). Included in the kit are the following components:

- ▶ Preassembled MaKey MaKey PCB

- ▶ Red Mini USB cable (you can also use this cable with the PicoBoard, by the way)

- ▶ Seven alligator clips

- ▶ Six connector wires

- ▶ Various swag (quick start guide, stickers, etc.)

Have you ever heard of Kickstarter (http://is.gd/YHGl3X)? This is a crowdfunding platform and is how the MaKey MaKey project received enough funding to manufacture and sell the units on a larger scale. In fact, check out the MaKay MaKey project's Kickstarter page to learn more about this fascinating story: http://is.gd/tIzxRv.

I just thought that because learning to program with Scratch is so centered on innovation and creativity, you'd like to know that you can have a great idea, add a proposal to Kickstarter, and potentially have a large-scale hardware and/or software success on your hands.

Building a MaKey MaKey Project

There is talk on the Scratch Forums that the MaKey MaKey works with Scratch 2.0. However, for the purposes of this text, I'd like to stay with Scratch 1.4. After all, the PicoBoard and other "Scratch and the Real World" hardware devices support only Scratch 1.4, so they've set a precedent for us. Finally, I want you to be proficient in both Scratch 1.4 as well as Scratch 2.0 in order to be a well-rounded Scratcher.

In any event, it's time to plug in the MaKey MaKey and build a test project or two. Or three.

The good news is that you don't need to install any drivers for your computer to recognize your MaKey MaKey. Just plug in the USB cable, and attach one of the alligator clips to one of the terminals that lines the bottom of the board; this is the ground circuit. Hold the other end of that alligator clip in your hand to complete the ground circuit.

NOTE

How the Contacts Work in the MaKey MaKey

What you're doing here in attaching an alligator clip to a pair of copper-lined holes on the MaKey MaKey is completing a circuit. Open the jaws of the alligator clip and clip in between a hole pair on the board. You then attach the other end of the clips to some other object. Thereafter, any resistance that is added to that circuit from the "object" end is registered by the connected computer as a specific key press or mouse action. From the perspective of your computer, the MaKey MaKey is nothing other than a tiny keyboard and mouse.

Now add one end of six alligator clips to the other terminals on the board:

- Up
- Left
- Right
- Down
- Space
- Mouse click

Now open Scratch 1.4 and start a new project. In the next Try It Yourself exercise, you create a paper joystick (!) with which you control the movement of the Scratch Cat sprite around the Stage.

▼ TRY IT YOURSELF

Create a Paper Joystick

In this Try It Yourself exercise, you use a piece of paper, a graphite pencil, the MaKey MaKey, and Scratch 1.4 to create a simple but unique project—a paper joystick! The completed solution file (such as it is; the code is extraordinarily pedestrian) is named `Hour23b.sb`. Complete the following steps to complete the exercise, and remember that, as always, the solution files can be found in the book's code listings archive:

1. First, let's create the paper joystick. Use scissors and a piece of white paper to fashion your joystick's "body." Next, use a graphite pencil to create a four-way gamepad, as shown in Figure 23.6. The point here, electrically speaking, is that graphite is a conductive material, so the MaKey MaKey can sense resistance along a graphite trail.

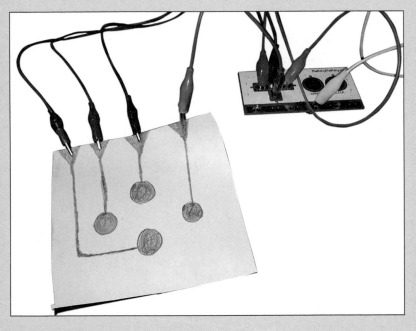

FIGURE 23.6
You saw it here first: a paper joystick created with MaKey Makey

2. Fill in four contact patches on the edge of the paper controller, and connect them to your gamepad buttons by using thick, heavy pencil lines. Think of current flow here, friend.

3. Connect one end of four alligator clips to the four directional contacts on the MaKey MaKey. Connect the other end of each clip to its corresponding graphite contact patch on your paper controller edge. We need four directions here to correspond to the UP ARROW, LEFT ARROW, RIGHT ARROW, and DOWN ARROW events.

4. Finally, connect a fifth alligator clip to one of the Earth terminals, and hold the other end in your hand. This grounds the system.

5. The code for the project is so simple I didn't even label the code. As you can see in Figure 23.7, you reset the Scratch Cat's size and position when the Green Flag is clicked. You then use four `when space key pressed` Hat blocks to detect when the arrow keys are pressed, and you move the Cat appropriately.

Remember that as far as Scratch and your computer are concerned, touching each of the four graphite pads on your paper controller is effectively the same thing as using an arrow key on your keyboard.

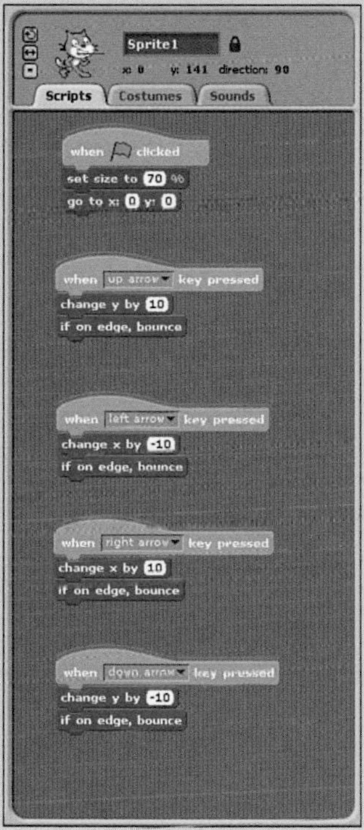

FIGURE 23.7
Source code for the Create a Paper Joystick Try It Yourself exercise.

6. Now it's time to test! Click the Green Flag, hold the ground clip with one hand, and tap the paper gamepad with your other hand. When contact is sensed by the MaKey MaKey, a light-emitting diode (LED) flashes on the underside of the board. Of course, you should also observe the Scratch Cat sprite moving on the Stage as well.

Summary

By now, you should understand what is meant by the statement "You can program Scratch to interact with the real world." I hope that you invest in a PicoBoard and a MaKey MaKey so you can work through this hour's two Try It Yourself exercises and springboard into experiments that are fueled by your own imagination, creativity, and newfound Scratch programming skills.

Workshop

Quiz

1. We say that real-world sensors operate in an analog fashion as opposed to a digital fashion because:

   A. Analog operates across a range of values.

   B. Analog operates across two values.

   C. Analog operates in a binary way.

2. The PicoBoard is a small circuit board that contains a number of sensor outputs.

   A. True

   B. False

3. How does the MaKey MaKey appear to Scratch?

   A. As a USB microcontroller

   B. As a keyboard/mouse input device

   C. As a digital synthesizer

Answers

1. The correct answer is choice A. Analog signaling involves a range of values, which occurs all the time in the real world. After all, the sound of that ambulance siren that you hear in the distance grows gradually louder as the vehicle gets closer to you, correct? By contrast, digital signaling has only two values: binary 0 or 1, also called low and high, off and on, and so forth.

2. The correct answer is choice B. The PicoBoard is a small circuit board that contains a number of sensor inputs. Scratch then performs detection and processing on that input data and gives you output on your computer screen or through a peripheral device such as a webcam or speaker.

3. The correct answer is choice B. From the perspective of your computer, the MaKey MaKey is simply a keyboard/mouse input device. This is somewhat of a trick question because you can indeed put the MaKey MaKey into so-called *Arduino mode*, which presents the device to your computer as a connected Arduino microcontroller.

Challenge

Your challenge for this hour, should you choose to accept it, is to make a Scratch 1.4 project that uses input from both the PicoBoard and the MaKey MaKey simultaneously. For instance, create a Scratch interaction or game that uses all of the following input types:

▶ Sound level

▶ Light level

▶ Slider control

▶ Button presses

▶ Movement

▶ Water flow

Capstone Project: Arcade Game

What You'll Learn in This Hour:

▶ Introducing *Dodgeball Challenge*

▶ Laying out the screens

▶ Wiring up the screen navigation

▶ Building the sprites

▶ Adding the main game logic

▶ Testing and tweaking the project

In colleges and universities, many professors use the capstone project as a way for students to demonstrate how much they learned over the course of the semester. A topic like computer programming lends itself to the capstone project format because, let's face it—you learned a *lot* of material over the past 23 hours. It's time to show off your new skills!

In this final hour, you build a game in Scratch 2.0 from beginning to end. One goal in this hour is to include as much functionality as possible into the game while at the same time limiting its size to what can be accomplished comfortably in an hour. Another goal for this hour is to program a game that incorporates the majority of the tools and skills that you've picked up thus far. Hopefully, you enjoy the result!

Introducing *Dodgeball Challenge*

Our capstone project involves the creation of a game called *Dodgeball Challenge*. Surely you have heard of the schoolyard game dodgeball, correct? In dodgeball, at least in the variant I played as a boy, a number of children stand lined up against the school's gymnasium wall, and a designated student hurls an air-filled rubber ball at said students with the goal of hitting one and knocking him or her out of the game.

The final student standing against the wall is declared the winner. Here is a basic schematic of how the computer-based version works:

▶ The player controls the avatar with the mouse, moving it around the playfield.

▶ At random intervals, ball sprites appear and bounce erratically around the playfield.

▶ A timer increments to a certain threshold value.

▶ The object of the game is to avoid the bouncing balls until the timer expires.

▶ The overall high score is posted on the Stage as a cloud variable, giving other Scratchers incentive to beat that high score.

A Bit of Storyboarding

Take a look at Figure 24.1, which uses the trusty Balsamiq Mockups tool (http://is.gd/gZstLx) to prototype how the game should look.

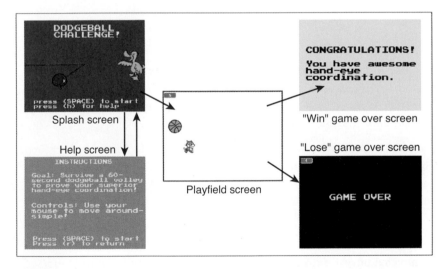

FIGURE 24.1
Storyboard schematic of the Dodgeball Challenge game.

To be honest, I cheated a bit here: I actually created the full game prior to beginning the composition of this hour. The screenshots you see in Figure 24.1 are taken from the game itself.

NOTE

Understanding Screen Captures

Screenshots, also called screen captures, are digital images that are produced by capturing all or part of what's on your computer screen. Software developers use screen capture software all the time to generate in-game pictures of their software projects, among other things. You can take screenshots for free on most operating system platforms, but if you're ever in the market for a top-shelf screen capture tool, then I recommend Snagit for Windows (http://is.gd/d2lfta) and Snapz Pro X for Mac (http://is.gd/TAOQej).

Extra Features

Besides the play mechanics of the game itself, it is important that you "dress up" the game to include several other hallmarks of a quality piece of software:

- ▶ A splash screen with a cool audiovisual effect to help gain player interest

- ▶ A navigation menu

- ▶ A help screen to provide the player with instructions

- ▶ A "Game Over" screen that includes a sound effect and a retro video game font

Being the prospective professional coder that you are, you'll develop *Dodgeball Challenge* in stages. Here they are:

- ▶ Laying out the screens

- ▶ Wiring up the screen navigation

- ▶ Building the sprites

- ▶ Adding the main game logic

- ▶ Testing and tweaking the project

Remember that the completed project is available online at the Scratch website (http://is.gd/cOWhMF) as well as in the book's solution files archive; the filename is `Hour24.sb2`. In addition, a copy of every named asset (graphic, font, sound file, and so forth) can be found in the code archive for your convenience.

Let's get to work!

Laying Out the Screens

As you saw in Figure 24.1, you'll need the following screens (which you know are technically Stage backdrops) to accommodate your project:

▶ **Splash screen:** This screen serves as the players' first impression and control panel for the game.

▶ **Help screen:** This screen provides the players with gameplay instructions and a navigation control to return to the splash screen.

▶ **Playfield screen:** This screen is where the game itself takes place.

▶ **"Win" game over screen:** If the player's avatar manages to avoid the bouncing balls for the duration of the timer, then he or she wins the game. To show this, you show the win screen.

▶ **"Lose" game over screen:** If the player's avatar connects with a ball, then the game is immediately ended, all scripts stop execution, and the "lose" screen appears.

▼ TRY IT YOURSELF

Create the Backdrops

In this exercise, we build some backdrops for our Scratch project. Set the stage (as it were) by logging in to the Scratch website, starting a new project, selecting the Stage, and navigating to the Backdrops tab. Follow these steps to complete the exercise:

1. To give you total control over the text that appears on your screens, bypass the Paint Editor and instead create your backdrops offline by using GIMP (http://is.gd/q8Axq1) or any paint editor with which you're comfortable.

2. Use Figure 24.1 as a guide to help you with text copy and placement. See the Note that follows this Try It Yourself exercise to learn how you can use the cool 8-bit video game font used for this project.

   As a reminder, use your paint editor program to specify a canvas size of 960×720, and save the finished backdrop as a `.png` file. Speaking of which, name your five backdrop images SplashScreen, HelpScreen, PlayfieldScreen, WinScreen, and GameOver, respectively.

3. When you're ready, click the Upload Backdrop from File [icon] button to import your custom playfields to the game. Be sure that the backdrop names in the Scratch Editor match the names given in the previous step. Figure 24.2 shows the backdrop upload process on a Windows 7 computer. To my readers with sharp eyes: yes indeed, I messed up the spelling on the SplashScreen.png filename. Showing you this mistake is important because in my experience as a programmer it's the "simple" stuff like this that can cause issues with your program execution. Watch your spelling and syntax, my friends!

FIGURE 24.2
Uploading custom backdrops to the Scratch project.

NOTE

A Cool, Retro 8-Bit Font

One of my favorite fonts in the world resembles the blocky text of the old 8-bit Atari, Coleco, Mattel Electronics, and Nintendo video games I grew up playing in the early 1980s. For *Dodgeball Challenge*, I downloaded the amazing Press Start 2P font from http://is.gd/d7ryMI. To save you some Internet download bandwidth, the font is included in the book's solution files archive. By the way, it's easy to install a new font on your system; for Windows users, see this tutorial: http://is.gd/dJmW5H. For OS X users, check out this tutorial: http://is.gd/8gDon9.

Excellent! By now, you have the road map of your project in place. It always gives me a warm and fuzzy feeling whenever I create a Scratch project that includes original, one-of-a-kind art assets. That's what it's all about!

Wiring Up the Screen Navigation

You'll make liberal use of broadcasts and other event blocks to orchestrate the player's movement through the game screens. Here's the high-level workflow:

▶ On the splash screen, the user can press the spacebar to start the game and press H to access the online help screen.

▶ On the help screen, the user can press the spacebar to start the game, or press R to return to the splash screen.

▶ On the playfield screen, you'll make sure that the backdrop shows up on Stage when the user presses the spacebar.

▶ You want an audio cue whenever you switch screens.

Just so you have them in your proverbial shirt pocket, drag a `broadcast message1 ▼` stack block to the Stage's Scripts pane and create all seven of the broadcast names that you need right now; their use will make more sense as you proceed through this hour:

▶ AddBall2

▶ AddBall3

▶ Crash

▶ GameLose

▶ GameWon

▶ MorphPlayfield

▶ StartGame

Also, go to the Sounds pane for the Stage and make sure to add the zoop and pop sound effect; these can be found in the All category of the Sound Library, as expected.

▼ TRY IT YOURSELF

Build Game Navigation

In this Try It Yourself exercise, you consolidate all screen-related code on the Stage. As usual, you can cross-reference the following steps with Figure 24.3. Complete the following steps to finish this exercise:

1. In the code section labeled A in Figure 24.3, you specify that when the user clicks the Green Flag, the SplashScreen backdrop appears on the Stage.

2. In the code section labeled B in the figure, you wait for the "spacebar is pressed" event, at which time you send out the StartGame broadcast message.

3. In the code section labeled C, the Stage responds to its own StartGame broadcast by switching to the PlayfieldScreen backdrop so the user can play the game.

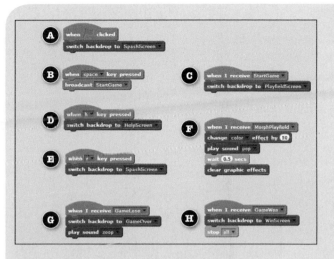

FIGURE 24.3
The relevant source code for the Build Game Navigation Try It Yourself exercise.

4. In the code section labeled D, you create an event handler with the 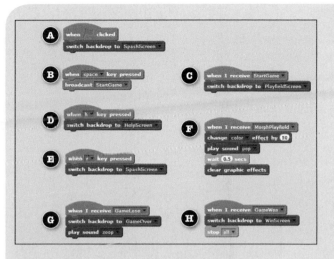 Hat block such that pressing the H key switches to the HelpScreen backdrop.

5. In the code section labeled E, you handle the R key press that takes the user back to the SplashScreen backdrop.

6. Later on, you'll send out a broadcast named MorphPlayfield such that the user receives an audiovisual startle whenever his or her avatar makes contact with the outer border of the Stage. Here, in the code section labeled F, you wait for the MorphPlayfield broadcast to fire and, when it does, you toggle a quick color effect to the Stage and play the pop built-in sound.

7. In the code section labeled G, you respond to the GameLose broadcast (which you'll create momentarily), where you switch to the GameOver backdrop and play the zoop audio clip.

8. In the code section labeled H, you respond to the GameWon broadcast by switching to the appropriate backdrop and stopping all script execution.

9. Click the Green Flag to test the project. What happens when you press the spacebar? Restart the project and press H, and then R. Do you return to the splash screen?

Building the Sprites

Now turn your attention to the sprites in *Dodgeball Challenge*. You need a grand total of six sprites, all culled from the built-in Sprite Library:

▶ Scratch Cat, renamed to PlayerIcon (shown in Figure 24.4)

▶ Basketball, renamed to ball1 (shown in Figure 24.5)

▶ Baseball, renamed to ball2 (shown in Figure 24.6)

▶ Beachball, renamed to ball3 (shown in Figure 24.7)

▶ Duck (shown in Figure 24.8)

▶ Apple (shown in Figure 24.9)

Examine the sprites' figure images and you'll see that the source code is provided in separate figures. Throughout the rest of this hour, these figures are referred to multiple times.

But Wait...What About the Timer?

In *Dodgeball Challenge*, the point of the game is to avoid the bouncing balls until the clock runs out. But where's the clock? In this section, you need to create a timer.

As you know by now, keeping time in Scratch can be accomplished in one of two ways:

▶ Using the built-in Timer object

▶ Creating a variable to store time

Although the built-in Timer is accurate, it is nowhere near as flexible as a variable-based timer. So that's what you use here. Create a global variable named Timer; you actually build the timer in the next section, but you need to reference it at this step.

See? Often, you have to think several steps ahead as a computer programmer. Get used to it!

▼ TRY IT YOURSELF

Set Up Your Sprites

In this Try It Yourself exercise, you are concerned with the housekeeping tasks behind these sprites, principally in terms of where they will appear on the Stage and when they should hide versus when they should show themselves. Work through the following steps to complete the exercise:

1. Program the sprites in the same order as listed in the previous unordered list. For the PlayerIcon sprite, you can see in the code section labeled A in Figure 24.4 that when the game is started, you hide the avatar and the timer variable. In annotation C, we reset the timer variable to zero.

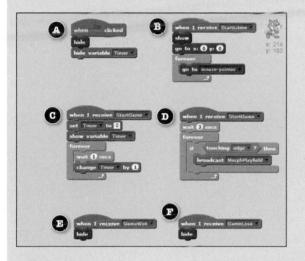

FIGURE 24.4
Source code for the PlayerIcon sprite.

In the code section labeled B in the figure, you respond to the StartGame broadcast (which occurs when the player presses the spacebar) by showing the PlayerIcon avatar and mapping its movement to the mouse pointer.

In the code sections E and F, you ensure that the avatar disappears when the game is over, regardless of whether the player wins or loses.

2. Now take a look at ball1. In the code sections labeled A, E, and F in Figure 24.5, you hide the ball at the start and end of the game.

A discussion of the remaining code is saved for the next section, in which you add the main game logic.

3. For ball2 and ball3, you have just more of the same. Add the relevant ![hide] code, as shown in Figures 24.6 and 24.7.

4. The Duck and the Apple sprite, whose code is shown in Figures 24.8 and 24.9, respectively, is a different story and bears further discussion. What you do with these sprites is create a simple splash screen animation to get the player's attention.

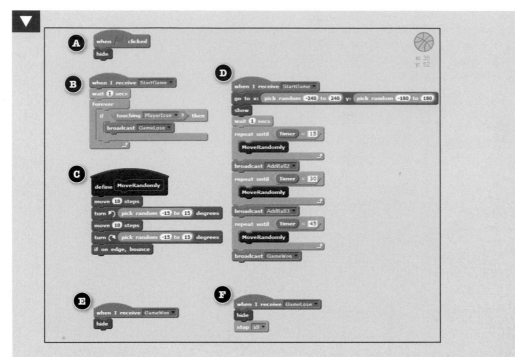

FIGURE 24.5
Source code for the ball1 sprite.

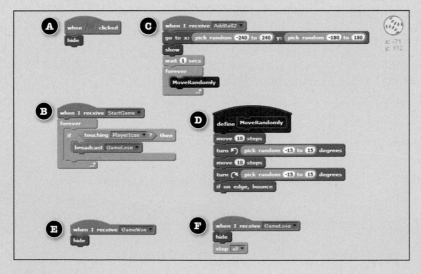

FIGURE 24.6
Source code for the ball2 sprite.

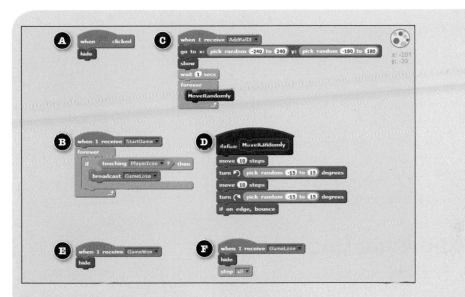

FIGURE 24.7
Source code for the ball3 sprite.

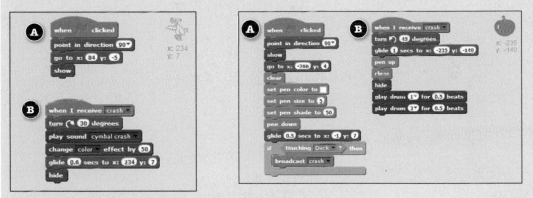

FIGURE 24.8
Source code for the Duck sprite.

FIGURE 24.9
Source code for the Apple sprite.

5. For the Duck, the code section labeled A in Figure 24.8 orients the Duck in its original location and places the sprite on the Stage at specific coordinates. In the code section labeled B, you respond to a Crash broadcast (which you create in the next step) that has the Duck tilt clockwise 30 degrees, play a cymbal crash sound, change its color effect, and glide offstage. Of course, you need to attach the cymbal crash audio clip to the Duck sprite (you should understand precisely how to do that at this point in the game).

▼

6. For the Apple, you have quite a bit of action happening in the code section labeled A in Figure 24.9. After initializing the sprite's position, you "launch" the Apple across the Stage, using the Pen tools to create a "trail" behind the object.

   The [if ⟶ then] block detects when the Apple makes contact with the Duck sprite, at which time you send out the Crash broadcast message.

   In the code section labeled B in the figure, you code the "bounce" animation for the Apple. Essentially, you shift its orientation, lift up the pen, and have it glide offscreen, followed by two strikes of the drum.

7. Run the project. How does the animation look? What room for improvement do you see?

Adding the Main Game Logic

Okay—now you finally reach the actual meat and potatoes of the *Dodgeball Challenge* project. Here's specifically how the gameplay will proceed:

▶ You create a timer and set the gameplay interval to 60 seconds.

▶ You program the three balls to appear at 15, 30, and 45 seconds into gameplay, respectively.

▶ You code that if the PlayerIcon hits the Stage border, the player is "zapped" with a multimedia wake-up call.

▶ You add logic such that if the PlayerIcon makes contact with a ball, the player loses. If the PlayerIcon makes it to the end of the gameplay duration, the player wins.

▼ TRY IT YOURSELF

Program the Game Logic

In this Try It Yourself exercise, you continue to use the labeled code sections in Figures 24.4 through 24.9 as you implement the main game logic in *Dodgeball Challenge*. Work through the following steps to complete the exercise:

1. Use the same order as you did for the previous Try It Yourself exercise. For the PlayerIcon (Figure 24.4), create the timer object in the code section labeled C. You could just as well have added the Timer to the Stage.

   In the code section labeled D, you define the MorphPlayfield routine. The [if ⟶ then] block detects whether the PlayerIcon hits the Stage border and, if so, you initiate the MorphPlayfield function on the Stage as previously described.

▼

2. Now for the ball1 sprite (Figure 24.5). In the code section labeled C, you create a custom block named MoveRandomly that defines the ball motion algorithm. The ball motion implemented here isn't necessarily realistic. This was by design to include some artificial wonkiness to the ball's motion to give the player a bit more of a challenge. The `if on edge, bounce` block is particularly helpful here.

The code section labeled D is really the heart of the entire game. The main purpose of this script is to set up the appearance of the three balls. You use `repeat until` blocks to fire the AddBall2 and AddBall3 broadcasts and reuse the MoveRandomly custom code to orchestrate their movement. Code reuse rocks, doesn't it?

3. The code for the ball2 and ball3 sprites (Figures 24.6 and 24.7, respectively) isn't anything new. Use the Backpack to copy the custom code block between the sprites. Implement the MoveRandomly function in the code sections labeled C in Figures 24.6 and 24.7, where the AddBall2 and AddBall3 broadcast event handlers are defined.

4. It's time for testing! Start the project, verify that the animation plays fully, and then press the spacebar to start the game. How does it work? Intentionally run the PlayerIcon into a ball. Does the game end with the correct backdrop?

   For testing purposes, you might want to lower the timer threshold to 10 seconds to ensure you can complete the challenge successfully. When you do this, do you see the win screen?

NOTE

On Creating Realistic Bounce Effects In Scratch 2.0

Creating realistic ball bounce effects is a work in progress in the Scratch community. What you've done with *Dodgeball Challenge* fits the goals of this game, but you might be interested in creating a more realistic bounce effect that perhaps takes gravity into account. For inspiration, draw your attention to the Scratch project Realistic Bouncing Ball (http://is.gd/5dcMmq) by funguy.

Testing and Tweaking the Project

If you've learned anything in this book, you've learned the importance of iterative software development. Recall that iterative development means that you test and retest every time you make a significant change to the program's code.

Another point that bears repeating is called unit testing. Here, you approach your game testing in a more structured, formal way. For example, you may have the following punch list of testing tasks to complete in the *Dodgeball Challenge* project:

▶ The opening animation plays correctly.

▶ Pressing the H key takes you to the help screen.

▶ From the help screen, pressing R takes you back to the splash screen.

▶ From the splash screen and the help screen, pressing the spacebar starts the game.

▶ The balls appear at their predefined time intervals.

▶ The timer resets and increments correctly.

▶ The game ends with a "lose" condition if the PlayerIcon touches a ball.

▶ The game ends with a "win" condition if the PlayerIcon survives the gameplay interval without touching a ball.

▶ The screen flashes and the audio clip plays if the PlayerIcon touches the border of the Stage.

If you decide to add a new feature to the game, you can buzz through the previous unit testing routine to ensure that your change hasn't broken anything in the game.

Speaking of new features, you may indeed want to add new and/or enhanced functionality to *Dodgeball Challenge*, especially if you want to remix my public project (http://is.gd/RvvRsT). Here are some ideas in closing:

▶ The player is allowed to touch a ball once, but when that happens, the ball clones!

▶ The balls increase their speed as they show up on the Stage.

▶ The PlayerIcon gets larger as the timer increments its value.

▶ The game ends if the PlayerIcon hits the Stage border.

▶ If the PlayerIcon hits the Stage border, the balls on the Stage clone.

You must always remember the Scratch mantra: Imagine, Program, Share!

Testing with the Beta Player

Software developers use the term *beta* to describe prerelease software that is currently undergoing testing. If you log in to the Scratch website and visit your Account Settings page, you'll see a tab called Beta Testing. Here, you can opt into enhancements that the MIT Scratch Team has in beta testing.

As you can see in Figure 24.10, I have the option to try out the beta Scratch project player. In my opinion, participating in these beta trials is a good idea for the following reasons at the least:

FIGURE 24.10
Sometimes Scratchers are invited by the MIT Scratch Team to participate in beta testing new products and features.

▶ By providing feedback on the beta features/products to the Scratch Team, you contribute to the Scratch community in general and the Scratch development platform in particular.

▶ By testing your own projects against beta versions of the player, you can get advance notice of incompatibilities and proactively address them in your project design.

As you work with beta features, especially the beta project player, you can learn how to send bug reports directly to the MIT Scratch Team by visiting this page: http://is.gd/0WuUjl.

Summary

In this hour, you had an opportunity to show off all your new programming skills. By now, I am entirely confident that you are a Scratch expert, and wholly worthy of the title "Scratcher." Your capstone project consisted of re-creating my original game *Dodgeball Challenge*. I dearly hope that you remix the project, make it your own, and republish it to the Scratch website. I look forward to playing it and seeing your other work!

Thanks, and Goodbye

Well, you've reached the end of the proverbial road, my friend. How does it feel to be a real, live computer programmer? Above all else, I hope that you discovered your interest and aptitude in programming. If you're looking for a next step after Scratch 2.0, take a look at JavaScript, if you are particularly interested in websites and web programming, and Python, if you are curious about building desktop applications (although Python is almost as well suited for web work as is JavaScript).

To help you along the way, please check out the following related Pearson titles:

▶ *Sams Teach Yourself JavaScript in 24 Hours* (Ballard and Moncur): http://is.gd/qGioN4

▶ *Sams Teach Yourself Python in 24 Hours* (Cunningham): http://is.gd/AQJoa5

Moreover, I hope that you are convinced that computer programming (1) isn't as difficult as you might have thought initially, and (2) isn't "for nerds" with no creativity. In fact, the process of designing and building a software application requires a high degree of creativity indeed.

Thank you so much for purchasing and reading this book. If it weren't for readers like you, I would have nothing to do professionally, so please know how much I value you. On that point, if you have any questions, comments, curiosities, complaints, or suggestions, then please don't hesitate to reach me at tim@timwarnertech.com. Happy programming!

Index

Sams **Teach Yourself**

When you only have time **for the answers**™

Whatever your need and whatever your time frame, there's a Sams **Teach Yourself** book for you. With a Sams **Teach Yourself** book as your guide, you can quickly get up to speed on just about any new product or technology—in the absolute shortest period of time possible. Guaranteed.

Learning how to do new things with your computer shouldn't be tedious or time-consuming. Sams **Teach Yourself** makes learning anything quick, easy, and even a little bit fun.

Python Programming for Raspberry Pi in 24 Hours

Richard Blum

Christine Bresnahan

ISBN-13: 978-0-7897-5205-5

JavaScript in 24 Hours

Phil Ballard

Michael Moncur

ISBN-13: 978-0-672-33608-9

Beginning Programming in 24 Hours

Greg Perry

Dean Miller

ISBN-13: 978-0-672-33700-0

C++ in 24 Hours

Jesse Liberty

Rogers Cadenhead

ISBN-13: 978-0-672-33331-6

Python in 24 Hours

Katie Cunningham

ISBN-13: 978-0-672-33687-4